The Frontier of Public Administration in China

The series focuses on the experience and cases of public administration in China, which holds the diversity on topics including land policy, real estate management, urban management, human re-source management. It aims to provide the overview as well as deep insight in this area as reading material and reference for the researchers and students.

Shukui Tan · Xianjin Huang
Editors

Land Policy in China

Issues, Analysis and Implications

華中科技大學出版社有限责任公司
Huazhong University of Science & Technology Press Co.,Ltd.

Springer

Editors
Shukui Tan
Huazhong University of Science
and Technology
Wuhan, Hubei, China

Xianjin Huang
Nanjing University
Nanjing, China

ISSN 2662-9917 ISSN 2662-9925 (electronic)
The Frontier of Public Administration in China
ISBN 978-981-19-9894-2 ISBN 978-981-19-9895-9 (eBook)
https://doi.org/10.1007/978-981-19-9895-9

Jointly published with Huazhong University of Science and Technology Press
The print edition is not for sale in China (Mainland). Customers from China (Mainland) please order the print book from: Huazhong University of Science and Technology Press.

This Springer imprint is published by the registered company Springer Nature Singapore Pte Ltd.
The registered company address is: 152 Beach Road, #21-01/04 Gateway East, Singapore 189721, Singapore

Editorial Board

Contents

1 **Land and Land Policies** 1
Xianjin Huang, Sujuan Zhong, and Taiyang Zhong

2 **Overview of China's Land Policies** 33
Xiao Lyu and Shandong Niu

3 **Land Tenure Policy** 97
Jun Yang

4 **Land Development Policies** 149
Siliang Wang and Shukui Tan

5 **Land Protection Policies** 217
Siliang Wang and Shukui Tan

6 **Land Administration Policies** 257
Shukui Tan, Siliang Wang, and Yang Liu

7 **Outlook of China's Land Policies** 283
Xianjin Huang, Xiao Lyu, Jun Yang, and Shandong Niu

Chapter 1
Land and Land Policies

Xianjin Huang, Sujuan Zhong, and Taiyang Zhong

Land is the foundational material not only for human survival and development but also for the emergence of culture and politics. With social and economic development, the connotations of land constantly change, and land classification evolves constantly. Rich social practices have given rise to diverse demands for land resource management, and land policies have become increasingly systematized, thus making them an important component of the national policy system. This chapter briefly clarifies the connotation and classification of land from the perspective of Chinese history, culture, and modern ecological civilization, and based on this, proposes an analytical framework for Chinese land policy and its underlying logic.

1.1 Definition and Attributes of Land

1.1.1 Land in China and Its Connection with Chinese Culture

(1) **Land as written in Chinese Characters**

"土" is a typical pictograph (Li 2012) first found in oracle bone and bronze inscriptions of the Shang Dynasty. The evolution of the character "土" can be seen in these oracle-bone and -bronze inscriptions, with the character resembling a mound of earth wherein the stroke "一" symbolizes the earth. The small seal script has the same character form as the modern "土," with the two horizontal lines indicating the two layers

X. Huang · S. Zhong (✉) · T. Zhong
Nanjing University, Nanjing, China
e-mail: sjzhong@smail.nju.edu.cn

X. Huang
e-mail: hxj369@nju.edu.cn

T. Zhong
e-mail: zty@nju.edu.cn

S. Tan and X. Huang (eds.), *Land Policy in China*, The Frontier of Public Administration in China, https://doi.org/10.1007/978-981-19-9895-9_1

of the earth, and the one vertical line indicating plants growing out of the earth. After the Li-variation, the regular script came to be written as "土," which is consistent with the current widely used "土." In Xu Shen's *Shuowen Jiezi*, the word "earth" is defined as follows: "Earth, the earth that gives rise to all things. The character '二' refers to 'below the earth' and 'in the earth.' The character '|' indicates that things emerge and grow from this. All that belongs to this world is from the earth." This short expression explains that the "earth" comprises four parts: the part above the ground, the topsoil layer, the part underground, and the subsoil layer. These parts highlight the productive function of the earth. In Zhou Yi's *Li—Tuan Chuan*, we find a similar expression, "the sun and the moon are beautiful to the sky, and the grasses and trees are beautiful to the earth," further explaining the ancient Chinese knowledge about the productive function of the land. The word "地" is derived from the character "土"; it is a synonym and a morphological character, first found in the small seal script. In *Shuowen Jiezi—Tubu*, it says, "all objects are presented on the earth. Sound also arises from the earth." In *Guanzi Xingshijie*, we find it written that "the earth produces and supports all things," thus providing a functional perspective as well showing how land is regarded as the basis for the growth and reproduction of all objects (Fig. 1.1).

(2) **China's agrarian civilization and the culture of worshipping land**

China is a vast country, with many of its regions topographically and climatically suited for growing different kinds of crops. In the case of an agrarian economy, which has predominated the national economy of China for a long time, land, as an important factor of agricultural production, is directly related to people's survival, and this is origin of the concept of valuing land in Chinese society. In the traditional small-peasant economy, farming production was closely linked to land, and land cultivation and reclamation was an important part of people's lives. In the long-standing production practice, the agricultural civilization of living in clans and intensive farming nurtured a self-sufficient way of life; further, it also gave rise to many

Fig. 1.1 Land in ancient Chinese script (top is "土" and bottom is "地")

cultural traditions, agricultural ideas, and rural management systems that are compatible with agricultural production. Therefore, the Chinese people's love and respect for the land is an important lens through which Chinese culture needs to be analyzed.

Among the many traditions, the most important is the concept of the vernacular and the concept of the regional, that is, being attached to the native land and unwilling to leave it. As Qian Mu said in his *Introduction to the History of Chinese Culture*: "Agrarian civilization is connected to its cultivated land; it is rooted to the land, cannot be moved away from it, originates from it, thrives on it, and disintegrates in it." Agrarian civilization, the backbone of rural society, has shaped the Chinese people's attachment to their native land and an unwillingness to leave it, thereby giving rise to the concept of geography and kinship. "The Chinese are not gypsies: we are a people that will carry their bones back even if they die on Mars."[1] To this day, homesickness, nostalgia, roots, and ancestral complexes continue to influence the life and behavior of contemporary Chinese people and are essential elements of Chinese "root culture," an important link in building a sense of community among the Chinese people.

The folk beliefs originating from the land are also an important part of Chinese folk culture. In China, land is the basis on which society survives; it is also the cause for the rise and fall of families. Tudigong, also known as the Mother of the Earth, the God of the Backlands, and the God of Soil, is often called the God of Soil and Grain, together with God of Ji, who represents the grains. The Altar of Land and Grain can be observed to have been built as early as in the Zhou Dynasty, the highest level of which was called Taishe, dedicated to the Great God of the Land who was in charge of the whole country. The five colors of the earth—green, white, red, black, and yellow—represent the five directions of the country—east, west, south, north, and center– which apart from being symbols of the country also represent the wishes of the supreme ruler for a good harvest. The Altar of Land and Grain has different levels below the Son of Heaven; however, after the Song Dynasty, the civil altars were gradually replaced by the Temple of the Land. Whenever there is an addition to the family, a house is built, a grave is erected, or someone is sick, people offer sacrifices to Tudigong, praying for blessings. The Chinese in Southeast Asia continue the custom of worshipping "Tudigong" even today, and the folk beliefs surrounding Tudigong are the cultural glue that unites and consolidates the Chinese nation's sense of community (Yang 2001). Even now there are Land Temples seen in the rural space at the head of fields and roads.

1.1.2 Ancient Chinese Perceptions of Land

(1) **Land as a symbol of power**

A major feature of Chinese history is its precocious and long-term continuation of autocratic kingship, wherein the land and the land system played an important role in the overall political system. Traditional Chinese land system and political system are

[1] Form Chinese Taiwanese writer Zhang Xiaofeng's essay "The October Sun.".

characteristically isomorphic systems. Unlike feudalization in Europe, where control of land and population was achieved through "feudal contracts," ancient Chinese rulers considered control over land a fundamental channel for the construction of imperial power. Moreover, the autocratic royals held the highest power of ruling and the highest power over land, even dominating and interfering with land relations at will. "Under the wide heaven, All is the king's land. Within the sea-boundaries of the land, All are the king's servants." During the Western Zhou Dynasty, the ownership of land belonged to the Son of Heaven, and vassals and lords used the land they were assigned, while the king's power was reflected and strengthened in the process of distributing and adjusting land rights. After Qin unified the Central Plains, the land system was organized such that "the feudal lords did not establish the feudal title over one foot of land" and instead "heavily rewarded the sons and ministers with the taxes collected from the public," thus realizing monopoly of power. At the same time, it was ordered that "those who had land should report the amount of land they possessed to the government (as the basis for taxation)," and the state would approve and collect taxes according to this, which placed both the "official system" and the "taxation system" of the state firmly in the hands of the emperor and made them mutually dependent and coordinated (Chen 2015). From having comprehensive control over land, ancient China completed the structure of absolute dominance of the imperial power and also made people recognize the ideological identity of "the king has the land," which solidified the ruling foundation.

(2) **Land as a means of production**

With agriculture dominating in ancient China, land was both a concrete object of labor and a means of production. During the Spring and Autumn Period and the Warring States Period, productive forces developed, and land privately owned by the people continued to emerge. The newly emerging landowning classes of the vassal states abolished the well-field system[2] after gaining state power and allowed land to be bought and sold freely, making China the first country in the world to have private ownership of land. Since then, the government actively encouraged land reclamation to increase the country's arable land area and enhance its financial strength. For example, the large-scale military and civilian cantonment systems of the Qin and Han dynasties and the merchant cantonment system of the Ming dynasty had all provided a solid material basis for promoting social production and national financial resources. At the same time, restrictions were imposed on the size of private land by various dynasties to consolidate power. For example, Dong Zhongshu, a famous thinker and politician during the Western Han Dynasty, wrote to Emperor Wu of the Han Dynasty to "restrict the amount of private possession of land" to prevent land annexation. Wang Mang, a politician and reformer at the end of the Western Han Dynasty, introduced the Wangtian system to limit private land holdings after usurping the Han Dynasty power and establishing a new dynasty. In the Western Jin dynasty, the occupation field system and the class field system were implemented to limit the amount of land held by peasants and different classes of clans. In the Northern Wei

[2] The well-field system was a form of land system in ancient Chinese society, which appeared in the Shang Dynasty and matured in the Western Zhou Dynasty. Since the roads and channels divide the land into squares and resemble the word "井" (well), it is called "well-field.".

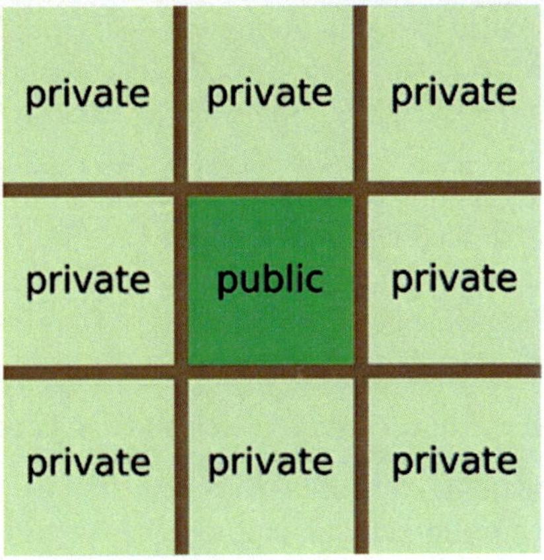

Fig. 1.2 Schematic diagram of the well-field system

and early Tang dynasties, the equal-field system was implemented, whereby peasants were allocated unowned land in equal order according to the strength of their labor force, which resolved the peasant land problem while limiting private ownership of land (Huang 2020a, b) (Fig. 1.2).

(3) **Land as a tax carrier**

As an important means of production and a major source of income, land was also the main vehicle for taxation in ancient China; hence, the taxation system often changed with changes in the land system. During the Xia, Shang, and Zhou Dynasties, when the well-field system was implemented, the three main forms of taxation were "*gong*, *zhu*, and *che*"[3]; rent was mainly paid in kind or through labor. There was no land tax or land rent at that time. At the end of the Spring and Autumn Period, the system of "levying different classes of agricultural taxes according to the different conditions of the land" in Qi and "primary tax mu" in Lu provided that both public and private fields were taxed according to the actual number of mu, which marked the beginning of land taxation in ancient China. In the Northern Wei Dynasty, Emperor Xiaowen introduced a rent modulation system in combination with the even-field system, which involved considering rural households as a unit, requiring farmers to pay a certain amount of rent in corn, silk, or hemp each year and thereby reduced the burden on individual farmers to a certain extent. The Sui and Tang dynasties started to levy "yong" on the basis of rent modulation, stipulating that farmers could pay silk or cloth in lieu of corvée, which ensured productivity of farmers. In the late Tang Dynasty, land annexation became a serious issue; the even-field system was destroyed, and the traditional rent modulation system became unsustainable. Hence, the ruling class started implementing "two tax laws," which considered assets and land as taxation standards. During the Song and Yuan dynasties, the share and fixed

[3] Both are ancient forms of taxation, in which "gong" is a fixed tribute to the ruling class, "zhu" represents the rent for labor, and "che" is the further exploitation of labor by linking the public and private fields.

land rent were implemented, wherein during the Southern Song dynasty, the fixed land rent was set according to land rank. With the increase in productivity, the Ming and Qing Dynasties implemented reforms in the taxation system (Guo 1998). The Ming Dynasty, in particular, implemented the "one whip" method based on the measurement of the entire country's land, combined the taxes, "integrated Ding (the poll tax) in the land tax," and uniformly collected taxes in the form of silver. Based on this, the Qing Dynasty implemented the land tax system, formally abolished the poll tax, implemented the unification of Ding and land, and started the single standard taxation of land.

(4) **Land as the object of household register and cadastre management**

To facilitate control, the ruling class used the system of linking households to land to fix people to the land and set up cadastres and household register specifically based on the land for management. In the feudal system of the Western Zhou Dynasty, the Son of Heaven gave the land to the vassals together with the people on the land, and the people were completely attached to the land (Jian 1979). In the late Warring States period, the Qin state established the "household register accompanying" system, which included the possession of land in the peasant household register and developed a formal household register system. During the Song Dynasty, private land ownership system was further developed, and the household registry was divided into the main and the clients' households according to whether they had land or not. Households were divided according to the amount of land (rural areas were divided into five classes) each household possessed; various single-line field and mu account books were set up. A trend leading to separation of cadastre and household registration was observed. In the Ming Dynasty, after a general household survey, a yellow book was set up in the household registry to register in detail the population and property of each place; in the cadastre management, a fish scale atlas was set up to record in detail the number of acres and scope of each township and the land possessed by each household, and this information was projected onto a map, which reveals the formal separation of the cadastre from the household registry. Both these worked in parallel to restrict the migration of people and exploitation through taxation and corvée (Fig. 1.3).

1.1.3 Perceptions About Modern Land Systems and Ecological Civilization

(1) **Evolution of the different connotations of land**

The creation of the words "土" and "地" shows that the ancient Chinese had a full understanding of the natural properties of land as a source of nourishment for all things and the concept of elemental stratification. Throughout Chinese history, land has long occupied an important position in Chinese political life as a means of production, a tax carrier, and a basis for cadastral and household management because of

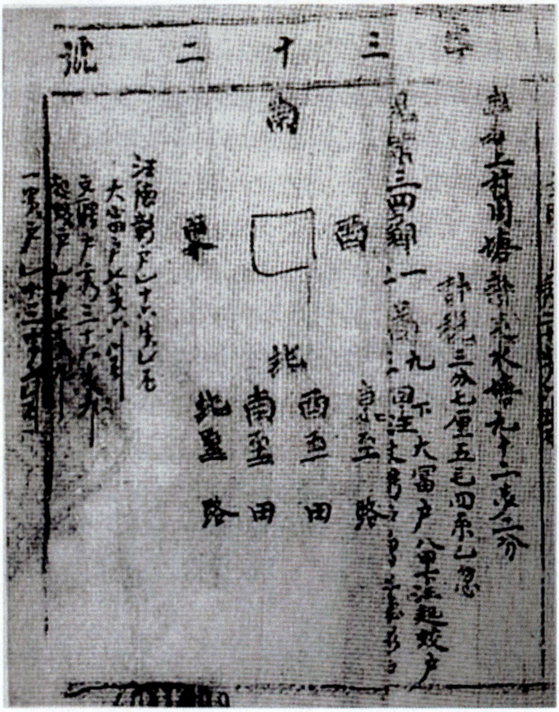

Fig. 1.3 Qimen County Fish Scale Atlas during the Shunzhi Period (Qing 1873)[4]

its functions of bearing, reproduction, and resource production (Bi 1996). The ruling classes of successive generations, from the perspective of maintaining political and economic interests, formulated a series of land policies and regulations to adjust land relations and rationally organize and supervise land use. This led to a strengthening of the Chinese people's land complex and deepened their perceptions about land. However, a gap still exists between the ancient Chinese people's perceptions about land and the modern concept of land.

In the modern disciplinary system, land has many definitions, but the understanding of land varies from discipline to discipline. The concept of "land" in economics is that land is nature, as Marx pointed out in *Capital*: "The soil (and this, economically speaking, includes water) … exists independently of him (man), and is the universal subject of human labour." It also focuses on the important role of land in social and economic development. As early as in the seventeenth century, the founder of classical economics, William Petty, had already proposed that "Labour is the Father and active principle of Wealth, as Lands are the Mother," and Adam Smith

[4] "The fish scale inventory of Qimen County in the sixth year of the reign of Shunzhi Sansi Du Ertu Yuezi" was hidden in the Institute of History, Chinese Academy of Social Sciences. The contents of the record include the name, name of the land, the name of the owner, the name of the family, the branch, the category of the land, the accumulation of the land, the tax mu, and the four points. In the lower left corner, the official seal of Qimen County is inscribed, and the specific contents of the fields are filled in with ink pen.

continued to develop on this, adding capital and labor as two factors of production, thus laying the theoretical foundation of classical economics to support economic growth. Land in the legal sense emphasizes more on people's right to use and control land, and land that human beings find difficult to control and use is not considered land in the legal sense (Shukui and Ying 2019). As Marshall argues, "the right to use a piece of land is the right to dominate a certain space—a certain part of the ground." In political science, land, people, and sovereignty are called the three elements of statehood, and a country's land is equivalent to its "national territory" (Li et al. 2000). The related land economics defines land as the place where the people of a country live, and all the land within the territorial limits of the country is the land (Yang 1986). For landscape scientists, land is synonymous with landscape, and according to the principle of landscape ecology, landscape is "the mosaic of ecosystems on the ground, a land that is a carrier of natural and cultural ecosystems" (Wang and Wang 2006).

The overall concept of land can be considered under two categories: broad and narrow, in which the narrow concept of land refers only to the terrestrial part, while the broader concept considers land as a three-dimensional spatial entity that includes the subsurface, surface, and upper layers of the earth. In the 1972 expert meeting on land evaluation, the FAO defined land as follows: "Land encompasses the atmosphere, soils, and underlying geology, hydrology, and vegetation at and above and below the surface of a given geographic region of the Earth. It also contains the results of past and present human activities within this geographic area, as well as the significant influence of animals on their current and future human use of the land." In 1975, the United Nations published the *Framework for Land Evaluation*, according to which, "land is an area of the earth's surface, the characteristics of which embrace all reasonably stable, or predictably cyclic, attributes of the biosphere vertically above and below this area, including those of the atmosphere, the soil and underlying geology, the hydrology, the plant and animal populations, and the results of past and present human activity, to the extent that these attributes exert a significant influence on present and future uses of the land by humans." *The Encyclopedia of China* defines land as a natural-economic complex that encompasses all types of land. In the *Land Dictionary* edited by Ma Kewei, land is defined as "the terrestrial part of the earth's surface, which includes inland waters and coastal mudflats" (Ma 1991). In *China's Natural Resources Series* (comprehensive volume), which was published in 1995, it is argued that "land is a natural complex formed by the combined action of natural elements such as climate, geomorphology, rocks, soil, vegetation and hydrology and the product of human productive labor" (Sun and Shi 1995).

From a comprehensive perspective, people's perception of land has gradually transitioned from considering land as a primitive means of agricultural production to a complex that includes both natural and human activities. Different understandings of land continue to persist in different disciplinary backgrounds and practical requirements, but, in general, land can be summarized as a natural economic complex containing natural elements such as climate, landforms, soils, hydrology, rocks, vegetation, and the results of human activities, which are distributed in a three-dimensional space of a certain geographical range on the earth's surface, are constantly occurring and developing over time (Lu 2015).

(2) Land system and ecological civilization construction

As a basic resource for human survival and an object of labor, land has multiple natural, economic, social, and cultural properties, and it can support socio-economic development in many ways, including economic, social, and environmental development (Chen et al. 2011). However, in the past, people tended to focus more on the socio-economic functions of land and ignored its ecological connotation; a systematic concept was lacking in its understanding and practice, thus leading to a recurring problem of unsustainable use of land resources (Rounsevell et al. 2012). In this context, an increasing number of scientists began to focus on land issues and thus emerged the discipline of land system science. This field of study considers land as a complex giant system with dynamic interactions within the social-ecological system and focuses on the changes in the interactions between human and natural environment and their social, economic, and political impacts to support the coordinated and sustainable development of social economy and resources and the environment (Verburg et al. 2013). The shift from land to land systems fully reflects the change in traditional land science from a focus on the natural properties of land characteristics to a focus on the interactions between humans and the natural environment, which includes not only land management but, more importantly, the ecosystem services that land provides.

In contemporary China, the construction of ecological civilization is considered a fundamental plan for the sustainable development of the Chinese nation. As a key element in the ecosystem, systematic cognition of land and the construction of a land ecological safety system have also become a practical need to serve the major strategy of national ecological civilization construction. At the Third Plenary Session of the 18th Central Committee of the Communist Party of China in 2013, President Xi Jinping pointed out in his "Decision of the Central Committee of the Communist Party of China on Some Major Issues Concerning Comprehensively Deepening the Reform" that "mountains, rivers, forests, farmlands, lakes and grasslands are a community of life." In July 2017, Xi Jinping, at the 37th meeting of the Central Leading Group for Comprehensively Deepening Reform, once again emphasized that all must adhere to the concept that "mountains, rivers, forests, farmlands, lakes and grasses is a community of life.". "Creating the life community of 'mountains, rivers, forests, fields, lakes, and grass'" is an important element of Xi Jinping's beliefs on ecological civilization and an important part of Xi Jinping's concept of "Socialism with Chinese Characteristics for a New Era," which promotes a systematic construction of China's ecological civilization to attain new heights.

Accordingly, the Central Committee of the CPC and the State Council issued *A Guideline on Building a National Territorial Space Planning System and Supervising the Implementation* in May 2019, wherein territorial space is elaborated as a dynamic and complex giant system of human-land relationship formed by the interaction of human elements such as population, society, economy, innovation, globalization, and infrastructure, and natural elements such as ecology, water resources, energy, land resources, environment, and climate (Zhang and Fang 2016). This aligns with the connotation of the concept of land system. In the framework of land spatial planning, the land system comprises an orderly ecological process and the process of human-land interaction, while the land ecosystem is a constantly developing and changing organic complex of energy flow and material circulation between inanimate objects (environmental conditions) and animate objects (plants, animals, humans, microorganisms, and other biological elements) on the land within a certain territorial scope (Lin and He 2002). In the context of ecological civilization construction, China's land spatial planning and the embedded land system concept within it will prove to be a sound basis for building a national ecological security pattern in the future (Chen et al. 2019).

1.2 Classification and Evolution of Land in China

1.2.1 Ancient Land Classification: Serving Agricultural Production and Feudal Rule

The concept of land type originates from a comprehensive understanding of land in the long-term production practice of human beings. In ancient China, classification of land mainly served two purposes: agricultural production and feudal rule. In the Western Zhou inscriptions, "Situ" represented both the "heir of the land" and "heir of the people" to manage land, agricultural production, and farming through fields, forestry, animal husbandry, and so on. In the second book of the *Rites of Zhou*, "The Land Official Situ," it is written that The Great Situ and the Little Situ are jointly responsible for management of various land resources and population, for division of land, and for the construction of the community (Guo and Wu 2017). From a traditional geomorphological viewpoint, land is to be divided into five categories: mountains and forests, rivers, hills, graves and marshes, also known as the five lands, and land division and layout is carried out accordingly. At the same time, as the land official, The Great Situ also used the methods of land discrimination, land suitability, and land evenness to divide the land into different grades, with the best graded land marked for the king of Zhou and the remaining grades of land to the vassals; this is the first indication of land classification practiced in China.

Written during the Warring States period, *Guanzi—Di Yuan* contains the earliest land classification section in China; it was already a highly systematic concept and widely used at that time. The book continues the previous geomorphological classification idea; first, it divides land into five major categories, namely Dutian (plains), Muyan (sloping land), Hills, Mountains, and Rivers and Lakes, and each major category is subdivided into 25 subcategories. It also contains analyses and measurements of 90 types of soils collected from across the nation according to soil guidelines and calls them "Jiuzhou Soil." Soils are meticulously classified into upper, middle, and lower classes based on their productivity, and each class contains six types of soils as signs; these six soil types are further subdivided into five types based on differences in soil traits (Zhou 2016).

1.2.2 *Modern Land Classification: Serving the Needs of Land Use Efficiency and Management*

With the founding of New China, a series of land resource surveys and evaluations were conducted for better planning and utilization of land, and a scientific land classification system became gradually established. In these surveys, land type classification focuses more on the natural attributes of land, while land resource classification is considered more from resource utilization value or functional differentiation (Tan and Chen 2019a, b, c).

(1) **Classification of land types in China**

In the 1950 and 1960s, natural zoning promoted land type survey and mapping, and the land classification system at that time followed the practice of the Soviet landscape school. Since the 1970s, large- and medium-scale land type mapping in China gradually adopted a three-level classification system combining the landscape school and the Anglo-Australian school. Since the 1980s, as a bottom-up geographical division, the link with natural zoning was strengthened, and two research directions of landscape ecology and environmental geomorphology were formed in theory. In 1985, the Institute of Geographic Sciences and Natural Resources Research of the Chinese Academy of Sciences presided over the development of the "classification system of land type map of 1:1 million in China." This is a typical systematic classification and a summary of the research on land classification in China, which is of pioneering significance. It divides land types into three levels: "land class, land category, and land type" and classifies the land in China into 12 land classes, 106 land categories, and 538 land types (Zhao 1989). This classification system is in line with the basic national conditions of China's vast territory, complex natural conditions, and diverse land types, and it is easy to grasp and apply in production practice. The method is simple and easy to operate, representing a research direction that is concerned with practicality.

(2) **Classification of land resource types in China**

The earliest classification system for land resources in China was first described in the 1930s in *China's Land Use* by Professor John Lossing Buck of Nanjing Jinling University. In the 1940s, Mr. Ren Mei E first proposed land use classification, and the land use survey conducted in Zunyi, Guizhou, divided land into six major categories: paddy fields, drylands, forests, roads and houses, wastelands, and others (Ren 1946). In 1981, the National Agricultural Zoning Committee and the Professional Group of Land Resources Survey proposed the *Classification of Current Land Use and Its Meaning (Draft)*, which was a comprehensive classification of land based on the economic use of land with appropriate reference to operational characteristics, utilization methods, cover characteristics, etc. The results of this classification were incorporated into the 1984 *Technical Regulations of Land Use Status Survey* as Chap. 1 after improvement. Specifically, a two-level classification was adopted, in which the first-level category was divided into eight subcategories:

arable land, garden land, forest land, pasture land, residential and industrial and mining land, transportation land, water and unused land, and this system was in use until 2002. In 1989, the *Urban Cadastral Survey Regulations* proposed for urban cadastral survey and urban cadastral change survey formulated "urban land classification and meaning," which divided urban land into 10 primary categories and 24 secondary categories based on the difference in land use: commercial and financial land, industrial and storage land, municipal land, public building land, residential land, transportation land, special land, water, agricultural land, and other land, and this system was in use until December 2001.

In 2001, the former Ministry of Land and Resources issued the *National Land Classification (Trial)* and the *National Land Classification (Applicable during the Transitional Period)* to meet the needs of land use control and for a scientific implementation of unified management of national land and urban and rural land administration. The primary category is divided into 3 categories: agricultural land, construction land, and unused land; the secondary category is divided into 15 categories: arable land, garden land, forest land, etc., and the tertiary category is divided into 71 categories. The Second National Land Survey was launched on July 1, 2007, and in the same year, the former Ministry of Land and Resources, together with the General Administration of Quality Supervision, Inspection and Quarantine and Standardization Administration of China, jointly issued the national standard "Current Land Use Classification (GB/T21010-2007)," with 12 primary categories and 57 secondary categories, which marked the first national unified land classification standard in China, wherein urban and rural land achieved a unified classification. In November 2017, the former Ministry of Land and Resources revised the "Current Land Use Classification (GB/T21010-2007)" to 12 primary categories and a total of 73 secondary categories (Tan and Chen 2019a, b, c).

1.2.3 Land Resources Classification in the New Era: Serving the Needs of Unified Natural Resources Management and Territorial Spatial Governance

(1) **The third national land survey work classification**

To meet the needs of the Third National Land Survey, the Ministry of Natural Resources released the *Technical Regulations of the Third National Land Survey* in 2019, which generally adopts a primary and secondary classification system, with 13 primary categories and 77 secondary categories (including 23 extended land categories). The third survey land classification was based on GB/T21010-2017. To strengthen land classification for ecological civilization construction to perform the basic support role, while ensuring the inheritance and stability of land classification, the third survey land classification was mainly modified in the following areas compared to the second survey: First, a new first-class category called "wetlands" was added as a primary land category. Eight secondary categories in the original classification were reorganized under the primary category of "wetlands" to highlight the importance of the "wetland" classification. Second, some of the secondary land categories were refined and adjusted. In adhering to the previous classification system based on the eight core categories—"arable land," "garden land," "forest land," "grassland," "urban, village, industrial and mining land, "transportation land," "water and water conservancy facilities land," and "unused land", some of secondary land categories such as, "commercial service facilities land," "special land," and "public administration and public services land," were refined and adjusted. At the same time, secondary land categories "wooded land," "shrub land," "natural grazing land," "mining land," "other garden land," "bare land," "street," "railroad land," etc. were specified and adjusted. Third, some tertiary land categories were refined and added. On the basis of secondary land category "science, education, culture and health land," "parks and green land," "pond water surface," and "ditches," tertiary land categories included "high education land," "square land,", "farming ponds," and "dry ditches," were refined and added respectively. For agricultural restructuring and change from arable land to other agricultural land, and for the cultivation layer to be not considered destroyed land, "the third survey" identifies it as an adjustable land class, as the next level of the corresponding agricultural land. For example, the tertiary category "adjustable orchard" was under the secondary category "orchard."

Considering the needs of the various departments for land-related management, the third survey regulations further strengthen the correspondence with relevant laws and regulations and classification standards. First, at the legal level, the three categories of "agricultural land," "construction land," and "unused land" in *The Third Survey Classification* are compared with the land use control requirements in the *Land Administration Law of the People's Republic of China* to clarify the land use of each secondary land category. Second, to strengthen the connection with related classification standards, first, the land type classification and land use code are fully connected with the national standard "Current Land Use Classification (GB/T 21010-2007)"; second, the types of wetlands included in the land surface establish a more complete correspondence with the "Wetland Classification (GB/T 24708-2009)"; third, a connection is established with the "Urban Land Classification and Planning and Construction Land Standards (GB 50137-2011)," and "streets" are divided into "urban and village road land," "transportation service station land" and "railroad land" into "railroad land" "rail transit land," respectively. Further, the interface with natural resource surveys such as forest land, water, and grassland is enhanced through refining the classification of "plantation land" and adding "rubber plantation" to meet the statistical needs of forestry coverage.[5]

(2) **Land and space survey, planning, and use control of land and sea classification**

China's new round of government institutional reform in 2018 unified the departments of land, planning, and ocean into a natural resources management department,

[5] Study on land classification of the Third National Land Survey [EB/OL]. [2021-08-21]. https://mp.weixin.qq.com/s/3tGK4GAQJp6ihImNpt8zbg.

which unifies the exercise of natural resources survey, evaluation, planning, supply, registration, and use control functions. In November 2020, to support the needs of land and space planning and unified natural resources management, the Ministry of Natural Resources issued the "The Classification Guide for Land and Space Survey, Planning and Use Control of Land and Sea (for Trial Implementation)." This guide is based on the integration of the original "Current Land Use Classification," "Urban Land Classification and Planning and Construction Land Standards," "Marine Use Classification," and other classification standards, unifying the status quo survey, planning and implementation, and use control of land and sea classification standards. The guidelines generally follow the basic principles of land and sea integration, urban and rural integration, and the integration of above and below ground space, dovetailing with the Land Administration Law, and "marine resources" are added related to the classification of sea use and divided according to the dominant way of resource utilization, setting a total of 24 primary categories, 106 secondary categories, and 39 tertiary categories.

In the terrestrial classification, the guide fully considered the interface with "the third survey (the Third National Land Survey)" work classification; land type is relatively consistent, with the same names of the first class used to connote unity. However, at the same time, it also incorporated the results of the "the third survey" practice based on the corresponding complementary improvements: in other words, to strengthen the focus on arable land resources. For example, the expression "cultivation of perennial crops in more than one season a year" was added to "arable land," and the land for growing greenhouses was transferred to the first class of "arable land," and the second class was determined according to the actual irrigation conditions. However, to further meet the demand for finer management of natural resources, the relevant land categories have been further refined, such as the subdivision of "rural roads" in the "*The Third National Land Survey Classification*" into "village roads" and "field roads" in the "*Classification Guide*" depending on whether the cultivated layer is destroyed for road hardening.

In the use of marine areas, the guidelines for the use of marine resources are divided into "fisheries sea," "industrial and mining communications sea," "transportation sea," "recreation sea," "special use sea," and "other sea," that is, six primary categories; these are further subdivided into 16 secondary categories of sea use. The land formed by reclamation is classified according to the main function of its surface land use or the main way of resource retention and protection according to the various types of land use in the land area. Nevertheless, the classification of sea use does not affect the relevant provisions of existing laws and regulations on the maintenance of marine rights and interests and on the implementation of island protection.

1.3 Framework for Analyzing China's Land Policy and Its Basic Logic

Land policy is a process of action undertaken by the state, political parties, the government, social groups, and even individuals to coordinate land relations at a certain stage or field and to achieve specific land rights and interests goals. The process of land policy formulation is also a process of coordinating diverse rights and interests claimed by multiple subjects, which includes not only direct interests such as land use and land revenue distribution, but also rights and interests such as land ownership, possession, and use. In the process of land policy implementation, the ruling party and the government play an important role, but specific decision makers also have the right to interpret and adjust the land policy. Under the influence of differentiated policy environments and different elements, the whole land policy process has a certain dynamic and monopolistic nature. To understand China's land policy, it is necessary to have some knowledge of the current land policy environment and the land policy elements within it.

1.3.1 China's Land Policy Environment

Land policy environment refers to the external environment that affects the whole process of land policy, including the socio-economic and political institutional environment as well as the background of economic and social development and other specific environments. The land policy environment is the prerequisite for the emergence and development of land policy, which determines and restricts the characteristics and functions of land policy. However, at the same time, land policy also has a certain degree of counteraction to the land policy environment and can also passively influence the land policy environment under the premise of adapting to land policy (Wang 2010). China, as the world's largest economy in transition, has a frequently changing policy environment. Specifically in the area of land policy, the economic development model, urban–rural relations, and institutional reform are the main influencing factors.

(1) **Economic status**

Since the reform and opening up in the 1980s, China's economy has become world-renowned for the stupendous achievements of the country. Industrialization formed the basis for China's economic take-off and is the key to understanding China's economic achievements. In the 70 years since the founding of New China, a historic leap was made from the early stage of industrialization to the late stage of industrialization, and the country has also achieved a historic transformation from being a backward agricultural country to the world's leading industrial country. In the first 30 years of reform and opening up, China established an independent and complete industrial system and national economic system with focus on industrialization, especially heavy industry, during the planned economy period, both of which laid the foundation for the later economic take-off (Lang et al. 2019). Since the reform and opening up, Chinese enterprises have helped China's economy grow continuously and rapidly by virtue of their traditional cost advantages in the pricing of various factors of production, such as labor, land, and energy. From the perspective of longitudinal comparison, China's GDP grew at an average annual rate of 8.1% from 1949 to 2008 and 9.8% from 1978 to 2008, showing a continuous high growth rate. From a cross-sectional comparison, the average annual GDP growth rates of the United States and Japan from 1978 to 2008 were 2.97 and 2.45%, respectively, while those of Brazil and India were 2.90 and 5.75%, respectively, China has a significant growth advantage over the world's major developed countries as well as developing countries. However, with the increasing economic volume, the problems of high resource consumption and high environmental pollution started becoming prominent (Fig. 1.4).

(2) **Urban–rural relationship**

The urban–rural relationship is the most fundamental economic and social relationship, and at different stages of development, different patterns of interaction are observed between urban and rural areas. In the early stages of the founding of New China, based on the experience of the Soviet Union, China undertook "Priority Development of Heavy Industry" as a strategic guideline and artificially restricted the flow of factors between urban and rural areas through the policies of unified purchasing and marketing, strict household registration and people's communes, forming the development model of "Assisting Industry with Agriculture and Supporting Cities with Rural Areas"; thus urban–rural development ran on separate course. During

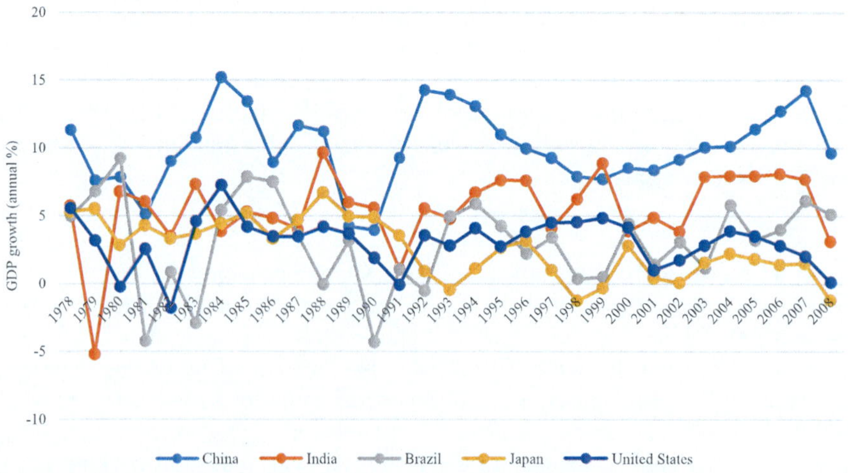

Fig. 1.4 Annual GDP Growth Rate of China versus that of the U.S., India, Brazil, and Japan, 1978–2008 (Source: Data retrieved from https://www.worldbank.org on May 16, 2022)

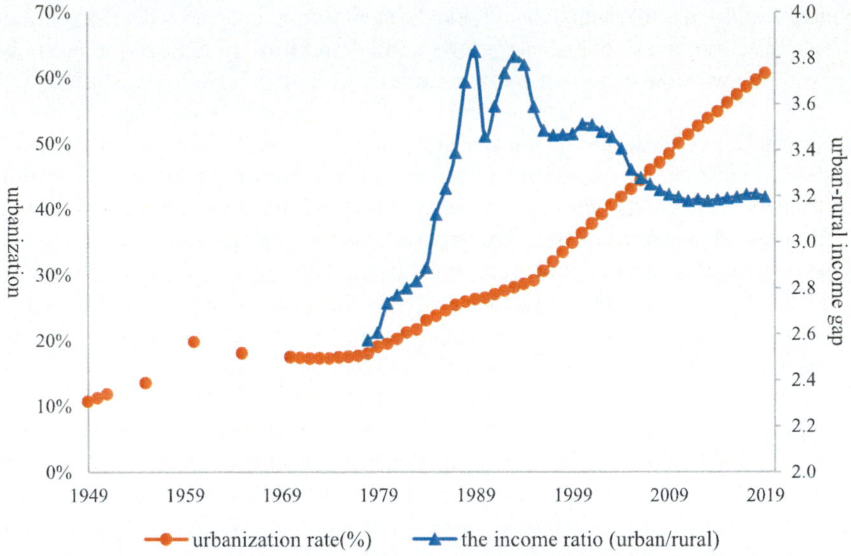

Fig. 1.5 Co-occurrence of fast urbanization and high urban–rural income inequality[6]

the early stage of reform and opening up, China mobilized farmers' enthusiasm for production and effectively promoted rural development through measures such as the system of household contract responsibility, liberalizing the operation of most agricultural products and promoting the transfer of surplus rural labor to non-agricultural industries or towns. However, after establishing a socialist market economy system in 1992, various resource factors again accelerated their gathering toward cities under the impact of market forces and the introduction of urban-biased policies. With the advancement of industrialization and urbanization, the gap between urban and rural development further widened (see Fig. 1.5). With the dawn of the new century, as China's industrialization entered the middle stage, the country is on the path to explore urban–rural integration and has proposed the strategic goal of achieving common prosperity in urban and rural areas by 2050 in the rural revitalization plan. To resolve the "Three Agriculture Issue" and narrow the gap between urban and rural areas, macro strategies, such as integrated urban–rural development, new rural construction, urban–rural integration, and new urbanization, have been proposed, but the results of these strategies and their progress are not obvious.

Presently, the imbalance between urban and rural development and inadequate rural development have become the most prominent structural contradictions in China. In 2017, the 19th National Congress of the Communist Party of China (19th CPC National Congress) explicitly proposed implementing rural revitalization, giving priority to development of agriculture and rural areas, establishing a

---

[6] Data from China Statistical Yearbook, calculated as the ratio of per capita disposable income of urban and rural residents, and deflated using 1978 as the base period.

sound institutional mechanism and policy system for the integrated development of urban and rural areas, and accelerating the modernization of agriculture and rural areas. This implies that the path of urban–rural development in China has shifted from "urban–rural planning" to "urban–rural integration." Under the dual land system of urban and rural areas, land is the key element connecting China's urban and rural systems; therefore, the reform of the land system with the protection and realization of farmers' land rights and interests as the core and the construction of a unified market for urban and rural areas are important policy tools to realize the integrated development of urban and rural areas. In 2008, the Third Plenary Session of the 17th Central Committee of the Communist Party of China proposed the policy goal of equal property rights for state-owned land and collective land with the policy "The Same Rights, The Same Prices".[7] In 2015, the Standing Committee of the National People's Congress authorized the State Council to carry out pilot projects in 33 pilot counties (cities and districts), including Daxing District in Beijing, on rural land expropriation, market entry of collective management construction land, and reform of the residential base system. The revised *Land Administration Law* in 2019 and the new *Implementing Regulations of the Land Administration Law* in 2020 both further emphasize the policy objective of urban–rural integration. For urban–rural integration development, further efforts are needed to reconcile several groups of contradictions, such as policy and regulations and development reality, government policy and collective action, government design and farmers' choice, government action and realization of rights and interests, and government action and lack of market.

(3) **Institutional reform**

China's natural resource management is mainly centered on the centralized state management system. With the recent socio-economic changes, the natural resource management institutions have undergone two transitions from "division" to "unification," which occurred in 1998 and 2018, respectively. In 1998, the Ministry of Land and Resources was formed from the Ministry of Geology and Mines, the State Land Administration, the State Oceanic Administration, and the State Mapping Bureau. Its main function was to be responsible for the planning, management, protection, and rational use of natural resources such as land resources, mineral resources, and marine resources. At the same time, the State Oceanic Administration and the State Bureau of Surveying and Mapping are retained as national bureaus under the Ministry of Land and Resources. The formation of the Ministry of Land and Resources has served as an effective institutional support to co-ordinate the management of natural

[7] *The Constitution of the People's Republic of China* stipulates that land in urban areas is owned by the state. The land in rural areas and suburban areas is collectively owned, except those that are owned by the state as stipulated by law. According to *Property Law*, collective landowners cannot establish the right to use construction land or mortgage property rights on collective land; besides, farmers do not have complete usufruct rights to collectively owned residential bases; hence, an obvious inequality persists in property rights between collective land and state-owned land under the dual land system of urban and rural areas.

resources such as land, minerals, and oceans. China has thus established a centralized and unified management from land to sea, from land to minerals, and has taken a key step forward in the management of natural resources from "division" to "unification." However, with the exception of a few important natural resources such as land, the management of other resources was still relatively fragmented, with problems in the setting up of management agencies, with management vacuums, or crossover of powers and responsibilities between different resource sub-management agencies. With the integration of economic and social development and the deepening understanding of the laws of nature, the unified management of only some natural resources could no longer adapt to the new requirements of ecological civilization construction under the new situation.

In 2018, the Ministry of Natural Resources was set up based on the requirement of "coordinating management of mountains, waters, forests, farmland, lakes and grassland," once again achieving a key leap from "division" to "unification" of natural resources management institutions (Dong 2018). After this, the Ministry of Natural Resources, in a unified way, performs its duties as the owner of public-owned natural resource assets, the duties of regulating the use of all territorial space and protecting and restoring ecosystems. China's land resource management is also undergoing a gradual shift to systematic governance of mountains, rivers, forests, farmlands, lakes, and grasslands. Spatial planning and use control are a new constraint mechanism for the central government to exercise proxy ownership over localities, while ecological protection and restoration is a new requirement for localities in the process of exercising proxy ownership. In the first half of 2019, the central government issued four important documents, including *A Guideline on Advancing the Reform of the Property Right System for Natural Resource Assets*, *A Guideline on Building a National Territorial Space Planning System and Supervising the Implementation*, *A Guideline on Establishing a System of Protected Natural Areas with National Parks as Its Mainstay* and *Opinions on the Establishment of a Sound Mechanism and Policy System for Integrated Urban–Rural Development*. These four documents can be considered the "multiple pillars"[8] of institutional design for natural resource governance in the new era, corresponding to the system of natural resource property rights, the construction of the government's public power in natural resources governance, the division of labor and collaboration between the central government and the countryside in the natural resources governance system, and the construction of the relationship between the government and the market, and between the city and the countryside in the unified urban and rural construction market, laying down a new order of relationship between the central government and the countryside (Tan 2021).

---

[8] In ancient traditional Chinese architecture, the four beams and eight columns represent the main structure of the building. Now, it is derived as a kind of reform thinking and reform methodology proposed by the Party Central Committee, with Xi Jinping as its core, emphasizing that reform should have a basic main framework.

1.3.2 *Land Policy Elements in China*

Land policy elements are the important components of the land policy system. All elements and the interactions between them constitute the land policy system and make it an organic whole that is interconnected and mutually constrained. Of all the land policy elements, land policy objectives, land policy instruments (tools), land policy subjects, and land policy objects are particularly crucial to understanding the entire land policy system.

(1) **Land policy goals**

Land policy goals are the requirements and objectives proposed by the state or land administration authorities to resolve land problems, usually set specifically according to realistic needs and constantly adjusted and updated in line with social and economic development and changes in people's perceptions about the role of land resources. Presently, China is still under pressure from its resource endowment of more people and less land, while it is also on a new journey to build a comprehensive socialist modern state. Therefore, it is particularly important to reconcile the relationships among population, resources, environment, and social economy. To this end, the goals of China's current land policy system include the following: (i) to harmonize land economic relations; (ii) to harmonize the relationship between people and land and people and nature; (iii) to achieve the optimal allocation of land resources through the development, utilization, and rational protection of land resources; (iv) to protect agricultural land, especially arable land resources, and (v) to guarantee the supply of agricultural products, especially food security. Future goals of the land policy system may be further adjusted as changes occur in the socio-economic development stages.

(2) **Land policy tools**

Land policy tools are the specific paths to achieve the goals of land policy and are a general term for various measures and methods. In terms of specific content, they can be divided into economic tools, administrative tools, legal tools, and so on. Under each of these, they are subdivided into a number of institutional norms and standards. For example, the economic tools of land policy include land financial tools, land market regulation, land administration, land rent, and land taxation policies, while the land financial tools themselves include collateral coefficients, discount rates, and so on. Since land policy tools are extremely abundant, they are often a combination of multiple tools in real life. To reduce the difficulty of policy makers in selecting policy tools, the classification method of policy tools by Michael Howlett and M. Ramesh can be borrowed to classify land policy tools into three major categories, namely, mandatory tools, hybrid tools, and voluntary tools, based on the degree of direct participation of the government, society, and the market (Howlett et al. 2009). Among them, mandatory tools mainly rely on direct government intervention, with less room for social and market discretion. They include planning control, behavioral regulation, legal responsibility, and direct provision, corresponding to the land planning system, land ownership registration and licensing, arable land protection responsibility system, and land allocation and expropriation systems, respectively. Hybrid tools are both voluntary and compulsory and are determined by both the government and the market. They include activities such as land title transfer or transaction, land-related urban land use taxes and fees, agricultural subsidies, land information disclosure, or information platform construction. Voluntary tools, on the contrary, rely on market and private forces to achieve the goals of land policy, such as voluntary participation of individuals in the protection of land resources and ecological environment, spontaneous monitoring of land pollution by the public, and voluntary rules and standards related to land formulated by relevant industry organizations, intermediary organizations, and other organizations (Cao and Du 2020).

(3) **Land policy subjects**

Land policy subjects are influenced by the characteristics of land itself. Specifically, land policy subjects involve individuals, groups, or organizations that directly or indirectly participate in and influence the land policy process in some way in a particular policy environment. In China, land policy subjects mainly refer to the ruling party, central and local governments, administrative departments, land economy or land property rights subjects, and the public. The government has the dominant power to allocate land resources and is the land policy subject with decisive influence. In the long-lasting economic development transition, the relationship between the central and local governments and the relationship among local governments become the key to influence land policy. The model of "administrative centralization + economic decentralization" is a generalization of the relationship between the central government and the local government in China, which corresponds to the centralized land administrative constraints and decentralized land economic management in the field of land policy (Tan 2021). Faced with the inequality of financial and administrative rights, with the central government having maximum power, and competition among local governments at all levels, local governments have adopted the strategy of land finance,[9] acquiring rural land at a low price, selling it as industrial land at a low price to attract investment and commercial and residential land at a high price to capture high value-added land revenue and gain an advantage in the development competition. In this process, it is worth paying attention to the interests between the central government and the local government, the government and the collective, the collective and the expropriated farmers, and the government and the market development entities.

(4) **Land policy objects**

The object of land policy is the object on which land policy acts, including the specific issue to be addressed and the specific group of land beneficiaries targeted by the policy (Chen 2003). Presently, the key land policy issues in China are as follows: First, to clarify land property rights, rapid urbanization has led to a large number of agricultural land conversions, and the lack of definition of rural land

[9] Land finance refers to the fact that under China's special tax sharing system, local governments rely on revenue from the sale of land use rights to meet their financial needs.

property rights affects the subsequent compensation and threatens social equity and stability.[10] Second, there is a need to levy property tax. The rapid economic development makes part of the wealth gather in the hands of a small group of people who get rich first in the form of assets. Hence, tax collection including real estate tax and inheritance tax becomes a powerful tool to reasonably regulate high income. Third, to strengthen the protection of arable land, from the latest release of the Third National Land Survey data in 2021, China's arable land area is 1.918 billion mu in 2019. Compared to the earlier survey in 2009, arable land area has decreased by about 113 million mu. Apart from the impact of statistical caliber, this is a reminder of the persisting serious issue of arable land protection in China. In the future it will be necessary to ensure systematic protection of arable land, quantity control, quality management, and ecological management as a whole. Fourth, with the optimization of urban planning and development, rapid urbanization is accompanied by urban poverty, high housing prices, and an imbalance between urban and rural incomes, with the need for more scientific and reasonable territorial spatial planning to lead urban economic growth while promoting socially equitable development. Fifth, to enhance environmental sustainability, under the constraints of carbon neutrality and carbon peaking goals, a key issue in future policy reform is on how to coordinate carbon sources and sinks through natural resource management and territorial spatial planning.

1.3.3 The Underlying Logic of China's Land Policy Analysis

(1) **Historical logic**

The historical logic in China's land policy is a summary of the inevitability and regularity of past policy practices and the practical basis for the emergence and development of the theoretical logic. The Communist Party of China pursued the method of historical materialism to summarize and analyze the core features of the different stages during a century of continuous temporal and spatial changes in the system and to delve deeper into the inevitable laws that remain unchanged (Yan et al. 2021). Throughout the development history of human society, the content of land policy has evolved and enriched through the process of "use—stable use—exclusive use—ownership—ownership system—separation of rights—formation of a system of rights—increasing prominence of the right to use" (Huang 2020a, b).

1921–1949 Before the founding of New China. Feudal land relations were abolished and land was realized for the cultivator. Since the founding of the CPC, the land issue has been considered the key to the rural revolution, and protecting the interests of the working people through land policy gradually became an important issue for the Party (Yu et al. 2021). The period from 1927 to 1937 was the ten-year agrarian revolutionary period in the history of the Chinese Communist Party, during

[10] Joyce Yanyun Man. Land policy issues in China [EB/OL]. [2021–08-21]. https://www.lincolninst.edu/publications/articles/land-policy-issues-china.

which a series of rural land policies were formulated and implemented, such as the *Jinggang Mountain Land Law*, *Xingguo Land Law*, and the *Land Registration Act*, all established considering the agrarian revolutionary task of changing the feudal and semi-feudal land ownership system into a peasant land ownership system. During the Second Sino-Japanese War from 1937 to 1945, to unite the peasants and landlords to fight against the Japanese, the CPC adopted the land policy of rent reduction and interest reduction for landlords and rent and interest payment for peasants. During the Liberation War of 1945–1949, people's desire and call for the abolition of the feudal land system and to gain access to land for cultivation became increasingly strong. The *Outline of China's Land Law* formulated by the National Land Conference in Xibaipo in 1947 clearly stipulated that "the feudal and semi-feudal exploitative land system should be abolished and the land system of land for the cultivator should be implemented," which fundamentally changed the land ownership system and fully stimulated the revolutionary enthusiasm of the masses of the rural proletariat, providing the impetus for victory in the Liberation War.

1949–1978 Before the reform and opening up: This period led to strengthening possession, using rights, and promoting equitable development. 1949 saw the founding of the People's Republic of China and the Communist Party of China became the ruling party. With development as the goal, exploration of the land system in all fairness began during the period of socialist construction. The promulgation and implementation of the *Land Reform Law of the People's Republic of China* in 1950 overthrew the feudal land ownership system and introduced the peasant class land ownership system. By the end of 1952, land reform was basically completed nationwide, and the feudal exploitative land system that had lasted for thousands of years in China was completely abolished. However, the peasants who owned land still faced many constraints such as fragmented production and operation, low technology, and lack of tools. The rural land system characterized by "collective ownership" and "unified management" was developed during this period. Supported by policy documents such as the *Resolution on Mutual Cooperation in Agricultural Production*, the *Model Statute of Agricultural Production Cooperatives*, the *Model Statute of Senior Agricultural Production Cooperatives*, and the *Resolution on the Establishment of People's Communes in the Countryside*, the rural cooperative movement emerged and eventually formed the "large in size and collective in nature" and " equalitarianism and unpaid appropriation " system of the people's communes.

1978–2012 after the reform and opening up: During this period, the emphasis was on the efficiency of factor allocation and achieving efficiency. China's economic system gradually shifted from a "planned economy" to a "socialist market economy," and efficiency became the key word in all policies. In rural areas, the household contract responsibility system promoted by the people of Xiaogang Village in Fengyang County, Anhui Province, pioneered the separation of land ownership and use rights in China, fully liberating and developing rural productivity. In cities, the first public auction of state-owned land use rights was completed in Shenzhen in 1987, providing an opportunity to promote the system of paid use of state-owned land in cities and towns. The amended *Land Administration Law* of 1988 clearly stipulates that "the State shall implement a system of compensated use of state-owned land in accordance with the law," marking the formal establishment of a market transaction system for the grant, transfer, lease, and mortgage of state-owned land use rights in China's urban areas, laying the institutional foundation for the rapid development of urbanization. At the same time, a series of land systems aiming to protect arable land and improve land use efficiency were introduced accordingly. In August 1998, the Standing Committee of the National People's Congress revised and passed the *Land Administration Law*, which clearly proposed the basic state policy of "cherishing and reasonably utilizing land and effectively protecting arable land" and improved the land use control system. On the basis of urban and rural land use control, housing system reform was also accelerated. In 1998, the *Notice of the State Council on Further Deepening the Reform of the Urban Housing System and Accelerating Housing Construction* marked the start of the reform of monetization of housing allocation and the rapid release of urban land rights.

2012–2021 New Era: In this period, reform of the factor market was deepened and modernization of land governance was promoted. Under the new economic normal, the ground realities of land resource allocation, utilization as well as protection, became more complex, and new requirements were proposed for territorial space planning and integrated management of natural resources in land resource work. In this period, China further explored innovations and actively piloted land policies with the goal of improving the efficiency of land use and enhancing the effectiveness of land governance through more comprehensive reforms. On the one hand, the rural land reform system was actively promoted based on the the three bottom lines: no change in the nature of public ownership of land, no breakthrough in the red line of arable land, and no damage to farmers' interests. On December 31, 2014, the General Office of the Central Committee of CPC and the General Office of the State Council jointly issued *Opinions on the Pilot Reform of Rural Land Acquisition, Market Entry of Collective Management Construction Land,* and *Residential Land System*, marking the official pilot stage of China's rural reform of "Three Pieces of Land (*sankuaidi*)". On October 30, 2016, the General Office of the CPC Central Committee and the General Office of the State Council issued *Opinions on Improving the Measures for Separating Rural Land Ownership from Contracted Management Right*, formally proposing the "Separation of Three Rights," which continued to expand the power of rural development. On the other hand, in response to urban housing tensions and real estate market problems, the supply-side structural reform of the housing system became strengthened. In 2017, the report of the 19th CPC National Congress proposed "putting in place a housing system that ensures supply through multiple sources, provides housing support through multiple channels, and encourages both housing purchase and renting." In the same year, the *National Land Planning Outline (2016–2030)* was published, and a long-term strategic plan was formulated for the land supply structure and utilization mode. In addition, market-oriented reform of land elements was actively promoted to further increase the productivity. In 2020, the Central Committee of the Communist Party of China and the State Council issued the *Opinions on Improving the Systems and Mechanisms for Market-oriented Allocation of Factors of Production* proposed to "promote the market-based reform of land elements" to achieve market-determined prices of land elements and the ensure flow of autonomous and orderly, efficient, and fair allocation (Fig. 1.6).

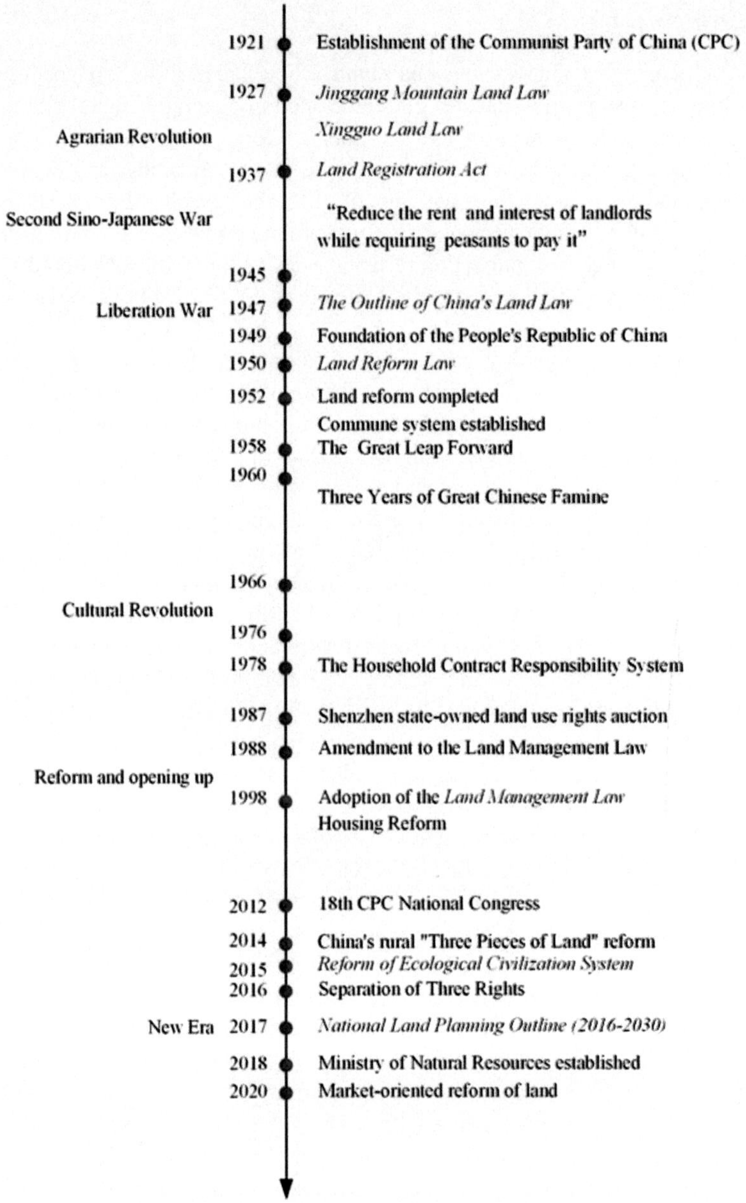

Fig. 1.6 Evolution of the Historical Logic of China's Land Policy Reform (Hand-drawn by the author)

(2) **Theoretical logic**

The theoretical logic contained in China's land policy analysis was born and informed by the logic of history; it was tested and developed in concrete practice. Its essence lies in the inevitable connection and the inner law operating between the intrinsic elements of each system, which determines the nature, meaning, and direction of the system and also guides the development of the historical and practical logic of China's land policy. The evolution and reform of land policy is essentially a process of continuous change and innovation of land policy in line with social productivity, and the change of land policy is closely related to the change of land system (Huang 2020a, b).

Land policies in China are based on the theoretical system of socialism with Chinese characteristics, which is the latest theoretical achievement of the Communist Party of China in combining Marxism with Chinese reality and realizing the Chinese-ization of Marxism, including Deng Xiaoping's theory, the socio-political theory of "Three Represents," the scientific outlook on development, and Xi Jinping's socialist thought with Chinese characteristics in the new era. In the socialist system with Chinese characteristics, the land system, as an important part of it, is characterized by people-centeredness, market economy, common wealth creation, fairness and justice, and democratic politics. Overall, it has the following characteristics: First, it realizes the socialist system of public ownership of land, with state-owned and collective ownership of land co-existing, and no organization or individual is allowed to appropriate, buy, sell, or otherwise illegally transfer land. Second, land ownership is separated from land use rights, and a land contractual management system is adopted in rural areas, granting farmers long-term and guaranteed land use rights, while state-owned land in cities is granted to land users for a fee. Third, to respect and protect land property rights, a legal system is formed to regulate land rights through the *CONSTITUTION OF THE PEOPLE'S REPUBLIC OF CHINA*, the *Chinese Civil Code*, *Law on Contracting of Rural Land*, *Land Administration Law*, etc., and thereby increase the rights and expectations of land users through a clear property rights system and an ideal property rights protection system. This helps promote economic development and optimal allocation of resources (Liu 2018). Additionally, as a socialist country, the Chinese government's role in regulating capital functions and market mechanisms differs significantly from that of governments in Western countries. As a major economic factor, land plays an important role in China's social economy, and the economic operation model associated with it is typical of the socialist market economy model with Chinese characteristics. On the basis of public ownership of land, "land capitalization" was the main source of capital accumulation in the early stages of China's urban development. The central government and local governments and their state-run enterprises, together with private enterprises, collaborated and shared profits in a market economy, jointly promoting China's urbanization and economic development. It is a new political and economic system that is neither a purely profit-seeking capitalist market economy nor a traditional "socialist" planned economy, but a combination of both (Huang 2021).

Land policies in China are guided by the theory of ecological civilization in the new era. Xi Jinping's thought on ecological civilization construction is the latest theoretical achievement of Marxism's Chinese-ization; it is also an enrichment and development of the path to socialism with Chinese characteristics based on the concept of human civilization. The concepts of (a) scientific development of "harmonious coexistence of humanity and nature," (b) green development of "clean waters and green mountains that are just as valuable as gold and silver," and (c) systemic and holistic development of "lucid waters and lush mountains that are invaluable assets" are all important guidelines for future land policy changes. In the previous land policy framework, China developed a land management system with protection of arable land as the primary goal and land use control as the core. In the twenty-first century, with increasingly serious environmental problems, China gradually expanded land use control to natural resources such as grasslands, waters, and wetlands, based on the experiences of other countries. In May 2019, the Central Committee of the CPC and the State Council issued *A Guideline on Building a National Territorial Space Planning System and Supervising the Implementation*, further pointing out the need to realize a territorial spatial governance system and governance capacity modernization, further expanding the object of control to the entire territorial space. With further promotion of ecological civilization, future land policy reform is expected to increase implementation of the concept of ecological civilization in a comprehensive manner, adhere to the policy of giving priority to conservation, protection, and natural restoration, actively respond to the needs of economic development and environmental protection through a full understanding of the laws of nature and ecological environment, and promote the synergistic management of various ecological elements such as mountains, water, forests, fields, lakes and grasslands while vigorously developing green industries to achieve a harmonious coexistence between man and nature in land use.

Land policies in China are guaranteed by the theory of modernization of state governance. China's national governance system has long been profoundly influenced by the centralized tradition and has evolved in response to economic and social development. In China, with its traditionally strong government and a communal system of urban and rural land ownership, land is often used as the main policy tool to achieve the corresponding spatial governance (Xia 2020). Land-related planning forms the basis of the process and plays an important role in coordinating the demands of multiple rights holders, such as the government, the market, and society, and in comprehensively distributing the use and benefits of spatial resources. Since the Third Plenary Session of the 18th CPC Central Committee, China has entered a phase of comprehensive deepening reform, with the overall goal of "upholding and improving the socialist system with Chinese characteristics and modernizing China's governance system and capacity.". This is not only different from the traditional Chinese "governance" under a single centralized system, but also different from the Western trend of decentralized government, polycentric governance, and social autonomy; moreover, it aims to establish a new national governance system that closely matches China's actual national conditions. Spatial planning is an important part of the national governance system, and in the new context of the requirements for the construction of ecological civilization, system reconstruction has become an inevitable task to enhance the national governance capacity (Zhang and Xia 2019). At the same time, land market is a specific object of national governance and an important component of the governance system. In the context of the long-standing urban–rural dual land system, land market involves not only the relationship between the government and the market, but also the development between urban and rural areas. In the future, urban–rural land management should be further strengthened, the value of collective land should be revealed, and the basic land rights of farmers should be guaranteed through the construction of a unified urban–rural land market.

(3) **Practical logic**

The practical logic underlying China's land policies revolves around the relationship between people and land at different stages of development, the essence of which is the objective relationship between productive forces and relations among production, the superstructure, and the economic base. Through clarifying the historical and theoretical logic of China's land policy changes, it is necessary to further explore how the two are unified in the practical logic to understand the specific reasons driving the evolution of China's land policies and provide a reference for future development. In terms of the relationship between people and land, China has roughly gone through three stages: "subsistence coercion," "development coercion," and "harmonious synergy."

"Subsistence coercion" was the form of relationship between the land and people from the early founding of New China up to the reform and opening-up period. During this period of a relatively low level of productivity and lack of obvious property rights constraints, the development and utilization of land was mainly subject to administrative or planning instructions from the higher authorities. To obtain more means of production, China engaged in "fighting with the sky and the earth," by "fencing rivers to make land, fencing lakes to make land, and reclaiming wasteland to make land," which increased the area of arable land, but still did not produce enough food to feed the hungry. It further aggravated the destruction of territorial space leading to conflict between human and land.

The second form of relationship between people and land was "development coercion," starting from the period of the reform and opening up to the early twentieth century. Although China had explored the establishment of a property rights system for natural resources earlier through the revision of the *Constitution*, the *General Principles of the Civil Law*, and the successive implementation of the *Forest Law of The People's Republic of China*, the *Grassland Law of the People's Republic of China*, the *Land Administration Law*, and other laws and regulations, the imperfections in the property rights system and the market mechanism for natural resources, as well as the excessive intervention of the "strong government" led to relations between people and land remaining tense. The rapid development of industrialization and urbanization increased consumption, occupation, or destruction of natural resources and the ecological environment, especially the universal "pie-spreading" urban expansion and the path dependence of the traditional development mode, which led to a sharp increase in the pressure on natural resources and the ecological environment.

The third period of the relationship between land and people is one of "harmonious synergy," from 2013 to the present. In 2013, the Third Plenary Session of the 18th Central Committee first proposed improving the property rights system and the use control system of natural resources assets; since then, the emphasis has been on the objectives of ecological civilization construction in the new era, further clarified in many documents, such as the General Plan for the *Reform of Ecological Civilization System* and the report of the 19th CPC National Congress. In the new era, the reform of the property rights system of natural resources assets and the market-oriented allocation of factors have become important institutional elements in building a new development pattern, and the revision of the *Civil Code* and the new *Land Administration Law* have further provided guarantees for the optimization of the territorial spatial development pattern. In the process of a series of policy advocacy and practice, a more effective adjustment has been seen in the relationship between people and the land (Huang 2021).

Under the framework system of the unified management of natural resources, the focus is on how to promote territorial spatial governance and the harmonious development of human and land through the reconstruction of property rights and innovation of property rights. The natural resources property rights system is an institutional tool to coordinate the development of different types of territorial space, a policy tool to realize the synergy between the subjects of interest, and an innovative tool to modernize the harmonious development of man and nature. A realistic territorial space development will have to balance between public interest and collective rights and interests, public power and individual rights, as well as between multiple property rights subjects and multiple types of property rights. Promoting territorial space governance and harmonizing the relationship between people and land through property rights innovation and building a new pattern of high-quality national spatial development and protection has become the main focus of future work.

References

Bi B (1996) Land economics. People's University of China Press, Beijing, China, pp 1–3 (in Chinese)

Cao X, Du D (2020) Research on land policy of functional zones from the perspective of policy instruments. Truth Seek (6): 30–41, 108 (in Chinese)

Chen M (2015) "Land politics": a political analysis of land issues in China. Nanjing Agricultural University, Nanjing

Chen M, Liang L, Wang Z et al (2019) Geographical thinking on the relationship between beautiful China and land spatial planning. Acta Geogr Sin 74(12):2467–2481 (in Chinese)

Chen R, Cai Y, Yan X et al (2011) The functions of land system and its sustainability assessment. China Land Sci 25(1):8–15 (in Chinese)

Chen Z (2003) Public policy analysis. China Renmin University Press, Beijing, China, p 50 (in Chinese)

Dong Z (2018) The improvement of territorial spatial governance capability from the perspective of institutional reform. China Land 11:4–9 (in Chinese)

Guo L, Wu T (2017) Identifying the region and order, shaping the cities and countryside: the ancient Chinese spatial planning system and the techniques in rites of Zhou. J Tsinghua Univ (Philosophy and Social Sciences) 32(6): 36–54, 194 (in Chinese)
Guo W (1998) A brief history of the development of agricultural science and technology in China. China Science and Technology Press, Beijing, China, pp 353–354 (in Chinese)
Howlett M, Ramesh M, Perl A (2009) Studying public policy: policy cycles and policy subsystems, vol 3. Oxford University Press, Oxford
Huaiyu Z (2016) The genesis of Chinese soil ecology theory: a brief exploration of Guanzi Di Yuan. Guanzi J 1:10–18 (in Chinese)
Huang X (2021) The reform of the natural resource property rights system and the innovation in territorial spatial governance. Urban Plan Forum 2:53–57 (in Chinese)
Huang X (2020a) Land policy science. China Agricultural Press, Beijing, China, pp 184–185 (in Chinese)
Huang X (2020b) Land policy science. China Agriculture Press, Beijing, China, p 81 (in Chinese)
Huang Z (2021) From the capitalization of land to the socialization of capital: the new political economy of China's development experience. Southeast Acad Res (3): 79–95, 247 (in Chinese)
Jian B (1979) An outline of Chinese history: Book I. People's Publishing House, Beijing, China (in Chinese)
Jingxiang Z, Tianci X (2019) The change and reconstruction of spatial planning system under the goal of modern national governance. J Nat Resour 34(10):2040–2050 (in Chinese)
Lang L, Zhou M, Liu Z (2019) The summary of the forum (2019) for China's economy growth and economic cycle. Econ Res J 54(10):204–208 (in Chinese)
Li X, Zi Yuan (2012) Tianjin. Tianjin Ancient Books Publishing House, China, p 1177 (in Chinese)
Li Y, Ma K, Lu X (2000) Land resources of China. China Earth Press, Beijing, China, p 1 (in Chinese)
Lin Q, He X (2002) Land policy. China Agricultural Press, Beijing, China, p 143 (in Chinese)
Liu S (2018) Land system and China's development. China Renmin University Press, Beijing, China, p 159 (in Chinese)
Lu H (2015) General theory of land management. China Agricultural Press, Beijing, China, pp 1–2 (in Chinese)
Ma K (1991) Land dictionary. Changchun Publishing House, Changchun, China, p 802 (in Chinese)
Qing T (1873) "Qimen Xianzhi," vol. 9, "Public Opinion and Geography—Ancestral Hall," engraved in 1873, p 6
Ren M (1946) Land use in the vicinity of Zunyi. Acta Geographica Sinica 12–13 (in Chinese)
Rounsevell MDA, Pedroli B, Erb KH et al (2012) Challenges for land system science. Land Use Policy 29(4):899–910
Songqiao Z (1989) Mapping specifications for 1:1 million land type maps of China. Survey and Mapping Press, Beijing, China (in Chinese)
Sun H, Shi Y (1995) China natural resources series-comprehensive volume//China natural resources series compilation committee. China Environmental Science Press, Beijing, China (in Chinese)
Tan R (2021) The central-local governance mechanism in China's land marketization. Int Econ Rev (2): 36–53, 5 (in Chinese)
Tan S, Chen Y (2019a) Land resources science. Fudan University Press, Shanghai, China, pp 1–3 (in Chinese)
Tan S, Chen Y (2019b) Land resources science. Fudan University Press, Shanghai, China, pp 87–93 (in Chinese)
Tan S, Chen Y (2019c) Land resources science. Fudan University Press, Shanghai, China, pp 87–93 (in Chinese)
Verburg PH, Erb KH, Mertz O et al (2013) Land system science: between global challenges and local realities. Curr Opin Environ Sustain 5(5):433–437
Wang W, Wang Q (2006) Land use planning. Science Press, Beijing, China, p 4 (in Chinese)
Wang D (2010) Modern public policy. Tsinghua University Press, Beijing, China, p 70 (in Chinese)

Xia Z (2020) Land system reform in the perspective of national governance. Seeker 2:143–150 (in Chinese)
Yan J, Guo D, Xia F (2021) The historical logic, theoretical logic and practical logic of the change of the land system of the communist party of China in the past 100 years. J Manag World 37(7): 19–31, 2 (in Chinese)
Yang S (1986) Land economics. Tianjin People's Publishing House, Tianjin, China, p 2 (in Chinese)
Yang C (2001) Affection towards the land: an important origin of Chinese culture. J Peking Univ (philosophy and Social Sciences) 5:104–113 (in Chinese)
Yongjiao Z, Chuanglin F (2016) A review on spatial planning coordination and China's "coordinated planning." Urban Plan Forum 2:78–87 (in Chinese)
Yu M, Gu Y, Li R (2021) The CPC's people-centered land policy: a century of evolution and development. J Manag World 37(4):24–35 (in Chinese)

Chapter 2
Overview of China's Land Policies

Xiao Lyu and Shandong Niu

Land is an important policy issue in China. The reform of land policy plays a vital role in the direction and track of China's economic and social development. This chapter provides an in-depth discussion on China's economic and social reform and land policy evolution, the strategic background of major land policy implementations since the reform and opening up, the legislative reforms and legal basis of land policy implementation, and China's land policy system in the relations between the central and local governments. The chapter analyzes the historical evolution of China's land policy, the internal logic of economic and social reform and land policy evolution, and the contribution of land policy innovation to economic and social development. It also combs the background of land policy implementation in the two stages from 1978 to 2012 and since 2012. The chapter explains the legislative reform process from decentralization to relative concentration and the implementation of the legal system and probes China's land policy system in different periods. It lays the foundation for an overall and comprehensive understanding China's land policy and its reform.

2.1 Evolution of China's Land Policies

2.1.1 Historical Evolution of China's Land Policy

(1) **Ancient land policy**

Mencius said, "Three of the dukes' treasures: land, people, and politics." As a traditional agricultural country, ruling classes in ancient dynasties always attached great importance to land issues, and from the perspective of safeguarding their own ruling interests, formulated a series of land policies to organize land development,

X. Lyu (✉) · S. Niu
Northeastern University, Shenyang, China

S. Tan and X. Huang (eds.), *Land Policy in China*, The Frontier of Public Administration in China, https://doi.org/10.1007/978-981-19-9895-9_2

utilization, management, protection, and other activities. Land policies are constantly changing and innovating with the development of social productive forces, and the land policies in each period have their specific process characteristics.

1) **Period of Primitive Society and Slave Society**. In the period of the primitive society, the land system was public ownership: land belongs to the gens, collective farming was practiced, and there was equal distribution. With the increase in productivity level, private ownership and national rudiment appeared toward the end of primitive society. The Xia Dynasty (c. 2070 BC–1600 BC) was the first slave-owning country in Chinese history. Ownership and use of land belonged to the slave-owners, and slaves were only obliged to provide labor. During the Shang and Zhou Dynasties (c. 1600 BC–256 BC), ownership of land belonged to slave-owning states, and the Jing-tian[1] distribution policy of public and private fields was implemented.
2) **Period of Spring and Autumn Warring States**. With the use of iron tools and the promotion of cattle farming, the social productive forces began to develop rapidly in the Spring and Autumn and Warring States Periods (770 BC–221 BC), and the number of private fields that were not taxed by the state, besides Jing-tian cultivated by slave owners, increased continuously. At the same time, frequent slave uprisings led to the waste of huge amounts of land, with slave-owners and nobles aggressively annexing and fighting for land violently. After gaining power, the new landlord classes in each vassal state implemented successive reforms. Various countries gradually abolished the Jing-tian system, allowed free sale of land, and promulgated a series of policies and laws. Soon, the private ownership of land of the new landlord class began to be established.
3) **Period of Feudal Society**. In 221 BC, Emperor QinShi Huang unified the six states and established the Qin Dynasty (221 BC–207 BC), which was the first unified feudal authoritarian and centralized state in Chinese history. This marked the entry of China into the feudal society period, which lasted more than 2,000 years. In China's feudal society, private land ownership and state ownership was practiced, and private land was divided into two types: owner-farmer private land ownership and landlord class private land ownership.
4) **Land Privatization in the Qin and Han Dynasties**. Toward the end of the Warring States Period,[2] private land existed, and land trading began to appear. Shangyang[3] introduced the reform to "abolish the Jing-tian system and begin to implement private ownership of land." Emperor Qin ShiHuang ordered the

[1] Jing-tian system: Land is divided into many squares, and the shape of the land is similar to the shape of "井," pronounced "jing" in Chinese; hence, it is called the Jing-tian system. A "jing" is divided into 9 squares, and the surrounding 8 fields are cultivated by 8 households, which are called private fields. All the harvests belong to the farming households; the middle is the public field, which is cultivated by the 8 households, and the income is owned by the feudal nobles.

[2] Warring States Period: The Warring States Period (476 BC, 453 BC or 403 BC ~ 221 BC) was the period of the Eastern Zhou Dynasty in Chinese history (before Qin unified the Central Plains); during this period, the countries fought endlessly, and hence, it was called "Warring States" by later generations.

[3] Shang Yang: (about 395 BC–338 BC), statesman, reformer, thinker, military strategist and representative of Legalism during the Warring States Period. In 356 BC and 350 BC, the reform he introduced is called the Shang Yang Reform.

common people to report the amount of land they possessed, conducted nationwide land registration to ensure tax revenue collection, and allowed land to be bought and sold. The Han Dynasty (206 BC–220 AD) did the same as the Qin Dynasty (221 BC–206 BC), and land was privately owned and could be bought and sold freely.

5) **Tuntian Policy during the Three Kingdoms Period.**[4] During the Three Kingdoms period (220 AD–280 AD), the Tuntian policy refers to the government's policy of encouraging land reclamation, whereby the reclaimed land belongs to the state. The Tuntian policy was founded in the Qin Dynasty, when the rulers mainly used sinners who had been exiled to the frontier to reclaim and cultivate the land. During the Two Han Dynasties, the Tuntian policy was developed on a large scale. Tuntian is mainly divided into two types: Juntun and Mintun. Juntun aims to consolidate and develop frontiers, so as to be self-sufficient or partially self-sufficient in agricultural products. During the Eastern Han Dynasty, the Central Plains area established the Tuntian base, which expanded the Tuntian area from the frontier to the interior. Mintun originated in the Han Dynasty. This system played a great role in the settlement of famine and refugees by the rulers at that time, stabilizing social order, and solving food problems. However, due to the continuous exploitation by the rulers, their plundering of a large number of fields, and the contradiction between the system in the Tuntian and the non-Tuntian areas, the Tuntian system was abolished during the Cao Wei period (AD 264).
6) **The Land Quota System of the Western Jin Dynasty and the Land-equalization System of the Northern Wei, Sui, and Tang Dynasties**. The Western Jin Dynasty (265 AD–317 AD) implemented the land quota system after the unification of the Three Kingdoms. The main idea in the land quota system is to allow people to occupy more land and pay less tax based on their farming ability so that the purpose of restoring agriculture is achieved. It further stipulates the maximum number of fields that may be occupied and the taxable area. For officials, the land quota system is meant to regulate the amount of land occupied and the number of Yinke[5] according to the level of the official's grade, so that tyrants may be controlled and land may be occupied widely; in other words, it involved restricting land. Compared with peasants under the Tuntian system, the burden on farmers under the land quota system was significantly reduced. In particular, the removal of forced labor under military control under the farmland system encouraged farmers for production. The land-equalization system is a system of allocating land according to the population. Some of the land that people cultivate will be owned by them after a certain number of years and some returned to the government after their death. On the basis of the land

[4] Three Kingdoms Period: A period of Chinese history after the Han Dynasty and before the Jin Dynasty. During this period, three main regimes, Cao Wei, Shu Han, and Soochow, appeared successively.

[5] Yinke: The Yinke system was a decree on household registration during the Jin Dynasties. The decree of occupying fields in the Western Jin Dynasty stipulated that officials could shelter relatives depending on the rank of the official.

occupation system in the Western Jin Dynasty, Emperor Xiaowen of the Northern Wei Dynasty promulgated the decree of equalizing land in the ninth year of Taihe (AD 485) and began to implement it. This land system went through the Northern Qi Dynasty (550 AD–577 AD), the Northern Zhou Dynasty (557 AD–581 AD), and the Sui Dynasty (581 AD–618 AD), and the scope of implementation was gradually extended from the Yellow River Basin to the whole country. The implementation of the land-equalization system affirmed the ownership and possession of land, reduced disputes over land properties, was conducive to the reclamation of unowned barren land, and played a positive role in the restoration and development of agricultural production. The land-equalization system was developed to the early Tang Dynasty. Due to the population growth, the land that could be distributed was limited, and the rulers used various means to plunder the land. At the same time, with social productivity improving and the commodity economy developing, land mergers became unprecedented. The heavy taxation was unbearable for the peasants; they either fled one after another or sold their land and joined the aristocratic bureaucratic landlords to become tenants, thus destroying the land-equalization system.

7) **Song to Ming and Qing Dynasties**. 1. Tax policy. The tax policy in Song and Yuan dynasties enforced split rent and fixed rent. Northern Song Dynasty mainly implemented split rent, generally more than 50%, and the common people who did not have cattle and farming tools had to pay more rent. During the Southern Song Dynasty (AD 1127–AD 1279), fixed land rent (Guo et al. 1988) was implemented in areas such as Liangzhe Road, where production was relatively well developed. Land was divided into upper, middle, and lower grades, and the fixed rents for each grade were different. In the Yuan Dynasty (AD 1271–AD 1368) too, the split rent was 50–80%. The fixed rent rice ranged from three dou per mu to one dan,[6] and three dou per mu and one dan to six dou for two dan. During the Ming and Qing Dynasties, taxation and the corvee labor system were reformed. In the Ming Dynasty (1368–1644), based on the measurement of land, the "one whip method" was carried out throughout the country, which mainly unified taxes and corvee labor, and unified payment in silver (Guo et al. 1988). In the Qing Dynasty (1636–1912), the man-land system was developed from the "one-whip method." In this way, the poll tax that had been in place for thousands of years was basically abolished, and from then on the corvée system was basically abandoned. The only thing that continued was dividing the land belonging to the landlords and extracting rent in kind or money from the peasants.
8) **Cadastral management policy**. During the Northern Song Dynasty, Wang Anshi began to implement reforms. Among them, the "Fang Tian Equal Tax Law" was enacted, which was to carry out large-scale land clearing across the country, dividing the land into five grades, square fields and four corners, standing soil as peaks, and planting trees as boundaries. On the basis of Qingzhang, land

---

[6] Mu: Mu is a unit of land area under the Chinese municipal system. One mu is equal to about 666.667 square meters and 15 mu is equal to one hectare. Dou and dan: Both dou and dan are units of capacity in ancient China. Ten dou are a dan and 10 L are a dou.

registration is carried out in terms of the quantity, quality, and use of land of each household according to the township, and a land account was established. During the Southern Song Dynasty, the "Jingjie Law" was implemented. Jingjie refers to the measurement of land boundaries. In the 12th year of Shaoxing of Song Gaozong (AD 1142), the Bureau of Jingjie was established in Pingjiang Prefecture of the Southern Song Dynasty. Each household in each township was ordered to create anvil land books (cadastral books) and based on the different shapes of the plots, different methods were used to measure and calculate the fields and acres. Area survey to determine the quality of the plot and a fish scales map mark the four corners to be mapped truthfully. In the Ming Dynasty, the cadastre was independent from the household registration. In the Ming Dynasty, a nationwide large-scale land survey was carried out successively, and a national general land register—the fish scales atlas—was compiled. The Qing Dynasty basically followed the cadastral management method of the Ming Dynasty, but the measurement was further standardized. In AD 1743, the *Rules for Measuring Fields* was promulgated, which introduced the casting standards and unified the standard size of field measurements in the whole country. At the same time, Western cartography and surveying were introduced into China. In the Qing Dynasty, Kangxi and Qianlong hired Western missionaries to conduct large-scale nationwide map surveying and mapping. In the late Qing Dynasty, the Bureau of Geodesy and the School of Surveying and Mapping were also established. The "Map of United Country of the Qing Dynasty" and "Qianlong Emperor 's Imperial Map" made during the Kangxi and Qianlong periods provided graphic materials for land management.

(2) **The period of the old democratic revolution: agrarian policy characterized as "average" (June 1840–1919)**

As land policy is related to the national economy and people's livelihood, it is an issue that cannot be ignored by any ruling power. During the Daoguang period of the Qing Dynasty (1821–1850 AD), the population of the whole country touched more than 400 million; wastelands were reclaimed, and the imbalance between people and land became increasingly serious. After the Opium War in 1840, the Western capitalist invasion and the deepening of domestic feudal exploitation further exacerbated the problem of land annexation. In a special period when the country's politics and economy were in turmoil, various political factions proposed their own policy plans to solve this problem.

1) **The Land Policy of the Taiping Heavenly Kingdom**. In March 1853, the Taiping army captured Nanjing, and the Taiping Heavenly Kingdom was established here. Hong Xiuquan[7] issued the most systematic and complete anti-feudal revolutionary program for the peasant class in Chinese history—*The Tianmu*

[7] Hong Xiuquan (1814–1864): King of the Taiping Heavenly Kingdom and leader of the peasant uprising in the late Qing Dynasty. The Taiping Heavenly Kingdom Movement led by him swept over more than half of China and lasted 14 years. It dealt a heavy blow to the reactionary forces at home and abroad and had a profound influence on the modern history of China.

System of the Celestial Dynasty—in accordance with the principles of "everywhere in the world, people in the world cultivate together" and "where the world is in the field, there is abundance and famine." The intention is to build an ideal society in which "all could farm their fields equally, share food, clothing, and money, and no one suffered from hunger or cold."

In terms of land distribution, the *The Tianmu System of the Celestial Dynasty* stipulates that land be divided into nine grades according to the level of production: in the morning and evening each year, those with a yield of 1,200 catties of grain per mu will be on the fields; Upper middle field, upper and lower field, middle upper field, middle middle field, middle lower field, lower upper field, lower middle field; a yield of 400 catties per mu is considered a lower field. Then, according to the population of each household, regardless of male or female, the fields are divided equally, combining both good and bad, and those under the age of 15 are halved. However, the ideal system of absolute egalitarianism of "equal and even," as proclaimed in the Taiping Heavenly Kingdom, failed to materialize.

2) **Sun Yat-sen's Land Policy Proposition**. On April 1, 1912, in his speech at the farewell meeting of the members of the Tongmenghui, Sun Yat-sen[8] proposed the idea of levying taxes according to price, buying according to price, and collecting "seal deed tax" to supplement the country's income. This basically established the theory system of equal land rights. Sun Yat-sen's system of the theory of average land rights includes four main aspects: approval of land prices, taxation according to price, purchase according to price, and return to the public after price increase. After the Revolution of 1911 failed, with the encouragement and help of the Soviet Union, the Comintern and the Communist Party of China, the Kuomintang and the Communist Party, achieved the first cooperation. Sun Yat-sen's land policy also underwent great changes from the old democracy to the new democracy. On the one hand, he reiterated the original claim of equal land rights, and on the other, he proposed the policy of "land to the tiller."
3) **The period of the new democratic revolution: establishment of peasant land ownership (1919–1949)**
   During the period of the New Democratic Revolution, China's land policy was aimed at safeguarding the interests of the peasants and promoting social and economic development; it established peasant land ownership. In 1921, the Communist Party of China was founded, and the exploration of a people-centered land policy was officially launched. Protecting the interests of the working people through land policy became an important topic of discussion within the party. In the August 7, 1927, meeting of the Chinese Communist Party, the general policy was determined as agrarian revolution and armed struggle. In 1928, the Communist Party of China promulgated the first land law in the history of the party, the *Jinggang Mountain Land Law*, which stipulated the confiscation and

[8] Sun Yat-sen (1866–1925): a democratic revolutionary in modern China, a forerunner of democracy, and the founding father of the Republic of China.

distribution system of land in the form of legal provisions. It aimed to fundamentally remove the feudal land relationship that has bound Chinese farmers for thousands of years (Yu et al. 2021a, b). During this period, the Chinese Communist Party established pioneering and beneficial practices in land policy, which won the support of the masses and consolidated the revolution.

From 1937 to 1945, the full-scale outbreak of the Second Sino-Japanese War marked the rise of ethnic contradictions into the main contradiction in Chinese society. During this period, the Communist Party of China adopted rent reduction and interest rate reduction as its basic policy to resolve farmers' problems during the War. In July 1937, the Party proposed stopping the confiscation of landlords' land in the *Declaration of the Central Committee of the Communist Party of China to Announce the Cooperation between the Kuomintang and the Communist Party,*[9] and then in August, in the *Ten Guidelines of the Communist Party of China to Resist Japan and Save the Nation*, the policy of "reducing rent and reducing interest" was proposed for the first time.

During the war of liberation from 1945 to 1949, the Chinese Communist Party's policy shifted to a more determined mass line, fulfilling the peasants' urgent need for land (Liu 2021). To this end, in 1946, the Central Committee of the Communist Party of China issued the "May 4th Directive," through which it was decided to change the policy of reducing rent and interest to confiscate the land of the landlord and distribute it to the farmers. In 1947, the Central Committee of the Communist Party of China promulgated the *Outline of China's Land Law*, which stipulated that the land system of feudal and semi-feudal exploitation be completely abolished, and implemented a land system wherein the cultivator had his own land.

4) **The period of socialist exploration: the establishment of public land ownership (1949–1978)**
The exploration of land policy in the period of socialist construction led to first uniting the farmers to transform private ownership of land to public ownership, and then to the cooperative movement to transform private ownership of farmers' land into socialist public ownership, so that rural land is collectively owned by the working people.

In September 1949, the *Common Program of the Chinese People's Political Consultative Conference* adopted by the Chinese People's Political Consultative Conference proposed to "step by step change the feudal and semi-feudal land ownership system to peasant land ownership".[10] In June 1950, the Central People's Government promulgated the *Land Reform Law of the People's Republic of China*, which further clarified the general principles of "abolishing land ownership by the feudal exploitation of the landlord class and offering land

[9] The Literature Research Office of the CPC Central Committee and the Central Archives: Selections of Important Documents Since the Founding of the CPC (1921–1949) (Vol. 14), Central Literature Press, 2011, p. 370.

[10] General Office of the Standing Committee of the National People's Congress, Literature Research Office of the CPC Central Committee: Selected major documents on the system of People's Congresses 1, China Democracy and Legal Affairs Press, 2015, p. 76.

ownership to peasants, so as to liberate the productive forces in the countryside, develop agricultural production, and pave the way for industrialization in New China." This included the confiscation, expropriation, and distribution of land, the handling of special land issues, the executing organs, and implementation plans of land reform and the relevant bylaws.[11] Later, land reform began to be carried out in stages and batches across the country, and peasant land ownership was established.

After the implementation of land reform, labor mutual aid organizations developed in rural areas, and the advantages of cooperative production gradually emerged. Soon, rural cooperatives were put on the agenda. The Central Committee of the Communist Party of China formulated the *Mutual Cooperation in Agricultural Production (Draft)* in September 1951, pointing out that farmers should be "organized" to carry out simple labor mutual assistance, develop perennial mutual assistance groups and agricultural production cooperatives with land as shares based on conditions and on the principle of voluntariness and mutual benefit.[12] In March 1956, the National People's Congress passed the *Model Statute of Agricultural Production Cooperatives*, marking the basic realization of primary cooperatives in the country. In January 1956, a nationwide campaign was launched for the vigorous establishment of senior clubs. The socialist transformation of agriculture led to the transformation of the rural land management system, which can be divided into the stages of primary agricultural production cooperatives, advanced cooperatives, and people's communes. By 1956, the agricultural cooperative movement had basically been completed, and the rural collective land ownership system had become established.

In 1957 the dire need to eradicate poverty and backwardness was recognized. To strengthen the collective cooperation ability, small cooperatives of advanced agricultural production cooperatives were merged into the large cooperatives. In 1958, the Central Committee of the Communist Party of China issued the *Resolution on the Establishment of People's Communes in the Countryside*, stating that "people's communes are an inevitable trend of the development of the situation" and that the establishment of people's communes should "accelerate the speed of socialist construction."[13] Soon, the country's rural areas realized communalization.

5) **Liberating and developing the productive forces of land elements in the period of reform and opening up (1978–1998)**
In December 1978, the Third Plenary Session of the Eleventh Central Committee of the Communist Party of China kicked off the reform and opening up. The socialist land system reform with Chinese characteristics also started in China's

[11] Legislative Affairs Office of the State Council: Compilation of laws and regulations of the People's Republic of China 1949-1952 (Vol. 1) 2nd Edition, China Legal Affairs Press, 2014, p. 17.

[12] Literature Research Office of the CPC Central Committee: Selected important documents since the founding of the People's Republic of China (Vol. 2), China Academic Press, 2011, pp. 451–452.

[13] Literature Research Office of the CPC Central Committee: Selections of important documents since the founding of the People's Republic of China (Volume 11), Central Literature Publishing House, 2011, pp. 384–388.

rural areas and cities during the same period, and the major reforms in which the ownership and use rights of state-owned land and collective land were separated successively entered the stage of exploration.

In November 1978, Xiaogang Village, Fengyang County, Anhui Province took the lead in launching rural land reform of ensuring that "the land distributed was to each household." With the affirmation and support of the central decision-making level, the household contract responsibility system became gradually promoted from local attempts to national exploration. In 1980, the Central Committee of the Communist Party of China issued the *Notice on Several Issues Concerning Further Strengthening and Perfecting the Agricultural Production Responsibility System*, which clarified that "production can be contracted to the household or work can be contracted to the household, and thus ensure stability for a long period of time."[14] Land ownership is of the collective, and land contractual management right belongs to farmers, thus forming the second-level land property right model of the collective and the farmers (Teng and Zhang 2021).

Guided by the efficiency of urban development, in December 1987, Shenzhen held the first public auction of land use rights in China's history, marking the precedent for the reform of market-oriented allocation of urban land in China. In 1987, the former State Land Administration reported to the State Council for approval to conduct pilot explorations in Shenzhen, Shanghai, Tianjin, Guangzhou, Xiamen, Fuzhou, and other places. In 1988, the *Constitution of the People's Republic of China* and *Land Administration Law of the People's Republic of China* were formally revised to establish the urban land transfer system in the form of a law, and further regulations on land transfer and transfer were made through a series of policies and regulations. The revised *Land Management Law* in 1988 clearly stipulates that "the state implements the system of paid use of state-owned land according to law." During the period of rapid urbanization in China, urban land use rights were separated from ownership; the market for urban state-owned land use rights began to be fully opened, and the system of "paid, limited-term, and allowed for transfer and use within the legal scope" of urban land in China was formally established.

At the same time, in response to the blind development of urban and rural land, the serious issue of protecting cultivated land, and the prominent contradiction between man and land, the Chinese government issued a series of land policies to protect cultivated land and improve the efficiency of land use. In 1986, the State Council promulgated the *Notice on Strengthening the Management of Land and Stopping Unauthorized Occupation of Cultivated Land*, the National People's Congress promulgated the *Land Administration Law of the People's Republic of China*, and in the same year, the State Land Administration was established to conduct unified management of urban and rural land administration. Urban development during this period benefited from the deepening of the reform of the

[14] Literature Research Office of the CPC Central Committee, Development Research Center of the State Council: Selected Important Documents on Agriculture and Rural Work in the New Era, Central Literature Press, 1992, p. 60.

land use system, especially the promotion of the "bidding, auction, and listing" transfer system for commercial land, which led to a substantial increase in land transfer income, and land capitalization and land mortgage financing for urban infrastructure. Construction provided huge sums of money (Liu 2021).

6) **Reform and adjustment of land policy in the period of rapid development (1998–2012)**
With the full release of the dividends of land policy reform, China's economy and society entered a period of rapid development, and the problem of the imperfect land management system became gradually exposed, thus starting a new round of land policy reform and adjustment.
The *Land Administration Law of the People's Republic of China* revised in 1998 proposed the basic national policy of "cherishing and rational use of land and earnestly protecting cultivated land," and it began to implement the land use control system. "The state formulates an overall plan for land use, stipulates land uses, and divides land into agricultural land, construction land, and unused land. The conversion of agricultural land into construction land is strictly restricted, the total amount of construction land is controlled, and cultivated land is subject to special protection." In 1999, the Ministry of Land and Resources issued the *Notice on Effectively Balancing the Occupation and Subsidy of Cultivated Land*, which connects the responsibilities, measures, management, and monitoring with the compensation system for cultivated land protection under the *Land Administration Law of the People's Republic of China*. In 2004, the State Council issued the *Decision on Deepening Reform and Strict Land Management*, emphasizing the revitalization of stock and the prohibition of idle land. In 2008, the *Decision of the Central Committee of the Communist Party of China on Several Big Issues on Promoting the Reform and Development of Rural Areas* adopted by the Third Plenary Session of the 17th Central Committee of the Communist Party of China proposed that while adhering to the strictest cultivated land protection system, the strictest land conservation system should be implemented. Under the implementation of a series of "strict" land systems, not only was national food security effectively guaranteed, but also liberation and development of productive forces became more efficiently supported.

7) **A new chapter of land policy reform in the new era (2012-present)**
Since the 18th National Congress of the Communist Party of China, China's economic development entered a new normal; this occurred during a critical period of profound changes in the international economic and political landscape. A bottleneck has been created due to the series of problems arising from resource supply and the contradiction between economic development needs, the uneven development of urban and rural areas, and the environmental carrying capacity, which has reached the upper limit. The reform has gradually entered a deep-water zone, where tough challenges need to be tackled (Yan et al. 2021).
The Decision of the Central Committee of the Communist Party of China on Some Major Issues Concerning Comprehensively Deepening the Reform in 2013 and the *Integrated Reform of Ecological Civilization System* in 2014 set the tone for the direction of land policy in the new era. In December 2014, the General

Office of the Central Committee of the Communist Party of China and the General Office of the State Council jointly issued the *Opinions on the Pilot Reform of Rural Land Acquisition, Market Entry of Collective Management Construction Land, and Residential Land System* to launch the reform of the "three parcels of land" in rural areas. In October 2016, the General Office of the Central Committee of the Communist Party of China and the General Office of the State Council issued the *Opinions of the General Office of the CPC Central Committee and the General Office of the State Council on Improving the Measures for Separating Rural Land Ownership from Contracted Management Right,* which clarified that the "three rights" of ownership; contracting rights and management rights were to be separated and parallelized for agricultural land. In 2018, the Central No. 1 document proposed to explore the "three rights separation" of ownership, qualification rights, and use rights of homesteads. In 2018, the *Action Plan for Deeper Reform of the Party and State Apparatus* reviewed and approved by the Third Plenary Session of the 19th Central Committee of the Communist Party of China and the State Council's institutional reform plan reviewed and approved at the first session of the 13th National People's Congress, established the Ministry of Natural Resources to promote systematic and holistic changes in natural resource management. In 2020, the Central Committee of the Communist Party of China and the State Council issued the *Opinions on Improving the Systems and Mechanisms for Market-oriented Allocation of Factors of Production,* which proposed to "promote the market-based reform of land factors" so as to realize market decision of land factor prices, independent and orderly flow, and efficient and fair allocation.

In the period of developing socialist modernization in an all-round way, land policy is based on the new development concept, and it comprehensively deepens the promotion of property rights, utilization, protection, and governance.

2.1.2 The Internal Logic of Economic and Social Transformation and Land Policy Evolution

Land policy makers have certain limitations in their cognition ability. This is because the level of development of social productive forces and their laws of development constantly change, and at the same time, human practice and social and economic development are a complex and comprehensive process of dynamic change. Therefore, the content of land policy is always largely incompatible with economic and social development. With the continuous development and change of the economy and society, it is bound to be necessary to continuously adjust and improve land policy to meet the requirements of productivity and land development and changes. Looking back at the evolution history of China's land policy, changes often occurred during the critical periods of major economic and social changes and contradictions, which also clarifies that the evolution of land policy is inextricably linked to the needs of economic and social change.

(1) **Political ideals are the fundamental driving force behind the evolution of land policy**

"Grain is what man lives on, and land is where millet grows; man is ruled by kings. These three are the urgent matters in governing the country" (Du 1984). The close connection among the land, the farmers, and the state is self-evident. Land is the material basis for constructing social and economic relations; it is crucial to economic development, social livelihood, and political struggle. The evolution of land policy is therefore a mirror of the social and economic changes. Different forms reflect different political ideals, and their evolution is also an important force in promoting social change. The achievement of political goals is subject to political, military, social, historical, and ideological influences. The need is to win the greatest political support through competition and cooperation of the property rights structure and obtain the core rights so as to maximize the benefits of representing interest groups. The victory of the Chinese Revolution, in the background of the feudal and semi-feudal land system, over the local tyrants to divide t land and distribute the land to the peasants for free, led to the cultivator obtaining his own land and private ownership of peasants' land. During the War of Resistance against Japanese Aggression, the Communist Party of China implemented the policy of "reducing rent and interest" to save the Chinese nation, which increased farmers' enthusiasm for production and improved farmers' lives. The "cultivator has his own land" policy greatly consolidated the foundation of the liberated areas, strengthened the people's support for the liberation war, mobilized the enthusiasm of the peasants for revolution and production, and played a decisive role in the victory of the liberation war. Practice has proved that to survive and develop, the land policies issued by the Communist Party of China during complex and changing situations are mostly temporary strategies, and this flexible adjustment of some policies highlights the importance of adaptive management.

(2) **Social equity is the value orientation of land policy evolution**

When the needs of social and economic development cannot be satisfied by the land policy of the time, a new land policy will inevitably emerge to replace it and carry the national livelihood to continue to move forward. From a historical perspective, the private ownership of peasants' land in the early days of the founding of the People's Republic of China and the change to collective ownership in the later period is the result of division of land by local tyrants; but it was also a means to achieve social equity. On December 29, 2005, the 19th meeting of the Standing Committee of the Tenth National People's Congress decided to abolish the *People's Republic of China on Agriculture Tax* from January 1, 2006. Since then, China no longer has a separate tax for agriculture; this marked the end of an ancient tax that has existed in China for more than 2,000 years. Reform of rural taxes and fees has reduced the burden on farmers, optimized the rural management structure, and provided support for the battle against poverty, alleviating social conflicts, and maintaining social equity. It should be noted that "giving more, taking less, and letting go" became the new mantra at this time, which laid an institutional foundation for building a socialist harmonious society and a new socialist countryside.

(3) **Food security is the bottom line for land policy evolution**

Food security has always been a strategic issue related to human survival and development and national stability and prosperity. Since the founding of the people's Republic of China, the national food security strategy has been adjusted many times, and a relatively stable national food security system has been gradually established. In this process, China's food security strategic guarantee objectives and scope, implementation methods and paths, and guarantee subjects have all undergone adaptive changes, and a corresponding evolution path has been formed. It is the contradiction between the "unchanged" national food security strategic thinking and the "changing" food supply and demand situation and production constraints that continue to promote the step-by-step evolution of China's 70-year food security strategy. Food security is of top priority in social security, emphasizing "adherence to the food crop production strategy based on farmland management and technological application, and implementing the strictest arable land protection system to ensure that the Chinese people's rice bowl is firmly in their own hands." With the policy support of the Central Committee of the Communist Party of China, farmers' enthusiasm for grain production has been fully mobilized, and the comprehensive grain productivity has greatly improved, although grain security has always been the bottom line of land policy adjustment. In the ever-changing situation of food supply and demand and production constraints, China has always adhered to the national food security strategic thinking and gradually promoted the adaptive adjustment of food security objectives and scope, implementation methods and approaches, and security entities.

(4) **The contradiction between man and land is the internal incentive for the evolution of land policy**

For a long time, China's land resources have faced the rigid constraints of "large total amount, small per capita possession, small high-quality arable land, and small reserve resources of arable land." In 2019, China's per capita arable land was only 1.4 mu (0.093 hm^2),[15] which was 0.4 times the world average. The total arable land was only 7.5% of the world's arable land, but it supported 18.7% of the world's population. The contradiction between man and land became the basic driving force for the evolution of land policy, and the tense relationship between man and land has become the main cause for the decline of agricultural production in China. The social security function of land for the rural population is greater than the production function. The per capita distribution reflecting the principle of fairness induces land fragmentation, and problems such as the inherent contradiction between "small household operation" and the development of modern agriculture are prominent.

(5) **Production efficiency is a key factor in the evolution of land policy**

The government achieves its economic and political goals through land policy innovation, and the government's institutional goals at different stages of development are different. The realization of economic goals follows the principle of prioritizing

[15] Ministry of Natural Resources of the People's Republic of China, http://www.mnr.gov.cn/dt/ywbb/202108/t20210826_2678337.html.

efficiency, aiming to improve the efficiency of land resource allocation and maximize the total social output by reducing transaction costs. After the reform and opening up, China has witnessed rapid development of industrialization and urbanization, and the contradiction between supply and demand of construction land is prominent. At the same time, the phenomenon of extensive use and waste of land is also serious. About 5,000 km^2 of urban industrial and mining construction land lie in a state of inefficient use, accounting for 11% of the national urban built-up area.[16] In this regard, based on the national conditions that the level of economical and intensive use of land and production efficiency need to be improved urgently, a policy for economical and intensive use of land has become inevitable for China's current economic and social development. In the process of agricultural modernization, adhering to strict land policies to ensure stable input of the most basic elements of agricultural production is compulsory. In the process of new urbanization, the structure of the land factor input should be continuously improved to change the degree of intensive use of land caused by the input of capital, labor, technology, energy, and other factors. Further, the level of technological progress in the process of spatial agglomeration of production factors must also be improved to promote reasonable allocation of production factors to achieve high-efficiency operation and high-quality development.

2.1.3 Contribution of Land Policy Innovation to Economic and Social Development

Land resources and their utilization management play an important role in social development, and land policy plays an important role in promoting social progress and economic development. Land policies that adapt to the conditions of social productivity and reflect the development requirements of social productivity include land use goals and land management tasks within a certain historical period, which are a series of guidelines centered on specific economic and social interests. Land policy plays the function of serving and promoting social and economic development in the process of solving multiple problems.

(1) **Solve the problem of contradiction between man and land and food shortage**

Before the first land reform in New China, the fertility of cultivated land was subject to natural disasters, agricultural science and technology, etc. The soil system was at the basic level of maintaining crop growth, and it was difficult to resolve the problem of farmers' food and clothing. After the land reform, the land of the landlords was confiscated and distributed to the peasants who had no land or had little land. The land and means of production were rationally distributed. This led to an enthusiasm among farmers to increase production, and the grain output continued to rise. In 1949, China's grain output was only 113.18 billion kilograms; it stabilized at more than

---

[16] Economic Daily, 2020, https://baijiahao.baidu.com/s?id=1670423589118062956&wfr=spider&for=pc.

150 billion kilograms in 1962 and exceeded 300 billion kilograms at the beginning of the reform and opening up in 1978.[17] In 1951, the national grain output increased by 28% compared with 1949,[18] and cotton and other industrial raw materials all exceeded the historical record. Water conservancy projects were built in many areas and farm tools were purchased leading to the development of related industries. After the reform and opening up, the household contract management system improved the supervision problems under the production team system, improved the incentive structure, stimulated farmers' motivation to consciously improve production efficiency, and had a significant impact on the growth of agricultural output. In 1993, "Several Policies and Measures of the Central Committee of the Communist Party of China and the State Council on the Current Agricultural and Rural Economic Development" clearly stated that "with the consent of the contracting party, the transfer of land use rights with compensation in accordance with the law is allowed." Since then, land transfer has significantly improved the labor productivity of farmers, increased their income, and improved their welfare, and the less restrictive land transfer rights have brought huge economic benefits. Simultaneous reallocation of land to those with lower initial endowments and higher agricultural capacity can help increase agricultural productivity.

(2) **Coordinate the contradiction between rapid development and resource shortage**

Rapid economic development is dependent on several production factors, and land is an indispensable resource. William Bidi said, "labor is the father of wealth, and land is the mother of wealth." However, land resources are limited and hence the need to rely on land policies to maximize the benefits of land elements. Therefore, land policy that is in line with social development can promote the rapid development of the economy and maximize the overall benefits. On the one hand, transforming the nature of land use, accelerating the change of economic development, and realizing the transformation of land use from extensive to intensive transformation can drive optimization and upgrading of the industrial structure. On the other hand, the impact of land policy on regional economic development is mainly achieved through land planning, land use control and land supply. Land planning combines the characteristics of the local area to formulate the most suitable solution for local development; land use control can stop unreasonable land use, offer guidelines for the correct use of land, realize the optimization and distribution of the industrial structure, and maximize benefits. The supply of land is a unified and reasonable plan based on the type of land supply, which in turn effectively relieves the contradiction between economic development and shortage of resources.

---

[17] Ministry of Agriculture and Rural Affairs of the People's Republic of China, http://www.moa.gov.cn/ztzl/70zncj/201909/t20190917_6328044.htm.

[18] Sourced from Compilation of cost-benefit data of main agricultural products in China (1953-1997) and Compilation of cost-benefit data of national agricultural products since the founding of the People's Republic of China.

(3) **Lay a solid foundation for the establishment of a better society (better standards of living) and the realization of new agricultural modernization**

Since the reform and opening up, a series of land policies have effectively promoted growth and prosperity of China's rural economy. Chinese farmers have overcome poverty and moved from the need for food and clothing to a comprehensively better standard of life. Since the 18th National Congress of the Communist Party of China, land policy has played a positive role in improving production and living conditions in poor areas and in alleviating poverty. During this period, China entered a new normal in economic and social development, and the shortcomings of rural development were to be addressed. The Communist Party of China has vigorously promoted modernization of agricultural and rural areas and the implementation of rural revitalization strategies in accordance with the requirements of "thriving businesses, pleasant living environments, social etiquette and civility, effective governance, and prosperity." The strategic goal of "strong agricultural, rural beauty, and peasant rich" has become a target to promote modernization of agriculture. Relevant departments such as the Ministry of Natural Resources and the Ministry of Agriculture and Rural Affairs have regarded poverty alleviation as a major political task, continuously innovated and improved land policies, implemented ultra -conventional and differentiated support measures, and established poverty alleviation policy systems such as, land use security, "linkage between urban-land taking and rural-land giving," and so on. The funds of projects such as rectification, geological survey, and ecological restoration lean toward poverty-stricken areas to ensure poverty alleviation and no return to poverty. It has laid a solid foundation for comprehensively building a well-off society and realizing agricultural modernization.

2.2 Strategic Backgrounds of China's Land Policies Since the Reform and Opening Up

2.2.1 1978–2012: Land Policy Reform with "Efficiency First, Equity Second"

During the period of socialist exploration, due to lack of experience in socialist construction, the egalitarian approach of decoupling labor from distribution was out of line with the laws of economic and social development, and the relations of production were out of line with the level of social productivity at that time. As China enters a new period of economic construction, there is an urgent need to shift from taking class struggle as the key link, as in the past, to economic construction as the center. In 1978, the Third Plenary Session of the 11th Central Committee of the CPC kicked off the reform and opening up of China, and China's economic system gradually shifted from a "planned economic system" to a "socialist market economy." The need to liberate and develop the productivity of the land factor, enhance the welfare of farmers, prioritize efficiency while considering equity, and serve the construction of a socialist market economy became urgent. The "lack of efficiency" in the land policy arrangements of the planned economy and the opportunity for social transformation led to the development of new property rights arrangements, resource allocation, and land use methods in land policy reform. Socialist land policy reforms with Chinese characteristics also originated in China's rural and urban areas during the same period. The reform of the rural land system began with the introduction of land contracting and farm output quotas fixed by households; the reform of the urban land use system began with the paid use of land and was aimed at the marketization of the allocation of land resources.

(1) **Historical choices of rural land contracting and urban land use with compensation**

1) **Historical choice of rural land contract management**. Dealing with the relationship between farmers and land has been the main line of reform and development of rural land policy, and the People's Commune movement, which began in 1958, centralized land through the merging of agricultural production co-operatives and the collective ownership of communes and equal distribution of products. However, this approach was out of line with the development of the rural productive forces and against the will of the peasants, inhibiting their enthusiasm for production and keeping the agricultural and rural economy in a state of slow development or even stagnation for a long time. With the successful achievement of the country's initial industrialization goal in 1978, and the completion of the original accumulation of industrialization, the most urgent reform task at that time was to correct the production relations that were incompatible with the productive forces, expand the autonomy of management, and stimulate the peasants' enthusiasm for production. The "farm output quotas fixed by household" created spontaneously in Xiaogang Village, Fengyang County, Anhui Province at the end of 1978 led to the basic impulse of Chinese farmers to pursue clear property rights (Luo 2008). As the peasant family contract for production developed into a contract for land management, the relationship between the collective and the peasant household in terms of land property rights was to some extent redefined.

After the Third Plenary Session of the 11th Central Committee of the CPC, the Party and the government began to examine the problems of rural land policy in the development of agricultural productivity and to confront the experience of peasants' spontaneous exploration. The direction of the state's property rights reform was gradually based on peasants' wishes, gradually recognizing peasants' spontaneous exploration of the contract system (Yu et al. 2021a, b). By 1981, the system of household contract responsibility had been promoted in most areas of the country. On January 1, 1982, the Central Committee of the Communist Party of China (CPC) approved the "The National Rural Work Meeting Minutes" of December 1981 and "Some Issues of Current Rural Economic Policy" issued by the CPC Central Committee in 1983, which formally established the system of household contract responsibility, further clearly affirming the system from practical, legal, and theoretical levels (Yu et al. 2021a, b). The socialist nature of the system of responsibility for joint family production was further affirmed at the practical, legal, and, theoretical levels. In 1983, 96.6% of production teams nationwide had implemented the "work contracted to households" system (Zhao 1989). In April 1993, the 8th National People's Congress amended the 1988 Constitution to include "the system of household contract responsibility" for the first time, making it a basic national economic system. The system of household contract responsibility, which combines the unified division and two-tier management, has become the main form of agricultural land system. In August 2002, the Standing Committee of the National People's Congress promulgated the Rural Land Contract Law, which legally ensures farmers' long-term contractual rights to operate rural land, and China's rural land policy entered a period of development, stability, and legalization.

In October 2008, the Third Plenary Session of the 17th Central Committee of the CPC adopted the Decision of the Central Committee of the Communist Party of China on Several Big Issues on Promoting the Reform and Development of Rural Areas, which clearly stated that "farmers should be given fuller and more secure rights to contracted land management, and the existing rural land should ensure stable and unchanged on a long-term basis." Since then, maintaining the "long-lasting" relationship between rural land contracts has become the direction of land system reform.

The system of household contract responsibility belongs to the smallholder family management method, which is to improve the productivity of the land by each farmer using intensive labor farming. With the changes in the rural market environment, this land system, which is characterized by a smallholder economy and compartmentalization, has shown certain drawbacks in adapting to the modernization of agriculture and large-scale operation. Coupled with the rapid urbanization and the non-agricultural transfer of surplus rural labor, the scattered state of farm households has become incongruous with the progress of modern agriculture, and the land rights and interests of some disadvantaged farmers have been damaged by the transfer of farmland under the coercion of multiple interest subjects; and the legal transfer of the management and use rights of farm contracted land has become a real demand and reform requirement. Rural Land Contract Law, which came into force in 2003, not only provides for the legal transfer of the right to use the contracted land, but also for the legal transfer of the right to use the contracted land. The Law on Rural Land Contracting, which came into effect in 2003, not only provides detailed regulations on the rights relationship, procedures, methods, and responsibilities of contracted land management in legal form but also provides detailed regulations and explanations on the principles and methods of transferring the right to contracted agricultural land management, which provides a clear legal basis for the transfer of agricultural land in China.

2) **Historical choice of urban land use with compensation**. China's urban land system has been continuously improved during the reform process and has successively undergone a mixed ownership system in which public and private

ownership of urban land co-existed in the early years of the founding of New China, that is, a system of free allocation of urban land and a system of paid use of urban land. The early stage of reform and opening up was the period when the system of unpaid allocation of urban land was transformed into a system of paid use of urban land. The system of unpaid allocation of urban land, like other institutional reforms in the economic field, was a product of the planned economic system, where land resources were allocated in full accordance with the provisions of administrative directive plans and physical targets on which all other resources depended, in line with the highly centralized and unified institutional background of the time (Wu 2019). In the course of the Chinese socialist revolution and socialist construction, allocation of land without compensation played an important role in consolidating the new red regime, combating the attacks of the domestic and foreign class enemies, and socially transforming the ownership of the means of production, carrying out large-scale socialist construction, and maintaining the stability of the urban socioeconomic order. However, at the same time, the administrative allocation and the prohibition of trade have led to a failure to separate the ownership and use of land, resulting in the repeated over-reporting and under-use of land, early occupation and late use, and occupation without use resulting in the waste and inefficient use of land resources (Wu 2019).

With the transformation from a socialist planned economy to a market economy, it has become increasingly difficult for the gratuitous urban land system to adapt to economic development. The development of a socialist commodity economy has brought serious challenges and good opportunities for the traditional urban land system, and reform has become an irreversible inevitable trend. In 1987, Shenzhen took the lead in carrying out the reform of separating ownership and use rights of state-owned land, and through the first public auction of state-owned land use rights, officially opened the reform of allocating land elements by market means instead of administrative allocation of land as in the past. It changed the situation of using land without compensation, indefinite periods, and mobility. Shenzhen's successful practice has promoted the reform of the land system at the national legislative level. In 1988, the Standing Committee of the National People's Congress amended the provision in the 1982 "Constitution" that "land belongs to the state and may not be leased" to read "No organization or individual may appropriate, buy, sell or otherwise illegally transfer land, and the right to use land may be transferred by the provisions of the law," only. The recognition and support of Shenzhen's land reform model from a legal perspective marked the full launch of the urban land system reform. To adapt to the new situation of the market economy, the "Land Administration Law" was also amended in December 1998: first, according to the "Constitutional Amendments," the content of "prohibiting the lease of land" was deleted, and second, it was added that "the right to use state-owned land and collectively owned land can be transferred following the law. The second is the addition of articles on "the right to use state-owned and collectively-owned land may be transferred according to law" and "the use of state-owned land for compensation," which clarifies the asset characteristics and rules of land transfer in the market economy. It implies the principle of separation of land ownership and use rights, and that the state, under the premise of retaining land ownership, will grant the right to use the land to users at a certain price, for a certain period, and for a certain purpose through auctions, tenders, and agreements, and that the land granted can be transferred, leased, and mortgaged according to law. It is a fundamental reform of China's urban land system, creating a new system of allocating land by market means, and the urban land system of allocation without compensation has since then retired from the historical stage.

(2) **The practical need to protect cultivated land and implement land use control**

With the full release of the dividends of land policy reform, China's economy and society have entered a period of rapid development. At this stage, the problems of unsound land management systems were gradually exposed, mainly as the blind development of urban and rural land, arable land protection, and the contradiction between people and land. After the reform and opening up, "the system of household contract responsibility," and the development of agricultural technology effectively enhanced the productivity of rural land, thus improving the long-standing problem of food shortage. With the rapid development of the economy, the amount of arable land has been rapidly reduced due to construction, and the protection of arable land has attracted social attention. As the conflict between economic development and arable land protection escalates, the state is placing increasing emphasis on the protection of the amount of arable land.

The Land Management Law of 1986 clearly states that "the indiscriminate occupation of arable land shall be stopped." In August 1998, the Standing Committee of the National People's Congress amended and adopted the Land Administration Law, clearly putting forth the basic state policy of "cherishing and reasonably utilizing land and effectively protecting arable land." It also proposed implementing a land use control system. The general objective of achieving a requisition-compensation balance of the total amount of arable land is clearly defined, and the responsibility of provincial governments for arable land protection is also clearly defined. A series of new legal systems, including planning control and control of the total amount of land for construction, are established with land use control and balance of arable land occupation as the core, basically building the current legal system of land management (Ye 2020). The protection of basic farmland was first proposed in this law and the simultaneous implementation of the "Regulations on Protection of Basic Farmland," which clearly requires provinces (autonomous regions and municipalities) to set aside a certain proportion of high-quality agricultural land as basic farmland for special protection in the form of a law. The establishment of the basic farmland protection system has brought arable land protection to a new level. In 2003, the Third Plenary Session of the 16th Central Committee of the CPC adopted the "Resolution to Perfect Socialist Market Economy System and to Remedy Some Problem Issued by the Central Committee of the Communist Party of China," which pointed out that "the strictest arable land protection system should be implemented to ensure national food security" and "the rights and interests of farmers should be protected and the scale of land expropriation should be controlled," further increasing the intensity of land use control in urban and rural areas. In the same year, the State Council issued the "Decision on Deepening Reform and Strict Land Management," emphasizing the work requirements for strengthening land management in the new era. Against the background of rapid economic development, contradictory land use in urban and rural areas, the severe situation of arable land protection, and prominent problems of human-land conflict, the promulgation, and implementation of a series of land policies effectively guarded the red line of China's arable land and guaranteed national food security.

Practice shows that the land use control system has established a structured and powerful land public authority system and ensured the orderly development of land use by compulsorily restricting the conversion of agricultural land to construction land, controlling the total amount of construction land, and providing special protection for arable land. Under the basic condition of China's long-term tension between people and land, the implementation of land-use regulation system has its historical selectivity and practical necessity (Zhang and Wu 2019).

2.2.2 *Since 2012: Promoting the Land Policy Exploration of "Comprehensively Expanding In-Depth Reform" in the New Era*

The reform of urban and rural land policies, mainly based on the separation of land ownership and use rights, has fully released the vitality of market factors and promoted the improvement of China's productivity and the process of industrialization and urbanization. However, at the same time, rapid social and economic development has aggravated the contradiction between resource supply and demand, and the improvement in productivity level brought by social and economic development has also provided new opportunities to solve the related problems. Since the 18th National Congress of the CPC, as economic development entered a new normal, the allocation, utilization, and protection of land resources have become more complex, their basic, global and comprehensive characteristics have become more significant, and the issues involved in coordinated development, economic transformation, social livelihood, and environmental protection have become more prominent. With the social transformation from food-oriented to economic construction-centered to ecological civilization and to building a community with a shared future for humanity, the exploitation of production materials has also shifted from a single element to a composite area, and from land resources to a three-dimensional space. In the new period of comprehensively deepening the reform comprehensively, the land policy reform is responding to the macro trend, continuously increasing its intensity, widening its depth, and improving its precision.

(1) The requirement of fairness and justice in the holistic design of land property rights

As an essential attribute and inherent requirement of socialism with Chinese characteristics, fairness and justice highlight the needs of people for a better life and manifest the pursuit of socialist values and moral spirit as well as the principles and norms, with Chinese characteristics in the new era. Since 18th National Congress of the CPC, in the face of the new problems that have emerged after a certain degree of economic development, the Party Central Committee, with Comrade Xi Jinping at its core, has profoundly recognized the changes in the major social contradictions and put forth five concepts for development to become "innovative, coordinated, green, open and inclusive." This has become the fundamental guideline of socialism with Chinese characteristics in the new era on the issue of how to develop, in which the concept of sharing is to focus on enhancing people's happiness and sense of access, aiming to solve the problem of social inequity and injustice. The prominence of social equity and justice issues can directly affect the realization of people's happiness. Therefore, improving land policies to overcome social phenomena that are against fairness and justice, and realizing fairness in terms of opportunity, distribution, and social security through the optimization of land property rights structure and holistic design become inevitable to guarantee social fairness and justice and the realization of people's happiness.

In the process of rapid industrialization and urbanization in China, land expropriation conflicts and contradictions have been the focus and hot issues affecting social stability. Therefore, upholding the concept of fairness and justice in compensation for collective land expropriation, effectively safeguarding the legitimate rights and interests of farmers, coordinating the interests of all parties, improving relevant laws and regulations, and regulating the legal procedures related to land expropriation play an important role in promoting a healthy and steady socioeconomic development and realization of fairness and justice. In 2013, the Decision of the Third Plenary Session of the 18th Central Committee of the CPC on the "Decision of the Central Committee of the Communist Party of China on Some Major Issues Concerning Comprehensively Deepening the Reform" proposed to "narrow the scope of land expropriation, standardize land expropriation procedures, improve the reasonable, standardized and diversified protection mechanism for peasants whose land has been expropriated; expand the scope of paid use of state-owned land, reduce the allocation of non-public-good land; establish a mechanism for distributing the value-added proceeds of land that takes into account the state, the collective and the individual, and reasonably increase individual income." 2014 The General Office of the Central Committee of the Communist Party of China and the General Office of the State Council "Opinions on the Pilot Reform of Rural Land Expropriation, Market Entry of Collective Management Construction Land, and Residential Land System" (Zhong banfa [2014] No. 71) were released, and 33 pilot reform areas across the country began pilot exploration on the reform of the land expropriation system in 2015. In 2019, the Land Administration Law set forth as law a number of innovative achievements that can be replicated, expanded, and amended. First, the scope of land expropriation is to be strictly limited to avoid generalization of the concept of public interest; second, the principles of compensation for land expropriation are to be clarified, and the compensation standard for land expropriation are to be improved; finally, the farmers' right to voice, participation, and supervision will be strengthened through procedural justice.

Under the dual land management system of urban and rural areas, collective construction land and state-owned construction land will have "equal land" but not "equal right." The dual market system of urban and rural construction land without "equal price" is not in line with the major strategic needs of China's rural revitalization and integrated development of urban and rural areas; nor is it in line with the premise of equality of land elements and rights between urban and rural areas. Therefore, it is necessary to seek a fundamental breakthrough in policy and law, reform the land ownership system, and realize "the equal land, the equal right, and the equal price" for rural collective construction land and state-owned construction land. In 2014, with the issuance of the Opinions on the Pilot Reform of Rural Land expropriation, Market Entry of Collective Management Construction Land, and Residential Land System (Zhong banfa [2014] No. 71), the reform of the three rural land plots was officially launched. In 2015, the Notice on the Issuance of the Implementation Rules for the Pilot Reform of Rural Land expropriation, Collective Management Construction Land in the Market and Residential Base System (Guo Tu Zi fa [2015] No. 35) clearly stated that the establishment of a collective management construction land in the market with "equal rights, equal prices, smooth flow, and shared benefits" is one of the important goals of China's reform of the rural land system. In 2019, the revised Land Management Law deleted the provision that "any unit or individual who needs to use the land for construction must use state-owned land," allowing collective business construction land to enter the market under the conditions of compliance with planning and legal registration, laying the foundation for promoting the establishment of institutional mechanisms for market-based allocation of land elements. In April 2020, the Opinions on Improving the Systems and Mechanisms for Market-oriented Allocation of Factors of Production called for further promoting market-based allocation of land factors by establishing a sound market for unified urban and rural construction land, encouraging the revitalization of stock construction land and improving the land management system. Collective operating construction land has the equal rights as state-owned construction land, and collective business construction land is included in the state-owned construction land market for public trading, giving full play to the decisive role of the market in the allocation of land resources and realizing equal access to the market and fair competition between urban and rural land.

Housing security is a matter of national importance and livelihood, to coordinate and strengthen the roles played by the government and the market, to solve the problem of housing shortage for the middle and low-income groups, and to promote the realization of housing equity, China's common property rights housing system is gradually taking shape through continuous exploration and practice. Shared-ownership housing is guaranteed to house invested by the government or provided by the government with policy preferences, raised and built following relevant standards, limited in size, restricted in the scope of use and the right to dispose of, with shared ownership between the government and the purchasing family, and supplied to the city's homeless families who meet the prescribed conditions. The Ministry of Housing and Construction announced the "Notice on ensuring housing security in 2014," in which six cities, including Beijing, Shenzhen, Chengdu, Huai'an, and Huangshi, were identified as pilot cities for shared ownership. In 2017, Beijing became the third city in China after Shanghai and Huai'an to issue a special document on shared ownership housing. The 19th National Congress of the CPC proposed to speed up the establishment of a housing system with multiple main bodies supplying, multiple channels guaranteeing and renting, and purchasing, so that all people can have a home. The National Housing and Urban–Rural Development Work Conference was held in Beijing in December 2018, in which the Ministry of Housing and Urban Development pointed out that in 2019, it should accelerate the solution of housing problems of low- and middle-income groups and develop shared property rights housing according to local conditions. "The Opinions of the General Office of the State Council on Accelerating the Development of Guaranteed Rental Housing," issued in June 2021, clearly proposed to improve the housing security system with public rental housing, guaranteed rental housing, and shared ownership housing as the mainstay, confirming for the first time from the national level that shared ownership housing is an important part of the current and future housing security system within a certain period of time. It is worth noting that there are still problems such as the single source of government funding, narrow coverage of the protection target, and imperfect access and exit mechanism of shared ownership housing in China, which need to be further explored and improved. The common property rights of shared ownership housing make fairness and justice manifest in the aspects of "fairness in the starting point" and "fairness in results" through housing allocation and housing property right distribution, which has far-reaching practical significance for improving China's housing security system and housing system, satisfying people's aspiration for a better life, and achieving social harmony and development.

(2) **Promote the separation of the three rights of the rural land, and the reform of "three pieces of land" as required by the rural revitalization strategy**

Modern urban–rural relationship has evolved from a stage of urban–rural dual structure with division of labor against each other to a stage of urban–rural integration and development with integration and symbiosis. The large number of farmers entering the cities to work and live has greatly promoted urban–rural integration, but it also inevitably brings problems such as the reduction of rural development resources and the decline of the countryside, which threaten stable socioeconomic development. However, in the socialist market economy environment, rural land, an important factor of production, cannot participate well in the market economy, which seriously restricts the realization of rural and farmers' development rights and interests. As urbanization and industrialization continue to advance rapidly, the massive outflow of the agricultural population not only generates abandonment and idleness of arable land but also leads to massive idleness and inefficient use of rural residential land. Productivity development and the transformation of rural human-land relations simultaneously require policy reforms and innovations in rural land systems. Optimizing the content and structure of land property rights is both an important means to promote the optimal allocation of land resources and a trend for land policy to evolve in the direction of social productivity. The 18th National Congress of the CPC and the Third Plenary Session of the 18th Central Committee of the CPC clearly pointed out the need to give farmers more land rights, to change the way rural land is operated through the confirmation of rights, and to fully stimulate the potential of innovation in rural land operation in agricultural development. Therefore, the 19th National Congress of the CPC proposed the rural revitalization strategy, with the overall requirement of "prosperous industry, pleasant ecology, civilized countryside, effective governance and, rich living." The introduction of the rural revitalization strategy requires land policies to provide land elements to guarantee comprehensive revitalization of the countryside. In this background, emerges the separation of the three rights of the rural land and the reform of "three pieces of land."

Some Opinions about Comprehensively Deepening Rural Reform to Accelerate Agricultural Modernization" issued by the Central Committee of the Communist Party of China (CPC) and the State Council in 2014 clearly pointed out that the right to contract land management remains unchanged in the long term and that transfer of land management rights is promoted in an orderly manner, while three policy bottom lines are set for rural land policy: the nature of land remains unchanged, the red line of arable land is not broken, and the rights and interests of farmers are not damaged, which has become a ballast for the comprehensive deployment and systematic promotion of rural land system and agricultural and rural reform. In 2016, the General Office of the Central Committee of the Communist Party of China and the General Office of the State Council issued the Opinions on Improving the Measures for Separating Rural Land Ownership from Contracted Management Right, which put forth the "separation of three rights" for the first time and emphasized the need to apply the theory of "separation of three rights" to guide the reform practice and continuously explore and enrich the specific forms of realization of "separation of three rights." Under the premise of separating ownership rights and contracting rights in the system of household contract responsibility, the "separation of three rights" by separating contracting rights and management rights of the land formed the rural land policy of separating ownership, contractual, and management rights. The newly amended and adopted Law of the People's Republic of China on Rural Land Contracting in 2018 affirmed the important value of the "separation of three rights," formally elevating it from policy to law and implementing more reliable legal protection and a certain degree of empowerment of land management rights utilizing term setting and property rights registration. Since 2018, the Central Document No. 1 has emphasized for three consecutive years that the main line of deepening rural reform is to deal with the relationship between farmers and land, improve the system of "separation of three rights," allow farmers to transfer their land management rights voluntarily, optimize the procedures for the transfer of land management rights, and give rural contracted land management rights financing guarantees according to the law. To increase farmers' property income, the "separation of three rights" is an innovation and development of the household contract responsibility system, which not only retains the collective ownership of rural land but also revitalizes the right to operate the land, giving farmers greater autonomy in choosing the use of land and playing an important role in increasing farmers' income and realizing agricultural modernization. This is both inevitable for the modernization of national governance and an added value of the times of the unique Chinese experience in the innovation of the property rights system (Deng 2017).

The implementation of the rural revitalization strategy requires that while the vitality of productive rural land is further released through the expansion of rights, the issue of the rights of collective business construction land and residential bases is resolved. The Decision of the Central Committee of the Communist Party of China on Several Major Issues Concerning Comprehensively Deepening the Reform, adopted at the Third Plenary Session of the 18th Central Committee of the Communist Party of China, proposed t "equal access to the market, equal rights, and equal prices," giving rural collective commercial construction land equal market status. In 2013, according to the spirit of the "Central Document No. 1," in the context of "establishing a rural collective property rights system with clear attribution, complete rights, smooth flow, and strict protection," comprehensive promotion of the registration and certification of rural land rights was undertaken. On December 31, 2014, the General Office of the Central Committee of the Communist Party of China and the General Office of the State Council jointly issued the "Opinions on the Pilot Reform of Rural Land Expropriation, Market Entry of Collective Management Construction Land, and Residential Land System," which marked China's "Trinity Rural Land Reform" officially entering the pilot stage. On June 30, 2020, the 14th meeting of the Central Committee for Comprehensively Deepening Reform considered and adopted the "Pilot Program for Deepening the Reform of the Rural House Base System." At the meeting, it was pointed out that "to deepen the reform of the rural residential base system, we should actively explore specific paths and methods to implement the collective ownership of residential bases, protect the eligibility of residential bases and the property rights of farmers' houses, and appropriately release the right to use residential bases and farmers' houses." It further promoted China's comprehensive reform to improve the system of rural land expropriation, market entry of collective operating construction land, and residential bases. By expanding the usufruct rights and security rights of related land, it is conducive to increasing the property income of farmers and eliminating the imbalance and inequality between urban and rural land markets. With a high degree of legalization and market-oriented mechanism, it further clarifies the direction, focus, and requirements of deepening the reform of the rural land system (Li et al. 2020) and promotes the requirements of the rural revitalization strategy of the separation of the three rights of the rural land and reforming the "Trinity Rural Land Reform."

(3) Give full play to the role of the government and promote the market to determine the requirements of the market-oriented reform of resource allocation

After the Third Plenary Session of the 18th Central Committee of the CPC in 1978, China gradually transitioned from a highly centralized planned economic system to a dynamic socialist market economy. In this process, the market-oriented reform of urban and rural land elements, which is mainly characterized by the separation of land ownership and use rights, has also been pushed out in a gradual and orderly manner. China's market-oriented reform of land factors has gone through three stages in which the market plays a supportive, fundamental, and decisive role in the allocation of land resources (Qian et al. 2021). Along with the process of marketization of land elements, China's land market has gradually opened up, and the right to trade land has undergone a loosening from restricting transactions to encouraging them and thus led to the current dual land market structure, Xisnqing and Zhonghao (2010) in which the government monopolizes the primary land market, and urban and rural areas are divided. Along with the establishment of China's socialist market economy system, under the dualistic socioeconomic structure, China's resource allocation method is generally changing from planned decisions to market decisions, and the land market is developing in parallel with the role of administrative intervention and market mechanisms (Chen and Long 2019). Over the past few decades, China has continued to explore and move forward with market-oriented reforms of land elements, and the gradual increase in the marketization of land has had a significant impact on the efficiency of land allocation and even national economic development. However, in the process of market-oriented allocation of land elements, there are still problems such as lack of institutional guarantee, imbalance of the institutional mechanism, the prominent contradiction between supply and demand, inefficient stock inventory, etc. The structural contradiction of market-oriented allocation of land elements is prominent, allocation efficiency is not high, the market transaction rules and service system are not perfect, the market price mechanism has not yet formed, and the market-oriented reform of land elements is urgent.

Under the new situation of economic adjustment and transformation and upgrading at home and abroad, China is at a critical point to deepen the reform of market-oriented factor allocation and promote quality change, efficiency change, and power change in economic development. To shift from high-speed growth to high-quality development, it is necessary to shift from government-led resource allocation to market-determined resource allocation and the role of the government should be better played. It is difficult to achieve optimal allocation of urban and rural land resources by relying solely on market mechanisms or government mechanisms (Cai and Long 2019). In 2013, the Third Plenary Session of the 18th Central Committee of the CPC adopted the Decision of the Central Committee of the Communist Party of China on Some Major Issues Concerning Comprehensively Deepening the Reform, which changed the "fundamental role" of the market in resource allocation to "decisive role" and proposed to "give farmers more property rights" and "promote the equal exchange of urban and rural elements and balanced allocation of public resources."

China's market-oriented reform of rural land elements is being fully explored in the form of the separation of the three rights of the contracted farm land, the separation of the three rights of the homestead, and the market entry of commercial collective-owned construction land. For contracted land, the 2013 Central Rural Work Conference proposed that "land contracted management right is divided into the right to contract land and the right to operate, so that the two rights can be separated in parallel." In 2014, it issued "About Guiding Rural Land Management Rights Transfer with the Opinions of the Development of Moderate Scale Management of Agriculture" to "adhere to the collective ownership of rural land, ownership, contracting rights, management rights 'separation of three rights.'" By further clarifying and improving the property rights system of contracted land, the contracting rights and land management rights were better utilized and the efficiency of land use effectively improved. At the same time, the pilot project of contracted land management mortgage was promoted, as per which contracted management rights become property and flow into the market, and the potential value of land effectively deployed. The 2018 Central Document No. 1 separated the ownership rights, qualification rights, and use rights for rural land designated for housing, and the Land Administration Law passed in 2019 formally recognized the feasibility of the market entry of collective business construction land from a legal perspective, further reinforcing the reform orientation of the release of the right to use residential bases. At the same time, the urban land market was optimized and upgraded, mainly focusing on industrial land allocation, inventory land revitalization, and improvement of the secondary market of urban land to promote the marketization of land elements to improve efficiency and quality. These measures highlight the importance of land system reform on the one hand and on the other they reflect the enormity and complexity of the land system reform. Although reform exploration has intensified, it is still necessary to further increase reform efforts and comprehensively promote the market-oriented allocation of land elements to meet the needs of further economic and social development.

(4) **Requirements for modernization of the territorial space governance system and capacity**

Entering a new era of socialist construction with Chinese characteristics, the fundamental changes in the main contradictions of society have put forth new requirements for public governance capacity. In the Third Plenary Session of the 18th Central Committee of the CPC, it was pointed out that the overall goal of comprehensively deepening the reform is to improve and develop socialism with Chinese characteristics and promote modernization of the national governance system and governance capacity. A spatial governance system is important to promote modernization of China's national governance system and governance capacity, and the establishment of a scientific system will regulate the use of all territorial space to enhance the capacity and level of spatial governance of the country, which directly determines the modernization construction of China's governance system and governance capacity (Chen 2020).

In the face of the new requirements for the rational use and optimal allocation of national spatial resources in the modernization of national spatial governance capacity in the new era, China has clearly defined the reform direction of natural resources development, utilization, and protection supervision as a "unified exercise of the responsibility of the owner of all natural resources assets for all people, the unified exercise of all national spatial use control and ecological protection and restoration," which has put forward corresponding demands for the regulated use of all territorial space systems. In 2018–2019, the State Council of the Central Committee of the Communist Party of China (CPC) promulgated the Opinions on Unifying the Planning System to Better Play the Role of Strategic Guidance of National Development Planning and Some Opinions on the Establishment and Supervision of the Implementation of the Land and Space Planning System, which require "the implementation of use control of all territorial space zoning based on territorial spatial planning." At this point, the traditional single-factor, sub-sectoral land use control began to transform into comprehensive territorial spatial land use control, and the top-level design of the management organization, control basis, and tools for spatial land use control were basically completed (Zhang and Lyu 2020). In the face of the demand for the construction of a national spatial governance system, China further improved its land policy in terms of reforming the management of land use plans and effectively linking land planning management with national spatial planning, thus giving play to the role of land policy in promoting modernization of national spatial governance capacity.

2.3 Legislative Reform and Legal Basis of Land Policy Implementation

2.3.1 Legal Basis System of China's Land Policy Implementation

The legal system of land refers to a system comprising interrelated, complementary, and mutually restrictive legal norms and other legal sources, which aim to adjust the social relations arising from the development, utilization, protection, and improvement of land and the land market. China's land legal system consists of three layers, namely, the fundamental law ("Constitution of the People's Republic of China"), the basic law ("Chinese Civil Code"), and the special laws, such as the "Land Administration Law of the People's Republic of China," "Law of the People's Republic of China on the Administration of the Urban Real Estate," "Law on Contracting of Rural Land," etc. (Fig. 2.1 presents the details.)

(1) **"Constitution of the People's Republic of China"**

The current Chinese Constitution is the 1982 Constitution. The Constitution is the fundamental law of the country, with the highest legal status, legal authority, and legal effect, which is fundamental, overall, stable, and long term. The Constitution

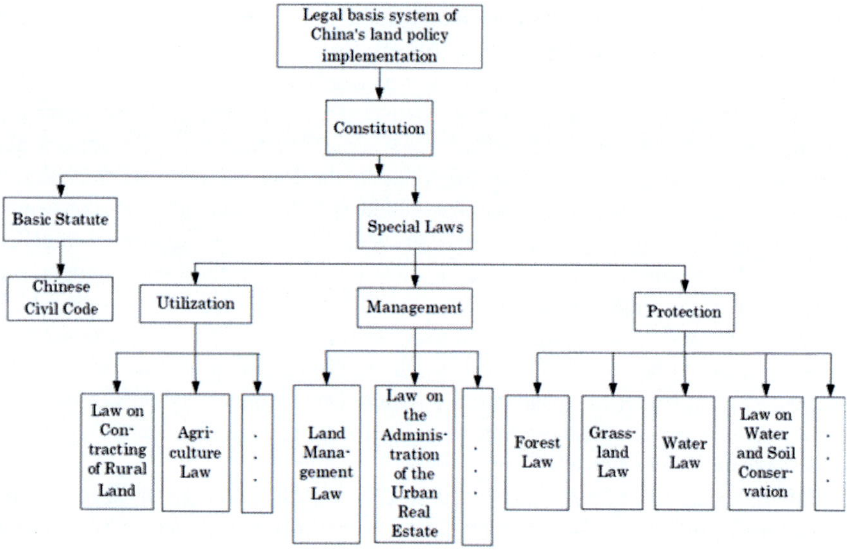

Fig. 2.1 Legal basis system of land policy implementation

plays a supreme legal position and role in the country's politics, economy, culture, and social life.

The implementation of socialist rule of law with Chinese characteristics is based on the implementation of the Constitution. The contents of the Constitution on land mainly include stipulating land ownership of the state and the collective, as well as the rights and obligations of the state in the rational development, utilization, protection, and improvement of land, which are instructive, principled, and policy-oriented. They form the constitutional basis of China's land legal system. In terms of politics, economy, culture, and social life, the Constitution, as the foundation of other land-related legislation, promotes and improves the legal basis system of China's land policy implementation and lays the foundation for the integrity of the country's legal system.

(2) **Basic Statute**

The "Chinese Civil Code" is the first law named after the code in Chinese history, which aims to ensure people's expectations for a better life in all aspects and to resolve the contradiction between unbalanced and inadequate development and the growing expectations for a better life. This code has Chinese characteristics, reflects the characteristics of the new era, conforms to the requirements of the times, and reflects the wishes of the people. It provides a complete civil legal guarantee for upholding and improving the socialist system with Chinese characteristics, achieving the "Two Century Goals" and realizing the Chinese Dream of national rejuvenation in the new era.

In accordance with the requirements of the CPC Central Committee to improve the property rights protection system and the modern property rights system with clear ownership, clear rights, and responsibilities, strict protection and smooth circulation, the property rights compilation of the "Chinese Civil Code" implemented on January 1, 2021, was revised and improved based on the original "Property Law," which further improved the property rights system. From houses to buildings, distinguishing ownership and the right of habitation, from neighboring relations to co-ownership, from land ownership to land contracted management right, right to use the land for construction, as well as real rights for security, etc., all kinds of rights embody the importance of the property rights compilation and form the legal basis for the implementation of land policies.

(3) **Important Special Laws and Regulations**

Since its promulgation in 1986, the "Land Administration Law" has been revised in 1988, 1998, 2004, and 2019. It is a special law that comprehensively regulates the management activities of the land property system and ensures rational use of land resources. Its latest content is about the reform of (a) marketization of collectively owned rural profit-oriented construction land, (b) the land expropriation system, and (c) the rural homestead land system. These reforms reflect the new achievements of Comprehensively Deepening the Reform and the national conditions and public opinion, break the institutional obstacles of land in Comprehensively Deepening the Reform, and meet the needs of current social and economic development. Meanwhile, they promote reform and innovation of the land system in a better way and speed up the establishment of a unified market for urban and rural land used for construction purposes.

The current "Interim Regulation of the Peoples' Republic of China Concerning the Assignment and Transfer of the Right to the Use of the Stated-owned Land in the Urban Areas" (Order No. 55 of the State Council) issued in 1990 established the national land use system in the form of administrative regulations for the first time. Since then, China has officially begun to implement the assignment and transfer system of the right to use state-owned land in the urban areas. The regulation explained in detail the assignment, transfer, mortgage, and allocation of rights to use state-owned land in the urban areas and provided legal support for reforming urban state-owned land use system, rationally developing, utilizing, and managing the land, strengthening land management, as well as promoting urban construction and economic development.

The current "Law of the People's Republic of China on the Administration of the Urban Real Estate" promulgated in 1994 has improved the socialist legal system with Chinese characteristics and reflected the process of China's reform and opening up and socialist modernization. Mainly from the perspective of urban land, it presents details of the regulations on the development, assignment, transfer, and mortgage of urban land, is in harmony with the "Land Administration Law" and other related laws, promotes reform and innovation of the land system, and provides legal support for the development of land policy.

The "Law on Contracting of Rural Land," which was implemented in 2002, focused on rural land contract, fully guaranteed farmers' right to contracted management of land, and was in line with China's rural reality and farmers' wishes. It is a solid foundation for stabilizing and perfecting the two-tier management based on household contract management and provided a strong guarantee for the long-term stability of rural land in contract relationship.

The "Grassland Law of the People's Republic of China," the "Water Law of the People's Republic of China," and the "Agriculture Law of the People's Republic of China," newly revised in 2002, as well as the "Forest Law of the People's Republic of China" newly revised in 2019, and the "Law of the People's Republic of China on Soil and Water Conservation" newly revised in 2010, not only stipulated the ownership of relevant land, but also prescribed cooperative utilization, protection, and management of all kinds of land (grassland, woodland, etc.) closely related to it.

Based on the legal system for the implementation of land policy, the following content takes all land-related laws as the analysis object, focuses on the land-related content, and introduces the processes and reasons of each law from its introduction to its revision, amendment, or repeal in detail.

1) **"Constitution of the People's Republic of China"**
   The "Constitution of the People's Republic of China" (hereinafter referred to as "the Constitution"), which is applicable to all citizens of the country and is the product of the comprehensive effects of specific social, political, economic, and ideological and cultural conditions, is the fundamental law of the country and the general charter for governing the country. It reflects the actual contrast of various political forces, confirms the victory of the revolution and realistic democratic politics, and stipulates the fundamental tasks and systems of the state, namely, the social system, the principles of the state system, the organization of state power, and the basic rights and obligations of citizens. After the founding of the People's Republic of China in October 1949, the First, the Fourth, and the Fifth National People's Congresses, respectively, formulated and promulgated four Constitutions in September 1954, January 1975, March 1978, and December 1982.

   On September 20, 1954, the Constitution adopted and promulgated at the first session of the First National People's Congress recorded the victory of the Chinese people's long struggle, pointed out the correct direction of socialist development, as well as established the political system, economic system, and other basic systems with Chinese characteristics, thus laying the basic structure of the Constitution of New China. There were some provisions for land in it. For example, first, "the state protects farmers' rights of land ownership and other means of production ownership in accordance with the law." Second, "For the needs of the national public interest, urban and rural land and other means of production may be requisitioned, expropriated or nationalized in accordance with the conditions prescribed by law." The 1975 Constitution is the product of China's specific historical conditions. It is an imperfect constitution with serious shortcomings and mistakes because it has too few clauses, has simplistic contents, omission of norms, and many other inaccuracies in the content. On the issue of land, it confirmed the economic system of "three-level ownership and team-based" people's commune but retained some basic principles of the 1954 Constitution, such as upholding the socialist public ownership of the means of production and the dictatorship of the proletariat.

After the Constitution was revised again in 1978, with the deepening of the Communist Party of China's "bringing order out of chaos," in 1982, an urgent need was observed to revise the original Constitution again to adapt it to the situation. After the promulgation and implementation of the 1982 Constitution, according to the practice and development of China's reform and opening up and socialist modernization, under the leadership of the CPC Central Committee, the National People's Congress made necessary and important amendments to the 1982 Constitution, that is, the current Chinese Constitution, five times, in 1988, 1993, 1999, 2004, and 2018. Among them, there were some amendments related to land policy. For example, first, paragraph 4 of Article 10 of the 1988 Constitution was amended as "No organization or individual may occupy, buy or sell or illegally transfer land in other forms. The land use right can be transferred in accordance with the law," and a new land use system was established. Second, in 1993, the Constitution deleted the reference of "Rural People's Commune" and established the legal status of the "system of household contract responsibility". Third, the 1999 Constitution amended China's rural production and management system, stipulating that "rural collective economic organizations shall implement a two-tier management system based on household contract management." Fourth, the 2004 Constitution amended the state's land expropriation system to "the state may expropriate or requisition land and give compensation according to the law for the needs of public interests." The 2018 Constitution made no specific changes to the land policy.

2) **"Land Reform Law of the People's Republic of China"**

The "Land Reform Law of the People's Republic of China" (hereinafter referred to as the "Land Reform Law") passed by the Central People's Government Committee on June 30, 1950, was formulated according to the domestic, political, and economic situation in the early days of the founding of New China and the urgent demands of the broad masses of peasants. It stipulated that the feudal system of land ownership that allowed for exploitation by the landlord class should be abolished, and that land ownership of farmers should be implemented to liberate rural productive forces, develop agricultural production, and clear the path for the industrialization of New China. It also stipulated confiscation and expropriation of land, mainly including confiscation of the land of the landlords and the expropriation of the land of ancestral halls, temples, monasteries, churches, schools and groups in rural areas. In addition, it also made specific provisions on the methods of land distribution, the handling of special problems in land reform, and the executing organs and methods of land reform.

Land reform was fully carried out in the newly liberated areas after the promulgation and implementation of the "Land Reform Law." By the end of 1952, except for some minority areas and Taiwan Province, land reform in the newly liberated areas was basically completed. Together with the old, liberated areas, the agricultural population in areas where land reform was completed accounted for more than 90% of the total agricultural population in China. In the whole process of land reform, more than 300 million landless peasants including those the old and new liberated areas got 700 million mu of land and other means of production free of charge, and feudal land ownership was completely destroyed.[19] This land reform completely overthrew China's feudal exploitation system that had lasted thousands of years, liberated the productive forces, and mobilized the productive enthusiasm of the peasants. With the gradual disappearance of the decay and rot in the countryside, ancient rural areas of China became fully vitalized and laid the foundation for agricultural cooperation in New China. Aimed at abolishing the feudal and exploitative land ownership of landlord class and implementing the land ownership of farmers, the law played a positive role in quickly restoring and developing production and ensuring the smooth completion of land reform. With the promulgation and implementation of "Land Administration Law of the People's Republic of China" (hereinafter referred to as "Land Administration Law"), the "Land Reform Law" became invalid toward the end of 1987.

3) **"Land Administration Law of the People's Republic of China"**
With the deepening of the economic system reform, the demand for land for national construction and people's living increased rapidly, and the problems of land management, utilization, development, and protection become increasingly prominent. To effectively utilize and protect land resources, it is necessary to "regulate the differences in the world to be consistent." The "Land Administration Law" passed in 1986 was a law in line with China's national conditions, which adapted to the objective requirements of the "Four Modernizations"[20] and was formulated on the basis of a scientific summary of China's land management experience. Its promulgation and implementation provided a strong legal guarantee for preventing and controlling land destruction and protecting land resources. It was also of great significance to guarantee socialist land ownership, rationally use land, guarantee land for national construction and village (town) construction, as well as promote the "Four Modernizations" construction. In 1988, to implement the provisions of the constitutional amendment of the same year, the "Land Administration Law" was amended for the first time, clearly stipulating that the right to use land can be transferred in accordance with the provisions of the law; the amendment made it clear that the right to use state-owned land should be paid for. It also responded to the need of land entering the market as a production factor in the transition from a planned economy to a market economy and played an important role in promoting the

[19] The magnificent 70 years - the new era of struggle: The glorious years of New China-abolish the feudal land system. People's Daily, 2019–09-05(06).

[20] The Four Modernizations, namely, industrial modernization, agricultural modernization, national defense modernization, and scientific and technological modernization, are the national strategic goals put forth by the Communist Party of China (CPC) and the People's Republic of China from the 1950s to the 1960s.

development of a socialist market economy. In 1998, the "Land Administration Law" was comprehensively revised to solve the problems of extensive land use and large-scale occupation of cultivated land in the process of rapid economic development and rapid urbanization in China. This led to the establishment of the strictest farmland protection system and improved the land use regulation system, ensuring food security and promoting the sustainable development of social economy. In 2004, the "Land Administration Law" was amended to distinguish the concepts of "expropriation" and "requisition," and the fourth paragraph of Article 2 was changed as follows: "The state may expropriate or requisite land according to law for the needs of public interests, and give compensation." Besides, the requisition of the original collective land was changed to expropriation, which improved the state expropriation and requisition system. In 2019, the "Land Administration Law" was revised again, which was an institutional innovation and improvement based on fully summarizing the successful experience of the rural land system reform pilot. First, it broke down the legal barrier of collective management construction land entering the market and realized the same price and rights in the same place. Second, it deepened the reform of the land expropriation system and more fully safeguarded the rights and interests of landless farmers. Third, it perfected the rural homestead system, which was conducive to the revitalization and utilization of idle homesteads. Fourth, it cleared the legal status of the land space planning system. Fifth, it reasonably divided the central and local examination and approval authority, in line with the requirements of a streamlined administration, delegated powers, strengthened regulations, and improved services. Sixth, it gave the land inspector a clear legal status. Overall, the amendment and revision of the "Land Administration Law" gradually reflected the new achievements of Comprehensively Expanding In-Depth Reform, reflected the national conditions and public opinions, removed the land institutional obstacles in Comprehensively Expanding In-Depth Reform, and met the needs of the current social and economic development. What's more, it even promote the reform and innovation of the land system and accelerated the establishment of a unified urban and rural construction land market (Meng et al. 2019).

4) **"Forest Law of the People's Republic of China"**
On September 20, 1984, the seventh meeting of the Standing Committee of the Sixth National People's Congress passed "Forest Law of the People's Republic of China" (hereinafter referred to as "Forest Law"). It was formulated in the background of a planned economy and in the context of the need to focus on wood production. It focused on the management of wood production, but there were provisions on land issues as well. First, in terms of land ownership, Article 3 clearly stipulated the ownership of forests and woodlands: "Forest resources are owned by the whole population, except those that are collective-owned as stipulated by law. The local people's governments at or above the county level shall register the forests, trees, and woodlands owned by the whole population and owned collectively and trees and woodlands owned and used by individuals and issue certificates to confirm the ownership or right to use. The legitimate

rights and interests of owners and users of forests, trees, and woodlands are protected by law, and no unit or individual may infringe upon them." As the socialist market economic system became gradually established, the original Forest Law needed to be revised, supplemented, and improved. In 1998, the "Forest Law" was amended, which mainly involved land protection, transfer of the right to use, etc. Specifically, it included strengthening the protection of natural forest land, transferring the right to use forest land, setting up a compensation system for ecological benefits, changing "owned by the whole population" to "owned by the state," changing "state-run" to "state-owned," and so on. Besides, detailed provisions were mentioned regarding the specific conditions and circumstances of the transfer of right to use forest land, which was in line with the improved land use regulation system proposed in the "Land Administration Law" of the same year.

Since the ideas it reflected were still based on traditional forestry and forest resources management and did not fully reflect sustainable development, the "Forest Law" amended in 2009 changed "expropriation" mentioned in Article 18 to "expropriation and requisition." In 2019, the newly revised "Forest Law" paid more attention to land ownership. For the first time, it listed forest ownership separately and as an independent chapter, emphasizing the foundation of forest ownership. Besides, according to the changes of state institutional reform and functional adjustment, it classified and standardized the registration of forest ownership and clearly defined ownership of forest land and trees, which was intended to promote the separation of ownership, contractual, and management rights. What's more, it promoted the rational flow of production factors, improved the efficiency of resource allocation, and enhanced enthusiasm in production management and protection. The revision of the "Forest Law" could thoroughly implement the decision-making arrangements of the CPC Central Committee, promote the construction of ecological civilization, and put into practice the notion that "lucid waters and lush mountains are invaluable assets." It was also of great significance to promote the modernization of the forestry governance system and governance capacity, Yu (2019) and plays an important role in promoting the development of China's land policy.

5) **"Grassland Law of the People's Republic of China"**

"Grassland Law of the People's Republic of China" (hereinafter referred to as "Grassland Law") is China's first agricultural industry law enacted in 1985. The implementation of this law has played a positive role in strengthening the protection, construction, and rational utilization of grasslands, protecting and improving the ecological environment; it also marked China's grassland management's entry to the stage of legalization with laws to follow. In terms of land ownership, its Article 4 made clear provisions: "The grasslands are owned by the state, that is, by the whole population, except those that are collectively owned by law. Grassland owned by the whole population can be fixed for collective long-term use. Grasslands owned by the whole population, grasslands owned by collectives and grasslands owned by the whole population that have been used by collectives for a long time can be contracted by collectives or individuals to engage in animal husbandry. Grasslands used by units owned by the whole population shall be registered by the local people's governments at or above the county level, and certificates shall be issued to confirm the right to use it. All grasslands owned by collectives and grasslands owned by the whole population that are permanently used by collectives for a long time shall be registered by the people's governments at the county level, and certificates shall be issued to confirm the ownership or right to use them. The ownership and right to use grasslands are protected by law, and no unit or individual may infringe upon them." In addition, Article 7 also made relevant provisions on the ways and conditions of land requisition: "The requisition of collectively-owned grasslands for state construction shall be handled in accordance with "Regulations on Land Requisition for State Construction." For the grasslands owned by the whole population for the use of collectives for a long time that was used in national construction, appropriate compensation shall be given according to the provisions of "Regulations on Land Requisition for State Construction," and the production and living of herdsmen shall be properly settled. In requisitioning or using grasslands in national autonomous areas for state construction, the interests of the national autonomous areas shall be considered and arrangements conducive to the economic construction of the national autonomous areas shall be made. The temporary use of grasslands for state construction shall be handled in accordance with the provisions of "Regulations on Land Requisition for State Construction." When the use period expires, the land use unit shall restore grassland vegetation.

However, with the deepening of reform and the development of the market economy, the economy and society in pastoral areas developed all round, population increased rapidly, and the pressure on grasslands touched the highest value in history. Therefore, in pastoral society, the concept of development and construction at the center gradually gave way to the protection of the ecological environment. The "Grassland Law" revised in 2002 stipulated the principles and conditions for the transfer of grassland contractual management rights and clearly put forward the national policy of scientific planning, comprehensive protection, key construction, and rational utilization of grasslands for the first time. It also clarified the legal provisions on grassland ownership and grassland contract management, planning, construction, utilization, and protection, which better reflected the basic requirements of grassland protection and rational utilization in China. The specific provisions were as follows: "Collectively owned grasslands or state-owned grasslands designated for use by collective economic organizations according to law may be contracted and managed by families or joint households within the collective economic organizations. Grassland protection, construction, and utilization planning should be linked with the general land use planning and coordinated with environmental protection planning, water and soil conservation planning, sand control planning, water resources planning, long-term forestry planning, general urban planning, village and town planning, and other relevant planning." However, many shortcomings persisted, mainly manifested in the failure to thoroughly implement the basic concept of "sustainable development." In 2009, articles 38, 39, and 63 of the "Grassland Law" was revised from "requisition" to "exploration and requisition." Subsequently, the "Grassland Law" was amended in 2013 and 2021, which was of great significance not only to the protection, construction, and rational use of land, but also to improvement of ecological environment, maintenance of biodiversity, and promotion of sustainable economic and social development.

6) **"Water Law of the People's Republic of China"**
The promulgation and implementation of "Water Law of the People's Republic of China" (hereinafter referred to as "Water Law") in 1988 marked China's entry into a new period of water control according to law. It was a law that suited China's national conditions and promoted reform and development of water conservancy. Its contents related were to land as well. First, article 41 clearly stipulated that land use and construction must meet the requirements of flood control in the flood control river channel and flood detention basin, which reflected coordination between the "Water Law" and the "Land Administration Law." As China's economy entered a period of rapid development and economic system transformation, the implementation of the "Water Law" encountered many new situations and problems. For example, in the development and utilization of water resources, people pay attention to opening up new sources while they neglected reducing consumption and protecting water. In addition, reform and opening up promoted the diversification of economic interests and made the relationship between water resources management more complicated.

The planning chapter was added to the newly revised "Water Law" in 2002. The land-related contents were as follows: "Regional planning within a river basin shall be subject to river basin planning, and professional planning shall be subject to comprehensive planning. The needs of various regions and industries, comprehensive river basin planning, and regional planning, as well as professional planning closely related to land use should be coordinated with national economic and social development planning, overall land use planning, overall urban planning, and environmental protection planning." It made great breakthroughs in both legislative concept and system design, and these breakthroughs created favorable conditions for water resources legislation and even other related legislation (Lyu 2006). Subsequently, the "Water Law" was further amended in 2009 and 2016, which was of great significance for the rational development, utilization, conservation, and protection of water and soil resources, and for adapting to the national economic and social development.

7) **"Law of the People's Republic of China on Soil and Water Conservation"**
On June 29, 1991, "Law of the People's Republic of China on Soil and Water Conservation" (hereinafter referred to as "Soil and Water Conservation Law") was promulgated and implemented. Its purpose was to prevent and control soil erosion, protect and rationally utilize soil and water resources, as well as to reduce water, drought, and wind-sand disasters and improve the ecological environment and develop production. Over the past 10 years, the work of soil

and water conservation has moved toward the track of legalization, which has played a great role in further improving the awareness of soil and water conservation in the whole society, paying attention to ecological construction of soil and water conservation while developing and constructing, and in controlling the existing soil and water loss. It mainly involved the planning, utilization, and protection of land resources. Specific provisions on planning were as follows: "The water administrative department of the State Council and the local people's government at or above the county level shall, on the basis of investigation and evaluation of water and soil resources, work out water and soil conservation plans with relevant departments. The water and soil conservation plan approved by the local people's government at or above the county level shall be reported to the water administrative department of the people's government at the next higher level for the record. The revision of soil and water conservation planning must be approved by the original approving authority." Specific contents related to land use protection were as follows: "To reclaim barren slope above five degrees and below the forbidden slope, it must be approved by the water administrative department of the people's government at the county level; To reclaim state-owned barren slope, it can apply to the people's government at or above the county level for land reclamation procedures, with the approval of the water administrative department of the people's government at or above the county level."

With the development of economy and society and the advancement of democracy and legal system, the "Soil and Water Conservation Law" was revised in 2010 after the first revision in 2009. The newly added planning and the newly revised governance chapter fully reflected coordination with land, and its specific provisions were as follows: "Soil and water conservation planning should be coordinated with the overall land use planning, water resources planning, urban and rural planning, and environmental protection planning. The state encourages and supports contracted management of barren mountains, barren gullies, barren hills, and barren beaches, prevention and control of soil erosion, protection and improvement of ecological environment, promotion of rational development and sustainable utilization of land resources, as well as protection of the legitimate rights and interests of the parties to the land contract according to law." They were of great significance to prevent and control soil erosion, protect and rationally utilize water and soil resources, alleviate disasters caused by water, drought and sand storms, as well as to improve the ecological environment and ensure sustainable economic and social development.

8) **"Agricultural Law of the People's Republic of China"**

"The Agricultural Law of the People's Republic of China" (hereinafter referred to as "Agricultural Law"), adopted by the Second Session of the Standing Committee of the Eighth National People's Congress on July 2, 1993, played an important role in further strengthening the basic position of agriculture, stabilizing agricultural production and the operation system based on household contract management, promoting the development and structural adjustment of agricultural production, strengthening agricultural science and technology education, safeguarding the legitimate rights and interests of farmers, and promoting the improvement of the overall level of agricultural production. With regard to the ownership of land resources, "Agricultural Law" stipulates the following: "Land in rural and suburban areas is collectively owned except for the land in these areas which belonged to the State as prescribed by the law. Natural resources such as forests, mountains, grasslands, wastelands, tidal flats, and water flows belong to the state; except for forests and mountains, grasslands, wastelands, and tidal flats that are collectively owned by law." It also stipulates the transfer of land use rights and the relevant content of farmland protection: "The right to use state-owned land and collectively owned land may be transferred according to law." No organization or individual may encroach upon, buy, sell, or otherwise illegally transfer land. People's governments at all levels must cherish and legally use land and earnestly protect cultivated land. Indiscriminate occupation and misuse of land are prohibited. In addition, it also involves more content on land contracting: "Collectively owned or state-owned and used by agricultural collective economic organizations, land, mountains, grasslands, wastelands, tidal flats, and water surfaces may be contracted by individuals or collectives to engage in agricultural production. State-owned and collectively owned barren mountains and wasteland suitable for forest cultivation may be afforested by individual or collective contracts. Individual or collective contract management rights shall be protected by law. The contractees and contractors should sign land use contracts to define each other's rights and obligations."

With the gradual improvement of the socialist market economic system, the operating mechanism and external environment of agricultural and rural economic development changed, and the traditional agricultural management and support model could no longer adapt to the new situation. The newly revised "Agricultural Law" in 2002 was revised, supplemented, and improved, stipulating that the state shall adhere to and improve the basic economic system with public ownership playing a dominant role and different economic sectors developing side by side, to revitalize the rural economy; the State adhered to the principle of rejuvenating agriculture through science and education and sustainable agricultural development; the State protected the property and other lawful rights and interests of farmers and agricultural production and operation organizations from infringement. The specific amendments to the land aspect are as follows: "The state implements the rural land contract management system, guarantees the long-term stability of the rural land contracting relationship according to law, and protects the farmers' right to use the contracted land. "Land Administration Law of the People's Republic of China" and "The Law of Contracted Management of the Rural Land of the People's Republic of China" shall apply to the methods and duration of rural land contract management, the rights and obligations of the contractees and the contractors, and the protection and circulation of the right to land contractual management." In addition, the new chapter on food security stipulates that "the state shall establish a system of farmland protection and implement special protection for basic farmland in accordance with the law," which puts forward higher requirements for farmland protection. Since then, in 2009 and 2012, the Agricultural Law has been amended, which is of great significance for consolidating and strengthening the basic position of agriculture in the national economy, deepening rural reform, developing agricultural productivity, and promoting agricultural modernization.

9) **"Law of the People's Republic of China on the Administration of the Urban Real Estate"**

In 1994, the Standing Committee of the Eighth National People's Congress adopted "Law of the People's Republic of China on the Administration of the Urban Real Estate" (hereinafter referred to as the "Urban Real Estate Administration Law"), the purpose of which is to strengthen the management of urban real estate, maintain the order of the real estate market, and protect the legitimate rights and interests of real estate rights holders. In terms of the setting of specific provisions, it is as consistent as possible with "Land Administration Law" that has been promulgated and implemented. Its promulgation and implementation indicate that the development of China's real estate industry has entered a new period of legal management. In addition to establishing the basic principles of China's real estate management, this law also establishes a series of basic systems and makes specific provisions on the main management links such as real estate development land, real estate development, real estate transactions, and real estate ownership registration. The content is rich.

In 2007, the "Urban Real Estate Administration Law" was amended for the first time, and the "General Provisions" of the first chapter were added: "For the needs of the public interest, the state may expropriate the houses of units and individuals on state-owned land and give compensation for demolition and relocation in accordance with the law so as to safeguard the legitimate rights and interests of the expropriated persons; when expropriating an individual's residence, the living conditions of the expropriated person shall also be guaranteed. Specific measures shall be formulated by the State Council." In 2009, the "Urban Real Estate Administration Law" was amended for the second time, and in article 9, "requisition" was amended to "expropriation." The second paragraph of Article 71 is amended to read: "When the staff of the real estate management department or the land management department use the convenience of their position to solicit other people's property or illegally accept other people's property to seek benefits for others, and if it constitutes a crime, criminal responsibility shall be pursued in accordance with law; when it does not constitute a crime, administrative sanctions shall be imposed." In 2019, the Third Amendment to "Urban Real Estate Administration Law" made certain restrictive provisions on the scope of collective land expropriation for commercial construction and amended Article 9 to read: "After the collectively owned land in the urban planning area is expropriated into state-owned land in accordance with law, the right to use the state-owned land can be transferred for a fee, unless otherwise provided by law." "There is room for narrowing the scope of collective land expropriation for real estate construction in urban planning areas." The gradual amendment of "Urban Real Estate Administration Law" comprehensively regulates the use of land for real estate development, real estate transactions, ownership registration management, and related legal responsibilities. This allows the construction, purchase and transfer of housing to follow the law, echoing the relevant provisions of "Land Administration Law" and promoting reform and innovation of the land system.

10) **"The Law of Contracted Management of the Rural Land of the People's Republic of China"**

In 2002, "The Law of Contracted Management of the Rural Land of the People's Republic of China" (hereinafter referred to as the "Rural Land Contract Law") was enacted to stabilize and improve the two-tier management system, which was based on household contract management and combined unification and division, to promote agricultural and rural economic development and social stability in rural areas. It guarantees farmers the right to contract land for 30 years and allows paid transfers to develop the land market. In addition to the right to use, farmers also have the right to transfer land, the right to inherit, the right to gain, and the right to dispose of products. "Rural Land Contract Law" consists of five chapters and 65 articles. It makes relatively comprehensive provisions on the protection of land contract management rights and the transfer of land contract management rights, mainly including the following aspects: it stipulates the rights and obligations of the contractees and the contractors; grants farmers long-term and stable contracted management rights; provides for the protection of contracted land management rights; provides the right to transfer contracted land management rights to the contractor according to law; and stipulates the legal responsibility for encroaching on contracted land management rights.

In the first amendment in 2009, "requisition" was revised to "expropriation and requisition." In 2018, the second key amendment focuses on the following major issues: the "three rights" of rural collective land ownership; land contract right and land management right are separated; the rural land contract relationship is to remain stable and unchanged for a long time, and the second round of land contract will be extended for another 30 years upon expiration, thus improving the rights of contracted land management, safeguarding the land contract rights and interests of rural migrant workers who have settled down in cities, clarifying that land management right can be financed and guaranteed; clarifying the right to buy shares of contracted management rights; clarifying the access supervision of the transfer of land management rights of industrial and commercial enterprises; and protecting women's land rights and interests. This amendment is basically in line with the reality of the development of contracted land in China's rural areas and provides for the "separation of the three powers" as the central government's spirit in promoting reform at the present stage. It is also in line with the development needs in the new era, and the central government's spirit and practical experience are translated as legal norms. The specific system design accords with the basic spirit of protecting farmers' interests.[21]

11) **"Property Law of the People's Republic of China"**
"The Property Law of the People's Republic of China" (hereinafter referred to as the "Property Law") passed in 2007 established the basic system of land legislation. Under the Property Law, the property right system on land includes land ownership, land usufruct right, and land security right. Among them, land usufruct right includes land contract management right, construction land use right, house land use right, and easement right; the real right of land security includes mortgage of the right to use construction land, mortgage of the right to contract and management of the land, and mortgage of the easement, forming a unified system of land rights and promoting the rational use of land. Specific rules on land ownership include: "Mineral deposits, water flows, and sea areas are owned by the state. The land in the city is owned by the state. Land in rural and suburban areas that is legally owned by the state shall be owned by the state. Forests, mountains, grasslands, barren land, tidal flats, and other natural resources shall be owned by the State, with the exception of those that are collectively owned by law." Specific provisions on usufruct right include: "Natural resources owned by the state or owned by the state and used by collectives or owned by collectives as stipulated by law may be possessed, used, and benefited by units and individuals according to law." The specific provisions on land contract management rights are as follows: "Rural collective economic organizations shall implement a two-tier management system based on household contract management and combine unification and division. Farmland, woodland, grassland, and other land used for agriculture that is owned collectively by farmers or owned by the state but used collectively by farmers shall be subject to land contract management system according to law," etc. Specific provisions on land use rights are as follows: "The person with the right to use the homestead has the right to occupy and use the collectively owned land according to law and has the right to use the land to build houses and their ancillary facilities according to law." "The person with the right to use construction land shall have the right to occupy, use, and benefit from the land owned by the state in accordance with the law, and have the right to use the land to build buildings, structures, and their ancillary facilities," etc.

The Third Plenary Session of the seventeenth Central Committee of the Communist Party of China adopted the "Decision of the Central Committee of the Communist Party of China on Several Big Issues on Promoting the Reform and Development of Rural Areas" (hereinafter referred to as the "Decision"), which focused on the issue of rural land. Combining with its important judgment and civil law theory, it can be found that the provisions of "Property Law" concerning the rural land system are not perfect. First, with regard to the ownership of farmland, Article 60 of "Property Law" did not dare to break through

[21] Land determines agricultural prosperity – Special report on the New Rural Land Contract Law. China Cooperative Economy, 2019, (01): 38–50.

the existing legal provisions, but faithfully extended the normative model of "three-level ownership," positioning "rural collectives" at all levels as the main body of rural ownership, and the corresponding "collective economic organizations" to exercise ownership on behalf of, so that the rural land ownership is still empty. Second, the property right attribute of the contracted management rights of rural land has not been implemented; the transfer of the contracted management rights of rural land is obviously subject to unreasonable restrictions; and the term of the contracted management rights of rural land and the provisions on the adjustment of rural land are confused and misunderstood. Third, there are problems about the use of homestead. "Property Law" does not indicate whether the right to use homestead land is paid for or acquired without compensation. There is a legal conflict between "one household can only apply for one homestead" and the redistribution of the right to use homestead. The law does not allow villagers to apply for the right to use homestead many times, but it does not forbid villagers from owning multiple homesteads at the same time. In addition, whether the right to use a homestead can be mortgaged is controversial. Fourth, there are problems with the expropriation of farmland. "Property Law" has too many references to public law provisions and policy directives; hence, it is difficult to grasp public interests in rural land expropriation. "Property Law" is based on the concept of "full compensation" for the compensation standard of farmland expropriation, which was different from the "complete compensation" standard adopted in the "Decision." In the future revision of relevant laws and legislation, the regulation of "Property Law" on the agricultural land system should conscientiously implement the requirements of the "Decision," make full use of the existing research results, respond to, and resolve the problems within the agricultural land system (Chen 2009a, b). "Property Law" is too conservative and lacks innovation in the regulation of the agricultural land system. In other words, as an unprecedented property code in China, the Property Law demonstrates its institutional value and normative purpose: paying attention to people's livelihood, publicizing private rights, and protecting farmers' land rights and interests. However, inherent lack of "Property Law" is obvious: the legislative technology is slightly crude, and the normative function is not completely reflected, revealing the characteristics of strong values and weak functions (Chen 2009a, b). In 2020, the "Civil Code" was issued, and when it came into effect, the existing "Property Law" became invalid.

12) **"Civil Code of the People's Republic of China"**
On May 28, 2020, the third session of the 13th National People's Congress voted to adopt "the Civil Code," ushering in a new era of the rule of law in China. On the basis of the current "Property Law," the property rights part of the Civil Code was further improved in accordance with the requirements of the Party Central Committee to improve the property right protection system, perfecting the modern property right system with clear ownership, clear rights and responsibilities, strict protection and smooth circulation, and combining it with the practical needs.

On the basis of "Property Law," it implements the land policy of "separation of three rights." The Civil Code includes the land management right into the classification usufructuary right, which confirms the property right attribute to a large extent. Article 339 stipulates that the owner of the contracted land management right may "independently decide to transfer the land management right to others by leasing, buying shares, or other means according to law." Article 341 clearly stipulates: "The land management rights whose transfer period is more than five years shall be established when the transfer contract becomes effective. The party concerned may apply to the registration organ for the registration of land management rights; without registration, it shall not oppose the bona fide third party." The system of expropriation has been improved: it is emphasized that expropriation can be carried out only "for the needs of the public interest and in accordance with the authority and procedure prescribed by the law." "Rural villagers' houses" were clearly listed as the object of compensation. It is emphasized that compensation must be paid in full and timely in accordance with the law to prevent the interests of the expropriated from being harmed by delay or insufficient payment. The Civil Code is an epoch-making declaration of rights, which is based on the people, comprehensively affirming and protecting private rights. Effective "Civil Code" planning of property ownership and distribution rules is the basis of a market economy. The "Civil Code" establishes the basic standards of administrative power, restrains public power from intervening in citizens' lives, and comprehensively promotes modernization of China's governance system and capacity. It is an important statute of governance.

2.3.2 *Legislative Reform Characteristics of Land Policy Implementation in China*

(1) The process of legislative reform from decentralization to relative concentration

From the promulgation and implementation of "Land Reform Law" in 1950 to the promulgation of the "Civil Code" in 2020, various relevant laws, such as "Constitution," "Land Administration Law of the People's Republic of China," and "Rural Land Contract Law," have gone through a process from promulgation to revision, amendment, or repeal. The legal basis of the implementation of China's land policy shows the process of legislative reform from dispersion to relative concentration, from initial establishment to gradual improvement.

From a deep historical perspective, we review and sort all the land-related laws issued since the founding of the People's Republic of China (Fig. 2.2). The horizontal axis represents the time when they were first promulgated, and the vertical axis represents the time when they were revised, amended, or abolished. It is not difficult to see that from 1950 to 1983, there were only two relevant legal reforms, "Land

Reform Law" and "China's Constitution." From 1984 to 2021, about 10 relevant laws went through the process of promulgation, revision, amendment, or repeal.

At the same time, subject changes in land policies of various land related laws are sorted out on the time axis (Fig. 2.3). The horizontal axis represents the time of initial promulgations, and the vertical axis represents the subject changes of various laws. It is clear that, except for the repealed "Land Reform Law," "Property Law," and the most recent "Civil Code" implemented in 2021, all other land related laws have undergone multiple subject changes in terms of land policy. Especially after 1990, policy subjects such as land use right transfer, land use control, land expropriation, and land protection gradually emerged. Among them, the subject of "Land Administration Law," "Real Estate Administration Law," "Rural Land Contract Law," and the latest "Civil Code" gradually focus on innovation and improvement of the land system in line with the development of the times, including the homestead "separation of three rights," and collectively-owned commercial construction land entered the market.

(2) **The process of legislative reform from focusing on public interests to considering personal interests**

During its 20 years of implementation, the people's commune system made some contributions to the country's original accumulation of industrialization, but it did

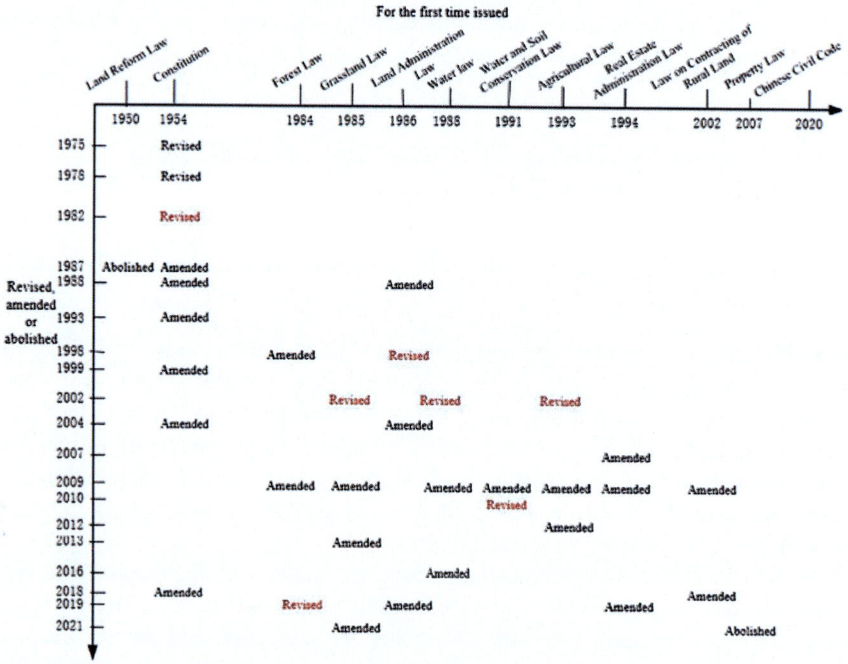

Fig. 2.2 China's land policy legislation reform context

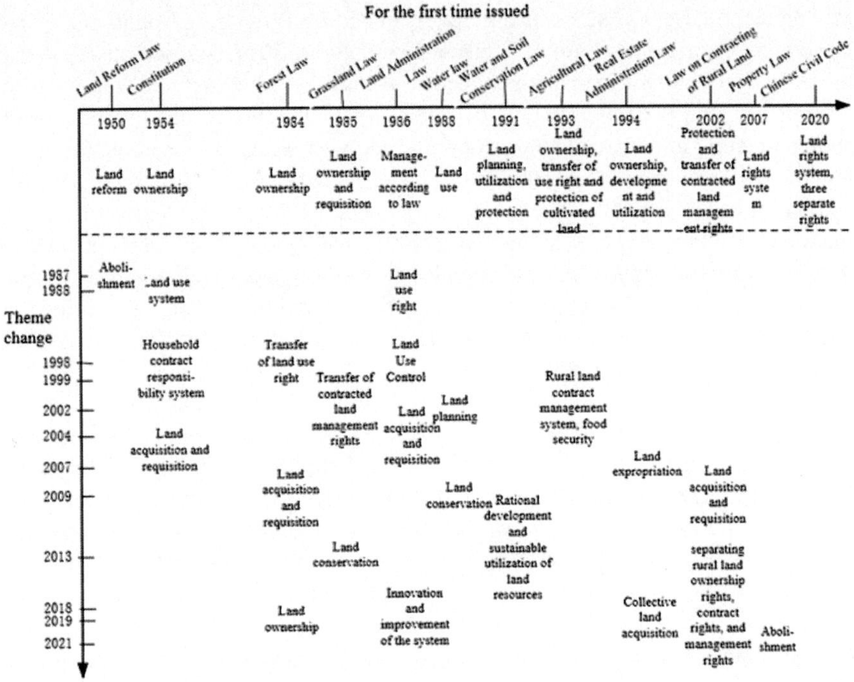

Fig. 2.3 Theme change in China's land policy

not handle the relationship between the public interests of the country and the collective and the individual interests of farmers well. Since the reform and opening up, farmers' rights and interests were gradually protected through legislative activities. In 1978, the system of household contract responsibility gave farmers autonomy and grassroots autonomy, and its gradual promotion launched the reform of the rural land property rights system. "Land Administration Law" passed in 1986 established the system of household contract responsibility in the form of law. "Rural Land Contract Law," promulgated in 2002, legally ensures that farmers have the right to contract rural land for a long time. After that, repeated amendments of the "Rural Land Contract Law" and the "Land Management Law" and the gradual advancement of land right confirmation work and provide legislative protection of individual rights and interests. The trend of reform is to ensure long-term and stable land use rights and the land earnings rights of farmers.

The land contract system implemented in China played a great role in the reform of farmland property rights. Therefore, this idea was introduced into grassland management and continues even now. "Grassland Law of the People's Republic of China," introduced in 1985, attempts to devolve state and collectively-owned grassland use rights to individuals and exemplifies the government's efforts to privatize grasslands. "Grassland Law of the People's Republic of China," revised in 2002, reaffirmed this principle once again and specified the provisions on contracted grassland management. "The Opinions of the State Council on Promoting Sound and Rapid Development of Pastoral Areas" released on June 1, 2011, also emphasized that the grassland contract management system should be stabilized and improved. In accordance with the requirements of clear ownership, standardized management, and contracting to households, we should actively yet prudently promote the determination and contracting of grassland rights. The ownership of grassland is clearly defined in accordance with the law, and the land, area, contract, and certificate of grassland contract are "four to one household," so as to keep the grassland contract relationship stable and unchanged for a long time. The grassland contract management system continues to this day, which is of great significance in safeguarding the equity of income opportunities for poor farmers and herdsmen and safeguarding the right to use grassland resources.

In 1982, "the Regulations on Land Requisition for State Construction" (hereinafter referred to as the "Regulations") were enacted to ensure the supply of land for State construction (Liu et al. 2018). Article 4 stipulates that "if the land requisitioned for national construction conforms to the provisions of these 'Regulations,' the cadres and masses of the requisitioned communes and brigades shall obey the needs of the state and shall not obstruct or hinder," which is the first time to put forward the mandatory characteristics of land acquisition. "Land Administration Law," passed in 1986, elevated most of the Regulations into law. In 1998, the newly revised "Land Administration Law" improved the expropriation system, such as expropriation procedure and compensation, making the government move from the background to the foreground in land expropriation work. The government decides on whether to start the expropriation process after judging whether it is in line with the public interest. The city and county governments should not only apply for land expropriation from the higher government, but also take specific responsibility for compensation and resettlement work. This significant change reflects that land expropriation is a kind of state behavior. Only the state can expropriate the land collectively owned by farmers for the public interest. The Constitution amended in 2004 changed "requisition" to "expropriation or requisition" to further clarify the connotation of land requisition and land requisition. The explicitly written "compensation" into the "Constitution," states that land expropriation compensation has been protected by "Constitution." In the same year, the "Land Administration Law" was amended to be consistent with the "Constitution." "Land Administration Law" and "Urban Real Estate Administration Law" were amended in 2019. The focus of the revision of the land expropriation system is to implement the Central Committee's decisions and arrangements, balance the protection of social development with the protection of farmers' rights and interests, highlight that land expropriation must be in line with the public interest, and work toward improving the land expropriation procedure and compensation and resettlement of land expropriation, ensure that the land expropriation procedure is open and democratic, and provide a reasonable, standardized, and diversified guarantee mechanism for farmers whose land is expropriated. It is also meant to ensure that the original living standards of farmers whose land has been expropriated are improved and their long-term livelihood is guaranteed (Shi 2020). Based on this, the reform of land expropriation system follows the legislative reform process from paying attention to the public interest of the construction land supply to considering the rights and interests of farmers who are expropriated (Zhou et al. 2020).

(3) **The legislative reform process of "scale—efficiency—quality"**

The legislation of land policy implementation in China originated from the recognition of the supporting role of land resources in economic and social development, especially the extreme emphasis on food security and farmland protection; it has always focused on the norms of rational utilization of farmland, woodland, and grassland. The value goal and overall process of the legislative reform also reflect the development of land resources from the initial stage of focusing on quantity protection to the development stage of combining quantity and quality, and then to the in-depth stage under the new situation of rapid urbanization. Presently, it is in the "trinity" stage of quantity, quality, and ecology, which has formed the third-order essential meaning of "strictly controlling quantity—simultaneously promoting quantity and quality—trinity." The management mode of land resources has gradually changed from simple quantity management to comprehensive management with equal emphasis on quantity, quality, and ecology. Based on this, the legislative reform process of China's land policy implementation can be divided into the following three stages:

Strict control of quantity—scale value target. "Forest Law of the People's Republic of China" passed in 1984 and "Grassland Law of the People's Republic of China" passed in 1985 emphasized the rational use of forests and grasslands, respectively. Article 3 of "Land Administration Law" promulgated in 1986 clearly states that "the policy includes cherishing and rational use of land, comprehensive planning, strengthening management, protection, and development of land resources, and stopping acts of misappropriation and abuse of land." In 1998, the "Land Administration Law" was comprehensively revised to address the problems of extensive use of land and excessive occupation of cultivated land in the process of rapid economic development and urbanization, establish the strictest possible farmland protection system, and improve the land use control system. During this period, the quantity of land resources was strictly controlled by establishing the "Law on Water and Soil Conservation," "Agriculture Law," "Real Estate Administration Law," and other relevant laws, administrative regulations, departmental rules, and other normative documents to achieve the goal of large-scale value of land resources.

Quantity and quality simultaneously, achieving the value target efficiently. "Land Administration Law" amended in 1998 established the use control system and the balance between occupation and supplement of cultivated land, which strengthened the quality control of cultivated land on the basis of strictly controlling quantity. The 2004 "Decision of the State Council on Deepening Reform and Strict Land Administration" explicitly implemented the strictest land administration system and strictly controlled the increase in land used for construction purposes. By 2012, the quality of land resources were strengthened mainly through the creation and revision of relevant laws, administrative regulations, departmental rules, and other normative documents. Among them, in 2004, 2005, 2007, the "Central Document No. 1" on "improving the quality of cultivated land" provided details of the behavior process for target positioning. In 2006, the "Central Document No. 1" provided the means for positioning of behavior process in "strengthening cultivated land quality construction." The "Central Document No. 1" in 2008 and 2010 gave a functional orientation to "supporting and attaching importance to the construction of cultivated land quality" (Zhao and Tian 2021). In this period, due to the fact that the demand for land for non-agricultural construction remained high for a long time and the phenomenon of the advantages and disadvantages of farmland occupation and compensation continued to occur, the emphasis on quantity protection of land resource gradually shifted to quality protection.

"Trinity"—the goal of quality value. "Forest Law of the People's Republic of China," "Grassland Law of the People's Republic of China," "Law on Water and Soil Conservation," "Rural Land Contract Law," and other laws, which have been amended many times and are now in effect, all clearly put forth rational use of land resources, improvement of the ecological environment, and promotion of an ecological civilization. In 2012, "the Ministry of Land and Resources' Notice on Improving the Level of Cultivated Land Protection and Comprehensively Strengthening the Construction and Management of Cultivated Land Quality" defined the connotation of cultivated land protection as cultivated land quantity, quality control, and ecological protection. According to the 2017 "Opinions of the Central Committee of the Communist Party of China and the State Council on Strengthening the Protection of Cultivated Land and Improving the Balance between Occupation and Supplement," the need is to adhere to the strictest cultivated land protection system and the strictest land saving system, striving to strengthen the "trinity" of protection of cultivated land quantity, quality, and ecology. The inclusion of ecological civilization in "Constitution" in 2018 meant that relevant laws should be formulated and amended in accordance with this constitutional concept. The newly revised "Forest Law of the People's Republic of China" in 2019 directly regards lucid waters and lush mountains as invaluable assets and ecological civilization as one of the legislative purposes and guiding ideology, which is an important embodiment of implementing Xi Jinping's ecological civilization and the rule of law. The revised "Land Administration Law" of the same year stipulated that "the contents of farmland rotation and fallow, high-standard farmland, and territorial space planning should be determined in a legal form," which further solidified the concept of protecting high-quality farmland (Wang et al. 2020). The "Trinity" protection is not a simple content superposition and mechanical combination, but it stands in the dimension of the whole natural system and uses the overall thinking to organically integrate the quantity, quality, and ecological protection of land resources throughout. To realize the trinity protection, we should, on the basis of ensuring the quantity of land resources, gradually improve the quality, constantly improve the ecological environment, coordinate the relationship among quality, quantity, and ecological environment, and promote the sustainable development of land resources and ecological environment.

2.4 China's Land Policy System Caught Between the Powers of the Central and the State Governments

Under the organizational structure of China's straight-line functional administrative system, the central government is the highest administrative organ of the state, and local governments are dispatched agencies of the central government to implement administrative management and provide public services on behalf of the central government. Over the past four decades of reform and opening up, this principal-agent system has produced good performance, but at the same time, it has also led to problems in the division and adjustment of administrative powers and financial powers between the central government and local governments, resulting in principal–agent problems. In the process of land policy implementation, under the strict control and incentive of the central government, local governments hold the power of decentralized land management but face the administrative constraints of centralization. As a result, there are differences in the action objectives of local governments and the central government, leading to a situation of a game played between the central government and the local governments (Tan 2021). Observing China's land management problems from the perspective of the game between the central government and the local governments can provide a better understanding of the formation and evolution logic of China's land policy system.

This section considers the change in the relationship between the central government and the local governments as the main theme, combs several changes in China's land policy system since the founding of new China, discusses the consistency of the objectives of the central government and local government in implementing land policies under the central local principal–agent system, and the performance of the implementation of land policies in the game between the central government and the local governments (Fig. 2.4).

2.4.1 Reform and Opening Up Toward the End of the Twentieth Century—The Initial Establishment of the Land Policy System with the Central and Local Governments Pursuing the Same Goal

After the founding of new China in 1949, under the guidance of the "Law of Land Reform of the People's Republic of China," land reform was carried out throughout the country. The feudal land ownership system was abolished, and the land ownership system of farmers was implemented. A wave of land equity participation and cooperative management was set up throughout the country. The establishment of primary agricultural cooperatives to a certain extent mobilized the enthusiasm of

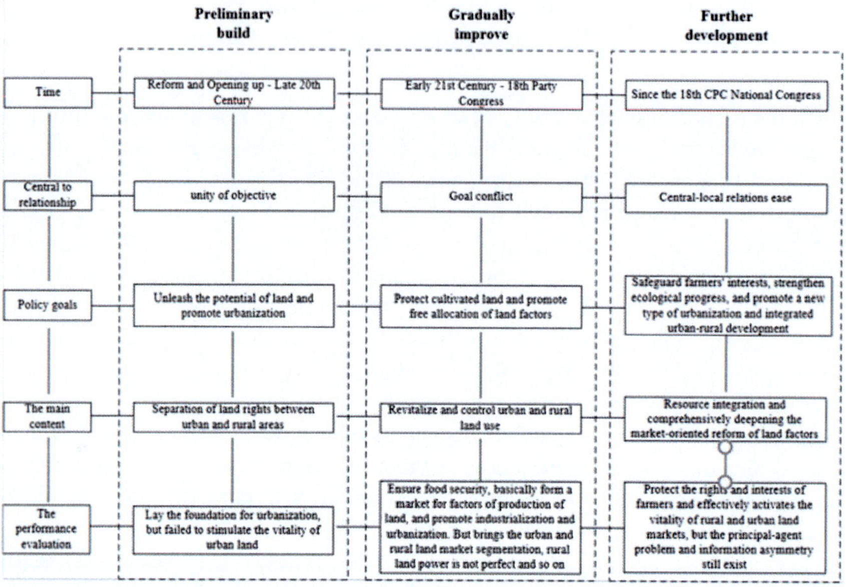

Fig. 2.4 China's land policy system in the game between the central government and the local governments

farmers for production and greatly liberated and developed social productive forces. After the completion of the "three great socialism reconstructions" in 1956,[22] China established its industrialization development strategy, decided to support industrialization development along with agricultural development, and established a system whereby rural land is owned by the production team. However, influenced by "left leaning" views, many overly radical policies damaged the interests of farmers and seriously dampened the development vitality of not only agriculture but all other forms of development in the country. Against this background, the Third Plenary Session of the 11th CPC Central Committee in 1978 led to the strategic decision of shifting the focus of work to socialist modernization and implementing reform and opening up. China then entered a new historical period of reform, opening up, and socialist modernization. The reform of the socialist land system with Chinese characteristics was also gradually promoted in China's rural and urban areas. The major reform of separating the ownership and use rights of state-owned land entered the exploratory stage. With economic construction as the center, the main objectives of the central government and local governments in this period were basically the same, and the urban–rural dual land system was established for the first time.

[22] The three great socialism reconstructions are the socialist transformation of the three industries of agriculture, handicrafts, and capitalist industry and commerce led by the Communist Party of China after the founding of the People's Republic of China.

(1) **Policy objective: release land potential and lay the foundation for urbanization**

After the reform and opening up, land policy was mainly used to ensure food security, liberate and develop the productivity of land factors, stabilize land property relations, and lay an economic foundation for urbanization. After the end of the "Cultural Revolution," innovative practices carried out from the bottom up in cities and rural areas promoted the reform of China's land system. The spontaneous institutional innovation at the grassroots level impacted and changed the consciousness and form of the central government. At this time, to ensure food supply, activate land production potential, and maintain the orderly use of urban land, the central government's "administrative" decentralization gave more autonomy to local governments. Meanwhile, the central government attached great importance to the stability of land property rights, encouraged farmers to increase their investment in land in rural areas, and put forth the policy of extending the land contract right of farmers for 30 years without change after the expiration of the motto, "increase the family population without increasing land, reduce the family population without decreasing land" to maintain the stability of the land contract right. In addition, the central government also put forward a series of state-owned land use policies in cities to promote the formation of the state-owned land market.

(2) **Main content: separation of urban and rural land rights**

With the continuous promotion of reform and opening up and the spontaneous transformation of farmers, China's land property rights were clarified, and the urban–rural dual land system was finally established. In December 1982, the promulgation of the "Constitution of the People's Republic of China" meant that state land ownership and collective land ownership were formally established. The central government completed the nationalization of urban land in the form of the Constitution and realized the separation of collective land ownership and land contracting rights. "The Land Administration Law of the People's Republic of China" promulgated in 1986 has clear provisions on land ownership and use rights, land registration, registration and certification, registration protection, etc., and required the preparation of land use master plans to coordinate the use of land by all parties. Overall, the land system arrangement after the reform guaranteed national food security. On the premise of adhering to the collective ownership and ensuring the interests of the state and the collective, the return of the land rights of collective members and family management was realized, and rural productivity has greatly improved.

Bottom-up spontaneous institutional innovation: Local exploration and central identification. In the backward period of social and economic development, to meet their own needs, farmers began to explore reform and practice of the land use system, and the household contract responsibility system came to the fore. The central government, the local governments, and the farmers held several discussions around this spontaneous and innovative land system reform. Finally, guided by common purpose and interests, the effectiveness of this system was tested through practice. The system directly combined farmers with land, greatly liberated rural productivity, fundamentally embodied the characteristics of socialist public ownership, and led to the second golden age of China's agricultural development. As a result, the attitude of central policy makers toward the household contract responsibility system changed from opposing to fully supporting, and the innovative measure of separating rural land ownership from contracting right rose to the level of becoming a national policy. In addition, according to "the Supreme People's Court on some issues of rural contract dispute cases opinions" in 1986, it mandated that rural land contract right can be obtained through inheritance, subcontract, person shares, and circulation; the road of substantial change of rural land policy thus ensued, and the people's commune ceased to exist. However, spontaneous land change also faced failure when central interests were threatened, such as after the household contract responsibility system, land fragmentation, small scale of farmers' operation, frequent land adjustment, and other problems resulted from the mode of subdivision of land and outsourcing of production to households. Pingdu in Shandong Province adopted the "two-field system" to make up for these shortcomings. It promoted the division of rural land into grain allowance farmland and responsibility farmland. Grain allowance farmland was contracted according to the average person, while responsibility farmland was contracted by paying agricultural tax. However, the "two-field system" not only does not meet the legal provisions of farmers to exercise the right to contract land, but also directly hinders the central tax reform. Since local governments were granted autonomy to a large extent, it affected the rights and interests of the central government, and the "two-field system" gradually became phased out. In view of the system defects caused by the household contract responsibility system, the central government successively proposed land policies such as "major stability, minor adjustment," extending the contract period of farmers for another 30 years after the expiration of 15 years and increasing the number of people without increasing the amount of land and reducing the number of people without reducing the amount of land to ensure stability of rural land. In addition, after the Third Plenary Session of the 11th CPC Central Committee, the rural areas were occupied in a disorderly fashion, the scale of construction land went out of control, local housing boom occurred, and commune and team enterprises were established. These behaviors disturbed the order of rural land use, and the area of cultivated land decreased sharply. Therefore, the central government issued the "Emergency Notice of the State Council on Stopping Rural Housing from Occupying Cultivated Land," "Notice of the CPC Central Committee and the State Council on Further Strengthening Land Management and Effectively Protecting Cultivated Land," "Regulations on the Administration of Land for Building Houses in Villages and Towns," "Interim Provisions on the Administration of Village Construction," "Emergency Notice of the State Council on Preventing Rural Housing Construction from Encroaching on Farmland," and "Regulations on Protection of Basic Farmland." These policies restrict the indiscriminate expansion of construction land, and the transfer of rural collective use rights is also strictly restricted. At the same time, "Land Administration Law" clarified the compensation system for occupied farmland and the protection system for basic farmland, strengthening the protection of farmland and restricting the acquisition of the right to use residential land by non-collective members. In addition, the Land Management Law clarified the compensation system for occupied farmland and the protection system for basic farmland. Therefore, under a common policy goal, with farmers exploring and the central and local governments continuously coordinating with them, the rural land policy system was set up.

Compared with the popular reform of the rural land system, reform of the urban land system is relatively slow. After the reform and opening up, economic development gradually increased the demand for land for industrial and housing construction in cities, and the value of land became increasingly apparent. With waste of farmland and free negotiation of construction land frequently occurring, the invisible market for land transaction spontaneously emerged under the control of national policies. To resolve these problems, the central government issued a series of policies to regulate the management of urban housing land ownership and the process of land expropriation, such as "Interim Provisions on the Administration of Property Rights and Properties of Urban (Town) Real Estate," "Measures on the Administration of Individual Residential Buildings in Urban Areas," "Regulations on Land Requisition for National Construction," "Notice on Stopping the Sale, Sale and Lease of Land," "Law of the People's Republic of China on the Administration of the Urban Real Estate" and through the "Land Administration Law," to standardize the compensation requirements of land expropriation and governance of the local invisible land market. In addition, the central government promulgated the Land Management Law to regulate the compensation requirements for land expropriation and control the local invisible land market. In order to revitalize land resources and reveal its economic value, Guangzhou, Shanghai, Shenzhen, and other regions began to explore the practice of paid use of land. In 1987, Shenzhen completed the first transaction of the public auction of state-owned land, officially opened the land market allocation mode. Local practices successfully promoted the reform of the state-owned land system at the central legislative level. The provisions prohibiting the transfer of land property rights in the Constitution and the Land Administration Law were amended to allow the transfer of state-owned and collective land use rights in accordance with the law, and pilot land system reforms were been launched in several regions to explore the separation of land rights between urban and rural areas. At the same time, to bring land transfer fees into the state financial system and strengthen management of the urban real estate market, the central government issued a series of notices, including "Notice on Strengthening the Administration of Income from the Paid Use of State-owned Land Use Rights," "Decision on Deepening the Reform of the Urban Housing System," "Opinions on Strengthening the Administration of the Housing Accumulation Fund," "Trial Measures on the Administration of Personal Housing Loan Guarantee," and "Law on the Administration of Urban Real Estate." In the face of huge economic benefits of land and with the support of local practice and the central government, the state-owned land system was established.

(3) The role, performance, and problems of the policy system

In the interactions between the central government and the local governments, the ownership and the use right of urban and rural land were separated, and land became the legal basis for entering the market. The productive potential of the land was effectively brought into play, and its economic benefits reflected, laying the economic foundation for urbanization. However, due to the imperfect supporting policies, problems such as the fragmentation, small scale, and encroachment of farmland in rural areas continued to prevail, and vitality of urban land did not receive proper stimulation.

2.4.2 From the Beginning of the 21st Century to the 18th National Congress: Gradual Improvement of Land Policy System Under Conditions of Conflicting Objectives Between the Central Government and The Local Governments

During this period, the central government began to attach importance to social goals such as food security and make adjustments to land management. It restrained local governments through land use control, farmland protection, and index control. Meanwhile, it also provided paths for local governments to develop the economy, industrialization, and urbanization through land expropriation and other systems. However, some problems such as extensive use of land and damage to farmers' interests by the urban–rural dual system also surfaced.

(1) **Policy objective: to protect cultivated land and promote free allocation of land factors**

With the increasingly mature urbanization and the implementation of the national tax sharing reform, local governments over-relied on land finance to pursue short-term interests and meet performance requirements, leading to a blind development of urban and rural construction land, serious loss of cultivated land, and disorder in the land market. In this context, the central government formulated a land policy with strict control and incentives to protect arable land and ensure food security, restrict the disorderly expansion of construction land by local governments, and alleviate the contradictions in urban land use.

(2) **Main contents: revitalize and control urban and rural land use**

After the dual land system was established, the central government strengthened the protection of basic farmland mainly through the farmland protection policy and the land use control system. By restricting local expansion of construction land, clear regulations were imposed on the circulation of rural land contracted management rights and collective construction land use rights, so as to promote agricultural development and revitalize idle rural land. At the same time, the government also standardized the development of urban land and the operation of the land factor market by means of planning, law, and administration, and encouraged local governments to excavate existing land to realize utilization and control of urban and rural land.

Land policy system with strict control and incentive: By the end of the twentieth century, the rural land policy system had been established stimulated by spontaneous system reform. However, due to the imperfect supporting policy system and the land finance attraction of local governments, farmland waste and occupation became increasingly serious.

To strictly control local behavior, strengthen the implementation of the compensation system for occupied land, and control the conversion of cultivated land into non-cultivated land, the central government promulgated a series of policies, such as:" Notice on Further Strengthening and Improving the Balance between the Occupation and Subsidy of Cultivated Land," "Decision on Deepening Reform and Enforcing Land Management," "Notice on the Basic Work of Converting the Quantity and Quality of Supplementary Cultivated Land into Grades," and "Technical Guidelines on the Basic Work of Converting the Quantity and Quality of Supplementary Cultivated Land into Grades."

To strengthen the protection of basic farmland, the central government promulgated "Regulations on the Protection of Basic Farmland," "Opinions on the Rectification of Relevant Problems in the Protection of basic Farmland," and the "Opinions on Further Improving the Work Related to the Protection of basic Farmland," to strengthen all-round protection of the quantity and quality of basic farmland. In addition, the central government explicitly implemented a land use control system in the "Land Administration Law" to further control encroachment on cultivated land. Besides the strict control of the central government, to realize sustainable development of agriculture, the central government successively promulgated the "Rural Land Contract Law" and the "Right to the Contracted Management of Rural Land Circulation Management Method," which were helpful in enriching the circulation of rural land contract right, motivating local agriculture to moderate scale management, and establishing and perfecting the contracted management of rural land circulation market. With the continuous development of agriculture, the central government promulgated the "Notice on Promoting the Policies of Land Use for Large-scale Livestock and Poultry Breeding" and "Several Opinions on Promoting the Stable Development of Agriculture and Continuously Increasing Farmers' Income to Promote the Balanced Development of Urban and Rural Areas," which gradually improved the concept and management policy system of facility agricultural land.

For the construction of the rural collective construction land market, the central government strictly controlled and encouraged local governments at the same time. Since 2003, the Central successively promulgated "Opinions of the CPC Central Committee and the State Council on Doing a Good Job in Agriculture and Rural Areas," "Opinions of the Central Committee of the Communist Party of China and the State Council on Several Policies to Promote the Increase of Farmers' Income," and "Decision of the State Council on Deepening Reform and Strict Land Management," and began to relax collective non-farming construction land control to explore methods and ways to enter the market, However, the rules were unclear. In 2007, the central Government issued the "Notice on the Strict Implementation of Laws and Policies Concerning Rural Collective Construction Land," which again strictly restricted the circulation of the right to use collective construction land: any other unit or individual carrying out non-agricultural construction must apply for the use of state-owned land according to law. No unit or individual may convert agricultural land or unused land into construction land by signing an agreement on its own. In 2008, the central government issued the " Decision of the Central Committee of the Communist Party of China on Several Big Issues on Promoting the Reform and Development of Rural Areas," which made it clear that rural collective land could be occupied with approval for commercial projects outside the scope of urban construction land defined in land use planning. Farmers were allowed to participate in development and management by leasing land or buying shares at a price. The decision separated rural collective construction land for business purposes from land for public welfare purposes and pointed the way to marketization of rural construction land. As for the management of homestead, the central government promulgated the "Opinions on Strengthening the Management of Rural Homestead" and the "Property Law" successively, which further standardized the acquisition of the right to use it. To sum up, under the strict control and incentive of the central government, agricultural land was protected, the rural land stock revitalized to a certain extent, and the rural land policy system became increasingly perfect.

In the background of rapid urbanization and the increasingly perfect paid use of state-owned land, land finance become the main source for local governments to seek financial resources. However, due to the imperfect land factor market, extensive use of state-owned land became increasingly serious and promoting intensive use of state-owned land became an urgent task for the central government to solve. The central government clarified the principle of intensive use of construction land in the "Land Administration Law" and the "Urban Planning Law" and controlled the blind expansion of construction land and its total amount through land use control policies and annual land use plans. Starting from ways and means of land acquisition, the central government corrected the excessive dependence of local governments on land finance, regulated the operation order of land factor market, and restricted local blind land acquisition. To further regulate the scope, price, procedure, and compensation standard of land acquisition, the central government promulgated "Opinions of the General Office of the State Council on the Implementation of the Outline of Comprehensively Promoting Administration in Accordance with the Law," "Opinions of the CPC Central Committee and the State Council on Several Policies for Further Strengthening Rural Work and Improving Comprehensive Agricultural Production Capacity," "Several Opinions of the CPC Central Committee and the State Council on Promoting the Construction of a New Socialist Countryside," and "Notice on the Work of Formulating the Standard of the Same Annual Output Value of Land Expropriated and the Comprehensive Land Price of the Area Expropriated." In addition, to improve the market-oriented level of land use, the central government issued the "Provisions on the Sale of State-owned Land Use Rights by Bidding, Auction and Listing." For the management of special industrial land, to limit the problem of extensive use and inefficient allocation of industrial land, the central government issued a series of policies, such as the "Control Index of Construction Land for Industrial Projects (Trial)," "Several Opinions on Strengthening Macro-Control of Real Estate Market and Promoting Healthy Development of Real Estate Market," "Measures for the Administration of Affordable Housing," "Notice of the General Office of the

State Council on Practically Stabilizing Housing Prices," and "Emergency Notice on Clearing Up All Kinds of Land for Industrial Parks and Strengthening the Control of Land Supply." Additionally, constrained by the rigid land policy of the central government, the contradiction between supply and demand of regional urban land became aggravated. Then, the central government issued the "Notice on Strengthening Land Management to Promote the Healthy Development of Small Towns" and the "Decision of the State Council on Deepening Reform and Strict Land Management," and put forth the construction land turnover index and the system linking the increase and decrease of urban and rural construction land to relieve the pressure on urban land use.

(3) **The role, performance, and problems of the policy system**

By gradually improving the land policy system, China guarded the red line of arable land to some extent, which effectively guaranteed China's food security. The disorderly expansion of construction land was curbed, the land factor market took shape, and urban land rights were rapidly released. The construction of industrial parks and economic development zones around the country promoted the construction and improvement of urban infrastructure and industrial supporting facilities, thereby further promoting the process of industrial clustering, industrialization, and urbanization. However, because the market mechanism was unsound, the problems remaining from history in the process of land development and derivative of social problems, such as reason, caused urban and rural land market segmentation. Rural land power did not come effectively into play. The interests of farmers, cultivated land quantity, quality, and ecology were damaged, and construction land sprawl failed to resolve such issues.

2.4.3 Since the 18th CPC National Congress—Further Development of the Land Policy System Under the Easing of Central and Local Targets

At this stage, the central government's evaluations of the local governments were no longer centered on the economy. Protecting farmers' interests, implementing ecological restoration, and spatial optimization became the new goals of the central government. In addition, the previous land finance model of local governments was transformed, which forced local governments to pay attention to the non-economic goals of land use without changing the incentive structure. During this period, the relationship between central government and land eased to a certain extent. How to use the market to adjust the allocation of land resources became the focus of the central government and the local governments.

(1) **Policy objectives: safeguard farmers' interests, strengthen ecological civilization construction, and promote new urbanization and integrated development of urban and rural areas**

The 18th CPC National Congress and the Third Plenary Session of the 18th CPC Central Committee clearly proposed to let farmers have more land rights, changed the rural land management mode by confirming the right, and fully stimulated the potential of rural land management mode innovation in agricultural development. The 19th CPC National Congress proposed the rural revitalization strategy. The main goal was to establish a land management system with equal rights, unified market, and fair sharing of value-added benefits, so as to effectively safeguard the interests of farmers, continuously expand their rights and empower them, strengthen ecological civilization construction, and promote the new type of urbanization and integrated development of urban and rural areas.

(2) **Main contents: land resource integration and comprehensively deepening the market-oriented reform of land factors**

Since the 18th CPC National Congress, the CPC Central Committee comprehensively deepened reform. The development goals of the central and local governments tended to be the same, and the relationship between the central and the local governments was eased to a certain extent. At this stage, land policies were improved, and a land policy system was formed with reform of land expropriation and compensation system, integration of rural land resources, and market-oriented reform of land factors as the main contents.

First, the land expropriation compensation system was reformed. After the 18th National Congress of the Communist Party of China (CPC), China committed itself to advancing the reform of the land expropriation system. To increase farmers' income and effectively protect their interests, China made efforts in the following areas: narrowing the scope of land expropriation, standardizing land expropriation procedures, increasing the proportion of land value-added income distributed to farmers, providing housing, old-age care, social security, and other security measures for land-lost farmers, and promoting pilot reform of the land expropriation system.

Second, it expanded rural land power and integrated rural land resources. In terms of expanding rural land rights and integrating rural land resources, China has made the following arrangements:

1) **Separation of ownership, contractual, and management rights.** Chinese president Xi Jinping creatively proposed the assumption of dividing land contract right and management right in 2013 while inspecting the Wuhan Rural Comprehensive Equity Exchange. The No. 1 Central Document of 2014 pointed out that the separation of rural land ownership, contract right, and management right is of great practical significance. In August 2015, the State Council issued "the Guiding Opinions on Pilot Mortgaging of Rural Contracted Land Management Rights and Farmers' Housing Property Rights" and clearly pointed out that China should give rural land contracted management rights mortgage financing function and implement the usufruct of rural land. From the "separation of the two

rights" to the "separation of the three rights," it essentially reflects the efforts made by the Party and the central government in promoting orderly transfer of management rights, promoting the appropriate scale of operation, and building a new agricultural management system.

2) **Reform of contracted land management rights**. To achieve the policy goal of ensuring that contracted rural land management rights remain unchanged in the long term, the central government issued several relevant documents to promote the confirmation, registration, and certification of contracted rural land management rights since 2008, when the pilot project was launched.
3) **Further promote reform of the market listing system for collective profit-oriented construction land**. Since the 18th National Congress of the CPC, China has continued to promote equal access to the market, equal rights, and equal prices, and granted rural collective commercial construction land equal market status with state-owned construction land. In November 2013, the Third Plenary Session of the 18th CPC Central Committee adopted the "Decision of the CPC Central Committee on Some Major Issues on Comprehensively Deepening Reform," which clearly stipulated that rural collective commercial construction land and state-owned land should be "equally available in the market, with the same rights and at the same price." In 2014, the No. 1 Central document further clarified that the reform of the rural collective profit-oriented construction land system should be accelerated. In December of the same year, the General Office of the CPC Central Committee and the General Office of the State Council jointly promoted the pilot work of rural collective commercial construction land and put forth corresponding solutions to problems such as incomplete ownership and unequal access to the market.
4) **The reform of the homestead system**. Both the No. 1 Central Committee documents in 2013 and 2014 gave important instructions on rural homestead allocation policies. In December 2014, the General Office of the CPC Central Committee and the General Office of the State Council jointly issued "Opinions on Rural Land Expropriation, Marketization of Collective Commercial Construction Land and Pilot Reform of the Homestead System," and the pilot work of rural homestead reform officially began, along with improvement of homestead rights and interests protection and acquisition methods. It also included diversified ways to achieve housing for farmers and voluntary paid withdrawal or transfer of homestead for farmers settled in cities. Subsequently, the First Central Document in 2015 and 2016 further made detailed provisions on pilot measures, right confirmation, registration, certification, and guarantee mechanisms for the reform of the homestead system. It is another creative measure taken by the central government to release rural land and protect farmers' interests by steadily and carefully carrying out the pilot reform of the homestead system and exploring effective ways to realize the separation of ownership, qualification, and use rights of the homestead. Third, it comprehensively deepened market-oriented reform of land factors. China's exploration of market-oriented reform of land factors can be traced to the early stage of reform and opening up. In the late 1980s, the household contract responsibility system in rural China and the practice of "land lease"

in pilot cities such as Shenzhen and Shanghai were both preliminary explorations of market-oriented reform of land factors. After more than 40 years of development, the market-oriented reform of land elements entered a comprehensive stage of deepening, with the central government continuously promoting market-oriented development of land factors in an all-round way by carrying out the "three rights and rights separation," establishing a unified urban–rural construction land market, deepening the reform of market-oriented allocation of industrial land, encouraging the utilization of existing construction land and improving the land management system. In April 2020, the party central committee and the State Council issued "Opinions on Improving the Systems and Mechanisms for Market-oriented Allocation of Factors of Production," clearly stating how the scale of construction land should be controlled, urban and rural construction land index approval rights lowered, etc., through these efforts. Thus, China further improved marketization of land policy and the land management policy system.

(3) **The role, performance, and problems of the policy system**

The land policy in the new era provides a land system guarantee for the construction of a modern socialist country, which is conducive to fully returning the rights and empowerment of farmers, protecting their rights and interests, and increasing their income, to better stimulate vitality of both rural and urban areas and drive high-quality and sustainable development in the region. The "three rights" of rural land can better protect the rights and interests of farmers to enhance the vitality of rural management subjects; Exploring and implementing the market system of rural collective commercial construction land and constructing a reasonable value-added income distribution mechanism can ensure that farmers enjoy equal income distribution rights. Promoting the reform of the land expropriation system is conducive to a more fair and reasonable protection of farmers' property rights; The reform of the rural homestead system has revealed the property attribute of the homestead, which is conducive to increasing farmers' property income (Liu and Liu 2021) and promoting the integrated development of urban and rural areas. It can be seen that the efforts of the central government in land policy since the 18th National Congress of the CPC have effectively protected the interests of farmers, which is conducive to the construction of an ecological civilization and the integrated development of urban and rural areas. However, the game between the central government and the land still affects the performance of the land policy system to a certain extent. For example, the reform of the land expropriation system is a key measure implemented by the central government to protect the interests of farmers. However, due to the inconsistency between the interests of the central government and local governments in the reform, the principal-agent problem lingers, and the reform is faced with heavy resistance. Under the "strict control" and "incentive" of the central government, local governments have a strong desire to expropriate land in the political tournament, and the reform of the land expropriation system means that the previous financial model of local governments has to undergo transformation, and that land financial behavior cannot be sustained. Therefore, it is inevitable that conflicting behaviors are seen in the implementation of land expropriation system reform. Due to the "asymmetric information" about the central land, it is often difficult for the central government to effectively restrict the land financial behavior of local governments, which leads difficulties int the effective implementation of the land expropriation system reform. To reduce local government incentives for land requisition, to ensure that the local governments adhere to the central land expropriation system reform intentions, the current land expropriation compensation price forming mechanism must be reformed, land increment income distribution mechanism must be reconstructed, and, additionally, supervision of local government must increase regarding the implementation of the land expropriation system reform. Further, there is a need to clarify the scope of land expropriation and land expropriation compensation price, etc., Local governments must push forward the reform of the land expropriation system in accordance with the central government's intention. Problems also exist in the market-oriented reform of land elements, such as the price difference between farmland expropriation and collective construction land, the conflict between the relatively high proportion of industrial land and low utilization efficiency, and the conflict between collective and state-owned ownership in the unified land market between urban and rural areas, which should be continuously optimized and improved in the subsequent reform (Rong 2019).

References

Cai L, Long K (2019) The logic, experience and reform proposals of the evolution of urban and rural land system in 70 years in New China. J Nanjing Agric Univ (Social Sciences Edition) 4

Chen K, Long H (2019) Impacts of land market on urban-rural integrated development in China. J Nat Resour 2

Chen M (2020) Construction of spatial use control system of China's national land in the new era. J Jishou Univ (Social Science) 41(02): 91–97, 143

Chen X (2009a) Analysis of property law norms of rural land system. Chin Procur 07:79

Chen X (2009b) Analysis of the property law norms of rural land system: thinking after learning the decision on some important issues of promoting rural reform and development. J Leg Bus Res 26(01):3–11

Deng D (2017) Experience and transformation of property rights in rural China: a national government perspective offering food for thought. Soc Sci China 1

Du Y (1984) Tongdian, vol. 1, Tian system. Zhonghua Book Company, Beijing, p 9

Guo W (1988) Brief history of development of agricultural science and technology in China. China Science and Technology Press, Beijing

Ji X, Qian Zhonghao (2010) Study on change of structure of farmland property rights in 30 years: a perspective of property rights. Nanjing Soc Sci 10

Li J, Xiong C, Cai J (2020) The land reform is stepping into a new chapter: the equalization of urban-rural land property rights and the marketization of resource allocation. Manag World 6

Liu W, Liu S (2021) Enlightenment from the CPC in promoting the land system reform in the past 100 years. Chinese Leadership Sci 02:26–30

Liu S (2021) Theoretical and practical exploration on the centenary of the founding of the Party and the change of land system. Econ Dly (10)

Liu D, Gong Q, Yang W (2018) China's farmland protection policy evolution and optimization path in the past 40 years of reform and opening up. China Rural Econ 12:37–51

Luo B (2008) The transformation and innovation of Chinese rural land institution. Southern Econ 11

Lyu Z (2006) Study on legislation of water resources protection in Yangtze River Basin. Wuhan University Press, Wuhan

Meng X (2019) Adhere to the lead of the rule of law, focus on implementation. China Nat Resour News (3)

Qian W, Zhu J, Qian Long, et al (2021) Qian Long, et al., Study on the rural land factor marketization reform in China. Agric Econ Issues 02:4–14

Rong C (2019) Market-oriented reform of land factors: Progress, obstacles and suggestions. Macroecon Manag 38(08):25–31

Shi C (2020) Innovation and development of land expropriation system in China in the new era. Adm Reform 06:51–59

Tan R (2021) Introduction to China's land system. Science Press, Beijing, pp 32–47

Teng M, Zhang Y (2021) From power structure to system perfection: the evolution logic of the rural land policy of the Communist Party of China in the past century and the prospect of the New Era. J Social Theory Guid 03:4–10

Wang W, Cao Y, Su R et al (2020) The evolution process of China's arable land protection policy based on policy quantification. China Land Sci 34(07):69–78

Wu S (2019) Review and implications of China's urban land system in the early reform and opening-up period. Law Soc 22

Yan J, Guo D, Xia F et al (2021) The historical logic, theoretical logic and practical logic of the change of the land system of the Communist Party of China in the past 100 years. J Manag World 37(07):19–31

Ye H (2020) The core objectives of land use control in China from the construction of the legal system over the past 30 years. China Land 6

Yu M, Gu Y, Li R (2021a) The CPC's People-centered land Policy: a century of evolution and development. J Manag World 37(04):24–35

Yu M, Gu Y, Li R (2021b) The CPC's people-centered land policy: a century of evolution and development. Manag World 4

Yu H (2019) "Overhaul" of the forest law: take two hands for releasing and controlling. People's Congr China 13:40–41

Zhang Q, Wu C (2019) The institutional evolution and optimization path of land use control in China. China Land 3

Zhang X, Lyu X (2020) The change and reconstruction of spatial planning system under the goal of modern national governance. J Nat Resour 35(06):1261–1272

Zhao Q, Tian H (2021) Forty years of arable land protection: the theory of change of terms and values. Res Real Estate Law China 24(02):105–134

Zhao D (1989) Economic history of the People's Republic of China (1967–1984). Henan People's Publishing House

Zhou Y, Li X, Liu Y (2020) Rural land system reforms in China: History, issues, measures and prospects. Land Use Policy 91:104330

Chapter 3
Land Tenure Policy

Jun Yang

Land is one of the most important elements in urban–rural relations; it is also the carrier of all economic and social activities. Along with the formation and development of the urwban-rural dualistic system in China, the urban–rural dualistic land ownership system in China also evolved and changed accordingly. This chapter introduces the urban–rural dualistic land ownership system and its formation process and discusses the reform direction of the urban–rural dual land system. Focusing on the characteristics of separation of the two rights of urban land and the separation of the three rights of rural land, the chapter analyzes the optimization path of the urban–rural land property right system and policies through an analysis of current policy situation and relevant exploration practices.

3.1 Urban–Rural Dualistic Land Ownership System

3.1.1 Basic Concepts of the Urban–Rural Dualistic Land Ownership System

1) **Land property rights.** Land property rights refer to the full exclusive rights that exist in the land and are the sum of all rights related to land property. Generally described as a "bundle of rights," land property rights include a series of distinctive rights that can be held in a discrete manner and when aggregated together represent a "bundle of rights" that includes ownership of land and the

J. Yang (✉)
China University of Mining and Technology, Xuzhou, China
e-mail: junyang@cumt.edu.cn

S. Tan and X. Huang (eds.), *Land Policy in China*, The Frontier of Public Administration in China, https://doi.org/10.1007/978-981-19-9895-9_3

various rights associated with it and are relatively independent of it.[1] In general, land property rights in China can be divided into three categories, land ownership, land usufructuary right, and other rights to land. Among them, other rights include land mortgage, land lease, land inheritance, easement, and other rights. Compared with the land property rights in western countries, the land property rights in China have their own characteristics. On the one hand, land ownership in China is highly centralized and lacks clear personalized representatives, The collective ownership of land gives each member of the collective organization equal right to own land, which nominally belongs to the collective. In fact, everyone has no share, thus seriously deviating from the principle of exclusivity of property right, that is, absence of ownership. This is why farmers are rarely willing to make long-term investments in land and tend to engage in predatory operations, leading to a disorderly allocation of agricultural resources. On the other hand, land use rights belong to different interest subjects without any economic and legal responsibility for the reasonable use of land and its owners, which leads to land resources not being fully and reasonably utilized used, thus causing waste of land resources and uneconomic use. Land property rights are the core issue around which the urban–rural dualistic land ownership system in China formed, evolved, and developed.

2) **State ownership**. State ownership is a form of public ownership in which the socialist state exercises ownership over the means of production on behalf of the whole population and is a form of common ownership of the means of production by the whole population. China's land ownership system refers to the system of land ownership vesting confirmed by the state under a certain social production mode. The land ownership system is an important part of the ownership system of the means of production and is the core and foundation of the land system. "Land Administration Law of the People's Republic of China" stipulates that "China implements a socialist system of public ownership of land, i.e., national ownership and collective ownership by the working masses. The ownership of land owned by the whole people, i.e., the state, is exercised by the State Council of the PRC on behalf of the state, and no unit or individual may encroach upon, buy, sell, or otherwise illegally transfer land. The right to use land may be transferred in accordance with the law, while the state may expropriate or requisition land for the needs of public interest and give compensation in accordance with the law".[2] In terms of scope, state-owned land includes land in urban areas and land in rural and suburban areas that are owned by the state as defined by law. In terms of use, state-owned urban land can be determined by law for use by units or individuals, and state-owned land used for agriculture by law can be contracted by units or individuals to engage in plantation, forestry, animal husbandry, and fishery production. The state ownership system forms the basis of China's urban–rural dual land system.

---

[1] Development Research Center of the State Council. Rural Department Subject Group. From urban–rural duality to urban–rural integration. Journal of Management World, 2014, (9): 1–12.

[2] The Law of Land Administration of the People's Republic of China, 2020.

3) **Collective ownership**. Collective ownership is a form of public ownership in which the means of production and the fruits of labor are collectively owned by some of the working masses in a socialist society. Compared with the state-owned system, the different characteristics of collective ownership are mainly the different scope of public ownership of the means of production. In agriculture, the collective ownership economy is absolutely dominant and undertakes the major task of strengthening the foundation of the national economy; in cities and towns, the collective ownership economy also occupies an important position and plays an important role in increasing production, booming markets, expanding employment, satisfying people's needs, and expanding exports. The realization of collective ownership is divided into two levels: institutional realization and operational realization. The legal system for the realization of collective ownership is collective ownership, which is essentially common ownership of collective members; however, the form of operation for the realization of collective ownership does not require collective labor and unified operation of collective members, but can take diversified forms of operation. For land, the collective land ownership system is a kind of collective ownership system, which refers to the system of the right to possess, dominate, use, benefit, and dispose of the land enjoyed by the peasants collectively in a certain geographical area. Both the "Land Administration Law of the People's Republic of China" and the "Regulations on the Implementation of the Law of Land Administration of the People's Republic of China" stipulate that "land in rural areas and suburban areas belongs to the peasants collectively, except for that which belongs to the state by law; residential bases and self-reserved land and hills belong to the peasants collectively." Similar to state-owned land, collectively owned land can also be determined by law for use by units or individuals and take the form of family contracting within the rural collective economic organizations. Collective ownership and the aforementioned state ownership system constitute the unique urban–rural dual land system in China.
4) **Land requisition**. Land requisition is an act of the state to compulsorily acquire the land use rights of civil subjects based on the public interest. As an administrative act, land requisition is compulsory, and its legal relationship between the two parties is specific; the requisitioning party can only be the state, while the object of requisition is collective land and the real or movable property of units and individuals. At the same time, land requisition is compensatory in nature, and the land use right will be transferred; while the land ownership still belongs to the peasant collective, the land must be returned to the peasant collective at the end of the requisition conditions. However, for a long time in the past, there was no clear distinction between expropriation and requisition in China, The "Constitution of the People's Republic of China" and "Land Administration Law of the People's Republic of China" directly referred to "land expropriation" as "requisition." As a result, in practice, some local governments, in the name of public interest, have transferred ownership in land requisition, infringing on the interests of farmers. Therefore, in 2004, the Chinese government amended the law to clarify the premise of land requisition and changed the word "requisition"

to "expropriate." Although land expropriation is not legally intended to convert ownership, it has for a long time been an "inappropriate" means of converting collectively owned rural land into urban state-owned land in the dual land system of urban and rural areas.

5) **Land expropriation**. Land expropriation in China has the same meaning as "compulsory purchase" in Britain, "expropriation" in France and Germany, "land purchase" in Japan, "exercise of supreme land rights" in the United States, and "resumption of government land" in Hong Kong, China (Li 2021). It is an important system of converting agricultural land into construction land by transferring collective land and its rights to the state under the condition of compensation in accordance with the law for public interest. Like the above-mentioned land expropriation, the subject of land expropriation is also the state, which is also compulsory, and the objects of expropriation can also be collectively owned land and organizations' and individuals' houses and other real estate. The difference is that land expropriation leads to ownership of the land. "The Civil Code of the People's Republic of China" provides that "the expropriation of collectively owned land shall be accompanied by full and timely payment of compensation for land, resettlement grants, and compensation for rural villagers' dwellings, other ground attachments, and seedlings, as well as arrangements for social security for the expropriated farmers, safeguarding the livelihood of the expropriated farmers and safeguarding their legitimate rights and interests." Expropriation of the houses of organizations and individuals as well as other immovable properties shall be compensated in accordance with the law, and the legitimate rights and interests of the expropriated persons shall be safeguarded; in case of expropriation of individual residences, the living conditions of the expropriated persons shall also be guaranteed. Land expropriation is the only legal channel to change rural land into urban land in China's urban–rural dualistic land ownership system.
6) **Land use control**. Land use control is a system whereby, the state, to ensure the rational use of land resources and the coordination of economic and social development and the environment, prepares a general land use plan, delineates land use areas, and determines land use restrictions so that landowners and users use land strictly in accordance with the uses determined by the state. It has the same meaning as "land use zoning control," "land planning permission system," and "construction and development permission system" of other countries (Yue and Wang 2019). Land use control consists of a series of specific systems and norms, which are legally valid and mandatory. Among them, land use classification is the basis for land use control; overall land use planning is the basis for land use control, prior approval is the key for conversion of agricultural land to construction land; strengthening land enforcement supervision and serious legal responsibility are the guarantee for land use control. It can be said that while the land use control system plays an important role in the allocation of land resources and the protection of arable land in China, it is also an invisible barrier in breaking down the urban–rural dualistic land ownership system.

3.1.2 The Evolution of Urban–Rural Dualistic Land Ownership System

China's urban–rural dualistic land ownership system became truly remarkable after the reform and opening up, when the "Constitution of the People's Republic of China," adopted in 1982, stipulated that urban land is owned by the state and rural land is collectively owned. This defined the land system at the highest legal level of the country as the two aforementioned public ownership systems of state ownership and collective ownership. In the subsequent evolution of the urban–rural dual land system, the main body that pushed forward the evolution of the system was the urban government. Under the condition that the state had limited funds to invest in urban construction, to obtain the funds needed for urban construction, the government had to find a way to the main body using the land in the city and make the users pay a certain cost for using the land. However, this is obviously not enough compared to the huge amount of money needed for urban construction. As a result, the urban–rural dual land system continued to evolve under the dual effect of the advancement of vested interests and the dependence of the reform path. The typical symbol was the adoption of "Land Administration Law of the People's Republic of China" by the National People's Congress in 1994. After the introduction of this law, urban land use fees were changed to land assignment revenue, which became an important part of the city government's fiscal revenue. With the increase in land use fee or land assignment revenue, the income from land use fee constitutes an important source of land revenue, and a cycle is formed between land assignment revenue and urban construction to promote each other. Especially after the tax sharing reform, land assignment has become the main source of fiscal revenue for local governments. Land assignment revenue accounted for less than 8% of the fiscal revenue in 2001 to nearly 34% in 2016, becoming an important pillar of government revenue, which is commonly known as land finance (Zhang and Yan 2020). Under the conditions of fiscal "separate kitchens for meals," local governments became strongly dependent on land finance. The dependence of local governments on land finance strengthened the government's incentive to acquire land and created a strong incentive to acquire and sell land, thus promoting the expansion of urban built-up areas and urban space. Thus, the government, especially the urban government, was the driver for the continuous evolution of the urban–rural dual land system.

Relevant policy interpretation:

"Land assignment".

1. Lei Xiaoyu, Gong Liutang's research considered that local governments in cities use the optimal land concession strategy to offer industrial land at low

prices and commercial and residential land at high prices to reduce enterprise costs and increase fiscal revenues and public expenditures, together to attract enterprises, promote production, and facilitate urbanization.

Source: Lei Xiaoyu, Gong Liutang. Industrialization and urbanization based on land assignment. Management World, 2014, (09): 29–41.

2. Liu Shouying, Xiong Xuefeng, Zhang Yonghui's research considered that the marketization of land assignment is conducive to improving the efficiency of land resource allocation, thus promoting economic development.

   Source: Liu Shouying, Xiong Xuefeng, Zhang Yonghui, et al. Land system and China's development mode. China Industrial Economics, 2022, (01): 34–53.

3. George C. S. Lin, Yi Fangxin's research considered that local governments acquire agricultural land at low prices and then sell it at high prices to urban construction, and areas with high growth rates of urban construction land tend to have higher inflows of land revenue. In this process, land becomes a "growth-enhancing" tool for local governments to pursue local financing for urban development.

   Source: George C. S. Lin, Yi Fangxin. Urbanization of capital or capitalization on urban land? Land development and local public finance in urbanizing China. Urban Geography, 2011, 32(1): 50–79.

The introduction of the "Real Estate Administration Law" transformed urban construction from relying mainly on state investment to relying mainly on corporate, social, and personal investment, and the funds for building cities from being allocated mainly through administrative allocation to relying mainly on market allocation. The implementation of the "Real Estate Administration Law" transformed the main promoting force of the urban–rural dualistic system from the city government to the state, the city government, and the real estate development enterprises. Real estate enterprises, as important benefit recipients, not only support the urban–rural dual land system, but also make their own statements on various occasions to guide the continuous evolution of the urban–rural dual land system and strengthen the urban–rural dual land system arrangement through some of their legal representatives or agents (Gui 2016).

After many evolutions, although China has repeatedly amended the "Constitution of the People's Republic of China," "Land Administration Law of the People's Republic of China," "The Civil Code of the People's Republic of China," and other relevant laws and regulations, the relevant legal provisions have not only failed to change the urban–rural dual land system, but also strengthened this institutional arrangement through the following aspects.

First, the use control system. Entity and individuals must use land according to the uses determined by land planning, and if they want to change the land use, this must be approved by the state land administration. In this way, rural land is mostly identified as inefficient agricultural land, while urban land is generally planned for more efficient land uses such as finance, commerce, industry, and real estate, Li et al. (2015) thus creating an urban–rural dual structure of land uses.

Second, the monopoly of the channel of transforming rural land into urban land. To convert rural collective land into urban land, it must go through the government or the state as an intermediate body, and rural collectives do not have the right to convert collective land into urban land. The government is the only compliant expropriator of collective land and the only land supplier after expropriation into state-owned land, forming a dual monopoly of the buyer's and seller's markets. This duopoly not only exacerbates the dualistic institutional characteristics of urban and rural land, but also enables the government to reap monopoly profits (Liu and Xiong 2018).

Third, the dualistic urban–rural institutional arrangement of land prices. In a general monopoly market, price negotiation between supply and demand is still possible through market mechanisms, but in the segment of government expropriation of rural land, there is no market mechanism. The price of expropriated land is regulated by the "Land Administration Law of the People's Republic of China." The reality is that after a farmer loses his land completely, he cannot maintain his standard of living even after being compensated at the highest rate. When rural land is transformed into urban state-owned land through government expropriation, the assignment price is mainly a monopoly price formed by the government as the sole monopolist, while competition can be very fierce as a demander. This often raises the price of land and pushes up the price of housing (Xia et al. 2020).

3.1.3 *Basic Characteristics of the Urban–Rural Dualistic Land Ownership System*

In the course of the evolution of the urban–rural dualistic land ownership system, the system developed its own inherent characteristics, whose main features are as follows:

1) **Urban–rural dual land rights system**. The first is the land rights structure of urban–rural division. In China, rural land contractors enjoy land use rights, income rights, and transfer rights within the scope of agricultural use of agricultural land. Once the conversion of agricultural land occurs, the former rural landowners lose not only their land ownership rights, but also their land use rights, income rights, transfer rights, and development rights after the land becomes non-agricultural. The second is the different empowerment of urban and rural construction land. Urban state-owned construction land allows institutions and individuals to have the right to use it. In contrast, the law limits the land that farmers can use as collective construction land to three categories: land for farmers to collectively establish enterprises or jointly hold enterprises with other units or individuals in the form of land use rights in shares or joint ventures,

land for the construction of collective public facilities and public welfare undertakings, and farmers' residential bases. Rural collective construction land is not allowed to be rented out, and residential bases are acquired as members of collective economic organizations, with one house per household and separate housing and land.

2) **Differential allocation of urban and rural land.** The first is, agricultural land is limited to being agricultural land for agricultural use under the main land lease, subcontracting, shareholding, transfer; second is the transformation of agricultural land into municipal land, whereby the city and county governments implement expropriation and transfer; third is the implementation of the dual system of allocation of state-owned land supply and paid use. In addition to land for state organs and military land, land for urban infrastructure and public welfare, and land for infrastructure such as energy, transportation, and water conservancy, supported by the state implements the allocation of land, and all other types of construction land is to implement the assignment, leasing, capital contribution, or equity, and any other compensable use; fourth is the implementation of state-owned operating land market allocation under the exclusive monopoly of the government. Industrial, commercial, tourism, entertainment, commercial, residential, and other operating land, as well as the same land has more than two intended land users, to take bidding, auction, and listing of assignment to the land. Urban land use rights can either be directly allocated to users or be granted to users for a fee through an agreement between the government and the users. Under the urban–rural division and different allocation methods, the land market has long been divided between urban and rural areas (Lu and Wang 2021).

3) **The distribution of land appreciation proceeds is seriously unfair between urban and rural areas**. The first is that in the process of converting agricultural land to non-agricultural land, government expropriation is mainly implemented. After receiving a certain amount of compensation in the distribution of value-added proceeds, the expropriated farmers lose the right to share future land value-added proceeds. The second is that since the municipal and county governments are the main body of land expropriation implementation and the only body of land supply in the primary market of land, the first line of value-added proceeds at the time of land use conversion goes to the local government for acquisition, use, and disposal. The third is that under the current market rules for state-owned construction land, the landowner has the right to occupy, use, gain, transfer, and secure the mortgage of the land during the annual period after obtaining the land use right according to the law. With the urbanization process, the value of the land rises dramatically, and the bulk of the future value-added revenue from the land goes to the land occupier, with the local government receiving part of the revenue in the form of taxes in the transaction. This system of land value-added revenue distribution is extremely inconsistent with the principle of generating land value-added revenue in the urbanization process, resulting in a huge inequitable distribution of land benefits.

4) **Deficiencies in land control have caused unequal development between urban and rural areas**. Through reforms of relevant laws and institutions, China gradually developed a unified land management model with relatively centralized management and top-down supervision of land. The State Council's administrative department of land and resources is unified and responsible for the management and supervision of land nationwide, with four levels of management: national, provincial, municipal, and county, In the management system of the leading bodies, the system of central and provincial double-layer management and vertical management below the provincial level is implemented. However, due to the existence of the urban–rural dual land system between urban and rural areas and the land sale model under the government's land finance dependence mentioned above, China developed a triple-controlled conversion of agricultural land, planning control, land use control, and ownership control, resulting in the process of urban–rural integration, which is the process of rural map reduction and rural development space compression. However, due to the failure of use control and the soft constraint of urban expansion by the overall land use planning, coupled with the low price land acquisition system that incentivizes local governments to acquire, occupy, and convert more rural land into urban land, the central government was required to strengthen the annual target and approval management of construction land conversion to restrain the scale of land use and urban expansion by the local governments. However, because the management of indicators and approval management showed strong planning, this top-down allocation of indicators fact resulted in the distribution of construction land indicators according to administrative levels, which not only makes it difficult to match the supply of its construction land indicators with the demand for economic development and to play a strong role in restraining local governments' land use, but also makes it difficult for lower-level county and township governments to be allocated indicators, and to develop, they can only resort to illegal and irregular use of land, and thus use it as another major path to land expansion (Feng and Wang 2019).

3.1.4 Problems Caused by the Urban–Rural Dual Land System of Urban and Rural Areas

1) **Eminent domain was applied to all agricultural land conversions, and urban–rural integration was distorted into land nationalization**. Under the dual land system pattern and the expropriation urbanization model, along with the urbanization process, peasant collective land became state land through expropriation. The implementation of urban–rural integration through the integration of urban and rural planning in various places increased the trend of turning rural land into state-owned land. According to statistics, between 2010 and 2012, the approved construction land nationwide increased from more than 7.2 million mu to more than 9.2 million mu. Among this, the amount of land converted

from agricultural land to construction land accounts for about 70%. At the same time, the scale of land acquisition during this period was around 4 million mu each year, and the amount of conversions from arable land to construction land accounted for more than 40% of the approved construction land (Yan and Feng 2019). Further, with the continuous expropriation of surrounding rural land and its inclusion in the urban construction area, urban boundaries began expanding outward as was the jurisdiction of urban governments. During 2005–2011, more than 15 million mu of rural land was expropriated and transformed into state-owned land for urban construction, with an average annual expropriation of rural land of nearly 2.2 million mu, which is basically in line with the growth area of urban construction land in the same period.

2) **The mismatch between land urbanization and population urbanization exacerbated the difficulty of urban management**. Unlike western countries that have moved from urban–rural fragmentation to urban–rural integration, China's urban–rural integration is urbanization driven by government land acquisition on the one hand, and spontaneous urbanization by farmers using residential base and collective construction land on the other (Liu et al. 2021). The two contributed to the unique phenomenon of urban–rural integration in China. In this, the urbanization driven by government land acquisition is characterized by expansionary urbanization, with various types of urban development showing a rapid outward expansion from the central city to the peripheral space. However, government-led urbanization did not achieve "synchronization of people and land" (Wu and Sun 2018). The development of cities attracted a large number of rural people who moved to live and work in cities, but they did not enjoy the same rights as urban residents in the areas of housing, social security, medical care, and education. At the same time, the spontaneous urbanization of farmers using residential bases and collective construction land led to increased difficulties in urban management, and the rural–urban fringe zone became the main vehicle for the urbanization of the mobile population (Zhao 2020). The self-induced sprawl of the rural–urban fringe zone created an extra-legal collective land and a housing rental "gray market" independent of the government land and housing market (before the newly implemented "Land Administration Law of the People's Republic of China" in 2020), and public services such as population, environmental management, and security maintenance in urban villages were not integrated into the urban public service system. Villages became overloaded and faced serious security problems.
3) **The legal market channel for collective construction land is basically closed, and the space for rural development is compressed**. First, under the control of construction land index, the amount of collective construction land became greatly reduced. To increase farmers' income and develop a collective economy, farmers' collectives had to take the risk of using collective land for non-agricultural construction on their own initiative, and many collective construction lands are in an extra-legal state. Second, the lack of mortgage financing function greatly limited the output level of collective construction land and farmers' property income, and the market valuation of collective construction land is much

lower than its real value, making it difficult to truly improve the utilization efficiency. Third, the reform of the governance structure of collective organizations is lagging behind, hindering the efficient allocation of collective construction land. Collective economic property rights are naturally ambiguous, and even after the rural collective land, factories, and other assets are converted into equity, "assets into capital and farmers into stock farmers," conflicts within rural collective organizations are still prominent. Eventually, the governance structure of collective economic organizations, which only shares dividends but not debts, is not conducive to industrial adjustment and upgrading on collective construction land and fundamentally restricts improving land use efficiency.

4) **The legal provisions of residential bases lag behind the reality, which is not conducive to both the realization of property rights of farmers in residential bases and to land management**. Rural residential bases form a unique category in China's rural land rights system and one of the most crucial institutional arrangements in the process of urban–rural integration. After China's residential base system experienced private ownership of residential bases during the period of land reform and agricultural cooperatives and collective ownership of residential bases during the period of collectivization, use by farmers and private ownership of houses, the system of residential base rights was systematically constructed since the reform, forming a basic system of collective ownership of residential bases and farmers' right to use residential bases and housing ownership. However, from the viewpoint of the actual effect of the rights, only the "right of possession and right of use" are legally assigned to the house bases as usufruct rights, and the "right of income" is missing, so that the property attributes of the house bases are greatly reduced, basically functioning only as residence. At the same time, the acquisition of residential land without compensation and one house per family are difficult practices to implement. On the one hand, the free acquisition of residential bases is considered the government's welfare for farmers, but with the dramatic increase in differential land benefit in the process of urbanization and the increasing tension of urban construction land, the free allocation of residential bases runs counter to the capitalization of land, especially in economically developed areas, where residential bases are no longer allocated free of charge. On the other hand, as the value of residential bases becomes more obvious, the expansion of residential bases and the building of houses by farmers are even more disorderly, and even have the tendency to spread. This has resulted in private building and unplanned construction in urban villages, inadequate infrastructure and public services, unorganized governance, and serious security problems, increasing the cost of urban management and difficulty of future renewal.
5) **Farmers' land rights became damaged and social instability caused by land issues increased**. However, the compensation for land expropriation kept moving toward marketization and property compensation (Liu 2020). In China, during the planned economy, farmers who lost their land due to land expropriation were resettled by the state. First, "agriculture to non-agricultural," and then from

agricultural household registration to urban household registration. Second, agricultural laborers were arranged to be employed as workers in urban enterprises and institutions. Under the urban and rural dual system at that time, this transformation led to a fundamental change in the identity of peasants. The peasants and their families were able to enjoy all the employment and benefits of the city people. Social contradictions caused by land expropriation were not common and acute, and most farmers welcomed and even looked forward to national land expropriation. In the period of the market economy, the implementation of monetary compensation made it impossible for farmers to work in agriculture once they lose their land completely, and subsequently a long or short process of employment outside agriculture, during which the cost of living became high and they found it difficult to maintain their normal life by merely the compensation cost of agricultural labor, which led to a de facto lowering of the living standards of the expropriated farmers, and social conflicts caused by land expropriation gradually became prominent (Chi 2021). With the further acceleration of industrialization and urbanization, farmers became more aware of their land rights and more dissatisfied with the unfairness of the compensation system for land expropriation. Further, the large and excessive speed with which land expropriation took place led to tens of millions of farmers losing the land on which they depended for their livelihood in the process of urbanization. The loss of land and the loss of livelihood, coupled with the lack of transparency in the land expropriation process, inadequate compensation for land less farmers and village collectives, and the huge gap between the compensation received for land expropriation and the government's proceeds from land concessions led to increased social instability and a growing sense of unfairness, thus intensifying the conflicts between rural residents and local governments and an increasing number of disputes surrounding land. Land-related disputes thus threatened the social stability of rural areas in China.

6) **The unreasonable degree of urban–rural distribution of land value-added income intensified**. Along with the urbanization process, with the value of land increasingly revealed, and the value-added income from land rapidly rising, the competition around land interests also intensified. First, consider the above-mentioned contradiction in interests between the expropriated farmers and the local government; the expropriated farmers do not share the fruits of urbanization, leaving most of them with no connection to the land appreciation income. Second, land assignment revenue mainly goes to local governments, and how farmers share in the land-grading income has not found a form of realization. Third, inequity persisted in the compensation of land benefits among farmers themselves, with the government's high compensation for farmers in the rural–urban fringe zone contrasting with the low and inadequate land compensation for farmers in agricultural areas. Fourth, the distribution of value-added gains between urban and rural areas became extremely unreasonable (Xu 2018). While there are certainly locational factors in the generation of land value-added gains, due to the dualistic land system of urban–rural division, China's land value-added gains were mainly obtained and used by cities, while rural areas did not receive

compensation based on land value when land is expropriated, and the value-add of land after non-agricultural use became irrelevant. Under the government's monopoly of the primary land market, the increase in land value-added revenue was mainly reflected in the growth of government land assignment revenue. As China's economy entered a new period of rapid growth, land assignment revenue also started rising rapidly. However, the portion of land assignment revenue spent on urban areas still accounted for the major share, while the portion spent on rural areas and agriculture was low. The imbalance in the distribution of land assignment revenue between urban and rural areas remained significant, and even the share of land compensation to farmers in land assignment revenue decreased instead of increasing. In fact, the increase in land assignment revenue implied that more land revenue is possessed and dominated by the local governments, which are eager to expropriate more and use less, and the mode of "making money from land" led to over-expropriation and inefficient use of land, which was not conducive to the protection of arable land. On the one hand, it was not conducive to the protection of arable land and the economical and intensive use of land, and on the other, it also seriously damaged farmers' property rights and interests.

3.1.5 *The Direction of Reform of the Urban–Rural Dualistic Land System*

(1) **Reforming the dual ownership structure of land with unequal rights**

First, to establish a system of equal rights for the two ownership systems of land, it was decreed that the same rights of possession, use, income, and disposal be given to collectively owned land and state-owned land and give equal protection to the rights enjoyed by the two ownership systems of land, so as to realize the same land and rights under the guarantee of the Constitution and relevant laws. Second, use control was considered the only access system. Under use control, peasant collective land and land of other subjects enjoy equal rights to enter non-agricultural use and equal rights to share the non-agricultural value-added income of land in accordance with the law. It was clarified that the main role of planning is to implement the spatial and functional layout and change the pattern of local governments turning peasant collectively owned land into state-owned and government-run through planning amendments. Third, it considered breaking the current policy of access to land within and outside the circle according to the different ownership systems because of the boundary between urban and rural areas, except for non-agricultural construction outside the circle that can be used for non-public welfare. The land collectively owned by farmers within the circle can be used for non-agricultural construction without changing the ownership system under the premise of use control. Fourth, it clearly limits the urban land state for the built-up area stock of land belonging to the state, new construction land for non-agricultural economic construction, except for public interest expropriation and can retain collective ownership. For the current status of collectively owned land in the built-up area, the "right to protect and share" or "transfer the right to protect" can be used to protect the land property rights and interests of farmers.

(2) **Establishment of a unified urban and rural construction land market**

Although the Third Plenary Session of the 18th Central Committee of the Communist Party of China at the end of 2013 had already proposed that "under the premise of conforming to planning and use control, rural commercial collective-owned construction land is allowed to be transferred, leased, or bought into the stock, and has the same access to the market, the same rights, and prices as state-owned land is implemented." Here, one is to define the scope of collective construction land allowed to enter the market for commercial collective-owned construction land. Second, it is the first time that the concept of equal land and equal rights is written into the highest document of the Chinese Communist Party. The biggest drawback of China's land system is that collective land and state-owned land have different rights to the same land, and this time, collective rural operating construction land is allowed to enter the market on an equal footing with state-owned land, which should contain the following layers of meaning: the same land and the same right. In other words, rural commercial collective-owned construction land can be transferred, leased or bought into the stock, breaking the ice that collective construction land cannot be leased and there is equal access to the market. In other words, commercial collective-owned construction land and state-owned construction land can be legally traded on the same platform, changing the current pattern that state-owned construction land is exclusively traded on the platform and collective construction land in the gray city of non-standard trading pattern; supply, and demand determine the price. The entry of commercial collective-owned construction land into the market will change the current situation of the government's exclusive offer to determine supply, resulting in price distortion, and multiple collective economic organizations to enter the market with the main body of commercial collective-owned construction land, truly forming a mechanism to determine prices by supply and demand and promote the healthy development of the land market (Huang 2019). Third, it must conform to planning and use control. Collective farmers can use commercial collective-owned construction land for non-agricultural economic activities only under the premise of conforming to planning and use control. This shows that there are strict limits on the entry of commercial collective-owned construction land into the market: first, it is not the same right and price of collective land as state-owned land into the market, but only an opening for commercial collective-owned construction land; second, even if it is collective management land, it must be subject to planning and use control. It is important to face the fact that the market entry of commercial collective-owned construction land through the pilot has encountered huge challenges. The reality is that collective construction land has actually been on the market for a long time, and it greatly exceeds the definition of collective management land under current law. First, the Pearl River Delta, the Yangtze River Delta, the Bohai Sea, and other coastal areas have a large proportion of collective construction land for industrial and industrial development, where there is both collective management land as currently defined by law, as well as collective public welfare and public utility land, and a large number of farmers' residential bases. Second, many of the collective construction land entering the market is in a gray state, and most of the collective construction land leased to enterprises by village organizations is a land lease contract signed privately between the two parties, and in the event of a dispute, the court deals with it as an invalid contract, leading to losses for both parties. Third, in the rural–urban fringe zone, a large number of collective construction land is engaged in business in the urban planning area, contrary to the law that urban land belongs to the state (Wu 2021). How can the spirit of establishing an integrated urban–rural land market be implemented and how can the stock of collective construction land in an operating state be resolved from a problem-oriented approach is an urgent issue to be addressed in the next step of implementation.

(3) **Effectively promote reform of the land acquisition system**

To put collective construction land on the market, it is necessary to resolve the issue of land acquisition. Since the 16th National Congress, the Chinese government has made painstaking efforts to promote the reform of the land requisition system and encountered a lot of resistance, the most important of which is the difficulty of changing the traditional way of development supported by this system. "The Decision of the Third Plenary Session of the 18th Central Committee" proposed to "narrow the scope of land acquisition, standardize land acquisition procedures, and improve a reasonable, standardized, and diversified protection mechanism for farmers whose land has been acquired." Specifically, the following reforms should be deepened and promoted in the future: first, narrow the scope of land expropriation. According to the principles of "The Constitution of the People's Republic of China," only land for public welfare purposes has to be expropriated. Although the "Land Administration Law of the People's Republic of China" in 2020 defines public interest in an enumerated manner, ambiguous situations persist for public interest in practice. It is recommended to refer to the practice of other reforms of negative lists and develop a negative catalog of land acquisition so that no land can be acquired as long as the use is for profit. Second, the procedure of land acquisition should be standardized (Du 2021). The new "Land Administration Law of the People's Republic of China" proposes issuing a pre-announcement for land expropriation, but it is not effective in the concrete implementation. It is suggested to further improve the grassroots constraint mechanism of land acquisition procedures to ensure that the statutory land acquisition procedures are implemented. Third, a reasonable, standardized, and diversified protection mechanism should be established. This is the core of the land acquisition system reform, and its connotation should be clarified in policy and law as soon as possible. The so-called reasonable is in terms of compensation price, that is, in adherence to the principle of use control, according to the locational conditions of the requisitioned land to implement market compensation; the so-called standardized is in terms of the act of land expropriation, with a clear scope of land expropriation, compensation price, and procedures, and must be implemented in accordance with the law of land expropriation. The so-called diversification refers to the resettlement according to diversified ways, to effectively resolve the problem of long-term livelihood of the landless farmers without guarantee, whereby the substantive institutional arrangement is to protect part of the land expropriated farmers' right to development, that is, when expropriating farmers' land to the expropriated farmers to reserve part of the land into urban planning, without changing the nature of collective ownership to participate in non-agricultural construction, which is the fundamental solution to the long-term livelihood of expropriated farmers (Xu 2021).

(4) **Reforming and improving the residential bases system**

As early as the Third Plenary Session of the 18th Central Committee, the Chinese government proposed to "safeguard the usufructuary rights of farmers' residential bases, reform and improve the rural residential base system, select a number of pilot projects, prudently and steadily promote the mortgage, guarantee and transfer of farmers' housing property rights, and explore channels to increase farmers' property income." The rural "three pieces of land" reform pilot started in 2015 marked the principles and scope for the next phase of the residential base system reform. From the practice of reform, the future residential base system should grasp the following points: First, it is meant to protect the usufructuary rights of farmers' residential bases. The bottom line of the reform of the residential base system is to guarantee the right to occupy, use, and strengthen farmers' rights to use residential bases in accordance with the principle of usufructuary rights of residential bases. The right of income and transfer should be truly given to the people who have the right to use residential bases. Second, it must reform and improve the rural residential base system. Presently, in the reform pilot in different types of areas of rural residential base system, although the focus is on exploring the acquisition and use of residential bases with compensation, residential base trading and transfer, etc., it is still limited to the internal members of the collective, and in the future, it is necessary to explore if we can break the boundary of residential base members and village communities, gradually realize the right to exchange property rights empowerment for the right to welfare distribution, realize the complete usufructuary rights of farmers to residential bases and promote the effective use of land. Third, the reform is meant to promote mortgage, guarantee and transfer of farmers' housing property rights in a prudent and appropriate manner. Presently, the relevant regions have given the right to mortgage, guarantee, and transfer to farmers' housing, but not to residential bases. Although it has its reasonableness under the current system and legal constraints, in the future, if the mortgage, guarantee, and transfer rights of farmers' housing and mansion bases can be clearly granted, it will be conducive to the more secure realization of farmers' property gains.

Relevant policy interpretation:

"three pieces of land".

1. Wu Bin, Zhang Wen, Zhang Zhanlu's research considered that land acquisition provides production factors such as land and capital for rapid economic development and speeds up the process of national industrialization and urbanization, but it also harms the interests of farmers to a certain extent.

   Source: Wu Bin, Zhang Wen, Zhang Zhanlu. Research on the reform of land expropriation system based on tradable property right. Modern Management Science, 2017, (04): 63–65.
2. Yan Jinming, Cai Dawei, Xia Fangzhou's research considered that the reform of land expropriation, market entry of collective management construction land, and residential base system has led to the continuous improvement of property rights, such as rural land ownership, usufruct and security rights, and enhanced market-oriented allocation efficiency of rural land elements, which has effectively contributed to the realization of poverty eradication and rural revitalization; thus, the reform has achieved remarkable results.

   Source: Yan Jinming, Cai Dawei, Xia Fangzhou. The reform of rural land system since the 18th National Congress of the CPC: Progress, achievements and prospect. Reform, 2022, (08): 1–15.
3. Han Wenlong, Zhu Jie's research considered that the "separation of three rights" of residential bases is conducive to solving the problem of idle rural residential bases and realizing the land property rights of farmers in the process of urbanization. The focus of the "three rights" subdivision of residential bases is to explore the mechanism to release the right to use, and the mortgage of the right to the homestead; use right is an important way to realize the economic value of the right to use residential bases.

   Source: Han Wenlong, Zhu Jie. Residential bases use right mortgage loan: practice mode and governance mechanism. Social Science Research, 2020, (06): 38–46.
4. Cui-ping Ma's research considered that the market entry of collective management construction land has, to a certain extent, solved the historically developed problem of unclear ownership of collective construction land assets, improved the fit between land supply and demand, helped to calm the current overheated land market prices and housing prices, and to a certain extent confirmed that the sharing of development rights of agricultural land contributes to the advancement of reform.

Source: Cui-ping Ma. Exploration and evaluation of collective operating construction land system: An analysis based on the first batch of pilot project. Chinese Rural Economy, 2021, (11): 35–54.

(5) **Establishing a fair and shared distribution system of land appreciation proceeds**

The issue of land value-added income distribution is a matter of social equity and has always been at the core of the land system reform. In 2013, the Third Plenary Session of the 18th Central Committee of the Communist Party of China called for "the establishment of a land value-added income distribution mechanism that takes into account the state, the collective and the individual, and a reasonable increase in individual income." This is important in increasing farmers' property income. In the future, the direction of reforming the distribution of land value-added income should be to change the current situation in which the first course of distribution of land value-added income is obtained by the government at the time of granting, which gets the future value-added part, and farmers have no share in the distribution of land value-added income. Since land value-added income is complex, it cannot be fully owned by the government, let alone by anyone, and certainly not by the landowners. Therefore, an important part of the future reform should be on how to truly implement "balance" in the distribution of land value-added income among the state, collective, and individual interests. A reasonable and fair distribution of land benefits should follow the principle of value-added income generation. The principle of reasonable distribution of land value-added income should be formulated to fundamentally reform the current situation of land value-added income going to the government and establish a mechanism for land value-added income to reach society, so as to ensure that the original landowners receive fair compensation and land differential rent, that the land and capital needed for urban infrastructure construction are guaranteed, and that the land value-added income is returned to society and shared by the citizens.

(6) **Promote innovation of land system in the rural–urban fringe zone**

Informal development on the urban fringe and in urban villages has spread to all types of cities in China. Land issues in these areas have become one of the sources of social stability and income distribution, posing significant challenges to inclusive and efficient urbanization. Both city governments and real estate developers have identified potential economic opportunities for redeveloping urban village areas. Informal development, underdeveloped public services, legal gaps in collective land use on the urban fringe, and increasing compensation and resettlement costs for city governments pose significant challenges to the financial balance. To address these issues, reforms, especially innovations in the land system, are urgently needed. First, there is a need to integrate urban villages into the overall urban planning. Based on the implementation of the integration of urban master planning and land use planning as well as the establishment of a unified urban and rural construction land market, integrating urban villages into the formal urban development process can increase the supply of land needed for urban development. This integration would not only provide housing accessibility for low-income people entering the city, but also enhance the strength of land property rights for collective economic organizations and indigenous people in urban villages. By taking the lead in implementing collective construction land access to the market in this area, it would allow expropriated farmers in this area to reap the economic benefits of urbanization and reduce conflicts between the government and farmers. Second, after allowing the stock of collective construction land in the rural–urban fringe zone to enter the market, the housing provision pattern in the future urbanization process will also change. Urban governments could, through more appropriate zoning plans, not necessarily follow the current model of providing tracts of land to developers; peasant collectives could form share cooperatives or provide land to other organizations to engage in development, thus solving the problem of building low-income housing on the one hand and allowing urban governments to avoid the resettlement and related costs they had to pay under the original land expropriation model on the other. Further, recognizing and legally protecting the property rights of housing on the collective stock of construction land in compliance with the plan would allow migrants who have moved to the city to integrate more decently into the city and change the current confusion and instability brought about by an entirely informal housing market. Third, consideration can be given to the introduction of a district expropriation law to provide a legal basis for urban renewal and urban village transformation. After a period of rapid expansion in some Chinese cities, it has become increasingly difficult to continue to rely on new land and expropriation of peasant land for expansion. In contrast, there is great potential to develop the stock of land, and the commercial value of these lands, which are located in better zones of the city, is increasing. The model of district expropriation in Taiwan, China, can be borrowed, that is, the original landowner is allowed to negotiate the price of the land directly with the developer under the premise of conforming to the overall urban plan, but since urban renewal requires the readjustment of land use, the government will require the original owner to put aside a certain percentage of the land for urban infrastructure construction and municipal land. At the same time, urban renewal also requires a certain amount of public investment, and the original landowner will also need to put up a certain amount of land for listing and trading to solve the problem. In this way, district expropriation essentially becomes a "cooperative development" model between the government and the owner to improve the quality of the city and increase the value of the land (Jiang 2015). Fourth, there is a need to consider the first property tax on collective construction land that is allowed to enter the market. A capital gains tax could be levied first on collective construction land that enters the urban land market to allow local governments to capture the value appreciation of such land and to collect additional annual property taxes on such collective construction land that enters the urban land market and is used for commercial purposes.

3.2 Urban Land Tenure Policy: Separation of Urban Land Tenure and Its Formation and Reform

The current "Land Management Law of the People's Republic of China" stipulates that land in cities is owned by the state. The state can grant its use rights to enterprises or individuals in the capacity of landowners. The relationship between urban land ownership and use rights has changed along with the development of China's urban land market.

3.2.1 The Connotation of the Two Rights of Urban Land and Its Formation

The so-called two rights of urban land refer to the ownership and use of land. Among them, urban land ownership refers to the right of the state, as the landowner, to possess, use, benefit, and dispose of the land it owns within the scope of the law, which is the legal expression of the land ownership system in a certain social form. Generally, urban land ownership belongs to the category of property ownership. However, the characteristics of land ownership in China are different from general property ownership, mainly in the following aspects: 1. Land ownership is an exclusive right, and the subject of its right is specific. The subject of land ownership can only be the state, and no other entity or individual can enjoy land ownership, which is determined by the socialist public ownership system of land in China. 2. The nature of the transaction is restrictive. Article 2, paragraph 3, of the "Land Management Law of the People's Republic of China" stipulates that "no unit or individual may appropriate, buy, sell, or otherwise illegally transfer land." Obviously, the sale, purchase, gift, and exchange of land ownership and the use of land ownership as investment are illegal and should be regarded as invalid as per civil law. 3. There is stability of ownership. Due to the specificity of the subject and the restriction of the transaction, the ownership of urban land in China is in a highly stable state. 4. With separability of rights and functions, land ownership includes the right to possess, use, gain, and dispose of land, which is the most comprehensive and fullest property right. In the case of highly stable land ownership, to realize the effective use of land resources, the law needs to separate land use rights from land ownership, making them a relatively independent form of property rights and tradable. Therefore, the modern concept of property law was transformed from "ownership-centered" to "utilization-centered" in the modern property law. (5) Exclusivity of land ownership prevails, that is, monopoly of land ownership exists. In China, the owner of urban land can only be the state. (6) As per the retroactive power of land ownership, if land is illegally possessed by another person, the owner can claim his rights against him regardless of the person or entity that has transferred control of the land (Lu et al. 2018).

The state, as the owner of urban land, does not use the land directly, but cedes the land use right to the land user for a certain number of years, and the land user pays the state for the land use right grant. From this, the right of use of urban land is derived. State-owned Land Use Rights refers to the right of the user of state-owned land to use the land and obtain income in accordance with the law. The subject of the State-owned Land Use Rights is broad. Any entity or individual, including enterprises, institutions, and individuals outside of China, can become a user of state-owned land in China if they meet the conditions for using state-owned land in China according to the law. The terms of use vary according to land use. The maximum term of the State-owned Land Use Rights is determined according to the following uses: 70 years for residential land; 50 years for industrial land; 50 years for education, science and technology, culture, health, and sports; 40 years for commercial, tourism, and entertainment land; and 50 years for comprehensive or other land. Land users who have obtained the right to use the land, within the life of the use can transfer, rent, mortgage, or use it for other economic activities, with legitimate rights and interests protected by the state law.

3.2.2 Urban Land Market and Two Rights to Land

From the above introduction to the two rights of urban land, we find that the ownership and use of urban land are separated in China, while the change of urban land use right forms the urban land market and plays an important role in the land market.

(1) **Overview of the urban land market**

An urban land market is a place where urban land ownership or use rights are transferred or ceded. In China, it is a place where urban land use rights are granted by city governments and urban land use rights are retransferred. The urban land market deals with the right to use land. The urban land market in China consists of a primary market (i.e., the land grant market) and a secondary market (i.e., the land transfer market). The urban land market has commonalities as well as differences with the general market system, which are mainly reflected in the following aspects.

First, let us consider the characteristics of coupling monopoly and competition. As a limited natural resource, urban land, as mentioned above, has monopolistic ownership and use rights, and the urban land market is a monopolistic market. Under the condition of state ownership of urban land, to ensure the rational use of urban land and realize the total control of non-agricultural construction land, the primary market of urban land in China is in the hands of the state, which authorizes the land management department to implement monopolistic operation for the granting of urban land use rights. The amount of land that enters the land transfer market, its use, the method of transfer, and the number of years of use are all controlled by the government. However, this is not the same as excluding competition, which manifests itself among land users for land use and price to obtain the right to use land. In the secondary market of urban land, the transfer prices are mainly formed by market competition.

The second aspect is the strong territoriality. Common goods can be transferred between different markets through complete spatial circulation and may form a national unified competitive market and market price. However, urban land is different, because the land location is fixed, and the land in different cities have different location characteristics and functional differences, so that the land in different cities, in addition to the common urban functions, does not have to flow; the differences in supply and demand cannot be transferred to each other. Even within the same city, different sections of urban land have their own characteristics, which cannot be replaced through market circulation. This makes it difficult to form a national unified urban land market and achieve competitive prices; instead, it can give rise to only local and imperfectly competitive markets, wherein land market prices and land rents are highly variable.

Third, we need to consider the diversity of the transaction methods and the multilevel nature of the market composition. The urban land market can adopt flexible and changeable operation methods. In terms of transaction methods, there are one-time sales and purchases, as well as phased leases, in the form of agreements, bidding, auctions, discounted shares, leases, and other methods. Leasing can be divided into long-term lease, short-term lease, sublease, and others. With the reform of the urban land system and the deepening of the reform of state-owned enterprises, new ways of operation will continue to emerge. The multi-level composition of the urban land market is manifested in the land acquisition market formed by the state's acquisition of rural collective land, the land use right assignment market formed by the state's transfer of land use rights to land users, and the land use right transfer market formed by the transfer of land use rights among land users. The degree and scope of competition in the various levels of urban land markets vary greatly, as do the difficulties in and methods of state macro-control.

Fourth, we need to consider the complexity of revenue distribution. Since China's urban land is state-owned, the distribution of proceeds from urban land become complicated: 1. The distribution relationship between the state and local governments. The state, as the owner of urban land, has to obtain the land revenue, while the local government, entrusted by the state to specifically exercise the right of land management, should also obtain part of the revenue. To protect and mobilize the enthusiasm of local governments, increase investment in urban infrastructure construction, and promote comprehensive urban economic and social development, there is a need to coordinate the interests of the central and local governments in the distribution of the urban land proceeds. 2. The interests between local governments at all levels. Provincial, municipal, and county governments at all levels undertake different land management tasks according to their land management approval authority, thus creating the problem of how to reasonably allocate and handle the allocation relationship between local governments at all levels. 3. The allocation relationship between the state land management department and the state-owned land development company of land revenue, which belongs to the allocation between the state and enterprises. 4. The complex allocation relationship in the use of land revenue. In other words, urban land revenue is used both for compensation of land capital depreciation costs and interest payments for urban construction and for reinvestment in urban development and old city renovation (Rong 2020). These pluralistic interest subjects and diverse use needs of urban land revenue mandate that the relationship between all parties must be considered in the distribution of land revenue, the enthusiasm of all parties must be fully mobilized, land revenue must be reasonably distributed, and preservation and appreciation of state-owned land assets must be promoted.

Fifth, is the aspect of diversity of prices. The formation of urban land prices is more complex than that of general commodities. Since land is a special commodity, many factors affect the market price of urban land, including economic, physical, and environmental factors, as well as policy factors and psychological factors. Thus, urban land has a special price formation mechanism, and the market price also presents diversity, constituting a multi-level and multiform urban land price system (Yao 2020). Further, the diversity of urban land prices determines that government management and supervision of urban land market is much more complicated than that of the general commodity market.

(2) **Ways of acquiring land use rights in the urban land market**

1) Allocation of urban land use rights: The allocation of state-owned land use rights refers to the act of the people's government at or above the county level approving, in accordance with law, the delivery of the land to the land user for use after the land user has paid compensation, resettlement, and other fees, or the delivery of the land use rights to the land user for use without compensation. The state restricts the establishment of construction land use rights by way of allocation; only land for state organs, military land, urban infrastructure, and public welfare undertakings, and land for key state supported energy, transportation, water conservancy projects, etc. can be acquired by way of allocation of land use rights. Allocated land may not change the use of land without authorization, while subject to the people's government on the right to use the land without compensation.
2) Urban land use right agreement assignment, similar to the concept of land agreement assignment, also refers to the state agreement to State-owned: Land Use Rights for a certain number of years to the land user, wherein the land user has to pay the state for land use right assignment. However, the agreement to assignment has restricted scope of use, mainly applicable to, (1) the supply of commercial, tourism, entertainment, and commercial residential, and other types of business land and industrial land (excluding mining land); also, other than the use of land, the supply of land plan after the announcement of the same land is restricted to only one intended land user; (2) the government to implement urban planning for the reconstruction of old urban areas, to relocate industrial projects in line with national industrial policy, after the city, county, Administrative department of the land and resources review and report to the city and county people's government for approval, the recovery of the original State-owned Land Use Rights, the agreement assignment or lease for the original land use rights

rearrangement of industrial land; (3) mining, quarrying, sand mining, salt pans, and other ground production and tailings piling land, to encourage the adoption of leasing, but also the agreement to transfer; (4) the original allocation, leased land use rights applied for agreement to transfer, and by law approved; (5) the transfer of land use rights for the transfer of the agreement, approved by law; (6) the application for renewal of the right to use the land granted, approved by the review of the renewal.

3) Tendering for urban land use rights: Tendering for the assignment of state-owned land use rights refers to the act of inviting specific or unspecified citizens, legal persons, and other organizations to participate in the bidding for state-owned land use rights by issuing a tender notice by the land administrative department of the municipal or county people's government and determining the land users according to the bidding results. It refers to the way in which units or individuals who meet the conditions for transfer bid for the right to use a certain plot of land within a specified period in the form of sealed written bids in accordance with the conditions proposed by the transferor, and the bidding team opens and evaluates the bids and finally determines the successful bidder on the basis of merit. The content of the bids is determined by the bidding team, which may specify only the bid price, or may specify both the bid price and a planning and design plan, and the bid opening, evaluation, and decision shall be notarized by a notary public. The method of tendering for the assignment is mainly applied to some large or critical development plans and investment projects.
4) Auction of urban land use rights: Auctioning of state-owned land use rights is an act of issuing an auction notice by the grantor, with bidders bidding publicly at a specified time and place and determining the land user based on the results of the bidding. The auction method introduces a competitive mechanism, eliminates artificial interference, and allows the government to obtain the highest revenue and increase fiscal revenue substantially. This method is mainly applicable to commercial, financial, tourism, and entertainment land with good investment environment, large profits and strong competition, especially in prime locations of large- and medium-sized cities.
5) Urban land use rights listing: Listing and transfer of state-owned land use rights is the act of issuing a listing notice by the transferor, announcing the transaction conditions of the land to be transferred to the designated land trading places according to the period specified in the notice, accepting the bidder's application for quotation and updating the listing price, and determining the land user according to the bid results at the end of the listing period.

In China, the following land must be acquired through bidding, auction, or listing: industrial, commercial, tourism, entertainment, and commercial residential land; same land having two or more interested parties; and land in which there is a change in the use of allocated land use rights. "State-owned land allocation decision" or laws, regulations, administrative provisions, etc., should clearly specify recovered land use rights, in the implementation of bidding, auction, and listing. If the land use right is transferred, the "State-owned land allocation decision" or laws, regulations, administrative provisions, etc. should be clearly withdrawn and the land use right put up for sale by bidding and auction.

(3) **Rights and obligations of the transferor and the transferee**

1) **Rights of the land use right grantor**: continued ownership of the land; collection of the land use right assignment; right of supervision and inspection; development and utilization of the land by the grantee in accordance with the period and conditions stipulated in the assignment contract; right to request administrative disposition; if the grantee does not develop and utilize the land in accordance with the statutory provisions and the period and conditions stipulated in the contract, the grantor shall, depending on the circumstances, give a warning, charge a land idling fee, or even take back the land without compensation The right to use the land shall be withdrawn. If the land user does not apply for renewal or the renewal is not approved after the expiration of the contractual term, the land use right will be withdrawn by the granting party without compensation or, under special circumstances and in accordance with the needs of the public interest, the land use right will be withdrawn in advance in accordance with the legal procedures and compensation methods; and the right to rescind the assignment contract according to law. After signing the land use right transfer contract, if the transferee fails to pay the land transfer fee as agreed, the transferor has the right to terminate the contract and the right to request compensation for breach of contract. If the transferee fails to perform its statutory and agreed obligations according to the contract, the transferor has the right to request the transferee to pay compensation for breach of contract and the right to request for arbitration or sue; and the right to submit disputes arising from matters such as land use rights to arbitration or to sue in the People's Court.
2) **Obligations of the land use right grantor**: First, the contract provides the land use right. The transferor must deliver the land use rights in accordance with the contract area and standards. Second, the land use right grantor is obliged to assist the transferee to register the land use rights in accordance with the law and receive the state-owned land use certificate. Third, the land use right grantor has to provide the transferee with relevant information and documents. The main information and documents must specify the location of the land, the surrounding environment, building density, plot ratio, environmental protection, landscaping, traffic conditions, firefighting facilities, power supply, water supply, etc. Fourth, the land use right grantor has to ensure that the transferee obtains the rights due to it. The transferor shall ensure that the rights acquired by the transferee in accordance with the contract shall not be interfered with by others.
3) **Rights of the transferee of land use rights**: The transferee has the right to use the land for a specific period of time in accordance with the law, including property rights such as possession, use, income, and disposal; the right to transfer, lease, and mortgage the land use rights in accordance with the law; the right to terminate the contract of transfer in accordance with the law (as opposed to the rights of the transferor); the right to request compensation for breach of contract

(as opposed to the rights of the transferor); and the right to bring arbitration or prosecution (as opposed to the rights of the transferor).

4) **Obligations of the transferee of land use right:** The transferee has to pay the land use right assignment and register the land in accordance with the law; develop, utilize, and operate the land in accordance with the contract and urban planning requirements; obtain the consent of the transferor and approval from relevant departments for any change in land use; return the land upon expiration of the land use term; and accept the transferor's supervision and inspection of the contract performance.

(4) **Transfer of urban land use rights**

Transfer of land use right refers to the act of land user transferring the land use right acquired according to law again, that is, the civil legal act of land use right holder transferring the land use right to others according to law within the validity of his/her right years, including as sale, exchange, or gift.

1) **Principles of land use right transfer**: First, the land is recognized, that is, all rights and obligations stipulated in the assignment contract are transferred at the same time with the land use right. Multiple transfers are possible, and the government and the new land user remain in an assignment relationship; second, property rights are consistent, that is, land use rights and ownership of buildings on the ground, as long as one is transferred, the other is also transferred with it; third, the benefits cannot be damaged, that is, the respective economic benefits must not be harmed; they must be equal, voluntary, equitable, and compensated (civil behavior). The principle of government supervision and management, that is, price declaration, tax payment (stamp duty, deed duty, VAT), and registration of transfer must be implemented.
2) **Conditions of land use right transfer**: land use right transfer, must sign the transfer contract, and transfer registration; land use right transfer, if there is a need to change the use of the original assignment contract, one must first apply to the competent land administration department and the planning department, and after examination and approval, adjust the land use right assignment before transfer; administrative allocation of land use right transfer, subject to approval by law. Land use must be in line with the "land allocation catalog," without paying the land premium, according to the transfer of registration; if it does not meet the "land allocation catalog," in line with the planning premise, the transferee to pay the land premium in accordance with the law; if land use rights transfer price is significantly lower than the market price, the city and county people's government has the right of first refusal.
3) **Ways of transferring land use rights**: First, sale and purchase. Sale and purchase is the most extensive way of transferring land use rights, and the payment of its price is the consideration of land use rights. Second, exchange. In the case of transfer of land use rights by way of exchange, the consideration for the land use rights is not the price but other property or specific property interests. The land user transfers the land use right to the transferee, thereby acquiring

other property or a specific property interest provided by the transferee. Third, it is a purchase for a price, which is between a sale and an exchange, and is similar to both a sale and an exchange. It is similar to a sale because the land use right is used as a price, and the price is like the price of a sale; it is similar to an exchange because the land use right is used as a share, and the share is like another property or a specific property interest. Fourth, as a gift. A gift is a legal act in which the landowner transfers his land use rights to the donee without compensation. If the land use right is transferred by way of gift, there is no direct consideration for the transfer of land use right, and it does not require the payment of price or the provision of property rights as the corresponding condition. Fifth, when the landowner is a natural person, the death of the landowner will cause his heirs to acquire the corresponding land use right. When the landowner is a legal person or another organization, its merger or separation will also lead to the acquisition of the corresponding land use right by the subject after the merger or separation.

3.3 Rural Land Tenure Policy Rural Land Tenure Policy and Its Practice of Separation of the Three Rights of Rural Land

China is currently promoting the reform of the rural land system, the most important of which is the "Separation of Three Rights" of ownership, contractual and management of rural contracted land, as well as the ownership, eligibility, and use of residential bases.

3.3.1 Urban–Rural Development Transition and Rural Land Policy Changes

Since the founding of New China, China's rural land system has undergone several changes, and the objectives of land policy adjustment and reform were changed from time to time. At the beginning of the founding of the country, the state carried out comprehensive land reform, abolishing the feudal system of land ownership that allowed for exploitation by the landlord class, and the peasants truly realized the ideal of "land to the tiller." The Party and the government won the support of the peasants, the largest social class at that time, and achieved the great goal of socialist revolution. During this period, land reform not only transformed agricultural production relations and liberated agricultural productivity, but also effectively consolidated the new people's power and reshaped rural social relations and rural social governance.

With the establishment of socialism, the state began to promote the transition from a traditional agricultural country to an industrialized country and established a development strategy that prioritized heavy industry. To this end, agriculture acted as a provider of primitive accumulation for industrialization, by providing low-priced agricultural products to secure low-priced food supplies, low wages, and low costs in cities (Liu 2018). Agricultural production began to unilaterally pursue large scale and communalization, and the agricultural mutual assistance and the movement of people's communes spread across the country, transforming rural land and other means of production in the direction of "large in size and collective in nature" and transforming rural land ownership from peasant to collective public ownership. The original intention of the land collectivization policy was to mobilize the maximum amount of rural labor into agricultural production, but because the agricultural collectivization movement deviated from the laws of social production development; it instead bound the agricultural production relations and reduced the efficiency of agricultural production instead of increasing it. During this period, to ensure intensive input of peasant labor on rural land and to maintain agriculture's ability to provide surplus for national consumption and national industrialization, the rural land policy revolved around the collectivization of agricultural production, and the system of collective ownership of rural land by the peasants was formally established through a series of laws and documents. Thereafter, with the country's ten-year "turmoil" until the Third Plenary Session of the Eleventh Central Committee of the Communist Party of China in 1978, which confirmed the shift of the center of national work to economic construction, originating from farmers' spontaneous practical experience of grouping, the exploration of land policy in the form of various responsibility systems, such as joint production and remuneration, became the starting point for the change in the rural land system. The country began to explore gradual, partially balanced, and diversified development of rural land system changes, and collective ownership and collective farming of the collectivization period began to change into the "dual-layer managing system" of collective ownership and farming by farmers, until the early 1980s when China established the basic rural management system with the system of household contract responsibility as the core. In the early 1980s, China established the basic rural management system with the family contract responsibility system as its core.

Relevant policy interpretation:

"the system of household contract responsibility".

1. Lin Yifu's research considered that during the period 1978—1984, the transformation of China's rural areas from the production team system to the system of household contract responsibility brought about a spectacular increase in the production of grain and other agricultural products, and the success of this reform drove market-oriented economic system reforms in both rural and urban areas.

   Source: Lin Yifu. Rural reforms and agricultural growth in China, American Economic Review, 1992, 82, 34–51.

2. Liu Shouying's research considered that the reform of the system of household contract responsibility realized the self-improvement and development of the collective ownership system and explored a new form of realization of the socialist collective ownership system in rural areas. The reform not only upheld the collective ownership system, but also changed the property rights structure of the collective ownership system of agricultural land through the "separation of the two rights" of land ownership and use. The establishment of the basic agricultural management system based on family management promoted the modernization of Chinese agriculture and became a management system adapted to the level of development of rural production at the primary stage of socialism.

Source: Liu Shouying. Rural land system reform: From the system of household contract responsibility to the separation of three rights. Economic Research Journal, 2022, 57(02): 18–26.

As the first step of reform and opening up, the reform of rural land management broke the system of collectivized agricultural production, and the adjustment of the rural land system continued the status quo of collective property rights of the "three-level ownership and team-based" ownership in which the ownership of land continued to be collectively owned by peasants, and peasant households acquired the right to use land by contract. The problem of collective members "piggybacking on this," which was common under the people's commune system, was solved. Since land policies were adjusted to suit the times and situations, the reform of the rural land system, with joint family production as its core element, was a great success, and agricultural production grew extraordinarily from the beginning of the reform to the mid-1980s. Insisting on collective ownership of land, by 1984, 99.1% of the country's basic rural accounting units had generally been contracted out to households, and the first Session of the Eighth National People's Congress in 1993 fundamentally established the legal status of the system of household contract responsibility for the first time. During this period, the state actively encouraged farmers to carry out internal restructuring of agriculture and develop the rural commodity economy, especially allowing farmers to set up enterprises on collective land, which greatly promoted the emergence of township enterprises, and China entered a period of rural industrialization. During the "golden period" of the development of rural enterprises (1978–1996), the added value of rural industries grew from less than 6% of GDP to 26% of GDP.[3] The development of rural enterprises in the countryside was facilitated by the opening of rural economic rights through reforms on the one hand and through the adjustment of rural land policies on the other.

The basic framework of the current land system in China is defined by the division of the attribution of state-owned land and rural collective land in Article 10 of the

[3] Data source: China Statistical Yearbook 2003, compiled by the National Bureau of Statistics, PRC, China Statistics Press.

1982 "Constitution of the People's Republic of China." With the all-round deepening of reform and opening up, land as a resource element began to participate in economic development and its asset capital characteristics gradually emerged. The state successively responded to the problems presented by the utilization of land resources at the policy and system level. To meet the needs of reform and opening up and the development of the market economy, many land policies began to be regulated and stabilized in the form of laws after continuous summary and adjustment in practice. In 1986, the "Land Management Law" was first promulgated; it was revised and amended four times in 1988, 1998, 2004, and 2019, thus legally regulating China's land property system and land resource utilization system. In particular, it established the basic land systems such as the state policy of arable land protection, land acquisition, land survey, land planning, and land use control, which prompted the use of rural land to be placed on the track of legalization. The year 2002 saw the introduction of the "Rural Land Contract Law," which stipulated and stabilized the rural land contract policy in the form of law and further regulated the rural contract management system.

After entering the new century, China's urbanization and industrialization accelerated, and with a large number of the rural population moving to cities and towns, a serious hollowing out problem emerged in rural areas, with the development difference between rural areas and cities under the urban–rural dual land system becoming increasingly prominent. In this context, the social and economic structure and system began to undergo a major transformation. To relieve the structural contradiction of the rural population moving to cities and towns, the state proposed a new urbanization strategy and to stop the decline of the countryside, the state proposed a rural revitalization strategy. In this process, the state began to pay increasing attention to the structural institutional mechanism concerning the protection of people's rights and interests; presently, deepening the reform of rural land system and improving the protection mechanism of farmers' land rights and interests have become the baseline of the current rural land policy reform and exploration. In 2013, the Third Plenary Session of the 18th CPC Central Committee made an overall plan to deepen reform of the rural land system, and the reform of the agricultural land system with "Separation of Three Rights" at its core in the current round of rural reform. Subsequently, the reform of land expropriation, collective management construction land into the market, and residential base system began to be piloted. In 2017, the 19th National Congress of the CPC proposed a strategy for rural revitalization and established the general requirements for the comprehensive revitalization of the countryside, under the guidance of which, the Central Document No. 1 in 2018 clearly put forth exploring the "Separation of Three Rights" of residential bases. Presently, the exploration of rural land policy reform continues to advance in depth, and pilot projects and practices are in full swing around the country; however, the summary of the policy experience needs to be refined although dealing with the relationship between farmers and land and safeguarding farmers' land rights have always been the basic principles of rural land policy reform.

3.3.2 *Exploring Rural Land Reform Policies in Different Development Periods*

Rural land policy during the land reform period (1949–1953): The "Land Reform Law of the People's Republic of China," promulgated and implemented in June 1950, clearly states that "feudal and exploitative land ownership system of the landlord class should be abolished and a peasant land ownership system should be implemented, thereby liberating the rural productive forces, developing agricultural production, and opening the way for industrialization in the new China." This law formed the legal basis for guiding land reform after the establishment of New China, and from the winter of 1950 to the spring of 1953, land reform was basically implemented in mainland China, except for some minority areas. The land reform completely destroyed feudal exploitation guidance and enabled 300 million peasants nationwide to share about 700 million mu of land and a large amount of production materials.[4] The land reform greatly mobilized the enthusiasm of the peasants, promoted the liberation of the agricultural productive forces, established the dominant position of the poor peasant-employee groups in the countryside, and consolidated the worker-peasant alliance.

Rural land policy during the collectivization period (1953–1978): After the completion of the land reform, the state put forward the general line and general task of socialist transformation. In this context, to enhance the productivity of the scattered and fragile individual agricultural economy, the Party and the government began to actively guide farmers to organize mutual aid and cooperation and take the path of collectivization. The year 1953 saw the issuance of the "Resolution of the Central Committee of the Communist Party of China on Mutual Aid and Cooperation in Agricultural Production" and the "Resolution of the Central Committee of the Communist Party of China on the Development of Agricultural Production Cooperatives," thus inaugurating the vigorous rural cooperative movement. The development of mutual agricultural production cooperatives went through the process of mutual aid groups to primary societies and then to senior societies. The primary society comprised Agricultural Production Cooperatives, characterized by land ownership and unified management, which were semi-socialist in nature. This led to the separation of land ownership and management rights; in the senior societies peasants' means of production, including land, were transformed into collective ownership of all members, which was completely socialist in nature. By the end of 1956, 96.3% of the total number of peasant households participated in primary societies, and 87.8%[5] of the total number of peasant households participated in senior societies, basically completing the socialist transformation of agriculture and the transformation from individual peasant ownership of land to socialist collective ownership. The second stage of agricultural collectivization was the period of people's communes, which

[4] Data source: The Archives of New China: The Land Reform Movement in New China, http://www.gov.cn/test/2009-08/20/content_1397342.htm, China Government Network, 2019–04-05.

[5] Data source: The Agricultural Cooperative Movement, http://cpc.people.com.cn/GB/64156/64157/4512295.html, People's Daily Online, 2019–04-05.

started from 1958 until the reform and opening up. According to the central government's thinking on agricultural and rural work at that time, people's communes were considered inevitable for the development of cooperatives, and therefore it was proposed that the transformation from small collective ownership of production teams to large collective ownership of people's communes should be actively promoted (Kong and Liu 2013). In August 1958, the central government issued the "Resolution on the Establishment of People's Communes in the Countryside," which guided the nationwide movement of people's communes. In less than three months after the Resolution was issued, the country's rural areas were basically transformed into people's communes. In the practice of people's communes, a three-tier ownership system of people's communes was gradually formed, namely, the people's commune ownership system of rural land and other means of production, the production brigade (formerly the senior commune) ownership system, and the production team ownership system, of which the production brigade ownership system was the dominant one. In September 1962, the "Draft Amendment to the Regulations on the Work of Rural People's Communes" (i.e., "Article 60" of the People's Communes) was published, which further strengthened the basic ownership system of production teams. Until 1978, when the rural reform was launched, the collective ownership system of "three levels of team-based ownership," was practiced in rural China, despite slight adjustments in between.

Rural land policy since the reform and opening up (1978–present): The reform and opening up were first explored and practiced in rural areas, and the reform in rural areas began from adjustments in the relationship between farmers and land. Dealing with the relationship between farmers and land has been the main line of the reform and development of rural land policy. After the Third Plenary Session of the 11th Central Committee of the Chinese Communist Party, the Party and the government began to examine the problems of rural land policy in the development of agricultural productivity and to face the experience of farmers' spontaneous exploration. Over the past 40 years of reform and opening up, with the country's forward social and economic development and strategic transformation, the exploration of rural land policy reform can be divided into the following aspects.

Rural land policy in the early stages of the reform and opening up (1978–1992): In the early stages of reform and opening up, the model of spontaneous exploration (contract production to households and contract work to households), which originated from the boldness of rural farmers, was recognized by the state. Thus, the system of household contract responsibility opened the prelude to the reform of the rural land system. The system of household contract responsibility is a form of agricultural production responsibility system in which peasant households contract the collective economic organization (mainly villages and groups) for production materials and tasks such as land. The system is a great creation of Chinese peasants and a product of the reform of the rural economic system. After the Third Plenary Session of the 11th Central Committee of the Communist Party of China, with the active support and strong advocacy of the central government, the system of household contract responsibility began to spread rapidly throughout the country. Central Document No. 1 in 1983 pointed out that the joint production contract system was a great creation of Chinese farmers under the leadership of the Party and a new development of the Marxist theory of agricultural cooperation in China's practice. Central Document No. 1 in 1984 emphasized that the contract period for arable land could not be less than 15 years and also encouraged the transfer of land use rights. In November 1991, the Eighth Plenary Session of the 13th CPC Central Committee adopted the "Decision of the CPC Central Committee on Further Strengthening Agricultural and Rural Work," which formally stabilized the system of household contract responsibility and the two-tier management system combining unification and division as a basic system of China's rural collective economic organizations for a long time, establishing for the first time the legal status of the family The legal status of the system of household contract responsibility was established for the first time. The system of household contract responsibility realized the separation of collective ownership of land and management rights and established a new agricultural farming model based on collective ownership of land and household-based family contract management. Compared with the collective farming model during the period of agricultural collectivization, the institutional innovation effect of family contract management is prominent, as farmers gained the right to use, profit, and transfer agricultural land for agricultural use. Under the contractual relationship of "what is handed over to the state, what is completed collectively, and the surplus is theirs," farmers are no longer bound by the collective management of production. This greatly liberated the rural productive forces, mobilized the enthusiasm of the peasants in production and management, and laid the foundation for economic development and subsequent reforms while changing the economic pattern of the countryside, which played an important role in lifting the peasants out of poverty and greatly changed the agricultural production and life of the peasants in China. In addition to the family contract responsibility system, two other important changes occurred on the road to the construction of the land legal system during this period. First, in 1982, the "Constitution" defined the framework of China's current land system in Article 10, which clarified the attribution of state-owned land and rural collective land. Second, in June 1986, China's first "Land Management Law" was introduced, marking the beginning of China's land administration toward the construction of a legal system. In addition to emphasizing the importance of arable land protection, the "Land Management Law" also allowed farmers to set up enterprises on collective land at that time, thus opening the door to rural industrialization and the emergence of township enterprises. The Party Central Committee, with Comrade Deng Xiaoping at its core, proposed to "apply the experience of rural reform to the cities and carry out a comprehensive economic system reform with emphasis on the cities." The great vitality released by the reform of the rural system in the adjustment of land relations stimulated the reform of the urban land system. In 1988, the State liberalized the restrictions on the transfer of land for compensation, breaking the shackles of the system of allocating land without compensation under the planning system and starting to establish an urban land market, thus laying a solid foundation for China's reform and opening up.

Rural land policy during the period of accelerated transformation from planned economy to market economy (1993–2002): During this period, the state accelerated the pace of development from a planned economy to a market economy, and the adjustment of rural land policy mainly centered on consolidating institutional innovation of the pre-reform and opening-up period and improving the way of land resource management. After the establishment of the basic system of joint family production and land management in rural areas, the property rights relationship between farmers and the collective as an important means of production was once again sorted out and reconstructed, after which farmers were most concerned about whether the duration of contracted land could be guaranteed by policies and institutions. By the early 1990s, the first round of land contracting was about to expire. To consolidate and stabilize the achievements of the institutional innovation of family contracted land management and encourage farmers to increase their investment in land, the "State Council of the Central Committee of the Communist Party of China on Several Policy Measures for Current Agricultural and Rural Economic Development" in November 1993 decided to extend the original land contract period for another 30 years unchanged after the expiration of 15 years; to prevent the scale of arable land operation from being constantly subdivided, it also advocated to implement the method of "increasing the number of people without increasing the land and decreasing the number of people without decreasing the land"; it also allowed land transfer and advocated a moderate scale operation (Wang 2020). In October 1992, the 14th National Congress of the Party formally proposed that "the goal of China's economic system reform is to establish a socialist market economic system," marking a new stage in the full establishment of a socialist market economic system in China. Driven by this, China's industrialization and urbanization began to develop rapidly, and the demand for land resources decreased sharply. In response to the land problems presented by the rapid economic and social development, especially the rapid loss of arable land resources and crude and wasteful land use, the "Land Management Law" was comprehensively revised in 1998, establishing a system of administrative management of land resources with arable land protection and use control as the main features (Wu 2020). This version of the "Land Management Law" also stipulates that all agricultural land converted to non-agricultural construction land be subject to land expropriation, and farmers be allowed to use collectively owned land only for the establishment of township enterprises and villagers' construction of residential houses and public facilities; further, only rural villagers can apply to obtain residential bases, thus strengthening control of rural land.

Rural land policies in the context of integrated urban–rural development (2003–2012): After entering the new century, the central government put forth the concept of scientific development by "adhering to the people-oriented approach, establishing a comprehensive, coordinated and sustainable development concept, and promoting comprehensive economic, social and human development." In response to the problems arising from the difference between urban and rural development, the state made significant adjustments to the relationship between urban and rural areas, and China's urban–rural relationship entered a stage of integrated urban–rural development. To reflect the stability and continuity of the state's policy on rural land contracting, the "Rural Land Contract Law," which came into effect in 2003, and the "Property Law" promulgated in March 2007 reaffirmed the 30-year contract period for arable land. In October 2008, the report of the Third Plenary Session of the 17th CPC Central Committee clearly stated that "farmers should be given fuller and more secure rights to land contracting and operation, and the existing land contracting relationship should be kept stable and permanent." Since then, keeping the contractual relationship of rural land "unchanged for a long time" has become the direction of development of future land system reform (Shen 2019). At the same time, the "Rural Land Contract Law" provides not only detailed regulations on the rights, procedures, methods, and responsibilities of land contracting and management, but also detailed regulations and descriptions on the principles and methods of transferring land contracting and management rights on agricultural land and replaces the previous term "land contracted management right circulation" with the term "transfer of use rights." This provided a clear legal basis for the transfer of agricultural land in China. Since 2003, China's urbanization has been developing rapidly, with the urbanization rate of the population rapidly increasing from 40.53% in 2003 to 46.99% in 2008, and the urbanization rate of the household population correspondingly increasing from 23.6% in 2003 to 33.28% in 2008, with a difference of 13.71% between the urbanization rate of the resident population and the urbanization rate of the household population in 2008. This shows the serious reality that the urbanization of land is faster than the urbanization of population, while a large number of peasants are moving into cities and towns (Qiao 2019). In this regard, the report of the Third Plenary Session of the 17th Central Committee of the Communist Party of China also proposed reform requirements in the following aspects: (1) improve the work of confirming, registering, and issuing certificates for rural land; (2) improve the right to contracted land management and guarantee farmers' rights to possession, use, and income of contracted land in accordance with the law; (3) establish and improve the market for the transfer of contracted land management rights and allow farmers to subcontract, rent, swap, transfer, share cooperation, and others; (4) improve the system of rural residential bases, strictly manage residential bases, and protect the usufruct rights of farmers' residential bases according to the law; and (5) reform the system of land acquisition, strictly define land for public welfare and business construction, gradually reduce the scope of land acquisition, and improve the compensation mechanism for land acquisition. Thus, rural land policy reform began explorations in the direction of visualizing and standardizing rural land rights, in preparation for the upcoming rural land system reform.

Rural land policy in the context of urban–rural integration development (2013 to present): The difference in development between urban and rural areas increased the state's attention and investment in rural development and rural system reform, and during this period, the state further strengthened its exploration of policies for urban–rural integration development. Since the 18th National Congress of the Communist Party of China (CPC), the process of deepening rural reform accelerated, and the implementation of the "separation of the three rights" of ownership, contracting, and management of rural land became clearly defined as the basic direction of the next stage of agricultural land reform. The "Decision of the Central Committee of the

Communist Party of China on Several Major Issues of Comprehensively Deepening Reform," reported at the Third Plenary Session of the 18th Central Committee of the Communist Party of China in November 2013, provides instructions for a comprehensive, holistic, and systematic deployment of the reform of the rural land system. The reform program of the "Decision" covers almost all aspects of land issues: (1) allowing rural collective land for business construction to be transferred, leased, or bought into the stock market, with the same rights and prices as state-owned land; (2) stabilizing the contractual relationship of rural land and keeping it unchanged for a long time, and giving the majority of farmers the right to possess, use, earn, transfer, and mortgage and guarantee the contractual land; (3) guaranteeing usufruct rights of farmers' residential bases, and reforming and improving the system of rural residential bases; and (4) guaranteeing farmers' fair share of the proceeds from land appreciation. Since then, the Central Economic Work Conference, the Urbanization Work Conference and the Rural Work Conference have developed clearer plans and arrangements for the reform of the rural land system.

In October 2017, the 19th National Congress of the CPC was held, which opened a new era of exploration of China's socialist road, and the reform entered a new journey toward the victory of building a well-off society in all aspects. To resolve the contradictions within unbalanced and insufficient development of China's urban and rural areas, the 19th National Congress report put forward the rural revitalization strategy, clearly requiring "deepening the reform of the rural land system, improving the system of separation of the 'three rights'; keeping the land contract relationship stable and unchanged for a long time, and extending it for another 30 years after the expiration of the second round of land contract," making strategic deployment and top-level design for the reform of rural land system in the new era. Under this guidance, Central Document No. 1 in 2018 calls for exploring the guarantee financing of rural contracted land management rights on the basis of improving the system of "separation of three rights" of rural contracted land, and promoting the "separation of three rights" of ownership, qualification, and use of residential bases. The 2019 Central Document No. 1 clearly puts forward the requirement to improve the construction of laws, regulations, and policy systems for implementing collective ownership, stabilizing farmers' contracting rights, and liberalizing land management rights. In November 2019, the "Opinions of the State Council of the Central Committee of the Communist Party of China on Maintaining Stable and Long-lasting Land Contracting Relations" was officially released, which clarified the basic principles of maintaining long-term stability of land contracting relations. The second round clarified that if the land contract expires, it is to be extended for another 30 years, and the contracted land shall not be disrupted and redistributed, to ensure that the vast majority of farmers' original contracted land continues to remain stable.

China is now in a period of development of historical change, and the arrangement and changes of rights of contracted land, residential land, and collective construction land in rural areas not only concern the basic rights and development opportunities of hundreds of millions of peasants, but also affect the direction of urban–rural relations and national transformation. The adjustment and institutional reform of rural land policy started early with the institutional change of reform and opening up and continues to this day, and division and reconstruction of rights are the basic thread of the reform and change of the rural land policy under collective ownership in China (Liu 2019). Currently, rural land policy reform is deepening in the direction of transformation of land assets and capital and advancing in the direction of institutional regulation and legalization. As the reform deepens, the rural land policy reform will reveal a strong vitality of institutional innovation, driving the country forward and its transformation.

3.3.3 *The Policy of "Separation of the Three Rights" Reform of Contracted Land*

(1) **Background and significance of reform**

Small-scale agriculture forms the basic national condition of China's agricultural production, and collective management and farming is inevitable in China's rural economy. The population is high in China's rural land while arable land is scarce, with about 1.4 mu of arable land per capita, which is only 40% of the world's per capita. Compared with European and American countries, China's average household cultivation land area is small, with more than 200 million farming households operating on less than 10 acres of land per household. In terms of the area of farmland operated by individual farmers, the EU is dozens of times larger than China, the US is hundreds of times larger, and Australia is thousands of times larger (Wang and Ma 2020). Resource endowment also determines the nature of small-scale agricultural production in China. Presently, with global trade integration, the prices of agricultural products in China are higher than the international market prices. While this is certainly related to the increasing cost of agricultural production, the fundamental reason is that the resource endowment of more people and less land determines that China's agricultural products do not have a comparative advantage in the international market for land-intensive agricultural products.

Small-scale agriculture has a series of drawbacks: fragmented family operations are not conducive to mechanized farming; there is low resistance to natural disasters and market risks; and there is lack of returns to scale and economic efficiency. To overcome the shortcomings of small-scale agriculture, collective management at the village and community levels must be prioritized, which is an important reason for China to insist on collective ownership of rural land. However, too much emphasis on collective management is not conducive to mobilizing farmers' enthusiasm and tends to create the problem of insufficient incentives for individual farmers. Therefore, under the constraints of China's national conditions, a balance is needed between collective management and peasant family management, and between the returns to scale of farmland management and the incentives of peasant family management. This is the basic problem facing the design and reform of China's farmland system.

With rapid urbanization, a large number of farmers are presently working in cities or moving into cities. The rural population, on the other hand, is on a continuous decline, having fallen from 796 million in 1980 to 560 million in 2020. This change in population distribution has led to a rise in the per capita area of arable land occupied by the rural population, providing an opportunity for the large-scale operation of rural land (Deng and Shao 2019). At the same time, the comparative returns of farming have declined, and new problems such as land abandonment, non-food, and non-farming have become increasingly prominent, highlighting the drawbacks of over-emphasis on decentralized farming. China's traditional institutional design of "separation of two rights" can no longer effectively respond to the real needs of rural land transfer and the expansion of the land management scale.

In this context, the reform of "separation of three rights" of contracted land is conducive to promoting appropriate flow of land, realizing large-scale operation of agricultural land, and injecting modern elements into rural development more quickly, which is a major institutional innovation in response to the changing conditions of the country. The "separation of three rights" refers to the division of land contracting and management rights into contracting and management rights, the implementation of ownership, contracting, and management rights in parallel, and efforts to promote agricultural modernization, which is another major institutional innovation in rural reform after the system of household contract responsibility. The "separation of the three rights" is a self-improvement mechanism of the basic rural management system, which is in line with the objective law of adapting the relations of production to the development of the productive forces and demonstrates the lasting vitality of the basic rural management system. It is conducive to clarifying land property relations and better safeguarding the rights and interests of farmers' collectives, contracted farmers, and business entities. It is also conducive to promoting the rational use of land resources, building a new agricultural management system, developing various forms of moderate scale operations, improving land output rate, labor productivity and resource utilization rate, and promoting the development of modern agriculture.

(2) **Objectives and principles of reform**

The objective of the reform of "separation of the three rights" of contracted land is to clarify the relationship between ownership and contracting rights, specify the relationship between contracting rights and management rights, stabilize farmers' contracting rights and guide the orderly withdrawal of contracting rights, and strengthen the control of land use and market supervision, so as to give farmers more property rights. This will gradually establish a rural land property rights system with clear attribution, complete rights, smooth flow, and strict protection, and provide a solid guarantee for developing modern agriculture, increasing farmers' income, and building a new socialist countryside.

In the reform of the "separation of the three rights," the following main principles should be followed: First, respect the will of the farmers. Adhere to the main position of the farmers, safeguard their legitimate rights and interests, give farmers the right to choose, and give full play to their initiative and creativity. Further, the need is to strengthen demonstration and guidance, not to engage in forced orders, and not to engage in one-size-fits-all policy. Second, maintain the policy bottom line. Adhere to (a) and improve the basic rural management system, (b) the collective ownership of rural land, (c) the basic status of family business, and (d) the stability of land contracting relations. It also mentions not allowing the collective ownership of rural land to collapse, not allowing reduction of arable land, not weakening food production capacity, and not do anything to the detriment of the interests of farmers. Third, adhere to the gradual. Fully understand the long-term nature and complexity of rural land system reform, maintain sufficient historical patience and prudence to promote reform, carry out reform point by point, not too hastily, and gradually upgrade the practical experience into institutional arrangements. Fourth, adhere to the local conditions. Take full account of local resource endowments and economic and social development differences, encourage practical exploration and institutional innovation, and summarize the formation of the "separation of the three rights" and identify specific paths and methods suitable for different regions.

(3) **Policy points of reform**

Continuously explore effective forms of collective ownership of rural land, implement collective ownership rights, stabilize farmers' contractual rights, liberalize land management rights, and give full play to the respective functions and overall effectiveness of the "separation of the three rights." These form the core of the "three rights of separate ownership" of contracted land in rural China. The main points of the policy are the following (Gong and Wang 2020):

1) **Always adhere to the fundamental status of collective ownership of rural land**. Collective ownership of rural land by peasants is the basis of the rural management system, which must be fully reflected and guaranteed and cannot be fictitious. People with collective ownership of land enjoy the right to possess, use, gain, and dispose of collective land in accordance with the law. The peasant collective is the subject of the right to collective ownership of land, and in the process of improving the "separation of the three rights" approach, it means to fully safeguard the peasant collective contracted land contracting, adjustment, supervision, recovery, and other rights and to give full play to the advantages and role of collective ownership of land. Peasant collective has the right to contract collective land in accordance with the law; no organization or individual may illegally interfere with it; it involves the right to adjust the contracted land due to natural disasters and other special circumstances; the right to supervise the use of contracted land by contracted farmers and business entities, and take measures to prevent and correct long-term abandonment, destruction of land, and illegal changes in land use. Contracted farmers' transfer of land contracting rights should be within the collective economic organization and agreed on by the collective farmers; transfer of land management rights must be recorded in writing to the collective farmers. If collective land is expropriated, the collective farmers have the right to comment on the compensation and resettlement program for land expropriation and other compensation in accordance with the law. By

establishing and improving the democratic deliberation mechanism of collective economic organizations, the right of collective members to information, decision-making, and supervision is effectively guaranteed to ensure the effective exercise of collective land ownership by farmers' collectives and to prevent a minority from making private grants and seeking private benefits.

2) **Strictly protect the contracting rights of farmers**. Farmers enjoy the right to contract land as per the basic management system in rural areas and to stabilize the existing land contract relationship and keep it unchanged for a long time. Land contracting rights to the contracted land offer farmers the right to possession, use, and income in accordance with the law. Collective land in rural areas is contracted by peasant families who are members of this collective economic organization, and the collective land contracting rights belong to peasant families regardless of how the management rights are transferred. No organization or individual can replace the land contract status of peasant families, and no one can illegally deprive and restrict the land contract rights of peasant families. In the process of improving the "separation of the three rights" approach, we must fully safeguard the rights of contracted farmers to use, transfer, mortgage, and withdraw from the contracted land. Contracted farmers have the right to occupy and use the contracted land, build the necessary agricultural production, ancillary and supporting facilities in accordance with the law, and organize production, operation, and disposal of products and income; farmers have the right to transfer the contracted land through transfer, exchange, lease (subcontracting), shareholding, or other means and obtain income, and no organization or individual can force or restrict the transfer of land; they have the right to set mortgage on the contracted land management rights in accordance with the law, and can voluntarily withdraw from the contracted land, with conditions to protect the contracted land to obtain the relevant subsidies. If the contracted land is expropriated, the contracted farmers have the right to receive the corresponding compensation according to the law, and those who meet the conditions have the right to receive social security costs. There is to be no illegal adjustment of farmers' contracted land and no withdrawal of land contract rights as a condition for farmers to settle in cities.
3) **Accelerate the release of land management rights**. Giving business subjects more secure land management rights is key to improving the basic rural management system. Land management rights holders have the right to possess, cultivate, and obtain corresponding income from the transferred land within a certain period of time in accordance with the law. Under the premise of protecting collective ownership and contractual rights of farmers in accordance with the law, the land management rights acquired by business subjects in accordance with the transfer contract are equally protected, and their stable business expectations are guaranteed. In the process of improving the "separation of the three rights" method, the rights required for the operation subjects to engage in agricultural production should be safeguarded in accordance with the law, so that land resources can be used more effectively and reasonably. The operating entity has the right to use the transferred land to independently engage in agricultural production and operation and obtain the corresponding income; with the consent of the contracted farmers,

it can improve the soil in accordance with the law, improve the ground, implement construction of agricultural production, ancillary, supporting facilities, and in accordance with the transfer contract obtain reasonable compensation; it has the right to renew the contracted land in accordance with the same conditions after the expiration of the transfer contract priority. The operating entity then transfers the right to operate the land or sets a mortgage in accordance with the law, subject to the written consent of the contracted farmers or their commissioned agents and to the farmers collective written record. When transferred land is expropriated, the ground attachment and seedling compensation fees should be determined in accordance with the transfer contract vesting. Contracting farmers who transfer out the right to operate the land should not prevent the operation of the main body from exercising their legitimate rights. Protection of land management rights must be strengthened and the flow of land management rights must be guided to capable cultivators and new business entities. New business entities must be supported to enhance land power, improve agricultural production conditions, and carry out mortgage financing for land management rights in accordance with the law. Use of land share cooperation, land trust, and farming on behalf of a variety of business methods must be encouraged besides exploring more effective ways to release the right to land management.

4) **Gradually improve the relationship between the "separation of the three rights"**. Collective ownership of rural land is a prerequisite for the right to contract land, and the right of farmers to contract management is a specific form of collective ownership; in land transfer, the right of farmers to contract management derives from the right to operate land. There must be support in practice to actively explore specific ways of farmers' collective exercise of collective ownership in accordance with the law, supervision of contracted farmers and business entities to regulate the use of land, etc. Encourage in-depth theoretical research on issues such as the boundaries of the rights of farmers' collectives and contracted farmers on contracted land and the rights of contracted farmers and operating entities in land transfer and the relationship between their mutual rights. Through practical exploration and theoretical innovation, the need is to gradually improve the relationship between the "separation of the three rights" and provide strong support for the implementation of the same.

3.3.4 The Policy of "Separation of the Three Rights" of Residential Bases

(1) **Background and significance of reform**

As a legacy and an innovation based on the "separation of two rights," the "separation of the three rights" of residential bases is necessarily related to the latter in terms of logical dependence and marginal changes. At the beginning of the founding of New China, residential bases in China were owned by farmers, and the subjects of ownership and use rights were both farmers. During the period of the people's commune, the ownership and use rights of the house bases and the houses on the land were gradually separated. The ownership of residential bases belongs to the collective, and the right to use them belongs to the farmers, but renting and buying are prohibited; the ownership and right to use the houses on the ground belong to the farmers, and the farmers have the right to buy, sell, or rent the houses. In the early stage of reform and opening up, the nature of collective ownership of residential bases was further consolidated, and the right to use was restricted; buying, selling and renting residential bases were strictly prohibited, but the scope of the subjects of residential bases was extended to some urban residents. After entering the new century, the subjects of the homestead use right bases were further strictly limited to members of the rural collective economy, thus gradually forming the current residential base system with the main features of "public ownership of residential land and separation of the two rights; specific subjects and welfare distribution; one household and one residential area; restriction on transfer and prohibition of mortgage" (Li 2021). This residential base system based on the dual structure of urban and rural areas has historically played an important role in guaranteeing farmers' housing and maintaining social stability in rural areas. With the profound changes in the economic, social, demographic, and spatial structures of urban and rural areas in China, the "separation of the two rights" residential base system, which is purely oriented to maintain fairness and justice, has been declining and has almost failed; gradually it has become the most backward institutional land arrangements in China. The problems of difficulty in approval, poor withdrawal, sloppy utilization, idle waste, invisible transactions, and illegal transfer became increasingly prominent (Shi 2020). Giving property value to residential bases, striking a balance between fairness and efficiency, and coordinating stability and liberalization became important value orientations of residential base reform. After the 18th Party Congress, China introduced a series of policies and measures around the reform of the rural house base system. From the reform of the rural land acquisition system to the exploration of the market of rural collective construction land, from the pilot mortgage loan for the property right of agricultural houses to the pilot of the house base system, the "separation of three rights and disposition" of house bases has gradually become an important issue in the context of rural revitalization. It gradually became the policy orientation of the reform of rural house base system in the context of rural revitalization.

The homestead system combines the dual attributes of an economic system and a legal right system. The root of the existing residential base problem lies in the hedge between historical welfare distribution and real land capital market, population mobility, and land consolidation, and the hedge between residential security function and property value function (Kang et al. 2019). Revitalizing idle land in rural areas, promoting the flow of land elements, expanding new rural industries, broadening the channels of farmers' income increase, and realizing the integrated development of urban and rural areas have become important goals in China's residential base reform. However, under the current institutional framework, the revitalization of residential bases and farmers' housing use rights face a dilemma: the homestead use right bases is an exclusive right enjoyed by members of rural collective economic organizations, and once social subjects outside of rural collective economic organizations directly acquire the homestead use right bases, it means loss of the advantage of membership in rural collective economic organizations. Directly expanding the scope of trading of residential base use rights and attracting urban capital and social capital to enter the residential base trading market may be conducive to releasing the property value of residential bases, but it can impact the nature of collective ownership of rural land in China. On the contrary, to simply limit the scope of the transfer of the homestead use right bases to the narrow space of "within the collective economic organization" is not only contrary to the policy intent of integrated urban–rural development, but also limited by the market space, which cannot realize the original reform intention of revitalizing idle residential bases. A legal system of rural residential land use rights that meets the real social needs of China cannot be replaced by other systems to achieve the most basic social equity and cannot completely disregard the efficiency of the residential land use system. The two value objectives must be realized in the same system, which is the basic requirement for the development of fairness and efficiency in modern society and is also a major theoretical problem facing the improvement of the legal system of the right to use rural residential bases in China.

(2) **Objectives and principles of reform**

The fundamental purpose of the "separation of the three rights" of residential bases is to reconstruct the bundle of rights of residential bases use rights, separate the qualification rights and use rights, balance the separation of security and property rights, and effectively coordinate the political function of ownership, security function of qualification rights, and property function of use rights, so as to achieve a balance among political stability, social equity, and economic benefits. According to the modern property rights theory, property rights (a) originate from scarcity of resources, (b) determine economic performance, and (c) are finely allocated to the corresponding subjects to achieve efficiency optimization. The essence of "separation of the three rights" of residential land is to refine the property rights of residential land into ownership, qualification, and use rights, and through the corresponding institutional arrangement, the rights are reasonably allocated among different subjects, so as to achieve the structural balance, functional balance, value balance, and income balance of the rights. From the perspective of institutional economics, the "separation of the three rights" of residential bases holds meaning in three levels: first, the property right bundle of residential bases is refined into ownership, qualification, and use rights, and the three rights are separated; second, the subjects of residential bases are expanded to provide a broader scope, going beyond the members of the rural collective economic organizations; third, the property right function of residential bases is expanded from the pure function of residence protection to the business functions of production, service, rental, and sale. As a kind of theoretical and practical innovation, the reform of "separation of the three rights" of residential bases has further enriched the property rights system of residential bases from the perspective of the optimal allocation of property rights and has resolved the dilemma of the reform of residential bases, laying the foundation for equal exchange and optimal allocation of urban and rural factors (Zhang 2019).

The main principles of the "separation of the three rights" are: 1. one house for one family, and the area does not exceed the standard; 2. in line with the planning, approval according to law; 3. after selling or renting, no further application, and residential bases cannot be used for mortgage; 4. urban residents are prohibited from purchasing residential bases in rural areas; 5. respect the will of the farmers. Prohibit the forced transfer of residential bases against the will of rural villagers, prohibit the withdrawal of residential bases as a condition for rural villagers to settle in the city, and prohibit the forced relocation of rural villagers to withdraw from residential bases.

(3) **Policy points of reform**

Similar to the reform of the rural contracted land "three rights separation," the core policy point of the reform of the "three rights of rural residential land" also lies in the implementation of the "separation of the three rights," that is, ownership, eligibility, and use.

1) **To implement the collective ownership rights**. According to the law, collective ownership rights include the four rights of possession, use, income, and disposal. However, due to the imperfections of peasant collective economic organizations and unsound governance mechanisms in many places in China, it is difficult to exercise the collective ownership rights in their entirety. In reality, peasant collectives have exercised rights of possession and distribution relatively adequately, but they lack effective mechanisms for exercising the rights of disposition and income, resulting in a certain degree of fictitiousness in collective ownership. To implement the collective ownership of residential bases, the core is to define the subjects of collective ownership at the legal level, to give complete rights, including income and disposal, and to improve the mechanism of exercising the rights. The basic path is to formulate the law on rural collective economic organization, improve the legal personality, clarify the relationship between rights and obligations, improve the governance mechanism, and implement its right to income and disposal of collective resources and assets, including rural residential bases.
2) **To protect the qualification rights of farmers**. After the reform of the residential bases' "three rights separation," the farmers' homestead use right bases under the existing pattern of "separation of two rights" will be carried by the farmers' qualification right, so as to realize the function of residential bases for residential protection. Presently, there is a wide divergence in the understanding of the attributes of farmers' qualification rights of residential bases. From the evolution of the residential base system, the farmers' residential base is a right based on the identity of collective membership and carries the function of residential security for farmers. In this sense, farmers' qualification right is not a brand new right, but a technical treatment of the identity right of members under the collective ownership system. In practice, since the actual situation varies greatly from place to place, the identification of qualification rights should be conducted in conjunction with the reform of the rural collective property rights

system, with emphasis on exploring the identification methods, exercise conditions, and realization methods of qualification rights, as well as the realization paths of special circumstances such as renunciation, loss, and reacquisition of qualification rights.

3) **The right to use should be appropriately released**. The use right is the focus of the reform of the "Separation of Three Rights" of residential bases, and the use right after relaxation carries the function of optimizing the allocation of resources and safeguarding farmers' property rights; its value can be realized only through transfer and transaction; the term "moderation" also provides the bottom line for the scope of residential bases. The use of the term "moderate" also draws the bottom line for the scope of release of the right to use. Therefore, the next reform path should be based on the bottom line and efforts should be made in two directions. The first is to improve the construction of the rural property rights transfer market by exploring various paths to release the residential bases use right, increase the export for the transfer of the homestead use right bases, optimize the efficiency of resource allocation, and realize the property rights of farmers' residential bases. The second is to combine reform matters such as the paid use of residential bases and voluntary paid withdrawal, to open up the conversion channel between residential bases and collective construction land, to improve the policy system of revitalizing idle residential bases and farmhouses, and to give complete rights to the main body of utilization.

3.3.5 Optimization of the Policy of "Separation of Three Rights" of Rural Land

(1) **Optimization of the policy of "separation of three rights" of contracted land**

The system of "separation of three rights" of contracted land in rural areas is significant in promoting standardized use and optimal allocation of land resources, protecting the legitimate rights and interests of operators, and enhancing their enthusiasm to engage in agricultural production and operation. To promote and improve the system of "separation of three rights" of contracted land and consider some problems encountered in China's current practice, the future policy of "separation of three rights" of contracted land should be improved and optimized at the following levels.

1) **Sound supporting laws and policy interpretations for the "separation of powers" reform**. Relevant departments and institutions should strengthen theoretical research, form a unified understanding of the "separation of the three rights," reform, clarify the interlocking relationships, and the rights boundaries of the "separation of the three rights"; continue to strengthen the top-level design of the "separation of the three rights" reform and improve the rigidity and authority of the policy interpretation in a timely manner; adopt the principle of "no change in ownership, stable contracting rights, and market access" as the basis for reform,

standardize land transfer procedures, protect and strengthen the legitimate rights and interests of the three parties; and establish as soon as possible a sound policy system to promote the development of business entities and carry out reform of agricultural subsidies. The state's agricultural inputs, subsidies, and insurance are more reasonable, targeted, and effective. Through the "stock adjustment, incremental tilt" subsidy policy, the existing policies are optimized and tilted to new business entities (Qu and Dong 2021). At the same time, the issue of land ownership after the end of the rural land contract period should be planned in advance.

2) **Speed up the registration of rural land circulation management rights**. The issue of confirming the rights of rural contracted land is not only a prerequisite for the "separation of the three rights" but also an institutional guarantee of farmers' property. Therefore, it is necessary to verify and accurately register the location, area, quality, ownership, and boundary of each plot of land and to apply new technologies to improve efficiency and reduce the cost of land titling in the process of land titling investigation, verification, and audit. Government departments should increase support, strengthen funding and fund management, and ensure that funds are earmarked for this purpose; and carry out extensive publicity to make farmers fully aware of their rights and interests involved in land titling to gain their support for the titling process. To gain farmers' support for the work of land titling, an arbitration body for land titling disputes should be set up, preferably jointly composed of personnel from the departments responsible for titling, so as to facilitate the arbitration of land with disputed titling. For those disputes that are difficult to resolve in the near future, identify the location, area and reasons for their formation, maintain the status quo for the time being and designate the disputed area, and wait until the dispute is resolved before publicizing and registering (Wang 2021).
3) **Construct and improve the market for land management rights transfer**. Relevant departments should take the opportunity of the "separation of the three rights" reform to improve the policies and mechanisms related to the land management rights transfer market, strengthen services and supervision, standardize the land transfer platform, and regulate the land transfer procedures. They also need to strengthen the policy propaganda and explanation work, enhance farmers' awareness of property rights, eliminate their ideological concerns, and increase their enthusiasm to participate in the transfer. The relevant departments need to improve the transfer method, on the basis of adhering to the farmers' voluntary, more collective entrusted transfer, whole piece transfer, to reduce disputes and improve transfer efficiency; the need is also to innovate the form of transfer, in the form of share cooperative transfer, shareholding guaranteed dividend transfer, etc., to build a community of interests between the operating body and the contracting body, and stabilize the transfer. The functions of the land transfer service department and the land arbitration department should be improved to give full play to their roles of transfer information dissemination, transfer value assessment, contract file management, and dispute mediation and arbitration. They must strengthen the supervision of land-transfer operators,

explore the establishment of a system of agricultural business qualification for land-transfer transferees, strengthen land use control, stop and investigate and deal with the "non-agriculturalization" of arable land and the destruction of arable land, and strengthen the supervision of the whole process of land transfer and post-event tracking (Chen et al. 2020). We should build a scientific and systematic evaluation system for the reform of the "separation of the three rights," summarize and promote the successful experiences of pilot areas, and timely identify and resolve the problems arising from the reform.

4) **Carry out mortgage financing of land contracted management right properly**. In addition to improving the laws and policies on mortgage financing of land contracted management right, ways must be explored to dispose of the collateral according to the degree of development of the mortgage market and standards constructed for evaluating the value of land management rights besides forming an institutional system. Rural credit guarantee entities must be supported, financial institutions guided to increase credit support for agriculture, and channels provided for financing new agricultural business entities. There is a need to construct a supervisory service platform for rural collective asset transactions, strengthen the dissemination of information on the transfer of rural contracted land and mortgages, regulate the transfer of rural contracted land and mortgage transactions, and improve the credibility of the supervisory platform.
5) **Vigorously cultivate new agricultural business entities**. The implementation of the "separation of the three rights," the release of management rights, and the development of modern agriculture all require the participation of new agricultural business entities. The requirement is to promote the joint development of new business subjects such as family farms, farmers' professional cooperatives, and leading agricultural industrialized enterprises, support the creation of model family farms with the policy system of land, capital, and talents, and improve the quality of farmers' professional cooperatives and cultivate leading agricultural enterprises. Further, the need is to guide new business entities and contracted farmers to establish a close interest linkage mechanism, so that farmers can also share the dividends of modern agricultural management; support the development of new agricultural business entities from the financial, credit insurance, taxation, and other aspects of mutual integration; strengthen agricultural policy insurance, rationalize the "common insurance body" work system, and further expand the coverage of agricultural policy insurance, and continuously improve the level of insurance.

(2) **Optimization of the policy of "separation of the three rights" for residential bases**

The "separation of the three rights" is not only an optimization of the property right system of residential bases, but also a reconstruction of urban–rural relationship in the new era. In view of the practical difficulties in the current "separation of the three rights" of residential bases in China, future policies related to the "separation of the three rights" of residential bases in China should continue to explore and improve in the following aspects.

1) **Construct a mechanism to balance interests**. Balancing the interests of the state, the collective and the individual, and fully protecting the rights and interests of farmers is the key to the reform of "separation of three rights." On the one hand, it is necessary to adhere to the market-oriented reform and improve the rural residential base trading market. With reference to the urban housing transaction system and the rural land contracted management right transfer system, the need is to establish the supply and demand, price, competition, and risk mechanisms for rural residential bases transactions, continuously improve the residential bases property rights transaction service system, and actively cultivate specialized service organizations such as residential bases property rights transaction witness, registration, consultation, evaluation, agency, conflict, and dispute resolution institutions and agricultural land transfer information network platform. On the other hand, we should further improve the rural social security system and establish a comprehensive farmers' residence protection system. Combined with national policies related to the construction of new-type urbanization, a housing security system for the agricultural transfer population should be established, and farmers who quit their residential bases to buy and rent houses in the city should be given preferential policies such as tax exemptions for house purchases and rental subsidies, and farmers who enter the city should be included in the scope of public rental housing and low-cost housing policies. At the same time, on the basis of the existing new rural cooperative medical insurance and new rural pension insurance, the social security system in rural areas should be improved, a unified social security system in urban and rural areas should be established, the level of social security for farmers should be improved, and the proceeds of rural collective land and assets, etc. must be used to pay social security contributions to farmers' collectives.
2) **Improve the rural grass-roots governance system** (Yang 2021). With the deepening of the reform of the "separation of the three rights" of residential bases, the basis, conditions, content, path, and mode of rural grassroots governance will undergo profound changes, and to effectively promote the reform of the "separation of three rights," the rural governance system must be improved. The first is to play the leading role of grassroots party organizations. Take the newly promulgated "Regulations of the Communist Party of China on the Work of Rural Grassroots Organizations" as a guideline, build a strong basic team, speed up the training of raw power, and let young and excellent power accelerate to become the backbone of the village party organizations. Second, we should integrate rural governance resources, place the subjective rights of peasant groups in the logic of rural social governance, improve the current plight of rural governance from the subjective needs of peasants, and ensure a benign interaction between the state and peasants, and peasants and grassroots power; focus on the cultivation of bottom-up endogenous autonomous organizations in rural society, and give full play to the mass mobilization advantages of various social organizations, especially in rural infrastructure construction, conflict and dispute resolution, and public service. Third, we should improve the level of rule of law in rural governance. Use the rule of law to build a rural governance system

with expected social behavior, open management process, and clear definition of responsibilities. Strengthen the legal constraints on the rural grassroots government and grassroots cadres, exercise their powers in accordance with the law, deal with affairs in accordance with the law, and strengthen the guidance of village governance, prevention, and supervision of various problems in rural areas in accordance with the law.

3) **Optimize national macro-control methods** (Wei 2021). As a kind of property rights system change, the "separation of the three rights" of residential bases requires the state to play an effective regulatory role in the use control, tax subsidy, and supervision and governance. First, according to the government's guidance, diversified capital participates in setting up a risk management fund for the "separation of the three rights" of rural residential bases to guarantee the risk prevention and benefit compensation of farmers who transfer the right to use residential bases in terms of housing resettlement. Further, the need is to improve the policy of insurance for residential bases ownership transactions, increase financial subsidies, encourage insurance institutions to develop the types and scope of insurance for residential bases ownership transactions, and gradually expand to home base replacement, guarantee, mortgage, transfer, withdrawal, and other aspects, and encourage areas with conditions to carry out pilot insurance for rural residential bases ownership transactions. Second, there is a need to set up special subsidies for residential bases retreat, and for farmers who voluntarily vacate their residential bases, with reference to the value of the residential bases, the local consumption level, urban and rural residents' income, and other factors, to give different levels of financial subsidies. The financial subsidies can be shared by the central and local finances. Third, to reduce or waive the tax on residential base transactions, to temporarily waive all kinds of transaction taxes in the preliminary residential base ownership transactions, and to appropriately reduce the corresponding taxes and tax amounts in the future in a gradual way. Further, the need is to establish a mechanism to return the tax on rural residential base transactions and return the collected tax on residential base transactions to rural infrastructure construction, public service supply, and the improvement of the human living environment. Fourth, the state must strengthen the planning to lead. It must connect the reform of "separation of three rights" with the spatial planning of rural revitalization, strengthen the planning and management of rural land use and rural construction, actively promote the "integration of multiple regulations," and prepare rural land use planning according to local conditions.
4) **Constructing a legal system of "separation of three rights"**. With the changes in the social foundation and value objectives of the land system, there is an urgent need to construct a legal system that is compatible with the reform of "separation of the three rights" of residential bases. First, we must systematically sort out the relevant provisions of the "Land Administration Law of the People's Republic of China," "The Law on the Administration of Urban Real Estate," "Property Law," "Security Law," "Inheritance Law," and other laws on residential bases, place the revision and improvement of these laws and regulations in the macro context of urban–rural integration and development, take the

free flow of elements and fair trade as the orientation, consider the elimination of conflicts and contradictions between various legal norms, and ensure that the residential bases conform to the unity and coherence of the laws related to the reform of "separation of three rights." Second, we must study and formulate the "Law on Rural Residential Bases and Farmers' Houses," to clearly stipulate in the form of law the nature and power of the right to use residential bases, the way to establish the right and the form of registration, the scope and conditions, rights and obligations of the right to use, the way to transfer the right to use house bases, the evaluation of land value, mortgage, and disposal, the supervision and management of the right to use house bases, the rights and obligations of industrial and commercial capital to obtain the right to use house bases, the rights and obligations of the right to use house bases, and the rights and obligations of the right to use house bases. The policies and regulations related to mortgage evaluation and disposal should ensure the smooth implementation of the reform of "separation of the three rights." Third, to speed up the formulation and introduction of the "Law on Rural Collective Economic Organizations," taking the newly promulgated "Civil Code" as the guiding principle and drawing on the experience of the pilot areas, there is a need to clarify the role, functions, attributes, status, and structure of rural collective economic organizations and to clarify the rights and obligations of rural collective economic organizations and other organizations and their members.

References

Chen S et al (2020) Property rights decomposition and policy improvement of "Tripartite Entitlement System" of farmland. China Land Sci 34(10):42–48

Chi Y (2021) Practice of social stability risk assessment of collective land acquisition under the new land law. Shanghai Real Estate 04:30–34

Deng H, Shao J (2019) Cultivated land protection zoning based on population flow and cultivated land location conditions a case study of Shizhu County. Chongqing Municipality J Southwest Univ (natural Science Edition) 41(03):40–48

Du W (2021) Reform of rural land acquisition system from the perspective of China's civil law. Rural Econ Sci-Technol 32(14):292–294

Feng Y, Wang X (2019) Land finance, financial development and urban expansion. J Guizhou Univ Financ Econ 01:25–36

Gong M, Wang T-H (2020) The influence mechanism of the separation of three rights of agricultural land on the endogenous development of agriculture in China. Reform Econ Syst 01:73–80

Gui H (2016) Discussing the legality of the dual system of urban and rural construction land–and the constitutional order of land in China. Law Rev 34(01):31–41

Huang X (2019) Establishment of the integrated urban-rural construction land market system. China Land Sci 33(08):1–7

Jiang W (2015) Considerations on the market entry of rural land for collective management and construction in China based on Taiwan's "sectional expropriation" system. Rural Econ Sci-Technol 26(07):27–29

Kang D et al (2019) Exploration on the utilization mode of residential bases in the context of "three rights separation." China Land 03:46–47

Kong X, Liu T (2013) On China's basic rural management system: history, challenges and choices. China Rev Polit Econ 4(04):78–133

Li J (2021) The connotation, practice and breakthrough of "three rights of rural residential bases"-based on the practice of residential base system reform in 15 pilot counties. J Shandong Agric Univ (social Science Edition) 23(03):24–28

Li L et al (2015) Breaking the urban-rural land use dichotomy: theoretical dilemmas and practical dilemmas. Rural Econ Sci-Technol 26(05):22–25

Liu S (2019) The changes in collective land rights system and agricultural performance-a review of research on agricultural land system during China's forty Years' reform. J Agrotech Econ 1:4–16

Liu S (2018) Land system and China's development. China Renmin University Press

Liu Y et al (2021) Research on the model and characteristics of in situ urbanization: a case study of four villages in Hebei Province. Urban Dev Stud 28(06):10–16

Liu S, Xiong X (2018) Dual-track urbanization under the dual land ownership system. Urban Plan Forum 01:31–40

Liu Z (2020) Reflections on legal issues related to land acquisition compensation and resettlement agreement. China Land 07:19–21

Lu M et al (2018) Institution and city: how traditional land property rights protection enhances the efficiency of new town construction. Econ Res J 53(06):171–185

Lu D, Wang S (2021) An analysis of the transfer of rural land contract management rights. Mod Agric 04:84–85

Qiao X (2019) Household registration system, urbanization and great population flow. J Popul Econ 2019(05):1–17

Qu Z, Dong K (2021) Perception and the context of Institution: the second-ordered deconstruction for institutional transition with constructivist institutionalism. Chin Public Adm 08:84–92

Rong C (2020) The orientation and initiatives of reforming the land revenue distribution system in China-based on the perspective of different interest subjects. Macroecon Manag 06:13–22

Shen S (2019) The introspection and reconstruction of entitlement relation on China rural land: perspective of the public ownership realization form. Issues Agric Econ 09:19–30

Shi C (2020) The connotation, obstacle and outlet of the separation of three rights of rural residential land. Nat Resour Econ China 33(10):39–43

Wang J (2021) On the idea of deepening the reform of the division of three rights under the goal of modernization of agricultural land system. J Shandong Agric Univ (Social Science Edition) 23(01):38–40

Wang Y (2020) An analysis of the transfer of rural land contract management rights in the context of rural revitalization. Agric Econ 09:80–82

Wang F, Ma S (2020) An analysis of the impact of arable land and population changes on the transformation and upgrading of smallholder economies in China. Rural Econ Sci-Technol 31(11):33–34

Wei L (2021) How to understand the "three rights of rural residential bases" and the outstanding problems in management. Chin Village Discov 01:46–51

Wu Y, Sun X (2018) The review and prospect of land use policy in China after the 40 years of reform and opening up: an urbanization perspective. China Land Sci 32(07):7–14

Wu Z (2020) Internal conflict and adjustment of land management right system. China Land Sci 34(07):9–16

Wu Z (2021) A brief discussion on the impact of collective management construction land in the market on rural development. Real Estate World 21:21–23

Xia F et al. (2020) Urban-rural land bank system: an exploration of new urban-rural land capitalization system. China Land Sci 34(04):48–57

Xu K (2021) A brief discussion on the practice of land acquisition after the implementation of the new land management law. China Land 01:48–50

Xu G (2018) The influencing factors of landless farmer' willingness to accept from the perspective of land attachment. J Land Econ 02:26–40

Yan J, Feng L (2019) Land supply regulation, housing supply elasticity and housing price fluctuation. China Land Sci 33(03):16–24
Yang T (2021) A study on the system of separation of three rights of rural residential bases in China. Mod Agric Res 27(08):147–148
Yao H (2020) Institutional roots of factor price distortions in China and ideas for reform. Econ Res Guid 05:6–7
Yiheng L (2021) Normative change and functional turn of land expropriation compensation clause in China. Nanjing J Soc Sci 11:83–91
Yong Z, Li Z, Shangui P (2021) Research progress and prospects for "Tripartite Entitlement System" of rural residential land: based on bibliometrics analysis. China Land Sci 35(06):105–114
Yue W, Wang T (2019) Rethinking on the basic issues of territorial and spatial use control in China. China Land Sci 33(08):8–15
Zhang L, Yan C (2020) Land renting tax and land financial evolution: economic logic based on public goods financing. J Yunnan Univ Financ Econ 36(06):3–16
Zhang L (2019) The function and realization path of "Three Rights Separation" of residential land in the context of new Urbanization. Rural Econ Sci-Technol 30(15):41–42
Zhao Y (2020) Research on the implementation in the path of urbanization urban-rural fringe area. Beijing University of Technology

Chapter 4
Land Development Policies

Siliang Wang and Shukui Tan

Land development is one of the key dimensions of land use, the purpose of which is to use land for a range of economic development activities related to urbanization, industrialization and agricultural modernization, including using land for the construction of various buildings and infrastructure, as well as using arable land for agricultural production. Under the institutional arrangement of dual urban–rural land ownership, following the unified requirements of the central government and exercising their own autonomy, local governments in China have implemented a set of land development policies to achieve economic and social development goals, with control of the land element at the core and relying on the institutionalized operation of government power. This chapter first outlines how the Chinese government controls land development under the framework of the major function zoning system, and then details the respective land development policies in urban and rural areas and policies involving the conversion of land from rural collective owned to the state-owned status, including, first, the market-oriented supply policies for urban land paid use; second, development policies corresponding to various types of rural land, namely the rural land contract management system and transfer policies, direct supply-to-market of rural profit-oriented construction land, and rural residential land system; and third, land expropriation system through which rural land can be converted to urban land for development. For each type of policy, this chapter integrates both historical and current perspectives, not only sorting out its historical evolves, but also highlighting how it operates in the present.

S. Wang (✉)
Hunan University, Changsha, China
e-mail: wangsiliang@hnu.edu.cn

S. Tan
Huazhong University of Science and Technology, Wuhan, China

S. Tan and X. Huang (eds.), *Land Policy in China*, The Frontier of Public Administration in China, https://doi.org/10.1007/978-981-19-9895-9_4

4.1 Major Function Zoning System and Land Development Control

Land space is the home and valuable resource for human beings to survive and reproduce. China has more than 9.6 million square kilometers of land territory and vast ocean territory. In order to scientifically develop and reasonably plan land space, China has pioneered the implementation of the major function zoning in the world as a fundamental system for regulating the development and protection of land space. In 2010, the State Council issued the National Plan for Major Function Zoning as a basic basis for promoting the formation of major function areas, providing a guide for scientific development of national land space and showing a visionary blueprint for this action. This plan is strategic, fundamental and binding, which means that, firstly, it is the general deployment of the future development of national land space from the perspective of the overall and long-term situations; secondly, it is prepared on the basis of a comprehensive evaluation of all basic elements of land space, and is the basic basis for the preparation of other types of spatial planning and a basic platform for the formulation of regional policies; finally, the scope, positioning and development principles of the major function areas specified in the plan are binding for all kinds of development activities. Overall, the plan clarifies the elements of the major function zoning system implemented in China. Although the *Opinions on Establishing a Territorial Spatial Planning System and Supervising its Implementation*, issued by the Central Committee of the Communist Party of China and the State Council in 2019, proposed to "integrate spatial planning such as major function zoning, land use planning, and urban–rural planning into a unified territorial spatial planning", the governance logic related to the major function zoning strategy, i.e. rational control of land development, continues to play an important role in the implementation of place-based development policies in China.

4.1.1 Definitions of Major Function, Major Function Area, and Major Function Zoning

The major function refers to the functional localization of a specific territorial spatial unit that matches the resource and environmental carrying capacity, existing development density and development potential of the region, which reflects the optimal function formed by the mutual coupling of human socio-economic and natural systems.

On this basis, the major function area can be defined as a spatial unit with a certain type of major function formed by determining the development concept, direction and mode according to the factors such as endowment base, resource and environmental carrying capacity and strategic positioning in the region at different scales.

The major function zoning can be described as the following: in order to achieve the top-down goal of national land space protection and utilization, by considering the natural and social conditions such as population, resources, environment and economic status, to determine the development orientation of different areas, to clarify the function and structure of spatial production, to formulate the development policy and intensity, to accelerate the transformation of economic development model and spatial structure adjustment, to promote spatial production within each function area, to form a pattern of national land space development that coordinates resource environmental protection and economic development needs, and to realize the efficient utilization of land space.

There are a series of benefits to implement the major function zoning, including being conducive to promoting the restructuring of economic structure, accelerating the transformation of the development mode and achieving scientific development; being conducive to promoting coordinated regional development, narrowing the gap across regions in terms of basic public services and living standards; being conducive to guiding the population distribution and economic layout to adapt to the carrying capacity of resources and environment, and promoting the spatial balance of population, economy, and resources; being conducive to reversing the trend of ecological and environmental deterioration at source, promoting resource conservation and environmental protection, coping with and mitigating climate change, and achieving sustainable development; being conducive to breaking the boundaries of administrative divisions, formulating and implementing more targeted regional policies and performance assessment and evaluation systems.

4.1.2 Backgrounds of Introducing and Implementing the Major Function Zoning System

The Chinese government's decision to introduce and implement the major function zoning system depends on the following background factors: inherent natural endowments, many challenges faced in the process of economic and social development, and the judgment of future trends.

(1) **Endowments**

According to the comprehensive evaluation of land resources, water resources, environmental capacity, ecosystem vulnerability, ecosystem importance, natural disaster risk, population concentration, as well as the level of economic development and transportation advantage, China's land space has the following characteristics from the perspective of promoting industrialization and urbanization:

1) **The land space is vast, but the area suitable for development is small.** China's land space is vast, ranking third in the world, but there are many mountains and few flatlands, and about 60% of the land space is mountainous and plateau. The area suitable for industrialization and urbanization has more than 1.8 million square kilometers, but after deducting the arable land and existing construction land that must be protected, only about 280,000 square kilometers can be used for industrialization and urbanization and other construction in the future, accounting for about 3% of the total land area of the country. The relatively small area of land suitable for development determines that China must take the development path of space conservation and intensification.

2) **The total amount of water resources is abundant, but the spatial distribution is uneven**. China's total water resources is 2.8 trillion cubic meters, ranking sixth in the world, but the per capita level is only 28% of the world's per capita possession. The spatial distribution of water resources is uneven, and does not match with land resources and economic layout. The amount of water resources in the southern region accounts for 81% of the country, while that in the northern region accounts for only 19%; the supply and demand of water resources in the northern region is tight, and the degree of water resources exploitation has reached 48%. Water pollution, water ecology and environmental degradation problems are prominent, and some water-abundant areas in the south even have a pollution-induced water shortage. Water shortage not only affects the economic development, but also restricts the balanced distribution of population and economy, and brings many ecological problems.
3) **Energy and mineral resources are abundant in variety, but relatively short in quantity overall**. China's energy and mineral resources are relatively abundant and complete in variety, but the per capita possession of major fossil energy and important mineral resources is much lower than the world average, making it difficult to meet the needs of modernization drive. Energy and mineral resources are mainly concentrated in ecologically fragile or ecologically important regions, and are distributed in the opposite direction from the main consumption areas. The energy structure is dominated by coal, with a serious shortage of high-quality fossil energy resources and huge potential for the development of new and renewable energy. The contradiction between the total amount, distribution and structure of energy and mineral resources and meeting consumption demand, protecting ecological environment and coping with climate change is very prominent.
4) **The ecological types are diverse, but the ecological environment is relatively fragile**. China has diverse ecological types, with forests, wetlands, grasslands, deserts, and oceans constituting a complete ecosystem. However, the ecologically fragile areas are vast and the factors leading to fragility are complex. Ecologically fragile areas above the medium level account for 55% of the country's land space, including 9.7% of extremely fragile areas, 19.8% of heavily fragile areas, and 25.5% of moderately fragile areas. The fragile ecological environment makes large-scale and high-intensity development for industrialization and urbanization can only be concentrated in the limited suitable areas.
5) **Natural disasters are frequent and the threat of disasters is high**. China has a large number of areas and populations affected by disasters, and the risk of catastrophes is high. Some of the county-level administrative regions are located within the areas with serious threats of natural disasters. Frequent natural disasters increase the cost of industrialization and urbanization and pose many hidden dangers to people's lives and property safety.

(2) **Challenges**

To promote industrialization and urbanization through economic development, it is inevitable to take specific land space as the carrier. In fact, industrialization and urbanization are essentially the process of transforming agricultural space and ecological space into urbanized space. On the one hand, China's development and utilization of land space has strongly supported the rapid development of the national economy and social progress, but on the other hand, some outstanding challenges have emerged that must be addressed with great attention and efforts.

1) **Arable land is decreasing too much and too fast, and the pressure to ensure food security is high**. The national arable land area decreased from 1.951 billion mu in 1996 to 1.826 billion mu in 2008, and the per capita arable land decreased from 1.59 mu to 1.37 mu, approaching the "red line" to ensure the security of China's agricultural supply.
2) **Serious ecological damage and degradation of ecosystem functions**. Global climate change and reckless development in some areas without regard to the carrying capacity of resources and environment have led to the destruction of forests, shrinking wetlands, drying up of rivers and lakes, soil erosion, desertification, rock desertification and grassland degradation, deterioration of the ecosystem of near-shore sea areas, and frequent meteorological, geological and marine disasters in some areas.
3) **The intensity of resource development is high, and environmental problems are prominent**. Rough and uncontrolled over-exploitation in some areas has led to water shortage, energy shortage and other problems becoming more and more prominent, bringing increasing pressure on large-scale long-distance water transfer, coal transportation, electricity delivery and gas transmission, as well as traffic congestion, ground subsidence and a sharp decline in green ecological space. Environmental pollution is serious, the overall condition of air and surface water environmental quality is poor, and the emission of major pollutants in many areas exceeds the environmental capacity.
4) **The spatial structure is unreasonable and the efficiency of space utilization is low**. Green ecological space is reduced too much, industrial and mining construction occupies too much space, and the development zones cover a large area and are too scattered. The output per unit area of urban construction space and industrial and mining construction space is low, and the space utilization efficiency of built-up areas of cities and established towns is not high.
5) **Urban–rural and regional development is not coordinated, and the gaps in public services and living conditions are large**. There is an imbalance between population distribution and economic layout, the working population and the supporting population live in different places, and the urban-rural and Interregional gaps in terms of public services and people's living standards are too large.

(3) **Trends**

China is at an important stage of promoting modernization, and therefore needs to accurately judge the trend of territorial spatial development and properly meet the new demands arising from it.

1) **The continuous improvement of people's lives leads to the demand for living space**. China is in a period of rapid upgrading of the consumption structure of the population, which has put forward new demands for expanding living space

such as housing, as well as higher requirements for the protection of arable land due to factors such as increased demand for agricultural products.

2) **The increasing level of urbanization leads to the demand for urban construction space**. China is in the stage of accelerated urbanization. The migration of rural population to cities has not only increased the demand for expanding urban construction space, but also brought about problems such as unused rural residential land, making new issues in the optimization of urban and rural spatial structure.
3) **The continuous improvement of infrastructure leads to the demand for infrastructure construction space**. China's transportation, energy and other infrastructure are still in the stage of continuous improvement. The construction of infrastructure is bound to take up more space, and even inevitably some arable land and green ecological space.
4) **The multi-polarization of economic growth leads to the demand for construction space in the central and western regions**. China's economic growth is increasingly multipolar. With the gradual saturation of the bearing capacity of resources and environment in some eastern regions, the accelerated expansion of economic activities to the central and western regions suitable for development requires continued expansion of industrial construction and urban construction space in these regions.
5) **The increasing conflict between water supply and demand leads to the demand for water conservation space**. China will face a serious shortage of water resources in the long term. With global climate change and increased water demand, water shortage will become more serious, and water for living, production and ecology are under great pressure. Meeting water demand should not only rely on water conservation and scientific allocation, but also on restoring and expanding water-conserving spaces such as rivers, lakes, wetlands, grasslands and forests.
6) **The increasing impact of global climate change leads to the demand for green ecological space**. Controlling greenhouse gas emissions has become a global consensus. China is still a developing country and needs to further develop its economy while making unremitting efforts and active contributions to combat global climate change. This requires changing past development patterns, altering the natural condition of the land as little as possible, expanding green ecological space, and enhancing carbon sequestration capacity.

In short, the Chinese government not only needs to meet the huge demand for land space from population increase, people's life improvement, economic growth, industrialization and urbanization, infrastructure construction, etc., but also needs to protect arable land to guarantee the security of national agricultural supply, and to protect and expand green ecological space to guarantee ecological security and people's health, cope with water shortage, environmental pollution, climate change, etc. These backgrounds in the field of territorial spatial development have driven the introduction and implementation of the major function zoning system.

4.1.3 *Guidance Ideology of Implementing the Major Function Zoning System*

In order to promote the implementation of the major function zoning system in practice, the central government has clarified the concepts and principles as the ideology to guide the practice.

(1) **Concepts**

The establishment of a new set of development concepts is the kernel of the implementation of the major function zoning system, and it should be noted that the development here refers specifically to large-scale and high-intensity development for the purpose of promoting industrialization and urbanization.

1) **The concept of suitability development according to natural conditions**. The natural conditions vary from one type of land spaces to another. Areas with very high altitude, complex terrain, harsh climate and other ecologically fragile or ecologically important functions are not suitable for large-scale and high-intensity development, and some areas are not even suitable for high-intensity agricultural and livestock development. Otherwise, it will cause damage to the ecosystem and damage to the ability to provide ecological products. Therefore, it is necessary to respect nature, respond to nature, and determine development contents according to the natural attributes of land spaces.
2) **The concept of distinguishing the major function**. In general, a certain land space always has multiple functions, but there is necessarily only one function that can be called the major function. From the perspective of providing products, the major function of a certain area is either to provide industrial and service products, or to provide agricultural products, or to provide ecological products. For example, for the area with decisive influence on the overall ecological security, the provision of ecological products should be taken as the major function, and the provision of agricultural products, service products and industrial products can only be its subordinate function, otherwise, the production capacity of ecological products may be damaged; while for the area with better conditions for agricultural development, the provision of agricultural products should be the major function, otherwise, the massive occupation of arable land for industrial development may damage the production capacity of agricultural products. Therefore, it is necessary to distinguish the major functions of different land spaces, and determine the main content of development and the main tasks of development according to the positioning of each type of major function.
3) **The concept of development according to the carrying capacity of resources and environment**. The major functions of different land spaces are different, and thus the scale of gathering population and economy is different. Ecological function areas and main agricultural production areas are difficult to carry a larger consumer population because they are not suitable or should not be developed for industrialization and urbanization in large scale and high intensity. In the process of industrialization and urbanization, part of the population will inevitably move

to urbanized areas where there are more job opportunities. At the same time, the excessive concentration of population and economy and the unreasonable industrial structure will also bring unbearable pressure on resources, environment and transportation. Therefore, it is necessary to determine the scale of population, economic scale and suitable industrial structure according to the "short board" factors in resources and environment.

4) **The concept of controlling the development intensity.**[1] China has a large proportion of land space that is not suitable for development. Although the plains and other spaces with good natural conditions are suitable for development, they are more suitable for agricultural cultivation, and in order to ensure the safety of agricultural products supply, the arable land cannot be excessively occupied to promote industrialization and urbanization. This determines that the land space available for promoting industrialization and urbanization in China is not abundant. Even in urbanized areas, it is necessary to maintain the basic arable land and green ecological space to meet the demand of the local population for agricultural products and ecological products to a certain extent. Therefore, all kinds of major function areas should be developed in a controlled manner and maintain an appropriate development intensity.
5) **The concept of optimizing the spatial structure.**[2] Spatial structure is the reflection of different types of space such as urban space, agricultural space and ecological space in the development of national land space. The change of spatial structure determines to a certain extent the way of economic development and the efficiency of resource allocation. Although the total area of China's urban built-up areas, built-up areas of established towns, independent industrial and mining areas, rural settlements and various development zones is already quite large, the spatial structure is unreasonable and the efficiency of spatial utilization is not high. Therefore, it is necessary to combine the optimization of spatial structure with the adjustment of economic structure, and shift the focus of land space development from occupying land mainly to optimizing the spatial structure and improving the efficiency of space utilization.
6) **The concept of providing ecological products.**[3] Human demand includes demand for agricultural, industrial and service products, as well as demand for

[1] Development intensity refers to the proportion of construction space in a region to the total area of that region. Construction space includes space for town construction, industrial and mining exploitation, rural settlements, transportation, water conservancy facilities and other construction land.

[2] Spatial structure refers to the composition of different types of space and their distribution in the national land space, such as the ratio of urban space, agricultural space and ecological space, as well as the ratio of urban construction space to industrial and mining construction space in the whole urban space.

[3] Ecological products refer to the natural elements that maintain ecological safety, guarantee ecological regulation and provide a good living environment, including fresh air, clean water and a pleasant climate. Ecological products, like agricultural products, industrial products and service products, are necessary for human survival and development. The major functions of ecological function areas in providing ecological products are: absorbing carbon dioxide, producing oxygen, nourishing water, maintaining soil and water, purifying water quality, preventing wind and sand, regulating climate,

ecological products such as fresh air, clean water and a pleasant climate. From the perspective of demand, these natural elements also have the nature of products in a sense. The process of protecting and expanding nature's ability to provide ecological products is also the process of creating value, and the activities to protect the ecological environment and provide ecological products also imply development. On the whole, China's ability to provide industrial products is rapidly increasing while its ability to provide ecological products is weakening, while people's demand for ecological products is increasing as their living standards improve. Therefore, it is necessary to make the provision of ecological products an important part of development and to make the enhancement of the production capacity of ecological products an important task of land space development.

(2) **Principles**

Based on the above concepts, the Chinese government has further defined specific principles for the implementation of the major function zoning system.

1) **Optimizing structure**. Shifting the focus of spatial development from the outward expansion through land occupation to the adjustment and optimization of spatial structure.
2) **Protecting nature**. In accordance with the requirements of building an environment-friendly society, according to the different characteristics of land space, taking the natural ecology protection as the premise, and based on the carrying capacity of water and soil resources and environmental capacity, to carry out moderate and orderly development and take the road of development in harmony with nature.
3) **Intensive development**. In accordance with the requirements of building a resource-saving society, taking the improvement of the space utilization efficiency as an important task of land space development, to guide the relatively concentrated distribution of the population and the economic activities and take the development path of intensive use of space.
4) **Coordinated development**. In accordance with the requirements of harmonizing population, economy, resources and environment as well as coordinating urban–rural development and regional development, to promote the spatial balance of population, economy, resources and environment.

4.1.4 Classification of Major Function Areas

At the specific operational level, the Chinese government has classified the types of major function areas based on two criteria.

---

cleaning air, reducing noise, absorbing dust, protecting biodiversity, and mitigating natural disasters. The "ecological compensation" for ecological function areas in some countries is essentially the purchase of ecological products by government on behalf of the citizens.

First, in terms of the development orientation, based on the resource and environmental carrying capacity, existing development intensity and future development potential, as well as the suitability to carry out large-scale and high-intensity development, the national land space is divided into four types of major function areas: optimized development areas, key development areas, restricted development areas and prohibited development areas.

Second, in terms of the functions carried, based on the types of main products provided, the national land space is divided into urbanized areas, main agricultural production areas and key ecological function areas, and the main functions of which are providing industrial and service products, agricultural products, and ecological products, respectively.

The endowments and development positioning of each type of major function areas are shown in Table 4.1.

It should be noted that all kinds of major function areas have the same important position in the overall economic and social development of the country, only that the major functions are different, the development orientations are different, the protection contents are different, the primary tasks of development are different, and the focus of national support is different. The central government supports the urbanized areas to agglomerate population and economy, supports main agricultural production areas to enhance comprehensive agricultural production capacity, and supports key ecological function areas to protect and restore ecological environment.

4.1.5 Policies to Support the Implementation of Major Function Zoning System

To support the implementation of the major function zoning system, the central government has introduced a series of policies, mainly in the following aspects.

1) **Fiscal policy**. Improving the central and sub-provincial financial transfer payment system with achieving equalization of basic public services as the goal, the focus of which is to increase the financial transfer payments for public services and ecological and environmental compensation for restricted and prohibited development areas.
2) **Investment policy**. Implementing the investment policy matching with the positioning of major function areas, with the government investment focusing on supporting the construction of public service facilities, ecological construction and environmental protection in restricted and prohibited development areas, and supporting the construction of infrastructure in key development areas.
3) **Industry policy**. Proposing industrial guidance directory and measures for different major function areas in accordance with the requirements of promoting the formation of the major function areas, to guide the optimized development areas to enhance the ability of independent innovation as well as the level of industrial structure and competitiveness, to guide the key development areas to

Table 4.1 Types of major function areas

Types	Endowments	Positioning
Optimized development areas (urbanized areas)	Such areas are more economically developed, more densely populated, with higher development intensity and more prominent resource and environmental problems, and thus should be optimized for industrialization and urbanization development	Important regions to enhance national competitiveness, leaders in driving national economic and social development, important innovation regions in the country, economic zones to participate in international division of labor and with higher-level global influence, and important densely populated and economically dense regions in the country
Key development areas (urbanized areas)	Such areas have a certain economic foundation, strong resource and environmental carrying capacity, greater development potential, and better conditions for gathering population and economy, and thus should be focused on industrialization and urbanization development	Important growth poles to support national economic growth, important support points to implement the overall regional development strategy and promote coordinated regional development, and important densely populated and economically dense areas in the country

(continued)

Table 4.1 (continued)

Types	Endowments		Positioning
Restricted development areas	Main agricultural production areas	Such areas have more arable land and better conditions for agricultural development. Although they are suitable for industrialization and urbanization, from the perspective of ensuring the security of national agricultural products and the sustainable development of the Chinese nation, it is necessary to make the enhancement of comprehensive agricultural production capacity a top priority for development, and thus large-scale and high-intensity industrialization and urbanization should be restricted	Important areas to ensure the safety of agricultural products supply, beautiful homes for rural residents to live and work in peace and happiness, and demonstration areas for the construction of new socialist countryside
	Key ecological function areas	Such areas have fragile ecosystems or important ecological functions, low resource and environmental carrying capacity, and do not have the conditions for large-scale and high-intensity industrialization and urbanization development, and must make enhancing the production capacity of ecological products a top priority, so that large-scale and high-intensity industrialization and urbanization development should be restricted	Important areas to ensure national ecological security and demonstration areas for people to live in harmony with nature

(continued)

Table 4.1 (continued)

Types	Endowments	Positioning
Prohibited development areas	Such areas are the areas established by law for the protection of various types of natural and cultural resources at all levels, as well as other key ecological function areas where industrialization and urbanization development are prohibited and need special protection, including national nature reserves, world cultural and natural heritage, national scenic spots, national forest parks and national geoparks, other natural and cultural resources protection areas at all levels, important water sources, as well as areas that must be prohibited from development as determined by governments at all levels	Important areas for the protection of natural and cultural resources, and places for the protection of genetic resources of rare plants and animals

strengthen the industrial support capacity as well as the ability to absorb industrial transfer and independent innovation, and to guide the restricted development areas to development special industries and to limit the expansion of industries that do not meet the positioning.

4) **Land policy**. Implementing differentiated land use policy based on the overall land use planning, to ensure that the quantity of 1.8 billion mu of arable land will not be reduced and the quality will not decline; implementing stricter control on the increase of construction land in optimized development areas, appropriately expanding the supply of construction land in key development areas, strictly enforcing the land use control in restricted and prohibited development areas, and strictly prohibiting the change of the use of ecological land.
5) **Population administration policy**. Regulating the total population in accordance with the major function positioning, guiding the orderly flow of population to gradually form a mechanism for the flow of population and capital and other production factors in the same direction. Encouraging optimized and key development areas to absorb population to settle down, guiding the population in restricted and prohibited development areas to gradually transfer voluntarily, smoothly and orderly, and easing the tension between human and nature.
6) **Environmental protection policy**. Proposing the environmental protection policy of classification management according to the environmental carrying capacity of different major function areas. Implementing stricter pollutant emissions and environmental standards to significantly reduce pollution emissions in the optimized development areas, maintaining the environmental carrying capacity to increase production and reduce pollution in the key development areas, adhering to the priority of protection to ensure the restoration of ecological functions and conservation in the restricted development areas, and strictly protecting by law in the prohibited development areas.
7) **Performance evaluation and assessment policy**. Implementing different performance evaluation indicators and performance assessment methods for the different positioning of the major functional areas. For the optimized development areas, strengthening the evaluation of economic structure, resource consumption, independent innovation, etc., and weakening the evaluation of economic growth; for the key development areas, implementing comprehensive evaluation of economic growth, quality and efficiency, industrialization and urbanization level and independent innovation in related fields; for the restricted development areas, highlighting the evaluation of ecological construction and environmental protection, and weakening the evaluation of economic growth, industrialization and urbanization level; and for the prohibited development areas, mainly evaluating the ecological construction and environmental protection.

4.2 Urban Land Paid Use Concept and the Market-Oriented Supply Policies

The urban land market did not exist previously under the socialist planning economy, and during that period before the reform and opening up, the basic features of China's urban land policy were public ownership, state control over land allocation, free use, and non-transferability, i.e., through a highly administrative process with every step controlling by the government, the state allocated the urban land it owned to entities to construct various types of buildings for free and without time limits, unless the government felt the need to pass on compensation to the expropriated peasants to them, and the transfer of land use rights between entities was restricted. Since the 1980s, the increased marketization and opening-up of the Chinese economy has brought about a great transformation of the urban space where labor, capital, and land are subject to commodification, and urban land is no exception. This perception has shaped the idea of paid use of urban land, in turn, influenced the approaches through which the urban land is supplied. Urban land supply policies centered on the conveyance system activate urban land market and generate a broader impact on the economic and social development. As a bottom-up process, urban land marketization in China is consisted of two important elements, namely, a pivotal and active role played by municipal governments as well as a variety of market mechanisms used by municipal governments to maximize their interests.

4.2.1 Introduction and Implementation of the Concept of Paid Use for Urban Land

(1) **Early exploration of urban land paid use in some cities**

With the passage of time, the urban land allocation and utilization policies under the planned economy system could no longer meet the needs of national economic and social development. At the early stage of reform and opening up, the Chinese government planned to reform the urban land supply system as an important part of the land system reform, and its basic starting point was to change the free and indefinite land supply into the paid and limited one. The force that triggered this idea came from the challenge posed by the entry of foreign capital.

In the late 1970s, with the introduction of foreign investment in the economic field, the provision of land for foreign-funded enterprises became an urgent and realistic need. In 1979, the *Law of the People's Republic of China on the Operation of Chinese-Foreign Joint Ventures* was promulgated, stipulating that "the right to use the site provided for the operation of the joint venture can be regarded as the investment of the Chinese side, and if the right is not part of the investment of the Chinese side, the joint venture shall pay land fees to the Chinese government", thus breaking the pattern of free use of urban state-owned land that had lasted for nearly

30 years. In 1980, the State Council promulgated the *Provisional Regulations on Land for the Construction of Sino-foreign Joint Ventures*, which further stated "The land for Sino-foreign joint ventures, regardless of whether the land is newly expropriated or the site of the original enterprise is used, shall be charged for the use of the site. The calculation of the site use fee shall include the compensation for the expropriated land, the demolition cost of the original buildings, and the personnel resettlement cost". The levy of site use fee solved the problem of land use for Sino-foreign joint ventures on the one hand, and highlighted the status of the state as the land owner on the other. From then on, urban state-owned land was no longer regarded as a mere means of production, and the understanding of its market value gradually developed from scratch, promoting the gradual formation of the urban land market.

In the early 1980s, some cities expanded the application of levying fees on the state-owned construction land use from foreign investment and Sino-foreign joint ventures to more areas in order to alleviate the shortage of investment in urban infrastructure construction. For example, the *Provisional Regulations on Land Management in Shenzhen Special Economic Zone*, which came into effect in January 1982, stipulated the maximum period of use of land for different purposes and charged land use fees at different rates according to the differences in use and region; Fushun City, Liaoning Province, introduced land use fees since January 1984; since the second half of 1984, Guangzhou City, Guangdong Province, introduced land use fees for economic and technological development zones, new projects, and foreign-funded projects. In 1986, Shanghai imposed land use fees on the land used by the foreign-funded enterprises. Although these local attempts did not fundamentally change the administrative allocation system for the construction land, they objectively became the germ of the urban land paid use system.

Following the introduction of land use charges, paid land conveyance and transfer have also begun to be conceived and explored. In April 1987, the State Council proposed that the right of land use could be transferred for a fee, and in September of the same year, Shenzhen took the lead in the trial of land use for a fee, and granted the right to use a piece of land of more than 5,000 square meters by closed-door negotiation for a period of 50 years, unveiling the prelude to the reform of the state-owned land use system. In November, the State Council approved the report of the State Land Administration and other departments, and decided to carry out pilot projects of land use reform in Shenzhen, Shanghai, Tianjin, Guangzhou, Xiamen and Fuzhou. In December of that year, Shenzhen publicly auctioned the right to use a piece of state-owned land with an area of 8,588 square meters for the first time in its history.

In terms of the institutional development, Shanghai stipulated the conditions, procedures and methods of urban land use rights transfer and the criteria for collecting land transfer fees in the *Measures for the Paid Transfer of Land Use Rights* in November 1987. Subsequently, Guangdong Province stipulated the relevant contents of the paid land conveyance in the Shenzhen Special Economic Zone in the *Regulations on Land Administration in the Shenzhen Special Economic Zone* released in December of the same year. Later, Tianjin and Xiamen also adopted relevant policy regulations. These regulations not only ensured the orderly implementation of the pilot reform, but also provided lessons for the introduction of national regulations and the nationwide extension of urban land system reform.

(2) Establishment of the urban land paid use system across the country

In the face of the growing tendency to follow Shenzhen's example, the Chinese central government initiated a revision of the relevant laws in order to break down the legal barriers to the development of the urban land market. The *Constitution* amended in April 1988 added the provision "the right to use land can be transferred in accordance with the provisions of the law", marking the confirmation of the legality of the transfer of land use rights in the form of the supreme law of the country, and in December 1988, the *Land Administration Law* was amended to add a new paragraph, stipulating "the State shall implement a system of paid use of state-owned land in accordance with the law, and the specific measures of paid use of state-owned land shall be separately prescribed by the State Council", marking the establishment of the system of paid use of state-owned land at the legal level.

In May 1990, the State Council, in accordance with the requirements of the *Land Administration Law* and on the basis of the experience of land use system reform in Shenzhen and other coastal cities, promulgated the *Provisional Regulations on the Conveyance and Transfer of Urban State-owned Land Use Rights*, specifying that "the conveyance of land use rights refers to the act of the State, in its capacity as the owner of land, convey land use rights to land users within a certain period of years and the land user pays the land conveyance revenue to the state". The regulations also put forward the equal, voluntary, and paid principles for the transfer of land use rights, as well as the three approaches, i.e., closed-door negotiation, tender and auction. The introduction of the regulation marks the beginning of the operation of the urban land paid use system at the national level, which is a fundamental reform of China's urban land system, creating a new system of land allocation by market means, which means that it has entered the era of the "dual-track" system of urban land allocation. Among them, the free administrative allocation approach is mainly applied to land for state agencies and military land, land for urban infrastructure and public welfare, and land for infrastructure supported by the state, such as energy, transportation, water conservancy; the paid conveyance supply approach is mainly used for meeting the land needs for commercial, office, industrial and residential and other operational projects.

Although the system of urban land paid use has been established at the national level and implemented one after another in various places, in terms of the nature of the various approaches, tender and auction are market-oriented, while the closed-door negotiation is non-market-oriented. In the 1990s, the real estate market witnessed the phenomenon of "land enclosure fever", multiple supply of land, low-priced land conveyance, rent-seeking and land speculation, etc. In order to avoid the loss of state-owned land revenue due to non-market allocation of urban land, the central government increased the enforcement of market-oriented land conveyance approaches, such as tender and auction, in an effort to better introduce market mechanisms into the land supply process. In January 1999, the Ministry of Land and Resources issued the *Notice on Further Implementation of Tendering and Auctioning of State-owned*

Land Use Rights, which fully affirmed the positive role of tender and auction, and required all places to strictly limit the scope of administrative allocation of land supply and strictly restrict the scope of conveyance by closed-door negotiation, but its actual implementation was not satisfactory, and closed-door negotiation was still the mainstream form of state-owned land paid use. In April 2001, the State Council promulgated the *Notice on Strengthening the Administration of State-owned Land Assets*, pointing out that no entity or individual may break through the relevant legal provisions of the scope of land administrative allocation, requiring all places to vigorously promote the tender and auction of state-owned land use rights, and the supply of land by closed-door negotiation must also be achieved on the basis of assessing land value, determining the price through a collective review, and making the results of the closed-door negotiation to the public.

In May 2002, the Ministry of Land and Resources issued the *Regulations on the Tender, Auction and Listing of State-owned Land Use Rights*, which introduced listing as a new market-oriented land supply approach beyond the tender and auction, and stipulated that all kinds of profit-oriented land such as commercial, tourism, entertainment and commercial residential land, as well as land for other purposes but with more than two interested parties, must be conveyed by tender, auction and listing. In March 2004, the Ministry of Land and Resources, together with the Ministry of Supervision, issued the "*Notice on Continuing the Law Enforcement Supervision of Tender, Auction and Listing of Profit-oriented Land Use Rights*", stipulating that after August 31 of that year, no profit-oriented land use rights could be conveyed by closed-door negotiation on the grounds of historical legacy issues. This policy regulation, known as the "831 deadline", had a fundamental impact on the subsequent urban land market and the broader real estate market, as the closed-door negotiation was withdrawn from the profit-oriented construction land supply channel and the supply of profit-oriented construction land was transformed into a fully market-oriented allocation. The *Notice of the State Council on Issues Related to Strengthening Land Control* issued in 2006 required that industrial land must be conveyed by tender, auction or listing, and the price of such land must not be lower than the lowest published price standard. In 2007, the Ministry of Land and Resources issued the *Regulations on the Conveyance of Land Use Rights for State-owned Construction by Tender, Auction and Listing*, which stipulates that "industrial, commercial, tourism, entertainment and commercial residential land, as well as land with more than two interested parties on the same parcel of land, shall be conveyed by tender, auction or listing". The shift of land conveyance approach from closed-door negotiation to tender, auction and listing reflects the principle of market economy, and the latter is conducive to letting the market mechanism play a fundamental role in the allocation of land resources due to introducing the open competition.

4.2.2 *Primary Land Market Mainly Supplied by the Government*

According to the *Implementing Regulations of the Land Administration Law*, the ways of state-owned land paid use include the conveyance of state-owned land use rights, the leasing of state-owned land, and the contribution of state-owned land use rights as capital. Among them, land conveyance activities in the primary land market are dominant, specifically, it refers to the act of the state, in its capacity as the land owner, ceding the land use right to the land user for a certain number of years, and the land user paying the land conveyance revenue to the state.

(1) **Duration of land conveyance**

According to the *Provisional Regulations of the People's Republic of China on the Conveyance and Transfer of Urban State-owned Land Use Rights*, the maximum number of years for the conveyance of land use rights is related to the purpose, which are: 70 years for residential land, 50 years for industrial land, 50 years for the land for education, science and technology, culture, health and sports facilities, 40 years for commercial, tourism and entertainment land, and 50 years for land for comprehensive or other uses.

(2) **Modes of land conveyance**

In practice, there are four modes of conveying land use rights, namely, close-door negotiation, tender, auction, and listing, as shown in Table 4.2.

1) **Close-door negotiation**. It refers to the act of the state conveying the state-owned land use right to the land user for a certain number of years by close-door negotiation, and the land user pays the land conveyance revenue to the state. In the case of land conveyance, the close-door negotiation is an exception. In

Table 4.2 Modes of land conveyance

Modes	Definition
Closed-door negotiation (xie yi)	Land use right is transferred to land users by one-on-one agreement and land users pay the state the agreed transfer fees
Tender (zhao biao)	Entails a local government's public invitation and takes the form of sealed-bid auctions. Winners are usually determined by the bidding price and the bidder's financial capability and reputation
Auction (pai mai)	Refers to a standard ascending bid auction with an open competing process. The highest bidder gets the land use right
Listing (gua pai)	Consists of two stages. In the first stage, bidders make entry decisions sequentially and the bids will be updated accordingly to the public. If there is only one bidder at the end of the first stage, the bidder is assigned the land use right; otherwise, the listing is converted to a public auction

other words, if tender, auction or listing should be used in accordance with the laws, rules and regulations, the conveyance by close-door negotiation shall not be adopted. On this basis, the regulations further stipulate that if the close-door negotiation is adopted to land conveyance, the land conveyance revenue shall not be lower than the minimum price determined in accordance with national regulations, and the minimum price shall not be lower than the sum of the land use fee for new construction land, compensation for land expropriation and relevant taxes and fees that shall be paid in accordance with national regulations, while in areas with benchmark land price, the minimum price shall not be lower than 70% of the benchmark land price of the level where the land is conveyed.

2) **Tender**. It refers that the department of land and resources at the municipal and county level issues a tender notice, inviting specific or unspecified natural persons, legal persons and other organizations to participate in the bidding towards the right to use state-owned construction land, and determines the holder of the right to use state-owned construction land according to the results of the tender.
3) **Auction**. It refers that the department of land and resources at the municipal and county level issues an announcement of the auction, and the bidders conduct public bidding at a specified time and place, and determines the holder of the right to use state-owned construction land according to the results of the bidding.
4) **Listing**. It refers that the department of land and resources at the municipal and county level issues a listing announcement, announcing the transaction conditions of the land to be offered for conveyance in the designated land trading places within the period specified in the announcement, accepting the bidder's application for quotation and updating the listing price, and determining the holder of the right to use state-owned construction land according to the results of the bidding at the end of the listing period or the results of on-site bidding.

(3) **Procedures of land conveyance**

1) **Compile annual plans for the conveyance of state-owned construction land**. According to the requirements of the central government, the local governments should plan to conduct tender, auction or listing activities for the conveyance of state-owned construction land. To this end, the departments of land and resources at the municipal and county level need to compile annual plans for the land conveyance according to economic and social development plans, industrial policies, overall land use planning, annual land use plans, urban planning and land market conditions, report to the government at the same level for approval, and then publicly release them to the public in a timely manner.
2) **Draw up the scheme for the conveyance of the land to be supplied**. The departments of land and resources at the municipal and county level shall, in accordance with the annual plans for land conveyance, together with urban planning and other relevant departments to develop a scheme for the conveyance of the land to be supplied, including the spatial scope, the use, the number of years, the mode of conveyance and other conditions, and implement after being approved by the government at the same level.

3) **Prepare the conveyance documents and determine the reserve price**. The organizer of the land conveyance shall, according to the situation of the land parcel, prepare the documents, which shall include the announcement of the conveyance, bidding instructions, land use conditions, bids or bid application, quotation, notice of award or confirmation of the transaction, the text of the contract for the conveyance of state-owned construction land use rights. In addition, the departments of land and resources at the municipal and county level shall, through collective decision-making, determine the reserve price based on a combination of land valuation results and government industrial policies. This price shall not be lower than the minimum price standard set by the state, and shall be kept confidential until the end of the conveyance activities.
4) **Announce the information on the conveyance**. The organizer shall publish the tender, auction or listing announcement at least 20 days before the start date in the land market or at the designated place or in the media, announcing the basic information of the land parcel, the time and place for implement the tender, auction or listing. The announcement shall include the following:

    i. The name and address of the grantor;
    ii. The area, the boundary, the spatial extent, the status quo, the use period, the purpose of use, planning requirements of the land offered for conveyance;
    iii. The qualification requirements for bidders, as well as the approaches to obtain qualifications;
    iv. The time, place and manner of requesting relevant documents;
    v. The time and place of tender or auction, period of tender or listing, bidding methods;
    vi. The criteria and methods for determining the winning bidder;
    vii. Bidding deposit;
    viii. Other matters that need to be announced.

5) **Receive the applications**. Natural persons, legal persons and other organizations within or outside the People's Republic of China, except as otherwise provided by laws and regulations, may apply to participate in the state-owned construction land conveyance activities. The grantor shall not set restrictions affecting fair and just competition in the announcement. For applicants who meet the conditions specified in the announcement, the grantor shall notify its participation in the conveyance activities. The departments of land and resources at the municipal and county level shall provide facilities for bidders to inquire about the land to be offered for conveyance.
6) **Determine the holder of the right to use state-owned construction land**.

    For the case of tender, the process to determine the holder is as follows:

    i. The bidders put their bids into the tender box before the deadline. If the tender announcement allows the bids to be mailed, the tenderer may mail it, but it is valid only if the bids is received by the grantor before the deadline. After the bids is put into the tender box, it cannot be withdrawn. Bidders shall be responsible for the bids and the relevant written commitment.

ii. The Grantor shall open the bids at the time and place specified in the tender announcement and invite all bidders to participate. The bidder or its elected representative shall check the sealing of the tender box, open the box in public and count the bids. If there are less than three bidders, the grantor shall terminate the tender activity. If there are not less than three bidders, the name of the bidder, the bid price and the main content of the bid document shall be announced one by one.
iii. The bid evaluation is carried out by a team, which consists of representatives of the grantor and relevant experts, the number of team members should be an odd number of five or more. The evaluation team may request the bidder to make the necessary clarifications or explanations of the tender documents, but the clarifications or explanations shall not exceed the scope of the tender documents or change the substantive content of the tender documents. The team shall evaluate the bid documents in accordance with the bid evaluation criteria and methods established in the bidding documents.
iv. The grantor shall determine the successful bidder according to the evaluation results. In the case of determining the successful bidder with the principle of the highest quotation, it is possible not to set up the team, but to determine the winning bidder by the tender presiding officer and based on the results of the bid opening. The successful bidder in the remaining cases shall be the one who can maximize the comprehensive evaluation criteria specified in the tender documents, or who can meet the substantive requirements of the tender documents and has the highest quotation.

For the case of auction, the process to determine the holder is as follows:

i. The moderator counts the bidders.
ii. The moderator introduces the area, boundary, spatial extent, status quo, purpose of use, tenure, planning requirements, commencement and completion time, and other related matters.
iii. The moderator announces the starting call price, the rules for incremental bids and the incremental range. If there is no reserve price, it should be clearly indicated.
iv. The moderator states the starting call price.
v. The bidder raises a price.
vi. The moderator confirms the price and continues bidding.
vii. The moderator announces the same price three times in a row and there is no further price, the moderator drops the hammer to indicate that the auction is sold.
viii. The moderator announces that the winner is the one who raise the highest price.
ix. When the highest price does not reach the reserve price, the presiding officer shall terminate the auction. The moderator may adjust the auction increment according to the situation during the auction.

For the case of listing, the process to determine the holder is as follows:

i. The grantor lists the area, boundary address, spatial scope, status quo, purpose of use, period of use, planning requirements, start and completion time, starting price, increase rules and price increase range in the land transaction place specified in the listing announcement.
ii. Eligible bidders fill out the quotation offer.
iii. The listing host update the listing price after confirming the quotation, and the listing time shall not be less than 10 days.
iv. When the listing period expires, the presiding officer of the listing announces the highest quotation, and ask the bidder whether he/she is willing to continue bidding. If a bidder expresses willingness to continue bidding, the listing will be transferred to on-site bidding, and the winner will be determined through on-site bidding. If no bidder expressed willing to continue bidding after the presiding officer of the listing has reported the highest quotation for three times, the transaction is determined in accordance with the following rules, first, if only one bidder quotes, and the quotation is not lower than the reserve price and meets other conditions, the deal is done; if there are two or more bidders quote, the winner is the bidder who reports the highest quotation, however, if two or more quotation are the same, the one who quotes first is the winner, except for those whose quotation are lower than the reserve price; if there is no quotation or all quotations are lower than the reserve price or do not meet other conditions, the deal is not done.

7) **Sign the contract**. After the successful bidder is determined, the grantor shall issue a notice of award to the successful bidder or sign a transaction confirmation with the successful bidder. The notice or confirmation shall include the name of the grantor, the name of the successful bidder, the subject of the conveyance, the time, place and price of the transaction, as well as the time and place of signing the contract for the conveyance of state-owned construction land use rights, which has legal force on both parties, meaning that once the grantor changes the result, or if the successful bidder abandons the land, they shall be liable for breach of contract according to law. The successful bidder and the grantor shall, in accordance with the time agreed in the notice or confirmation, sign the contract for the conveyance of state-owned construction land use rights. In addition, after the end of the conveyance activities, the grantor shall announce the results of conveyance in the land market or the designated place or the media within 10 working days.

4.2.3 Secondary Land Market Mainly Participated by Market Entities

After the conveyance of the construction land use rights by the local government to a user through one of the above four channels, the land use can further transfer, lease or collateralize the right to use the land in the open market, a market that is known as the secondary land market. According to the *Guidance on Improving the Secondary Market for the Transfer, Lease and Collateral of Construction Land Use Rights* issued by the General Office of the State Council in 2019, the Chinese government's governance goal on this topic is to establish a secondary land market with clear property rights, market pricing, information gathering, safe transactions and effective supervision, and to form a modern land market with coordinated development of primary and secondary markets, regulation and order, and intensive and efficient resource utilization. To this end, the central government has formulated appropriate policies for land transfer, lease and collateral respectively.

(1) **Land transfer policy**

The land transfer refers to all kinds of acts that lead to the transfer of the right to use construction land, including the sale, exchange, gift, and contribution of capital, as well as other relevant kinds involved in the judicial disposal, asset disposal, merger or separation of legal persons or other organizations. It should be noted that when the transfer of the right to use construction land occurs, the ownership of buildings and other attachments on the ground should be transferred together.

1) **The necessary conditions**. There are differences in the necessary conditions that need to be met when transferring the right to use construction land, depending on the approaches to acquire it. If the right to use construction land is acquired by administrative allocation, and the use after transfer still meets the requirements of allocation, it is possible not to pay the land conveyance revenue and go through the procedures of transfer registration; if it no longer meets this requirement, the party who obtain the use right should pay the land conveyance revenue in accordance with the law and regulations. If the right to use construction land is acquired by conveyance, the freedom of transaction should be fully guaranteed under the premise of conforming to the laws and regulations and the agreement of the transfer contract; if the original conveyance contract has an agreement on the conditions of transfer, it is necessary to comply with this agreement. If the right to use construction land acquired by way of capital contribution, the relevant provisions on the construction land acquired by conveyance can be referred to when transferring, without the need to report to the relevant departments for approval, and the right to use construction land after transfer is retained as either capital contribution or can be directly changed to the way of conveyance.
2) **Transfer of divided or merged land**. Divided or merged parcels should have the conditions of independent subdivision. If the construction and use of public facilities are involved, both parties to the transfer shall specify the relevant rights and obligations in the contract. If the parcel to be divided has been pre-sold or there are multiple rights holders, the consent of the relevant rights holders shall be obtained and the legitimate rights and interests of the rights holders shall not be harmed.

(2) **Land lease policy**

Land lease refers to the act of the land user as the lessor leasing the land use right along with the buildings and other attachments on the ground to the lessee for use, and the lessee paying rent to the lessor.

1) **Regulating the management of leasing the construction land acquired in paid approach**. If the right to use the construction land for lease is acquired in a paid manner by conveying, leasing, making capital contribution or equity participation, the lease shall not violate the relevant agreements of laws and regulations and paid use contracts.
2) **Regulating the management of leasing the construction land acquired in allocation approach**. If the right to use construction land for lease is acquired by way of administrative allocation, the land revenue included in the rent should be paid, and this part of the revenue should be included in the management of land conveyance revenue. If such land is prepared to be leased for a long time, or part of it for leasing and the lease of this part can be divided from the whole, the procedures for conveying, leasing and other paid use should be supplemented according to law.
3) **Creating an environment that facilitates the lease of the right to use construction land**. Local natural resources authorities should provide conditions and venues for the release of information on supply and demand for the lease of construction land use rights, develop standardized text of lease contracts, provide transaction authentication services, protect the legitimate rights and interests of rights holders, and provide statistics and analysis on the lease of construction land use rights and market-related data, and regularly release dynamic information and guidelines for the land lease market.

(3) **Land collateral policy**

According to the policy, the construction land use right can be mortgaged. When the land use right is mortgaged, the buildings and other attachments on the ground are mortgaged with it. When buildings and other attachments on the ground are mortgaged, the land use rights within the scope of their use are also mortgaged.

1) **The necessary conditions**. There are differences in the necessary conditions that need to be met when mortgaging the right to use construction land, depending on the approaches to acquire it. If the right to use construction land is acquired by administrative allocation, the mortgage of land shall be given priority to pay the land conveyance revenue when it is realized. The right to use construction land acquired by way of conveyance, contribution or equity can be set up as a mortgage. If the right to use construction land is acquired by lease, after the lessee pays the rent of the land and completes the development and construction as required, the buildings and other attachments on the land can be mortgaged together with the land according to the lease agreement.
2) **Relaxing the restrictions on the mortgagee**. Both natural persons and enterprises can apply for real estate mortgage with the right to use construction land

and the ownership of buildings and other attachments on the ground as mortgage holders, and if it involves debt contracts between enterprises, the mortgage needs to comply with the provisions of relevant laws and regulations.

3) **Guaranteeing the right to mortgage in accordance with the law**.Exploring the possibility of allowing enterprises in the social sector such as pensions and education that do not aim at public welfare, to mortgage their property such as the right to use construction land and facilities obtained in a paid way to finance. Further improving the supporting measures to ensure the continued stability of the original business activities after the realization of the mortgage, to ensure that the purpose of land use does not change, the rights and interests of stakeholders are not damaged. Exploring the establishment of risk alert mechanism for construction land use rights mortgage and supervision mechanism for mortgage funds to prevent and control market risks.

4.3 Rural Land Contract Management System and Transfer Policies

Land reform adapting to the development of productive forces can stimulate farmers' enthusiasm, initiative and creativity, thus promoting the development of productive forces. China's agricultural production mode is changing from traditional slash-and-burn cultivation to more dependent on mechanization, and urban–rural factors such as population, land and capital flow more frequently. China's rural reform originated from its rural land system reform, and the latter leads and promotes the former. The household contract responsibility system, the core of China's rural land reform and marketization, separated land management and ownership, established new production relations based on family units, liberated productivity, motivated agricultural labors effectively, and brought rural households with stable income. At the same time, it was conducive to optimizing labor resource allocation and forming diversified income sources, thus promoting poverty alleviation. In the new era, this system has been continuously adjusted along with the optimization of the contracted land rights system. The policy and practice of agricultural land transfer based on the separation of the three rights of contracted land has been developing, and promoting the organic linkage between small farmers and modern agriculture has become a new policy objective.

4.3.1 Household Responsibility System

(1) **Background**

After its founding in 1949, the People's Republic of China initiated the structural transformation of an old agricultural country into an industrial country, and set the goal of building a modern and powerful socialist country. The Communist Party of China realized the transformation from landlords to peasants regarding the owner of rural land through land reform, completed the socialist transformation of agriculture in 1956 through the cooperative movement in rural areas, and culminated the cooperative movement by establishing people's communes. In the early 1960s, the central government transformed the institutional arrangement of rural land into a collective ownership system. This shift led to incomplete rural collective ownership, use and revenue rights on the one hand, allowing the state to use the collectivization system to convert a large amount of agricultural surplus into industrial accumulation, and on the other hand brought about difficulties in monitoring and distributional egalitarianism in collective agricultural production, making incentives for farmers insufficient, resulting in dilemma in terms of agricultural performance such as declining agricultural productivity, shortages in the supply of agricultural products, and slow growth in the per capita consumption level of farmers. With the launch of reforms in the 1970s, this situation urgently needed to be broken.

(2) **Dynamics**

1) **The establishment of household responsibility system**

In the late 1970s, the state began to resume a series of policies aimed at stimulating rural vitality, including respecting the autonomy of production teams, reducing the burden on farmers, raising the purchase price of agricultural products, promoting family sideline businesses and diversified operations, and restoring and appropriately expanding self-reserved land. At the end of 1978, Xiaogang Village in Fengyang County of China, as the archetype of China's rural reform, took the lead in breaking through the traditional system and realized the contractual responsibility system with the main contents of "contracted production to household (*baochan daohu*)", i.e., the household responsibility system. Although the Third Plenary Session of the Eleventh Central Committee of the Party held in December 1978 still emphasized the maintenance of the existing system in the rural areas, and explicitly stipulated that "it is forbidden to transfer the production to households and to divide the land into separate units", the policy environment was gradually relaxed with the introduction of "emancipating the mind and seeking truth from facts".

In September 1979, the central government lifted the ban on "not allowing to contract production to household", but stressed that "except for the special needs of certain sideline production and single households in remote areas with difficult transportation, the production should not be contracted to the household". However, the interaction between local governments and the grassroots in some regions has led to a variety of practices of contracting to the household. In September 1980, the Central Committee of the Communist Party of China allowed the existence of "multiple forms of business operation, multiple labor organizations, and multiple methods of remuneration" and affirmed the form of "professional contracted joint production and remuneration responsibility system". Since then, the household responsibility system has spread rapidly throughout the country.

In 1982, the Central Committee of the Communist Party of China (CPC) issued a document affirming that the "contracted production to the household" is the production responsibility system of the socialist collective economy, which is different from the small private individual economy before the cooperation, and emphasizing that the rural policy should continue to be relaxed. The central document issued at the beginning of 1983 clearly stated that the household responsibility system was "a great creation of Chinese peasants under the leadership of the Communist Party of China and a new development of the Marxist theory of agricultural cooperation in Chinese practice". By the end of that year, the proportion of contracted households in China's rural areas had expanded to more than 95 percent, and against this background, peasants urgently demanded the stability of the household responsibility system.

2) **The legalization of household responsibility system**
The central document issued in 1984 focused on stabilizing and improving the production responsibility system, helping peasants improve their productivity and developing rural commodity production, and stipulated that "the contract period for land should generally be more than 15 years. The central document issued in 1985 emphasized that "the household responsibility system and family farming will remain unchanged for a long time". From that year onward, the state no longer gave farmers the task of collective purchase of agricultural products, and they became relatively independent commodity producers and operators. At this point, the rural system basically broke away from the original "three-tier ownership, team-based" system and started the "household contracted production, collective land ownership" model with Chinese characteristics.

The *Decision on Further Strengthening Agricultural and Rural Work* issued by the Central Committee of the Communist Party of China in November 1991 and the *Opinions on Strengthening the Management of Agricultural Contracts* transmitted by the State Council in September 1992 both proposed to make the responsibility system based on the family contracted production and the two-tier management system combining unification and division a basic system for long-term stability, and to bring it into the legal system, improve and strengthen the management of contracting. In April 1993, the family contracted production was written into the revised *Constitution*, and in November 1993, the Central Committee of the Communist Party of China and the State Council issued the *Policy Measures on the Current Economic Development of Agriculture and Rural Areas*, which proposed that "in order to stabilize the contractual relationship, encourage farmers to increase input and improve the productivity of land, the contractual period of arable land will be extended for another 30 years after the expiration of the original contractual period", and advocated that the contracted land area should not be adjusted due to changes in family size during the contractual period. The *Land Administration Law*, as amended in 1998, legally specifies that the term of land contracted production is thirty years.

In the twenty-first century, a series of laws and regulations related to the agricultural land system, such as the *Rural Land Contract Law*, the *Measures for the Administration of the Certificate of Rural Land Contract and Management*

Rights, and the *Measures for the Administration of the Transfer of Rural Land Contract and Management Rights*, were promulgated and implemented, initially forming a relatively complete legal system for agricultural land contracting. The *Property Law*, which came into effect in October 2007, further defined the right to contract and manage land as a usufruct right, clarifying that peasants have the right to possess, use and earn income from their contracted land in accordance with the law. The report of the 19th National Congress of the Communist Party of China in 2017 proposed to "keep the land contract relationship stable and unchanged for a long time, and extend it for another 30 years after the expiration of the second round of land contract". The document issued by the central government in 2018 called for the "articulation and implementation of the policy of extending the land contract for another 30 years after the second round of which expires". The *Rural Land Contract Law* and *Land Administration Law* amended in 2019 clarified the policy of extending the land contract for another 30 years after the second round of which expires from the legal level. In 2019, the Central Committee of the Communist Party of China and the State Council issued the *Opinions on Maintaining Stable and Long-lasting Land Contracting Relationships*, which require the implementation of the long-lasting land contracting relationships to be promoted steadily. The central document issued in 2020 proposed to carry out pilot projects on extending the land contract for another 30 years after the second round of which expires, and to formulate specific measures based on the experiences concluded from the implementation of pilot projects.

(3) **Operation**

The *Rural Land Contract Law* makes a series of provisions regarding the operation of the household responsibility system.

1) **The rights and obligations of the owner and contractor**
The owner of rural land in the contractual relationship can be a rural collective economic organization, villagers' committee, or villagers' group. The owner enjoys the following rights: to issue contracts for land owned by the collective, or land owned the state and used by the collective in accordance with the law; to supervise the reasonable use and protection of the land by the contractor in accordance with the purpose agreed in the contract; to prevent the contractor from damaging the contracted land and agricultural resources; and other rights stipulated by laws and administrative regulations. The owner undertakes the following obligations: to maintain the contractor's right to contract and manage land without illegally changing or canceling the contract; to respect the contractor's autonomy in production and management without interfering with the normal production and business activities of the contractor in accordance with the law; providing production, technology, information and other services for the contractor in accordance with the contract agreement; implementing the land use planning and organize the construction of agricultural infrastructure

within the collective economic organizations; and other obligations under the laws and administrative regulations.

The contractor of rural land in the contractual relationship is the peasant households in the collective economic organization. The contractor enjoys the following rights: to use contracted land, obtain income and transfer the contract and management right, to independently organize the production and operation and dispose products; to receive the appropriate compensation in accordance with the law in the case that the contracted land is expropriated; and other rights provided by laws and administrative regulations. The contractor undertakes the following obligations: to maintain the agricultural use of the land without using it for non-agricultural construction; to protect and reasonably utilize the land in accordance with the law without causing permanent damage to the land; and other obligations stipulated by laws and administrative regulations.

2) **Principles and procedures of contracting**

Land contracting should follow the following principles: the issuer in accordance with the provisions of the unified organization contracting, members of the collective economic organization to exercise the right to contract land equally in accordance with the law, but also can voluntarily give up contracted land; democratic consultation, fair and reasonable; contracting program should be agreed by more than two-thirds of the members of the villagers meeting of the collective economic organization members or more than two-thirds of the village representatives; contracting procedures are legal.

The implementation of land contracting should follow the following principles: first, the owner shall, in accordance with the provisions, uniformly organize contracting, and members of the collective economic organization exercise the right to contract land equally in accordance with the law, they can also voluntarily give up the right to contract land; second, democratic consultation, fair and reasonable; third, the contracting scheme should be agreed by more than two-thirds of the members of the villagers meeting of the collective economic organization members or more than two-thirds of the village representatives; and last, the contracting procedures should be legal.

Land contracting shall be carried out in accordance with the following procedures: first, the collective economic organization organize the members to participate in the meeting to elect a team that undertakes the contracting work; the team develops and publishes the contracting scheme in accordance with the provisions of laws and regulations; convening a meeting attended by members of the collective economic organization to discuss and adopt the contracting scheme; publicly organize and implement the contracting scheme; and signing the contract.

3) **Duration of contracting and contents of contracts**

The duration of contracting for arable land, grassland, and forest land is thirty years, thirty to fifty years, and thirty to seventy years, respectively; and the contract period of forest land with special forest trees can be extended with the approval of the forestry administrative department under the State Council.

The owner should sign a written contract with the contractor, and the contract should generally include the following provisions: names of the owner and the contractor, the name of the person in charge of the owner and that of the contractor's representative and their addresses, the name, location, area, and quality level of the contracted land; the duration of contracting as well as the start and end date; the purpose of contracted land use; the rights and obligations of the owner and the contractor; liability for breach of contract.

The contract is effective from the date of establishment, and the contractor acquires the right to contract and manage the land from the time the contract takes effect. After the contract has come into effect, the owner shall not be changed or cancelled due to a change in the person in change, or shall not be changed or cancelled due to the separation or merger of the collective economic organization.

4) **Protection of the right to contract land**

During the contracting period, the owner shall not take back the contracted land. If the family of the contractor moves to a town to settle, the right to contract land should be retained or be allowed to transfer in accordance with the law, depending on own wishes, however, if the family of the contractor moves to a city to settle, the contracted arable land and grass land should be returned to the owner, while if the contractor does not return, the owner can take back the contracted arable land and grass land. If this happens and the productive capacity of the land is improved by the contractor's input, the contractor is entitled to receive the corresponding compensation.

During the contracting period, the owner shall not adjust the contracted land. If there is a need for appropriate adjustment of contract between individual farmers due to special circumstances such as serious destruction of contracted land by natural disasters, it must be agreed by more than two-thirds of the members of the villagers meeting or more than two-thirds of the village representatives, and approved by the township government and the departments in charge of agriculture and other affairs at the county level.

The following kinds of land should be used to adjust the land contract: mobile land reserved by collective economic organizations according to law; land increased through legal reclamation and other means; land returned by the contractor. If the contractor voluntarily returns the contracted land back to the owner, he/she should notify the owner in writing six months in advance. Once handed back, no further claims to contracted land may be made during the contracting period. Women's right to contract land is fully guaranteed by relevant laws.

4.3.2 Encouraging Land Transfer to Adopt the New Mode of Organization in Agriculture

(1) **Motivation and actions to promote land transfer**

The implementation of the household responsibility system has made great achievements in China's agricultural development since the reform and opening up, however, its impact on agricultural output is also marginally diminishing. With the rapid industrialization and urbanization, the rural population and agricultural labor force have decreased drastically. Between 1978 and 2017, the rural population decreased from 790 million in 1978 to 577 million in 2017, and the urbanization rate increased from 17.92% to 58.52% accordingly. Although the number of people employed in rural areas has increased, from 306 million in 1978 to 352 million in 2017, the share of people in the primary industry sector has decreased significantly, from 92.4% to 59.5% over the same period.

In terms of the disadvantages of the household responsibility system, although it achieves economic incentives through clarifying property rights, it does so at the expense of large-scale operation. Given that an efficient property rights system and large-scale operation are the twin foundations of agricultural production, the fragmentation, parcellation, and miniaturization of arable land under collective ownership and household contracting arrangements have thus become bottlenecks in China's agricultural production, which, when combined with the low prices of agricultural products, have led to serious land abandonment. Considering that agricultural mechanization and technological advances have expanded the minimum optimal size of arable land, this has further amplified the negative effects of the household responsibility system.

In fact, the informal transfer of agricultural land in China began in the 1990s for the following reasons: First, with the disintegration of the urban–rural dual management system, the surplus rural labor force was gradually allowed to work in the cities, so the original contracted land of peasants faced the problem of being abandoned. Second, under the reform of the market economy system, plain areas suitable for the development of large-scale agriculture have higher requirements for agricultural production efficiency, and in this case, there is a need to centralize farmland production to obtain economies of scale. However, Chinese peasants, who are obsessed with land, are extremely reluctant to see this happen and transfer their contracted land to their relatives to continue farming. Second, under the reform of the market economy system, the plain areas suitable for the development of large-scale agriculture have higher requirements for agricultural production efficiency, and in this case, there is also a need to centralize agricultural land to obtain economies of scale.

In the twenty-first century, rural land transfer began to develop in the direction of institutionalization and standardization, and the central government issued relevant laws and regulations to build a formal system. the *Rural Land Contract Law* adopted in 2002 defined the main status of peasants in the transfer of land contracting rights, and the *Measures for the Administration of the Transfer of Rural Land Contracting Rights*, which came into effect in 2005, further stipulated the mode of transfer, that is, the rural land contracting rights acquired by the contractor in accordance with the law may be transferred by subcontracting, renting, swapping, transferring or other means that comply with the relevant laws and national policies.

Since the 18th National Congress of the Communist Party of China, along with industrialization, informatization, urbanization and agricultural modernization, China's rural labor force has migrated to cities in large numbers, and the problems of part-time agriculture, aging farmers and hollowing out of the countryside have become prominent, making the construction of a new agricultural management system and the development of moderate scale operations an inevitable trend, thus requiring that granting more secure land management rights to operators while safeguarding the rights and interests of contracted land for peasants. To this end, the central government has expanded the rights and empowerment in the reform of the rural land system, implemented the parallel separation of land ownership, contracting rights and management rights, and encouraged the transfer of contracted land to new agricultural business entities.

(2) **Approaches of land transfer**

According to the relevant regulations, the contractor can take the leasing (subcontracting), shareholding or other ways that are complied with the relevant laws and national policies to transfer land management rights.

1) Leasing (Subcontracting). It refers that the contractor leases part or all the land management rights to others to engage in agricultural production and operation.
2) Shareholding. It refers that the contractor contributes part or all the land management rights for a price and becomes a shareholder or member of a company or a cooperative economic organization, and uses it for agricultural production and operation.

If the contractor takes the leasing (subcontracting), shareholding or other ways to transfer part or all of the land management rights, the contracting relationship between the contractor and the owner remains unchanged, and the rights and obligations of both parties remain unchanged.

If the contractor voluntarily shares the right to operate the land in the company to develop agricultural industrialization, preferred shares and other ways can be took to reduce the risk of the contractor. When the company is dissolved, the shareholding land should be returned to the original contractor.

(3) **General policies about the rural land transfer**

The central government has made several policies regarding the transfer of rural land.

1) **Principles**

First, land transfer should adhere to the basic system of collective ownership of rural land and household contracted operation, to maintain a stable and permanent rural land contracting, to be in accordance with the law, voluntarily, the principle of compensation, any organization and individual shall not force or hinder the contractor to transfer the right to operate land.

Second, land transfer shall not harm the legitimate rights and interests of rural collective economic organizations and stakeholders, shall not damage the comprehensive agricultural production capacity and agricultural ecological environment, shall not change the nature of ownership of contracted land and its agricultural use, shall ensure that agricultural land is used for agriculture, shall give priority to food production, shall stop the "non-agriculturalization" of arable land and prevent arable land "non-food".

Third, land transfer should be appropriate to local conditions, be implemented step by step, grasp the degree of transfer, concentration, and the scale of operation. The scale of transfer should be compatible with the process of urbanization and the scale of rural labor force transfer, with the degree of progress in agricultural science and technology and improved means of production, with the level of agricultural socialization services to improve, and encourage the establishment of various forms of land management rights transfer risk prevention and protection mechanisms.

2) **Requirements for contractor and transferee**

Contractor in the contracting period has the right to decide independently whether to transfer the land management rights, as well as the object, way and duration of the transfer. The proceeds from the transfer of land management rights belong to the contractor, and no organization or individual may retain or withhold them. If the contractor voluntarily entrusts the owner, intermediary organizations or others to transfer its land management rights, the contractor should issue a letter of entrustment, which shall set out the matters entrusted, authority and duration, and signed or sealed by the principal and the trustee. Without the written commission of the contractor, no organization or individual has the right to decide to transfer the contractor's land management rights in any way.

The transferee of the land transfer should be organizations and individuals with agricultural business capabilities or qualifications. Under the same conditions, members of the collective economic organizations enjoy priority. The mode, duration, price and specific conditions of land management rights transfer shall be determined by equal consultation between the parties to the transfer. After the expiration of the transfer period, the transferee enjoys the right to renew the contract on equal terms and priority. The transferee shall protect the land in accordance with relevant laws and regulations, not to change the agricultural use of the land, not to make the land idle, barren, not to occupy arable land to build kilns, graves or unauthorized construction of houses sand mining, quarrying, mining, soil extraction on arable land, not to occupy the permanent basic farmland to develop forestry and fruit industry and digging ponds for fish farming.

If the transferee re-transfers the land management rights as well as use it for financial guarantees to financial institutions, it shall obtain the prior written consent of the contractor and file with the owner. If the transferee invests in soil improvement, construction of ancillary and supporting facilities for agricultural production as well as facilities directly used for crop cultivation and livestock and poultry aquaculture in agricultural production after the consent of the contractor and the contractor takes back the contracted land at the expiration of the land management right transfer contract or in advance when it is not due, then the transferee is entitled to reasonable compensation.

3) **Land transfer contract management**

If the contractor transfers land management rights, it shall sign a written transfer contract with the transferee on the basis of consensus and record it with the owner. If the contractor entrusts the contracting party, intermediary organization or others to transfer the land management right, the transfer contract shall be signed by the contractor or its trustee entrusted in writing. Land transfer contract generally includes the following: the name, residence, contact information of the parties; the name, four areas, area, quality level, land type, and plot code of the transferred land; the term and start and end date of the transfer; the approaches of transfer; the use of the transferred land; the rights and obligations of the parties; the transfer price or share dividends, and the payment method and payment time; the disposal of the attached objects on the ground and related facilities after the expiration of the contract; the vesting of relevant compensation fees when the land is expropriated or occupied according to the law; and the liability for breach of contract.

The contractor shall not unilaterally terminate the land transfer contract, except for the transferee has one of the following circumstances: unauthorized changes in the agricultural use of the land; abandoned for more than two consecutive years; caused serious damage to the land or serious damage to the ecological environment of the land; other serious violations of the contract. With the above circumstances, if the contractor does not terminate the land transfer contract within a reasonable period of time, the owner has the right to request termination of the land transfer contract. The transferee shall compensate for the damage caused to the land and the land ecological environment in accordance with the law.

4) **The role of government**

The departments in charge of agriculture and rural affairs at the county-level play an important role in promoting and regulating the transfer of agricultural land, and their responsibilities are mainly reflected in the following areas.

Encouraging the establishment of land transfer market or rural property rights trading market, and being responsible for strengthening business guidance, supervising the establishment of sound operating rules and the implementation of services such as policy consultation, information dissemination, contract signing, transaction authentication, equity assessment, financing guarantee, and file management.

Establishing rural land contracting information application platform with the interconnection of national, provincial, municipal and county in accordance with unified standards and technical specifications, improving the online signing system for the land transfer contract, and improving the standardization and information management level of land transfer.

Strengthening services to encourage the transferee to develop food production; encouraging and guiding industrial and commercial enterprises and other social capital (including legal persons, unincorporated organizations or natural persons, etc.) to develop modern breeding and raising industries suitable for entrepreneurial operation.

Guiding the transferee to develop moderate scale operation according to the natural economic conditions, the transfer of rural labor, the level of agricultural mechanization and other factors.

Establishing a graded qualification review and project audit system in accordance with the law for the transfer of land management rights by industrial and commercial enterprises and other social capital.

Establishing a risk prevention system for industrial and commercial enterprises and other social capital through the transfer of land management rights, strengthening supervision in the aftermath, timely investigating and correcting the violations of the law.

(4) **New mode of organization in agriculture**

1) **Direction**

In recent years, the Chinese government has emphasized the importance of cultivating new agricultural business entities engaged in agricultural production and services on the basis of adhering to family contract management, accelerating the formation of a three-dimensional and complex modern agricultural business system based on farmers' family operation, tied by cooperation and association, and supported by socialized services, which is considered a major strategy for China's agricultural modernization and is of great significance in promoting structural reform on the agricultural supply side, leading the development of moderate scale agricultural operations, driving farmers' employment and income, and enhancing new dynamics of agricultural and rural development.

In general, new agricultural business entities and service entities include family farms, farmers' cooperatives and agricultural socialized service organizations.

Family farms, with family members as the main labor force and families as the basic business unit, are engaged in large-scale, standardized and intensive agricultural production and operation, which is the main mode of operation of modern agriculture.

Farmers' cooperatives refers to mutual economic organizations established voluntarily and democratically managed by production operators of agricultural products or providers and utilizers of agricultural production and management services.

Agricultural socialized service organizations refer to social and economic organizations that provide various services to meet the needs of agricultural production for the business subjects of agricultural production. The socialized services in rural areas are generated along with the transformation of agricultural production from a scattered, isolated and self-sufficient small production mode to a commercialized society with a fine division of labor and extensive collaboration, which is an objective requirement for the industrialized development of agriculture and the integrated development of urban and rural areas.

2) **Cultivating and developing family farms**

The Chinese government has implemented the following policies to accelerate the cultivation and development of family farms.

First is to establish and improve the family farm directory management system, improving the conditions and procedures for inclusion in the directory, guiding the majority of farmers and various types of talent to create family farms, while including the professional households that meet the conditions and family farms that has been registered in the market supervision department into the directory management, and establishing a complete list of family farms, implementing the dynamic management to ensure quality.

Second is to increase efforts to create model family farms, reasonably determining the model family farm assessment criteria and procedures according to the region labor force status, productivity levels, agricultural regional characteristics, family farm business categories, and based on management capacity, physical equipment conditions, moderate scale of operation, production and operational efficiency and other factors. Strengthening demonstration guidance and exploring the policy framework and working mechanism to promote the development of family farms.

Third is to strengthen the guidance, services and support for family farms, exploring a set of support policies that meet the characteristics of family farms in terms of cost saving and efficiency, green ecology, improving facilities and capacity. Focusing on promoting the establishment of financial subsidies, credit support and insurance protection policies for family farms. Guiding family farms to adopt advanced technology and production means to carry out standardized production. Strengthening the family farm statistics and monitoring.

Last is to encourage the formation of family farm associations or alliances. According to the breeding species and other industry characteristics and the needs of different industries and regions, orderly forming a number of family farm association or alliance with outstanding driving ability and obvious demonstration effect, and gradually building a family farm association or alliance system.

3) **Promoting the standard development of farmers' cooperatives**

The Chinese government has implemented the following policies to promote the standard development of farmers' cooperatives.

First is to improve the standardization of farmers' cooperatives, guiding farmers' cooperatives to develop bylaws that meet their own characteristics, to strengthen file management, to implement open social affairs, to establish and improve organizational bodies such as general meetings, councils and supervisory boards in accordance with the law, to implement financial accounting system, to establish members' accounts in accordance with the law and strengthen internal audit supervision, and to establish a surplus distribution plan in accordance with the law and the articles.

Second is to enhance the service driving ability of farmers' cooperatives, encouraging farmers' cooperatives to make use of local resource endowments to drive members to carry out continuous planting and large-scale breeding, as well as to grow advantageous industries with special characteristics and cultivate agricultural brands. Encouraging farmers' cooperatives to strengthen the capacity building of key links such as primary processing of agricultural products, storage and logistics, technical guidance and marketing. Encouraging farmers' cooperatives to extend their industrial chains and broaden their service areas. Encouraging farmers' cooperatives to build and operate agricultural waste, rural toilet manure, domestic waste treatment and resource utilization facilities, and to participate in the construction and operation of rural public infrastructure management, as well as in rural cultural construction.

Third is to promote the union and cooperation of farmers' cooperatives. Encouraging farmers' cooperatives in the same industry or closely related industries to restructure their organizations and integrate their resources through mergers and consolidations on a voluntary basis, so as to strengthen a number of highly competitive single farmers' cooperatives. Supporting farmers' cooperatives to voluntarily form a federation in accordance with the law, so as to expand the scale of cooperation, improve the level of cooperation, and enhance market competitiveness and risk resistance.

Last is to strengthen the demonstration and leadership of the pilot. Deeply carrying out the pilot project of quality improvement of farmers' cooperatives in the whole county, developing and strengthening single farmers' cooperatives, cultivating and developing farmers' cooperative associations, and improving the level of county guidance and support services. Continuously carrying out the evaluation of model cooperatives, establishing the directory of model cooperatives, and promoting the creation of model cooperatives at four levels of national, provincial, municipal and county. Summarizing the experience and practices of the whole county in promoting the quality improvement of farmers' cooperatives and the creation of model operatives, and introducing and recommending a number of typical cases of farmers' cooperatives with sound systems and standard operation.

4) **Promoting the diversified and integrated development of agricultural socialized service organizations**

The Chinese government has implemented the following policies to promote the diversified and integrated development of agricultural socialized service organizations.

First is to accelerate the cultivation of socialized agricultural service organizations, in accordance with the principles of diversified subjects, diverse forms, professional services and full competition, accelerating the cultivation of various types of service organizations and giving full play to the respective advantages and functions of different service subjects. Supporting rural collective economic organizations to play its unified management function through the development of agricultural production services; encouraging farmers' cooperatives to provide members with various types of production and management services, to play its role of the link in servicing members and leading farmers to the market; guiding the leading enterprises to provide full service for farmers through the base construction and orders, to play its service driven role; and supporting the development of all kinds of professional service companies to give full play to their advantages of mature service mode, flexible service mechanism and high service level.

Second is to promote the joint and integrated development of service organizations, encouraging all kinds of service organizations to strengthen joint and cooperation to promote the horizontal expansion and the vertical extension of the service chain, as well as to promote the multi-faceted interaction, functional complementarity, and integrated development of the main body. Guiding all kinds of service subjects to actively develop service consortia, service alliances and other new organizational forms around the same industry or the production of the same product, with capital, technology, services and other elements as a link, to create an integrated service organization system. Supporting various types of service subjects and new agricultural business subjects to carry out various forms of cooperation and association, to establish a close interest linkage and sharing mechanism. Guiding all kinds of service subjects to actively carry out scientific research and talent cooperation with higher education institutions, vocational colleges and research institutes, and encouraging banks, insurance, postal services and other institutions to cooperate with service subjects in depth.

Third is to accelerate agricultural production hosting services. Adapting to the needs of different regions, different industrial farmers and new agricultural business entities in agricultural operations, and developing various trusteeship models such as single link trusteeship, multi-link trusteeship, key link comprehensive trusteeship and full trusteeship. Supporting professional service companies, supply and marketing cooperatives specialized service organizations, service-oriented farmers' cooperatives, rural collective economic organizations and other service entities to carry out hosting services by focusing on small farmers engaged in the production of bulk agricultural products such as grain, cotton, oil and sugar, as well as new agricultural business entities.

Last is to promote the normative development of socialized services. Strengthening the management of the agricultural production service industry to effectively protect the interests of small farmers. Accelerating the construction of service standards, by encouraging relevant departments, units and service organizations, industry associations, standards associations to study and develop service standards and service specifications that meet local realities. Strengthening the dynamic monitoring of service organizations, supporting the exploration of the establishment of a socialized service organization directory, and promoting the credit records of service organizations into the national credit information sharing platform. Establishing a credit evaluation mechanism for service entities and hosting service entities directory management system, focusing on support for the inclusion of directory management, strong service capacity, good service results of the organization. Strengthening guidance on service price, adhering to the principle of service prices determined by the market, and guiding service organizations to reasonably determine the price of each operational service link. Strengthening the supervision of service contracts, strengthening the guidance and management of contract signing, and actively playing its important role in regulating service behavior and ensuring service quality. Accelerating the development of standard form contracts, standardizing service behavior, ensuring service quality, and protecting the interests of farmers.

4.4 Direct Supply-To-Market of Rural Profit-Oriented Construction Land

The rural profit-oriented construction land is the land that used for industrial, commercial, and other business purposes conforming to the territorial spatial planning and has been registered for ownership according to the law. Unlike rural residential land, which is welfare in nature and can only be occupied by the collective members, and land for public facility construction, it is rural collective property with the function of commercial value creation, and its typical features are profitability, liquidity and capitalization.

4.4.1 Evolution of Policies on the Rural Profit-Oriented Construction Land Supply

The direct supply-to-market means that rural profit-oriented construction land is traded directly on the open market by way of conveyancing, leasing or shareholding, rather than having to be converted to state-owned construction land by the local government before it can be used by entities other than the collective itself for non-agricultural construction, as was previously the case. Unlike the establishment of the market for the paid use of urban profit-oriented construction land since the early 1980s, the development of the rural profit-oriented construction land market has been rather choppy, experiencing the dynamics of absolute inadmissibility, to strict restriction, then to conditional permission, and then to granting the same rights as state-owned land.

(1) **The scale of de facto rural profit-oriented construction land rapidly expanded, but the conveyance of such land was absolutely prohibited by law (late 1970s to 1990s)**

In the late 1970s, the large-scale industrialization in the countryside in China's coastal areas directly induced the emergence of rural profit-oriented construction land, as evidenced by the fact that some collective land was used to build rural enterprises and develop secondary and tertiary industries, and thus had profit-oriented attributes. The *Minutes of the National Rural Work Conference* issued by the central government in 1982 explicitly encouraged collective members to operate the business on contracted land, an attitude that continued to be reflected in the central documents in subsequent years. The implementation of the *Land Administration Law* in 1986 provided a legal guarantee for the development of rural enterprises, and the law introduced an application-approval system for the use of land needed for the construction of rural enterprises, but which still needed to be strictly controlled. Due to the simple operation and low comprehensive cost of using rural land, the reliance on rural profit-oriented construction land for industrial and commercial operations increased significantly. In addition to land for rural enterprises, some local governments, when implementing land expropriation, left some construction land for the development of secondary and tertiary industries for the collectives whose land was expropriated, which was also of a profit-oriented nature.

Despite this, the central government's attitude toward the conveyance of rural profit-oriented construction land remained subordinate to its attitude toward the transfer of all types of rural land, i.e., the absolute prohibition. While the previously mentioned *Minutes of the National Rural Work Conference* encouraged collectives and their members to operate on contracted land, it emphasized that contracted land was not allowed to be bought, sold, rented, or transferred. Later, although the *Constitution of the People's Republic of China* adopted in 1982 allowed the right to use land to be transferred in accordance with the law, no specific provisions were made for the transfer of the right to use rural construction land. In 1992, the State Council issued the *Notice on Several Issues Concerning the Development of the Real Estate Industry*, which clearly stated that "collectively owned land must first be expropriated and converted to state-owned land before it can be conveyed.

(2) **The supply of rural profit-oriented construction land was strictly controlled, and the conveyance of such land was still prohibited (1990s to early 2000s)**

The scale of agricultural land deagrarianization in China during this period was large, especially in the relatively economically developed coastal and eastern regions, which posed a challenge to China's food security and rural order. In response, the general provisions of the *Land Administration Law*, as amended in 1998, explicitly restricted the conversion of agricultural land to construction land. Although the establishment of rural enterprises could still use the land owned by the collective economic organization, the control of this behavior became increasingly strict. In 1999, the General Office of the State Council issued the *Notice on Strengthening Land Transfer Management and Strictly Prohibiting Land Speculation*, which stated that land for rural enterprises should be strictly limited to urban, village, and township construction land as determined by the overall land use planning, and that buildings and structures that do not conform to the overall land use planning should not only not be altered or expanded, but should also be gradually adjusted and concentrated in conjunction with the reform of rural enterprises and land consolidation. In addition, the *Land Administration Law* revised in 1998 also clearly stipulated for the first time that the right to use collectively-owned land should not be conveyed, transferred or leased for non-agricultural construction, with subsequent regulations and documents reinforcing this provision, which means that during this period, the closed mode of operation characterized by self-use of rural profit-oriented construction land was implemented.

Since non-agricultural use of land has a higher rate of remuneration compared with agricultural use, it inevitably triggered the spontaneous transfer of agricultural land to the non-agricultural sector. Especially in those areas with rapid economic development and better development of private economy, illegal and irregular land use was very common. For example, in the coastal areas, it was a more common practice at that time that rural collectives transferred the right to use collective construction land for a certain period of time to rural enterprises, with the collectives receiving transfer payments as land owners. Driven by interest, the subject of the land transfer gradually expanded from the rural enterprises to individual industrial and commercial households, and even urban enterprises.

(3) **Two-way exploration on the transfer of rural profit-oriented construction land (2000~2012)**

Rapid changes in the economic situation brought calls to change the definition of existing laws regarding the right to transfer rural land. To this end, the issue of legal access to market for rural profit-oriented construction land supply was explored at the local level and the national level in both directions, from the bottom up and from the top down, respectively. In the economically developed Pearl River Delta region, the *Measures for the Administration of the Transfer of the Right to Use Collective Construction Land in Guangdong Province* was issued as early as 2005, explicitly proposing that the right to use collective construction land can be transferred by way of conveyance or lease for commercial, tourism, entertainment and other business projects with reference to the management of state-owned land, thus breaking the tradition that no agricultural land can be legally converted to non-agricultural use unless it has been expropriated by the government. Meanwhile, the central government also adopted the approaches of issuing documents and conducting pilot projects to encourage and regulate the transfer of rural profit-oriented construction land. For example, the *Opinions on Several Policies to Promote Farmers to Increase Income* issued by the CPC Central Committee and the State Council in 2004 proposed to actively explore ways and means for collective non-agricultural construction land to supply on the open market. In 2008, the Third Plenary Session of the 17th CPC Central Committee proposed to gradually establish a unified urban and rural construction land market and allow the transfer of land use rights for rural profit-oriented construction land acquired in accordance with the law, breaking the restrictions on the entry of rural profit-oriented construction land into the market for the first time at the national level. However, because there has been no corresponding change in the relevant laws, the local reform exploration has not made a major breakthrough.

(4) **Reform on the direct supply-to-market of rural profit-oriented construction land (2013)**

A systematic reform on the supply of rural profit-oriented construction land was really put on the agenda after the 18th National Congress of the Communist Party of China, and its basic direction was to establish a market for the direct supply of such land by collectives. In 2013, the Third Plenary Session of the 18th Central Committee proposed to allow rural profit-oriented construction land to be conveyed, leased, or capitalized, with the same rights as state-owned land, under the premise of compliance. Subsequently, after exploratory practice in dozens of pilot areas, the latest revision of the *Land Administration Law* in 2019, for the first time, explicitly allows rural profit-oriented construction land to be directly supplied on the open market in the form of a higher law, stating that for those rural profit-oriented construction land that is identified to be used for industrial, commercial and other operating purposes by the overall land use planning and urban and rural planning, and registered in accordance with the law, the land owner can convey or lease it to entities or individuals to use, once it is agreed by more than two-thirds of the members of the meeting of the collective or more than two-thirds of the collective representatives, and the user can still be transferred or mortgaged after obtaining the right to use the land, thus clearing the legal obstacles to the direct supply of rural profit-oriented construction land on the open market.

4.4.2 Policy Issues in the Direct Supply-To-Market of Rural Profit-Oriented Construction Land

The direct supply-to-market of rural profit-oriented construction land is still a field that is being explored and promoted, and the corresponding institutional system is being established and improved. Overall, there are the following key policy issues that deserve attention.

(1) **Subjects: entities that are qualified to supply the land**

In general, the subjects leading the direct supply-to-market of rural profit-oriented construction market are the rural collective economic organization such as a township, village or village group that owns the land. Authorized by the collective land owners, the land share cooperatives, land franchise or joint venture companies, collective asset management companies with legal personality may act as agents to implement the direct supply-to-market of rural profit-oriented construction land within the scope of authorization.

(2) **Objects: features of land that can be directly supplied**

To ensure that the risks are controllable and prevent large-scale land direct supply-to-market from impacting urban land markets and threatening rural production and social order, relatively stringent conditions have been set for identifying rural profit-oriented land that can be supplied on the open market. The first and most important is that the land has been identified in the general land use planning and urban and rural planning for industrial and mining warehousing, commercial services and other business purposes. Then, the land should, in principle, be the existing construction land. However, there are exceptions, for example, some pilot areas in Guangxi allow new rural profit-oriented construction land to be supplied on the open market. There are also some areas that have converted some of their rural residential land into profit-oriented construction land when conducting the second or third national land survey, so that they can legally transferred on the open market.

(3) **Patterns: the practical operation of the direct supply-to-market**

There are three patterns for supplying the rural profit-oriented land on the open market at the practical level.

1) in-site supply-to-market (*jiu di ru shi*), which means that rural profit-oriented construction land parcels can be directly supplied on the local land market if they meet the eligibility requirements and have the infrastructure and other conditions required for development.
2) supply-to-market with off-site adjustment (*yi di tiao zheng ru shi*), which refers that the collective first reclaim sporadic or scattered rural profit-oriented construction land into arable land according to the overall land use planning and land remediation planning, to ensure that the quantity of arable land is not reduced, and the quality of which is improved, and then the higher-level government gives the collective a considerable amount of land quota in the industrial concentration areas or other qualified areas within the administrative jurisdiction to be supplied on the open market.
3) supply-to-market with comprehensive remediation (*zong he zheng zhi ru shi*), which refers to the unified reclamation of rural profit-oriented construction land and infrastructure construction in urban villages and contiguous rural areas, followed by parcel reallocation and property rights determination, and the direct supply of rural profit-oriented construction land that has not been expropriated or not included in the scope of land reserves on the open market.

(4) **Purposes: types of projects that can be developed using the land**

The rural profit-oriented construction land needs to be used for the development of industrial warehousing, commercial, tourism, entertainment, services and other productive and business projects. Except for some pilot areas in Guangxi and Shanxi, it is basically explicitly prohibited everywhere to use such land for the development of commercial housing. It is important to note that, combined with the reform on establishing a new housing supply system by multiple subjects, many regions allow the use of the land to develop rental housing, joint-ownership housing and other affordable housing projects.

(5) **Approaches: ways to supply the land**

There are three general ways of supplying the rural profit-oriented construction land on the open market, namely, conveyance, lease, and make capital contribution, of which, as the most important form, land conveyance can be done through tender, auction and listing, which is similar to the conveyance of state-owned land use rights.

(6) **Benefits: allocation among stakeholders**

The direct supply-to-market of rural profit-oriented construction land generates a certain number of value-added benefits, so a very important issue is how such benefits be distributed among stakeholders, including local governments, collectives and their members.

First, following the guiding opinions released by the central government, local governments obtain a certain share of value-added benefits by differentially levying the so-called adjustment fee from the collectives who have conveyed, leased, or capitalized the rural profit-oriented construction land. The starting point of this policy is to make the share of land value-added benefits between the state and the collectives roughly balanced and to protect the interests of farmers, and the key points are the calculation and allocation of the adjustment fee.

For the calculation of the adjustment fee, it is generally made in two ways. The first one is levied according to a certain percentage of the total transaction price, which is simple and easy to operate; the second one is levied according to a certain percentage of the net value-added benefits, i.e., the proceeds after deducting the expenses of land acquisition cost, land development cost and related taxes and fees from the revenue, which has better reasonableness.

For the allocation of the adjustment fee, most regions have stipulated that the adjustment fee should be used at the county level in a coordinated manner, that is, the government at the county level aggregates and arranges for the construction of local infrastructure and public welfare facilities.

Second, as the value-added benefits go to the rural collective economic organization that exercise the collective land ownership, so the distribution of value-added benefits mainly occurs between the collective and households, and between the village collective and the village group. From the practice of the pilot areas, the value-added benefits are generally used for two purposes: investment and operation, and public expenditure. Among them, investment and operation mainly involve the development of production and investment, purchase of properties, shareholding cooperation, purchase of government bonds and other aspects that are conducive to the development and growth of the collective economy; expenditure is mainly used for infrastructure, public welfare, and protection of basic farmland.

4.5 Rural Residential Land System

Rural residential land is land acquired by rural residents in accordance with the law for the construction of residential buildings and their ancillary facilities, including land for housing, auxiliary houses, and small courtyards, as well as land for greening in front of and behind houses. As an important type of rural land, the scale of rural residential land is large. The Ministry of Natural Resources estimated that in 2016, the per capita area of rural residential land was about 204 square meters, and there were about 184 million mu of residential land nationwide, accounting for 57.5% of the collective construction land area and nearly 1/3 of the national construction land area. Rural residential land is not only closely related to the vast number of rural residents to build their shelter and achieve a peaceful life, but are also their very important and increasingly important property. At the same time, the residential land system is the most special institutional arrangement in the rural land system, with a special system of rights arrangement, a special system of acquisition and a special social objective, the basic content of which is collective ownership, long-term use by collective members, exemption from land price, and prohibition of rent and sale. This system was formed during the People's Commune period and played an important role in guaranteeing the most fundamental housing and livelihood needs of peasants, facilitating agricultural production under traditional farming civilization, maintaining social harmony and stability in rural areas, and consolidating the collective ownership of rural land. However, after the initiation of reform and opening up, this system has become increasingly incompatible with the new situation of faster economic growth, unbalanced regional development, massive migration of rural labor and differentiation of different generations of rural workers, resulting in many outstanding problems in practice. Improving the rural residential land system has become one of the important elements of rural land system reform in recent years.

4.5.1 Evolution of Rural Residential Land System in China

The rural residential land system in China has undergone many adjustments, all closely related to the economic development, political stability, and social construction characteristics of the corresponding period, involving behavioral choices among different subjects such as the central government, local governments, collective economic organizations, and peasants. The changes of the rural residential land system can be divided into different stages according to the nature of residential land rights, the national economic system, and the land administration system.

(1) **Private ownership of residential land (1949~1962)**

At the beginning of the foundation of the People's Republic of China, in order to consolidate the new regime and promote the recovery and development of agricultural production, a nationwide land reform campaign was launched to confiscate the land of the feudal landlords and return it to the peasants, to realize the goal of "land for the cultivator and house for the dweller". The *Constitution* promulgated in 1954 stipulated that the state would protect the peasants' ownership of land and houses in accordance with the law, and that the right of inheritance of private property would also be protected by the state law. At this stage, the peasant land ownership system was established, and the ownership and use of residential land belonged to the peasants, and both land and houses could be freely bought, sold, rented, and inherited. The peasants enjoyed absolute freedom of circulation and complete disposal rights. At that stage, based on the political consideration of gaining peasants' support and maintaining rural stability, the design of the rural residential land system followed the concept of guaranteeing peasants' right to housing, emphasizing equal and gratuitous distribution, and the residential land was regarded more as a basic means of living, with welfare at the level of right content and guarantee at the level of social function. However, the private ownership of rural land is incompatible with the ideology of socialist public ownership, so the central government tends to support the development of mutual and cooperative agricultural production methods, and the policy of rural residential land has gradually shifted from free trade to restricted trade, which has laid the groundwork for the collectivization of rural residential land and the restriction of residential land transactions.

(2) **Separation of ownership and use rights of rural residential land (1962~2017)**

With the consolidation of the regime, the establishment of a national industrial system and industrialization became the strategic goal of the new stage. Due to the domestic and foreign macro environment, the endogenous path of industrialization became the inevitable choice. The wealth of agriculture and rural areas was gradually transferred to industry and towns through the "scissors difference" between industrial and agricultural products, accumulating primitive capital for the priority development of urban heavy industry. The relationship between industry and agriculture and between urban and rural areas became dichotomized at the national strategic level. However, the decentralized small farmer economy, backward agricultural production technology, and limited rural production conditions greatly limited the efficiency of agricultural production. In order to improve rural productivity, socialist transformation and agricultural cooperative movements were implemented nationwide to transform privately-owned rural land, production tools, and other agricultural means of production into collective ownership. As the most important means of livelihood for peasants, restricting the transfer of residential land was crucial to stabilizing rural society and the agricultural population. In 1962, the central government promulgated the *Regulations on the Work of Rural People's Communes*, which stipulated that "the rural residential land belongs to the production team and are not allowed to be rented or bought and sold" and that "the members have the right to buy, sell or rent houses". In 1963, the *Notice on Some Supplementary Provisions on the Residence Land of Community Members* was issued, introducing for the first time the concept of "the right to use the residence land" and stipulating that "after the house is sold, the right to use the residence land will be transferred to the new homeowner". These two documents marked the transformation of rural residential land system from private ownership by peasants to collective ownership, with peasants enjoying only the right to use them, basically establishing the property right structure of "separation of ownership and use rights" for residential land, which has continued for decades at the legal level. Since then, the state has adopted a series of supporting policies to consolidate the framework of the residential land system, with different degrees of restrictions on the use of residential land and the transfer of houses at different times.

(3) **Separation of ownership, qualified and use rights of rural residential land (2018~)**

After the 18th National Congress of the Communist Party of China, the central government has accelerated the pace of reform of the rural land system by issuing special policy documents, among which the main contents of the reform of the rural residential land system are: safeguarding the usufruct rights of peasants' residential land, safeguarding the property rights of peasants' housing, exploring new mechanisms of housing security for peasants, exploring the system of paid use of residential land and voluntary paid withdrawal mechanisms, revitalizing the use of vacant rural houses and residential land. The basis of these reforms is the "separation of three rights" of residential bases. The basis of these reforms is the separation of ownership, qualified and use rights of rural residential land. In general, the reform in the pilot areas has achieved some results, but there are still some theoretical problems and practical difficulties that have not yet been solved, and need to deepen the reform exploration work in a targeted manner.

4.5.2 Current Situation of the Reform of Rural Residential Land System

(1) **Reasons to reform**

1) **Problems with the rural residential land system itself**

For a long time, the core of the rural residential land system implemented in rural areas in China is: collective ownership, use by members, free allocation, long-term occupation, and prohibition of transfer. Its main contents include: (1) rural residential land is owned the collectives and used by peasant households for a long time without cost; (2) a household can only occupy one parcel of rural residential land and the area of which cannot exceed the specified standard; (3) peasants cannot apply for residential land after renting or selling their houses; (4) rural residential land cannot be rented, transferred, or bought and sold. (5) If there is redundant residential land, it shall be taken back by the collective. However, the system itself suffers from the following problems.

First, many rural collectives lack the ability to exercise ownership rights. Faced with the inherent demand for optimizing the resources of residential land triggered by the increasingly prominent contradiction between people and land, many rural collective economic organizations are incapable of exercising the right of distribution and lack the ability to or execute the right of supervision and revenue. For much residential land that have been idle for a long time or the houses built on which have collapsed or been demolished for more than two years without being restored to use, collective economic organizations simply do not have the ability to recover them, and even if some plots can be recovered, they lack the management ability to allocate and reuse them.

Second, the qualification of the so-called members of collective economic organization is rather vaguely defined. Since the use of residential land is limited to members of collective economic organization, it makes peasants more restricted in choosing sites for their residences, which aggravates the small and scattered layout of rural settlements and seriously affects the rational allocation and use efficiency of rural living infrastructure and public services. In addition, the qualification right of residential land is determined by households, but the definition of "household" is not clearly defined in the relevant laws, which leads to various ways in the actual implementation in various regions, which also means that the use and management of residential land are quite confusing.

Third, the long-term occupation without payment makes it difficult to realize the optimal allocation of rural residential land resources. The indefinite possession of residential land seriously hinders the optimal allocation of residential land resources and intensifies the contradiction between supply and demand. On the one hand, the long-term solidification of the right to use residential land means that even if the actual user disappears, it cannot be transferred and revitalized, resulting in the continuous creation of vacant residential land and vacant houses, and the situation of "multiple sites of residential land for one household" naturally formed by inheritance is contrary to the current regulations, and the use of residential land is very sloppy and increasingly inefficient; on the other hand, with the increasing number of collective members and the limited land area, the contradiction between supply and demand of residential land is becoming more and more prominent, the reasonable demand for residential land is not guaranteed, and the fairness of collective land use is becoming a prominent contradiction in rural society.

2) **Incompatibility between the rural residential land system and development needs**

Beyond that, there is still a large incompatibility between the rural residential land system and China's current economic and social development needs.

First, it is difficult to meet the demand for factor security to implement rural revitalization strategy. The implementation of rural revitalization strategy is an inevitable choice to solve the main social contradiction and achieve common prosperity in the new era, while land factor guarantee is an important support for the implementation of rural revitalization strategy. As the main system of land factor guarantee, the existing residential land system can hardly meet the needs of rural revitalization strategy. Firstly, under the background of industrial integration, the residential land not only plays the function of residence, but also plays the function of production and operation, and under the condition that the residential land cannot be transferred, the demand for land for the industrial integration cannot be guaranteed. Secondly, the lack of optimal allocation mechanism of residential land restricts the construction of rural living infrastructure and public service facilities, and fails to meet the villagers' demand for a livable living environment. Thirdly, unfair allocation of residential land and disputes over residential land have become one of the major social problems in rural areas, weakening villagers' sense of identity with collective organizations and restricting the realization of the goals of "civilized countryside" and "effective governance".

Second, the rough use of residential land and the difficulty in obtaining reasonable land for peasants to build houses coexist. In the continuous promotion of industrialization and urbanization, most of the rural migrant population has become "urban–rural amphibious" population. These people have a foothold in the city and a parcel of residential land in the countryside, but they live and work in the city all year round, leaving the rural residential land unused for a long time. At the same time, out of a traditional plot, this population is eager to increase their family property by constantly building new houses, especially among the first and second generation of migrant workers, who spend most of their income from working outside for building houses, resulting in the reverse growth of rural residential land areas as the rural population decreases, and the phenomenon of rough use of rural residential land becomes increasingly serious. Given that the permanent basic farmland and ecological red line designated by the state restrains the space of village outreach expansion, resulting in the reasonable demand for land for many newly established villagers to build houses cannot be met. This contradiction between supply and demand is not only manifested within a village, but also in the imbalance between different regions. The contradiction between supply and demand of rural residential land is more prominent in villages located in the combination of urban and rural areas, major transportation routes and other areas with obvious advantages, or villages with developed non-agricultural industries, as well as villages with relatively complete living infrastructure and public service facilities; on the contrary, in villages located in remote mountainous areas, with small population size, poor industrial economy, the contradiction between supply and demand of residential land is relatively moderate. However, the design of the rural residential land system, which is limited to the use of the members of the collective, cannot be coordinated among different regions, which exacerbates the already acute contradiction between the supply and demand of rural residential land.

Third, it is difficult to realize the function of bringing property income carried by the rural residential land. The rural residential land has the innate property of being a means of production, and it is an inherent requirement of social development to improve farmers' property income by realizing the property value of the residential land. The development of industrial integration in today's era has given rise to new industries and new business modes such as rural electric business, platform-mediated short-term rentals and rural tourism, which provide an opportunity to obtain property income through the optimal use of rural residential land and houses. However, due to the unsoundness of the rural residential land system, a large amount of real demand for obtaining property income from residential land can only be met through so-called invisible transactions, especially in some places with good location conditions.

(2) **Aim of the reform**

The goal set by the central government for the reform of the rural residential land system is to build an orderly and efficient system of rural residential land utilization and management on the basis of the separation of ownership, qualified and use rights of rural residential land, so as to meet the needs of the rural revitalization strategy, optimize the spatial pattern of rural land utilization, enhance the vitality of rural development and improve rural governance; to facilitate the realization of property income from rural residential land and promote the increase of farmers' income; and to promote the transformation of rural residential land utilization from crude to intensive, improve the level of intensive and economical utilization of rural residential land, and effectively protect the villagers' demand for land for reasonable housing construction.

(3) Contents of the reform

The reform of the rural residential land system is one of the most unique, sensitive and difficult to decide among the rural land system reforms. In order to achieve the above goals, the reform of the rural residential land system promoted by the Chinese government mainly includes the following specific contents.

1) **Reform of the rural residential land distribution system**

According to the law, a rural household can only own one parcel of residential land, and the area cannot exceed the standard set by the provincial government. The exception is that in areas where a household cannot be guaranteed one parcel of residential land due to the small amount of land per capita, the county government can take other measures to arrange the allocation of residential land with full respect for the wishes of rural villagers. The purpose of this regulation is to ensure that rural households have a home and that the resources of the residential land are not wasted at the same time. Therefore, the reform of the rural residential land allocation system involves the recognition of membership in collective economic organizations, the recognition of a household, and the limitation of area.

In terms of membership recognition, there are usually five types of ways to obtain membership in a rural collective economic organization: the first is acquired due to the initial establishment of the collective economic organization, i.e., they were already members when the organization was established; the second is acquired due to the reproduction of members of the collective economic organization, i.e., children born to members of the collective economic organization are automatically qualified since birth; the third is acquired by moving in by legal marriage and adoption; the fourth is acquired by moving in by law or policy, and the fifth is acquired by moving in by negotiation, i.e., a member of other collective economic organizations is allowed to become a member of the organization after negotiation. Accordingly, the following four situations lead to the loss of membership, namely, death, acquisition of membership in other collective economic organizations, failure to live and work in the collective economic organization, and dissolution of the collective economic organization.

In terms of the recognition of a household, a household can be identified as a new one that is qualified to be allocated a new parcel of rural residential land if: first, a male member reaches the legal age of marriage; second, a female member of a purely female household is married and her spouse has registered with the organization; third, after the parents and one child are combined into one household, one of the other children really needs to be identified as a new household.

In terms of the standard of a parcel of rural residential land, the regulations of provincial governments are not consistent. In Beijing, for example, the municipal government requires that the area of rural residential land for each household in suburban areas and distant suburban areas where there are many people and little land shall not exceed 0.25 mu, while that of rural residential land for each household in other regions shall not exceed 0.3 mu.

2) **Reform of rural residential land approval and house-building planning permission**
According to the policy requirements by the central government, when preparing territorial spatial planning and village planning, local governments should give comprehensive consideration to the production and living needs of rural residents, follow the principles of economy, intensive, and adapting to local conditions, make reasonable planning for the layout of rural settlements and the scale of construction land, arrange construction land quotas in accordance with national regulations, reasonably guarantee the demand for residential land for rural residents in the administrative region, and improve the living environment and conditions for rural residents. Specifically, in the planning, the permanent basic farmland shall not be occupied, and the existing residential land and vacant land in the village shall be gave priority to the use.

The township government is responsible for reviewing and approving applications submitted by rural residents for the use of residential land, and if it involves the occupation of agricultural land, the approval procedures should be carried out in accordance with the provisions of the *Land Administration Law*. Township governments are responsible for fulfilling their local responsibilities, optimizing the approval process, improving the efficiency of the approval process, strengthening supervision in and after the event, and organizing the work related to the approval of rural residential land and planning permission for building houses, providing peasants with convenient and efficient services.

The application procedure is as follows: peasants who meet the conditions for applying for a parcel of rural residential land shall submit a written application to their village group as a household unit. After receiving the application, the village group shall submit the application to the village group meeting for discussion and publicize the reasons for the application, the location and area of the proposed land, the proposed building height and area within the group. If there is no objection or objection is not established, the village group submits the application, minutes of the villager group meeting and other materials to the village collective economic organization for review. The village organization focuses on reviewing whether the materials submitted are real and valid, whether the proposed land for building the house is in line with the village plan, whether the views of adjacent rights holders have been consulted. If the review approved, the village organization signs the opinion and submits it to the township government. If the organization is not divided into village groups, or related matters have been handled by the village-level organizations, peasants shall apply directly to the village-level organization, and after discussion and approval by the village representatives meeting and public display within the scope of the collective economic organization, the application should be signed by the village organization and reported to the township government.

With regard to the review of the above applications, agriculture and rural affairs, natural resources and other relevant departments perform their respective work responsibilities in the material review, site inspection and other aspects. The department of agricultural and rural affairs is responsible for reviewing whether the applicant meets the application requirements, whether the proposed land meets the requirements of a reasonable layout and the area standards of the residential land, whether the residential land and building applications are audited and publicized by the village group, and make recommendations for approval with the comprehensive views of other relevant departments. The department of natural resources is responsible for reviewing whether the land for building houses in line with the territorial spatial planning, use control requirements. According to the results of the joint examination of various departments, the township government approves the application for rural residential land and issues the approval letter.

Housing construction activities of rural residents are subject to the whole process of management. In detail, rural household who has got approval for land to build house should apply to the township government or the lead department authorized to delineate the scope of residential land before the start of construction, the township government timely organizes agriculture and rural affairs, natural resources and other departments to the site for the inspection and measurement. After the completion of the construction, the township government organizes relevant departments for acceptance, field check whether the peasant uses the residential land in accordance with the approved area, the four areas and other requirements, whether the construction of house in accordance with the approved area and planning requirements. Peasants who pass the acceptance can apply to the real estate registration department for real estate registration.

3) **Reform of paid use of rural residential land**

The implementation of paid use of rural residential land is an ongoing experiment by local governments in some areas of China. Generally, rural households are not charged for the use of residential land if they meet the criteria. The following are the main situations for the paid use: a rural household occupies more than one parcel of residential land, the area of the residential land occupied by the rural household exceeds the standard, the person occupying the residential land is not a member of the collective economic organization and the occupation of the residential land is caused by the inheritance of a house, the residential land is occupied or transferred across collective economic organizations, the residential land is converted to business use, the location of the residential land has good locational advantages, the local government approved the construction of houses on the residential land without the farmers actually building them, instead leaving the residential land vacant for a long time; the parcels of rural residential land is developed by the collective economic organizations at the townships level.

The paid use fee of rural residential land is uniformly collected by village-level organizations according to the standard and manner prescribed by the government, and is mainly used for the cost of residential land repurchase, development and finishing, the expenditure of public welfare undertakings in the village and the distribution of members' income. From the current pilot implementation, on the one hand, the paid use is conducive to solving the historical legacy problems and achieving the goal of land conservation, while on the other hand, the farmers' acceptance of the policy of paid use of rural residential land is not high.

4) **Reform of withdrawal from rural residential land**
The withdrawal from rural residential land means that the person who has the right to use residential land voluntarily gives up the application for residential land and returns the legally obtained right to use residential land to the collective, or there is a change in the use of residential land. There are five common situations of rural residence land withdrawal as follows. First, the household returns the right to use the rural residential land to the owner, in a free or paid way; second, the household transfers the right to use the rural residential land to members of the collective economic organization within the same township or even others; third, the household transfers the right to occupy and use the rural residential land for a certain period of time to the lessee by way of rent and receives rent; fourth, the rural residential land is first converted into collective profit-oriented construction land and then transferred to other entities for use; fifth, one or more households operate with the right to use the rural residential land solely, or jointly with social capital, and obtain income.
The state allows rural residents who have settled in cities to withdraw from their residential land voluntarily and with compensation according to law. The rural government and rural collective economic organizations, villagers' committees shall give priority to the withdrawal of residential land to meet the needs of the members of the rural collective economic organizations. Relevant laws and regulations also provide that the residential land obtained in accordance with the law and the rural villagers' houses and their appurtenances on the residential land are protected by law, the forced transfer of rural residential land against the will of rural villagers is prohibited, the illegal recovery of residential land obtained by rural villagers in accordance with the law is prohibited, the withdrawal of residential land as a condition for rural villagers to settle in cities is prohibited, and the forced relocation of rural villagers to withdraw from residential bases is also prohibited.
5) **Reform of the activation of idle rural residential land and housing**
The central government hopes that local governments take into account the location conditions, resource endowment, environmental capacity, industrial base and historical and cultural heritage to develop new industries and new business modes using the idle rural housing, such as leisure agriculture, rural tourism, catering and lodging, cultural experience, creative office, e-commerce and other new industries that meet the characteristics of the countryside, as well as industrial integration development projects such as cold chain, primary processing and storage of agricultural products, and also supports the adoption of finishing, reclamation, greening to carry out idle rural residential land rectification, providing land element for farmers to build houses, rural construction and industrial development.
Under the premise of fully protecting the legitimate rights and interests of farmers' residential land, the central government supports rural collective economic organizations and their members to adopt various ways to revitalize and utilize idle residential land and housing in rural areas, such as self-operation, leasing, shareholding and cooperation; encourages rural collective economic

organizations with certain economic strength to revitalize and utilize idle residential land and housing in a unified manner; supports returning villagers to develop suitable rural industrial projects based on their own and idle housing; guides enterprises with strength, willingness and responsibility to participate in the revitalization and utilization work in an orderly manner; protects the legitimate rights and interests of various subjects in accordance with the law, and promotes the formation of a good situation of multi-participation and win–win cooperation.

The central government supports local governments at all levels to coordinate the arrangement of relevant funds for the use of incentives and subsidies for revitalizing the idle rural residential land and housing; encourages financial and credit products and service innovation to provide support for the revitalization and utilization of idle residential land and housing in rural areas. The central government also emphasizes the need to further strengthen the management of rural residential land, regulating the utilization methods, business industries, lease terms, and transfer objects, preventing encroachment on arable land, large demolition and construction, and illegal development, and ensuring that the revitalized and utilized idle rural residential land and housing is obtained in accordance with the law and has clear ownership.

4.6 Land Expropriation System

The land expropriation system has long existed in almost all countries, and under China's dualistic urban–rural land ownership system, it refers specifically to a series of policy arrangements for the conversion of rural land into state-owned construction land led by local governments, involving the following practical matters: the scope of land expropriation, i.e., the situations under which local governments can initiate land expropriation; land expropriation procedure, i.e., what necessary process local governments should go through to complete land expropriation; and compensation for land expropriation, i.e., what kind of compensation the expropriated rural collectives and farmers can receive for the loss of land and the amount of each kind. The following will first review the evolution of China's land expropriation system over the decades, and then focus on the current set of policy elements.

4.6.1 Evolution of Land Expropriation System in China

China's land expropriation system has roughly undergone a process of change from the planned economy, when absolute government dominance and low compensation were emphasized, to the reform and opening up, when land expropriation procedures and compensation standards were gradually adjusted, to the new era, when market-oriented allocation of urban and rural land elements and a sound mechanism for distributing land value-added benefits have been promoting. Since the economic and social development at different stages have different requirements for land management, China's land expropriation system has evolved with the times. For example, during the stage of rapid economic growth, the policies of construction land reserve, with land expropriation as the main approach, provided space security for the rapid industrialization and urbanization of China, but also led to a fragmented and dualistic urban–rural land market, which to a certain extent caused restrictions on rural development and damage to the interests of farmers, resulting in the Chinese government to pay attention to the protection of rural land rights and interests of collectives and farmers, and to make it the core objective of the reform of land expropriation system.

(1) **Land expropriation system before the reform and opening up (1949~1978)**

The land expropriation system after the founding of the People's Republic of China was created to meet the needs of socialist construction and evolved along with the extremely high political prestige of the nascent regime and ideological education in the context of public ownership transformation. This institutional arrangement ensured that the construction of infrastructure and industrial systems operated at a lower cost, strongly supporting the implementation of the priority development strategy of heavy industry during the planned economy.

The *Law of the People's Republic of China on Land Reform* issued in 1950 contains many provisions on "confiscation and expropriation of land". In order to speed up the process of getting rid of the backward situation of poverty, China studied the Soviet experience and aimed to establish a highly centralized planned economic system, giving priority to the development of heavy industry. In order to guarantee the demand for land for economic activities, the state designed a system of land expropriation, and the *Measures on Land Expropriation for Construction* issued in 1953 initially stipulated the procedures and compensation standards for land expropriation, making it clear that not only should the land necessary for construction be guaranteed, but also the interests of local residents should be taken care of, and production and living should be properly settled. The first *Constitution of the People's Republic of China*, adopted in 1954, clearly stipulated that "the State may, for the needs of public interest, expropriate, requisition or nationalize land and other means of production in urban and rural areas in accordance with the conditions prescribed by law". In 1958, the amended *Measures on Land Expropriation for Construction* was published, and the compensation standard was adjusted downward from the total production value in the last three to five years to that in the last two to four years, and this policy continued for more than 20 years.

Overall, during this period, the consensus on the objectives and meaning of land expropriation reduced the cost of institutional design, allowing the land expropriation system to be introduced quickly and to meet construction needs; the consensus on the rules, contents, and procedure of land expropriation reduced the cost of negotiation between the government and farmers during its implementation, ensuring that governments at all levels and entities could efficiently obtain the land needed for construction.

(2) Partial adjustments of the land expropriation system (1978~1998)

After the launch of reform and opening up, with the emergence and development of market economy and rapid industrialization, the value of land has become increasingly visible, and group interests and social ideology have become increasingly diversified, the social consensus to maintain the original land expropriation system has been weakening, and transaction costs have continued to rise, triggering partial policy adjustments.

In 1982, the State Council issued the *Regulations on the Expropriation of Land for Construction*, which refined the procedures, approval authority and compensation standards for land expropriation and proposed that the compensation standard for the expropriation of arable land should be three to six times the annual output value of the expropriated land. The *Land Administration Law*, which was adopted by the Standing Committee of the National People's Congress in 1986, further clarified that the resettlement subsidy for farmers whose land is expropriated was also calculated with reference to the multiple of the annual output value of the land, and the sum of land compensation and resettlement subsidy shall not exceed 20 times of the annual output value of the expropriated land. The revised *Land Administration Law in 1998* raised the upper limit of the sum of land compensation and resettlement subsidy to 30 times the annual production value of the land, but the revision did not make significant reforms to the scope of land compensation and compensation standards, but instead shifted the land compensation procedure from mutual agreement to unilateral announcement by the local government.

The practice of this period showed that although the passive policy adjustment of simply raising the compensation standard as the main content had alleviated the pressure in the short term, it could not fundamentally solve the contradiction resulted by land expropriation, and even led to the dissatisfaction of the peasants whose land was expropriated in the early days due to the change of compensation standards, so that the reform of the land expropriation system was put on the agenda.

(3) Initial exploration of reforming the land expropriation system (1998~2012)

At the end of the twentieth century, with the accelerated development of market economy and rapid urbanization, China's economy maintained high growth. The relatively crude development model coupled with the inadequate design of the relevant system has led to the increasing scale of land expropriation, and factors such as non-compliance with legal procedures, illegal forced expropriation, unreasonable compensation and resettlement, and misconduct of a few cadres have made land expropriation conflicts one of the major issues affecting social stability. Under the situation that land expropriation activities were becoming the main growth point of social conflicts, the social consensus that the land expropriation system must be reformed was gradually formed.

In 1999, the former Ministry of Land and Resources organized a research group whose task was to study on the reform of the land expropriation system, and since 2001, two batches of pilot projects on the reform had been launched nationwide, aiming at exploring feasible compensation standards, resettlement approaches and management procedures for land expropriation, but none of them involved the deeper issue of the scope of land expropriation. In 2003, the Third Plenary Session of the 16th CPC Central Committee proposed the direction of land expropriation reform as to improve the procedures, strictly distinguish the land for public welfare and business construction purposes, conform to the overall land use planning and use control, and give the farmers reasonable compensation in a timely manner, in accordance with the principles of protecting the rights and interests of farmers and controlling the scale of land expropriation. The 2004 amendment to the *Constitution* amended the relevant article as "The state may, in the public interest, expropriate or requisition land in accordance with the provisions of the law and pay compensation". In the same year, the *Land Administration Law* was constitutionally amended, and the State Council issued the *Decisions on Deepening Reform and Strict Land Management*, which required local governments to ensure that the living standards of farmers whose land had been expropriated were not lowered due to land expropriation and that their long-term livelihoods were guaranteed, while to improve land expropriation procedures and strengthen the supervision of land expropriation implementation.

Previously, the former Ministry of Land and Resources had issued a series of documents such as the *Notice on Strengthening the Management of Land Expropriation* (1999), the *Measures on the Announcement of Land Expropriation* (2001), the *Notice on Effective Compensation and Resettlement for Land Expropriation* (2001), and the *Notice on Effectively Safeguarding the Lawful Rights and Interests of Expropriated Farmers* (2002). The *Law of the People's Republic of China on Property Rights*, issued in 2007, clearly stipulates that in addition to the compensation for land expropriation, arrangements should be made for the social security costs of farmers whose land is expropriated. In order to implement the requirement of "reforming the land expropriation system, strictly defining land for public welfare and business construction purposes, gradually reducing the scope of land expropriation, and improving the compensation mechanism for land expropriation" as proposed by the Third Plenary Session of the 17th CPC Central Committee in 2008, in 2010, the former Ministry of Land and Resources launched a new round of pilot projects to reform the land expropriation system in 11 cities and began exploring ways to reduce the scope of land expropriation. Although the outcomes of the reform were relatively limited, it has to a certain extent alleviated the intensifying conflicts over land expropriation and accumulated a social consensus for the reform, laying the foundation for the subsequent comprehensive deepening of the reform.

(4) **Deepening reform of the land expropriation system (2012~)**

Since the 18th National Congress of the Communist Party of China, socialism with Chinese characteristics has entered a new era. With the changes in economic and social development, including the decline in economic growth speed, the weakening of the function of land as an economic "engine" and the widening of the gap between urban and rural areas, the construction of a modern market economic system and the promotion of high-quality development have become the themes of the times, and the social consensus of promoting the sharing of land value-added benefits through the reform of the land expropriation system has been established and continuously consolidated.

In 2012, the 18th National Congress of the Communist Party of China (CPC) explicitly proposed "reforming the land expropriation system and increasing the proportion of farmers' share in the land value-added benefits", making it clear for the first time at the central level that farmers should share in the value-added benefits from land, providing an important foundation for the formation of a new order for the distribution of value-added benefits from land that integrates the interests of the state and farmers, with fairness and justice as the guide. In 2013, the Third Plenary Session of the 18th CPC Central Committee proposed the establishment of a unified urban–rural construction land market, which, on the one hand, allows rural collectively owned profit-oriented construction land to be directly transferred or leased in the open market to obtain the same treatment as state-owned construction land, on the premise of compliance with planning and use control, and on the other hand, narrows the scope of land expropriation, standardizes land expropriation procedures, and improves a reasonable, standardized and diversified protection mechanism for farmers whose land is expropriated. This means that the state-led reform of the land expropriation system has taken a major turn and has begun to focus on giving farmers a greater share of land value-added benefits through the free flow and equal exchange of land elements.

The *Land Administration Law* amended in 2019 absorbed the outcomes of land expropriation system reform in pilot areas during the period from 2015 to 2018, and promoted some reform experiences with high social consensus through legal forms, such as clearly defining the scope of public interest, calculating compensation for land expropriation by the integrated land price method instead of the production value multiplier method, and guaranteeing the right of land-deprived farmers to obtain information and participate in. Subsequently, the central government proposed a new round of general deployment and top-level design to deepen the reform of the land expropriation system in accordance with the requirements of building a new development pattern, continued to promote the reform of market-oriented allocation of land elements, and accelerated the establishment and improvement of a unified urban and rural construction land market. In 2020, the Fifth Plenary Session of the 19th CPC Central Committee proposed the establishment of a mechanism for identifying public interest situations in which land expropriation could be initiated, and in the same year, the Ministry of Natural Resources issued the standard for land expropriation for comprehensive development purpose, which are practical initiatives to achieve the goal of narrowing the scope of land expropriation.

The reform of the land expropriation system in this period has been promoted in depth, showing the following characteristics: First, in terms of reform objectives and value orientation, it goes beyond the instrumental rationality and respond positively to the value rationality that should be embedded in the land system, aiming to reshape the pattern of distribution of land value-added benefits; second, in terms of reform content, more attention has been paid to the systemic, holistic and synergistic nature of the reform, and within the framework of establishing a unified urban and rural land factor market, it has integrated the reform of land expropriation, marketization of rural collectively owned profit-oriented construction land and the rural residential land reform, and the reform of the scope of, compensation standards for, and procedures of land expropriation has be comprehensively promoted; third, in terms of the way to promote the reform, more attention has be paid to the combination of top-level design and grassroots exploration, with the central government specifying the general direction and bottom-line principles of reform, authorizing the local governments to carry out innovative pilot projects, and timely absorbing the experiences that have achieved greater social consensus into laws, so that the central and local governments have formed a positive interaction. Overall, the change in the reform mode of the land expropriation system is not only a positive response to the transformation of China's major social contradictions and national strategies such as rural revitalization and high-quality development, but also the inevitable result of the accumulation of experience and the enhancement of social consensus in the adjustment of land expropriation policies.

4.6.2 Current Policy on the Implementation of Land Expropriation System

China's current land expropriation policy builds on the amendments to the Land Administration Law in 2019 and focuses on three issues: Situations in which land can be expropriated, compensation for peasants whose land is expropriated, and the procedures to conduct the land expropriation.

(1) **Narrowing the scope of situations in which land can be expropriated**

Defining the scope of the government's power to expropriate land involves a trade-off between the interests of urban development and those of rural development, and thus has been the focus of debate in the reform of the land expropriation system. According to the *Constitution*, the state may expropriate land to meet the public interest needs in accordance with the law. It is clear that the situations for permitting land expropriation are that for public interest needs, however, the definition of public interest has long been rather vague. In recent years, the central government has been working to narrow the scope of land expropriation by clearing defining the situations that are related to public interest needs.

1) **Situations in which land expropriation can be implemented**. According to the provisions of the *Land Administration Law*, the expropriation of land owned by rural collectives may be carried out in accordance with the law under one of the following situations: land needed for military and diplomatic purposes; land needed for infrastructure construction such as energy, transportation, water conservancy, communications and postal services organized and implemented by the government; land needed for public affairs in the fields such as science and technology, education, culture, health, sports, ecological environment and resource protection, disaster prevention and mitigation, cultural relics protection,

comprehensive community services, social welfare, municipal public utilities, mercy and resettlement, martyr protection organized and implemented by the government; land needed for poverty alleviation and affordable housing construction organized and implemented by the government; land needed for comprehensive development within the scope of the overall land use plan, approved by the government at or above the provincial level and organized and implemented by the local government at or above the county level; and other situations in which land is needed for meeting the public interests needs.

2) **Comprehensive development with land expropriation can be implemented.** With regard to these situations listed in the *Land Administration Law*, there is no controversy about the need for land expropriation other than in the case of the comprehensive development. Critics have suggested that local governments could abuse the provision, making it difficult for the central government's efforts to narrow the scope of situations in which land can be expropriated to work. In light of this, the central government has further clarified what constitutes the comprehensive development that meets the needs of the public interest. The general requirement is that land expropriation for comprehensive development should adhere to the new development concept, be people-centered, focus on protecting arable land, focus on safeguarding peasants' legitimate rights and interests, focus on the economical and intensive use of land, focus on ecological and environmental protection, and promote sustainable development of local economy and society.

   Based on this requirement, before applying for land expropriation on the grounds of comprehensive development, local governments above the county level should organize to prepare a comprehensive development plan based on the local economic and social development plan and territorial spatial planning, incorporate it into the local economic and social development annual plan, and submit it to the provincial government for approval.

   The comprehensive development plan should include the following: the basic situation of the comprehensive development about the location, area, scope and infrastructure conditions; the necessity, main uses and functions to be achieved of the comprehensive development; construction projects to be arranged for comprehensive, the development timing and annual implementation plan; the proportion of land for infrastructure, public service facilities and other public welfare purposes within a complete comprehensive development scope determined by the territorial spatial planning, which is generally not less than 40%; assessment of the land use benefits as well as economic, social and ecological benefits of comprehensive development.

   According to the requirements of the central government, local governments at or above the county level should fully listen to the opinions of People's Congresses deputies, People's Political Consultative Conference members, the public and relevant experts and scholars when preparing the plan of comprehensive development for land expropriation. After preparing the plan, they should also fully consult the rural collective economic organizations and peasants within the area of comprehensive development and obtain the consent of more than two-thirds of the members of the villagers' meeting or more than two-thirds of the villagers' representatives who are members of the collective economic organizations. Otherwise, no application for land expropriation for comprehensive development shall be made.

Upon receipt of a comprehensive development plan submitted by a local government at or above the county level, the provincial government shall organize a committee of experts, which shall consist of representatives of the People's Congress, members of the People's Political Consultative Conference and experts in land, planning, economics, law, environmental protection, and industry, to demonstrate the scientificity and necessity of the comprehensive development plan for land expropriation. The conclusion of the demonstration should be used as an important basis for approving the plan. Besides, National natural resources inspectors, the Ministry of Natural Resources, the provincial government should strengthen the supervision of work of comprehensive development for land expropriation.

For the existence of one of the following situations, the provincial governments shall not approve the comprehensive development plan for land expropriation: involving the occupation of permanent basic farmland; the existence of a large amount of unprovided or idle land in the city and county areas; the land use efficiency in various types of development zones and new urban areas is relatively low; the local government has not completed the annual implementation plan for two consecutive years in terms of the approved comprehensive development plan.

(2) **Improving the compensation for peasants whose land is expropriated**

Given that land is the most basic means of production on which Chinese peasants depend for survival, land expropriation means the loss of the most important income and security sources for most of peasants, compensation for land-deprived peasants is therefore the most concerned element of the land expropriation system. In the process of reforming the land expropriation system, the Chinese government has paid an increasing attention to performing its redistribution adjustment function, emphasizing the improvement of a reasonable, standardized and diversified protection mechanism for the land-deprived peasants, so that they can share more of the value-added benefits of land development. The basic principle is to give fair and reasonable compensation to the land-deprived peasants, and to ensure that the living standard of land-deprived peasants does not drop below original and that their long-term livelihood is guaranteed.

1) **Composition of compensation**. The main components that constitute compensation for peasants whose land is expropriated are the following: land compensation, resettlement subsidy, compensations for dwellings, other attachments and crops, and the costs required to integrate the land-deprived peasants into the social security system.

2) **Land compensation and resettlement subsidy**. Land compensation is the compensation for the loss of land owners and land users due to their input into the land that is expropriated by the state. Settlement subsidy is the subsidy granted by the state to settle the agricultural population who use the expropriated land as the main means of production and the source to maintain a livelihood.

   According to the current law, the land compensation and resettlement subsidy granted by the local government to the collectives and peasants whose land is expropriated is calculated based on an established standard. This standard is reflected as the comprehensive land price at the block scale set and announced by the provincial government, specifically, it refers to the compensation standard directly used for land expropriation, which is formulated by dividing blocks by considering the factors such as land type, production value, location, grade, as well as the amount of local arable land per capita, land supply and demand, the level of economic development and the level of minimum living security for urban residents. According to the requirements of the central government, the comprehensive land price at the block scale should be set with a comprehensive consideration of the original use of land, land resource conditions, land production value, land location, land supply and demand, population and the level of economic and social development, and should be adjusted or re-announced at least every three years. The principles to be followed for such adjustment include:

   First is the principle of reasonable security. The comprehensive land price at the block scale should be adapted to the local economic and social development level, and the division of the blocks and the calculation method should be scientific and reasonable, so as to ensure that the living standard of the land-deprived peasants will not be reduced and their long-term livelihood will be guaranteed.

   Second is the principle of smooth transition. The new comprehensive land price at the block scale needs to be formulated in accordance with the requirements of the law by adopting scientific and reasonable technical methods, so as to ensure its full convergence with the existing compensation standards for land expropriation and the smooth promotion of practice of compensation and resettlement for land expropriation.

   Third is the principle of regional coordination. The comprehensive land price at the block scale between adjacent areas should be appropriately balanced to avoid excessive differences. When carrying out the balancing work, the differences in social security and resettlement approaches between different regions should be taken into account in an integrated manner, so that the overall level of compensation for land expropriation is reasonable.

   Last is the principle of public participation. When formulating the comprehensive land price at the block scale, the views of relevant departments, villagers' committees, rural collective economic organizations, peasants and various sectors of society should be widely heard to ensure public participation.

3) **Compensations for dwellings, other attachments and crops**. The standards for this type of compensation are, again, set by the provincial government. It is worth noting that the current policy distinguishes peasants' dwellings from other attachments, reflecting the protection of peasants' right to live and their

legitimate housing property rights and interests. Specifically, if the dwelling of land-deprived peasants is built on the expropriated land, fair and reasonable compensation should be given in accordance with the principles of compensation before relocation and improvement of living conditions, respecting the wishes of peasants and adopting such means as rearranging residential bases to build dwellings, providing resettlement dwellings or monetary compensation, and compensating for the costs of relocation and temporary resettlement caused by the expropriation.

4) **Integrating the land-deprived peasants into the social security system**. According to the law, local governments at or above the county level shall include land-deprived peasants in the social security system in the fields such as pensions. The social security costs for land-deprived peasants are mainly used to provide subsidies for eligible land-deprived peasants to pay social insurance such as pension insurance. Provincial governments are responsible for formulating the collection, management and use of social security fees for land-deprived peasants.
5) **The availability of compensation is a prerequisite for the approval of land acquisition applications**. According to the requirements of the central government, local governments above the county level that apply for land expropriation should raise all types of compensation in a timely manner, including land compensation, resettlement subsidy, compensation for dwellings, other attachments and crops, and social security costs, and ensure that the full amount is in place and earmarked for the purpose. In the case that the relevant compensation is not fully in place, their applications for land expropriation will not be approved.
6) **Distribution of compensation for land expropriation**. According to the law, the compensation paid for the attachments and crops belongs to their owners. As for the distribution of land compensation and resettlement subsidy, the central government authorizes the provincial governments to formulate corresponding methods. Based on the nature of these two types of compensation, the allocation of the resettlement subsidy is less controversial and usually goes to the land-deprived peasants. The focus of the controversy is on how to allocate the land compensation between the collective and the land-deprived peasants. In fact, there are many disputes arising from this in practice.

Since the compensation for land expropriation is the compensation for peasants and rural collective economic organizations whose land is expropriated by the state due to the public interest and social development needs, the proper management and use of this fund is an important measure to safeguard the rights and interests of rural collective economic organizations and land-deprived peasants, which concerns the stability of rural social development, so the central government has always attached great importance to it. In 2005, the Ministry of Agriculture formulated the *Opinions on Strengthening Supervision, Management and Guidance of Land Expropriation Compensation for Rural Collective Economic Organizations*, proposing that the allocation of land compensation after 2005 should be distributed in accordance with the standards set by the provincial governments, and especially emphasizing that land expropriation compensation should be mainly used for the production and living needs of the land-deprived peasants, and should be regulated in strict accordance with the principles of special account storage, special account management, and special use of funds. The land compensation that is reserved for the land-deprived peasants belongs to themselves; the land compensation that is reserved for the rural collective economic organizations belongs to the collective assets and should be used to develop production and increase accumulation, and should not be used to issue compensation to cadres, pay for hospitality and other non-productive expenses. Resettlement subsidies belong to the peasants who lost their land, must be earmarked for special use, not diverted for other purposes. The plan about the allocation and use of the land compensation shall be approved by the general meeting or representative assembly of the members of the rural collective economic organization, and the actual expenditure and management of the land compensation shall be reported to the general meeting or representative assembly of the members of the rural collective economic organization afterwards. At present, more than ten provinces have formulated documents about the management of land compensation allocation, with corresponding regulations on the allocation standards, scope of use, accounting methods, and approval procedures. In general, the land compensation is allocated to peasants in a proportion of not less than 70% to 80%, and the remaining portion is reserved for the operation and management of collective economic organizations for the development and growth of the collective economy or village public welfare undertakings.

(3) **Regulating the procedures to conduct land expropriation**

Land expropriation procedures are an important part of the land expropriation system. In order to improve the land expropriation system, the Chinese government has been committed to exploring to establish land expropriation procedures that better meet the needs of economic and social development, with the basic direction of expanding citizens' administrative participation, promoting consultation and cooperation between the government and citizens, and guaranteeing the right to equal participation of land-deprived peasants in the decision-making and implementation of land expropriation. The revision of the *Land Administration Law* in 2019 reflects this direction; before that, the provisions of the law on expropriation procedures were relatively simple and the design of the procedures was not perfect, especially lacking the contents on how to restrain the government's behavior and guarantee the expropriated peasants' rights to know, participate, express and supervise, which led to the failure to define the substantive rights given to the expropriated peasants by laws and regulations as well as relevant documents issued by the central government. The revised law fills the gap regarding the pre-approval procedure of land expropriation, strengthens the peasants' right to know and speak, and also increases the content of social risk assessment with the times, and makes whether or not to sign compensation and resettlement agreements as an important basis for approving land expropriation applications. According to the latest law, the following legal procedures are required to conduct land expropriation.

1) **Issuing pre-announcement of land expropriation**. If the local government at or above the county level considers that it should apply to the higher level of government for the expropriation of land in situations that meet the needs of the public interest, it shall first issue a pre-announcement of the expropriation of land, which shall include the scope of the expropriation, the purpose of the expropriation, and the arrangements for conducting a survey of the current status of the land. Pre-announcement of land expropriation shall be made in the township, village and village group where the land is to be expropriated in a manner conducive to public knowledge, and the pre-announcement duration shall not be less than ten working days. It should be noted that from the date of issuing the pre-announcement of land expropriation, no entity or individual shall be allowed to plant and build within the proposed area of expropriation; if they do so in violation of the provisions, no compensation shall be paid for the new planting and building.
2) **Conducting survey on the current status of the land to be expropriated and social stability risk assessment**. While issuing the pre-announcement of land expropriation, the local government should also carry out a survey on the current status of the land to be expropriated and social stability risk assessment. Through the former, the location, ownership, type and area of the land, as well as the ownership, type and quantity of rural villagers' residences, other above-ground attachments and crops, should be identified. The latter means to conduct a comprehensive study and judgment on the social stability risk situation of the land expropriation, determining the risk points, and proposing risk prevention measures and disposal plans. It should be noted that when carrying out the social stability risk assessment, the rural collective economic organizations and their members, villagers' committees and other stakeholders of the land expropriation should be invited to participate, and the assessment results should be used as an important basis for the application for land expropriation.
3) **Drafting compensation and resettlement solution for land expropriation**. Local governments at or above the county level should organize the natural resources, finance, agriculture and rural affairs, human resources and social security, and other relevant departments to draft compensation and resettlement solution for land expropriation, which shall be based on the results of social stability risk assessment and combined with the status of land survey. The solution should include such contents as the scope of expropriation, the current state of the land, the purpose of expropriation, compensation method and standards, objects to be resettled, resettlement approach, and social security plan.
4) **Issuing announcement of compensation and resettlement for land expropriation**. After drafting the compensation and resettlement solution for land expropriation, the local government at or above the county level should announce it within the scope of township, village and village groups where the land is to be expropriated, and the announcement should last no less than thirty days. And within this period, the local government should listen to the views of the rural collective economic organizations and their members, villagers' committees and other interested parties. This announcement should also contain the way

and period for the registration of compensation, as well as the feedback channel for objections.

5) **Organizing hearing (optional)**. If the majority of the members of the rural collective economic organizations whose land is expropriated believe that the compensation and resettlement solution does not comply with the laws and regulations, the local government at or above the county level shall organize a hearing and modify the solution in accordance with the provisions of laws and regulations and the feedback from the hearing.
6) **Signing compensation and resettlement agreement for land expropriation**. The owner and the holder of the right to use of the land to be expropriated should register for compensation with documents proving real estate ownership within the period specified in the announcement. Local governments at or above the county level shall organize the relevant departments to calculate and raise the compensation to ensure that the full amount will be available for distribution in the future. Local governments above the county level should organize the relevant departments and the owner and the holder of the right to use of the land to be expropriated to sign the compensation and resettlement agreement, according to the compensation and resettlement solution determined. The model text of compensation and resettlement agreement for land expropriation should be formulated by the provincial governments. If there are indeed cases where some individuals are unwilling to sign compensation and resettlement agreements for land expropriation with the local government, the local government should truthfully explain this when applying for land expropriation.
7) **Submitting land expropriation application for approval**. Local governments at or above the county level may submit applications for land expropriation to higher-level governments with approval authority for their approval only after completing the above-mentioned preliminary work on land expropriation. According to the law, the State Council's approval is required if the expropriation is for the following types of land: permanent basic farmland, arable land over thirty-five hectares that is not permanent basic farmland, and other land over seventy hectares; while other types of land expropriation require the approval of the provincial government. When the State Council or provincial governments review the application for land expropriation, the main contents of the review are: the necessity and reasonableness of the land expropriation, whether it is consistent with the situations that require the expropriation of land in the public interest and whether it conforms to the legal procedures.
8) **Issuing announcement of land expropriation**. If the submitted application for land expropriation is approved, the local government at or above the county level shall, within fifteen working days from the date of receipt of the approved document, publish a notice of land expropriation within the village group, the village, and the town where the land to be expropriated is located, announcing the specific work arrangements including the scope of expropriation, the time of expropriation, and for individuals with whom no agreement on compensation and resettlement for land expropriation has been reached, the local government shall make a decision on compensation and resettlement for land acquisition, and organize the implementation in accordance with the law.

Chapter 5
Land Protection Policies

Siliang Wang and Shukui Tan

Land protection is another important dimension of land use in the broad sense, aiming at preserving land resources, restoring and improving their material production capacity, and preventing environmental pollution existing in land use, so that they can be used sustainably and meet the long-term needs of human beings for their own survival and development. The Chinese central government has been attaching great importance to the sustainable protection of land resources, and is constantly updating the protection philosophy, enriching the policy framework and optimizing the policy tools portfolio. This chapter introduces China's land protection policies in three main areas: first, cultivated land protection policies for food security strategies; second, industrial and mining land reclamation and ecological restoration policies to address the land pollution problems accumulated during the rapid industrialization and urbanization; and third, policies related to integrated ecological protection and restoration of territorial space based on system perspective. For each type of policy, this chapter systematically describes its history and outlines its whole picture, i.e., why it is implemented, how it has been evolved, and what are the key actions currently being taken to implement it.

S. Wang (✉)
Hunan University, Changsha, China
e-mail: wangsiliang@hnu.edu.cn

S. Tan
Huazhong University of Science and Technology, Wuhan, China

S. Tan and X. Huang (eds.), *Land Policy in China*, The Frontier of Public Administration in China, https://doi.org/10.1007/978-981-19-9895-9_5

5.1 Cultivated Land Protection

5.1.1 *Policy Outline*

(1) **Fundamental intention: ensuring food security**

The people are the foundation of a country, and food is the primary need of the people. As food decides national prosperity and the people's wellbeing, food security is a major prerequisite for national security, for China is no exception. Since the founding of the People's Republic of China (PRC) in 1949, China has always prioritized food security in state governance and treated food security as a top state issue. Despite a weak agricultural foundation and extreme poverty, the Communist Party of China (CPC) has led an unremitting campaign of hard work over the past 70 years that has made China basically self-sufficient in food supply. China now has enough food to feed its nearly 1.4 billion population, and has remarkably improved the people's nutrition and life quality. China's food security is a success of worldwide significance.

As the basis of food production, cultivated land is a scarce resource with fixed location and sustainable use, and is the core element to ensure food security. Compared with many countries in the world, China's cultivated land resources are characterized by less cultivated land per capita, less high-quality cultivated land and less cultivated land reserve resources. For example, China's per capita cultivated land level is less than 40% of the world average, the results of cultivated land quality classification according to the ten-grade system show that the highest three grades of cultivated land account for less than one third. Thus, cultivated land protection is an overall strategic issue related to China's sustainable economic and social development. Especially in the process of rapid urbanization, the loss of high-quality cultivated land has aroused the great attention of the Chinese government and the public to food security.

Therefore, although the implementation of cultivated land protection has economic, social, political, environmental and other considerations, for China, the largest developing country, ensuring food security is undoubtedly the most important fundamental policy intention. It is precisely out of following the principle of basic grain self-sufficiency based on domestic grain production that China has practiced the strictest farmland protection system, a strategy of sustainable farmland use, and innovative application of agricultural technology to increase farmland productivity, which has achieved positive results. In 2019, the country has 134.88 million hectares of cultivated land, an increase of more than 4.8 million hectares over 1996. There are more than 117 million hectares sown with grain, an increase of about 4.5 million hectares over 1996. The foundations of grain production have been strengthened.

Although China has embarked on a road to establishing food security in its own way based on its own national conditions and food availability, making historic achievements in feeding nearly 20% of the world's population with 9% of the world's cultivated land, it still has a long way to go in ensuring sustainable food security. Nowadays, in order to achieve the strategic goal of "ensuring basic self-sufficiency of grain and absolute security of staple food", the basic supporting role of cultivated land protection policy is still needed to be constantly played.

(2) **Evolving goal: from single to trinity**

The establishment of China's cultivated land protection policy system started in the 1980s. At that time, with the economic and social transformation brought about by reform and opening up, the cultivated land resources experienced a sharp decline, which was not only directly caused by the disorderly occupation of cultivated land for urban and rural construction purpose, but also indirectly related to the lack of cultivated land use management system. In fact, one of the legislative purposes of the *Land Administration Law* deliberated and adopted in 1986 was to effectively protect cultivated land resources. Since then, the Chinese central government has successively issued a series of policy documents related to cultivated land protection, according to the statistics of some scholars, from 1978 to 2019, the number of cultivated land protection policy documents issued by the central government was more than 450, which indicated that promoting the implementation of the world's strictest cultivated land protection system has become one of China's important national strategies for a long time.

Generally, it is acknowledged that the evolution of China's cultivated land protection policy has experienced three stages: formation stage (before 2003), improvement stage (2003–2013), and maturation stage (after 2013). This phased evolution not only reflects the changing situation faced by cultivated land protection, but also related to the deepening understanding of the concept of cultivated land protection by all sectors of society. The policy goal of cultivated land protection set by the Chinese government in this process are also not invariable, but have experienced changes from single to trinity.

In the formation stage, the most important consideration of the Chinese government in the decision-making of cultivated land protection is to slow down the sharp decline of cultivated land resources and protect national food security. Therefore, for the decision-makers in this period, the protection of cultivated land quantity is the first. The Chinese government put forward the idea of "dynamic balance of total cultivated land" in 1996 and officially wrote it into the *Land Administration Law* in 1998. In short, the "dynamic balance of total cultivated land" refers to the balance between supply and demand of cultivated land in both quantity and quality aspects under the condition of meeting the growing demand for cultivated land by population growth and economic development. In the view of the Chinese government, the scale of cultivated land that needs to maintain at a dynamic balance level is 120 million hectares. Therefore, in 1997, it proposed to implement the policy of balancing the occupation and replenishment of cultivated land, that is, if non-agricultural construction does need to occupy cultivated land, it must replenish cultivated land that is not less than the occupied area and meets the quality standards. With the introduction of a series of subsequent supporting policy documents, this policy has played a positive role in protecting cultivated land, stopping the indiscriminate occupation of cultivated land and the abuse of land. By 2002, all provinces in mainland China have achieved the balance of occupation and replenishment of cultivated land in their own regions.

However, although the policy design requires that the quality of replenished cultivated land should be equal to that of occupied cultivated land, in actual implementation, the central government only requires local governments to submit the quantity when making statistics on the situation of balancing the occupation and replenishment of cultivated land, so that local governments have no incentive to supervise how land users replenish cultivated land. For profit reasons, the quality of the cultivated land replenished by land users often just meets the minimum standards of the local government, which is far from that of the cultivated land occupied by the construction, because the construction usually occurs in areas with high-quality cultivated land around the city. As this situation occurs in many regions, the quality of cultivated land throughout the country has decreased. Moreover, although the policy intended to limit unreasonable land use, many people misunderstood that the reserve resources of cultivated land were unlimited, and as long as cultivated land could be replenished in other places, cultivated land could be occupied all the time, which made the blind demand for land expanded invisibly.

This grim situation promoted the central government to further improve the cultivated land protection policy. During the improvement stage, the policy goal developed from a single focus on quantity to taking into account quantity and quality. On one side, the central government improved the policy of balancing the occupation and replenishment of cultivated land by putting forward specific operable requirements for the balance of quality. Weight is given to the recognized quantity according to the quality of replenished cultivated land. If the quality grade of replenished cultivated land is lower than that of occupied cultivated land, it is required to replenish more cultivated land than the absolute quantity of occupied cultivated land. Moreover, in order to ensure that this requirement is fully implemented, the central government also requires that cultivated land be permitted to be occupied only after the cultivated land meeting the quality and quantity standards is replenished. On the other side, the central government has launched the project to develop large-scale high standard farmland, through the introduction of advanced agricultural technology for land remediation, the quality of cultivated land in China has been greatly improved.

Since 2013, the Chinese government has further improved the setting of cultivated land protection objectives, brought ecological considerations into the scope, and proposed to establish a trinity cultivated land protection objective system, involving quantity, quality and ecology. There are two main reasons for this decision. The first aspect is still related to the problems exposed in the operation of the policy of balancing occupation and replenishment of cultivated land, that is, some places take the development of ecological land as the source of replenished cultivated land, which makes the newly reclaimed cultivated land at the cost of pasture, forest land and wetland, resulting in serious losses of the ecological environment, including desertification, soil erosion, biodiversity damage, etc. On the other hand, blindly pursuing the balance in the terms of quantity and quality makes the use of cultivated land tend to exceed its own capacity, resulting in serious cultivated land ecological environment pollution. Consequently, cultivated land rehabilitation has become another key word in China's cultivated land protection in recent years.

It should be noted that the trinity of cultivated land protection policy goal is not a simple superposition or mechanical combination of three single goals, but reflects the overall thinking of decision-making based on the whole natural system. Among them, the protection of cultivated land quantity is the premise of protecting cultivated land quality and cultivated land ecology, and the protection of cultivated land quality and that of cultivated land ecology interact and rely on each other. This trinity goal means that on the basis of ensuring the quantity of cultivated land, cultivated land protection should gradually improve the quality of cultivated land and continuously improve the ecological environment of cultivated land, so as to coordinate the symbiotic relationship between the quantity, quality and ecology of cultivated land.

(3) **Basic principles: fourfold requirements**

The Chinese government has set four basic principles for formulating and implementing cultivated land protection policies, requiring relevant localities and departments to adhere to them in their specific work.

1) **Strictly protecting and administrating**
The Chinese government has been devoting to widely spread and shape the awareness of cultivated land protection in the whole society. It requires the central departments and local governments at all levels to strengthen land use control, pay attention to improving the quality of cultivated land, prevent the problems of insufficient replenishment in quantity or quality aspect as well as the phenomena of "occupying more but replenishing less", "occupying good quality but replenishing poor quality", "occupying paddy fields but replenishing dry lands" in implementing the policy of balancing the occupation and replenishment of cultivated land. In particular, it is emphasized that the established red line of cultivated land must not be crossed in any time, and the designated permanent basic farmland parcels around the city must not be arbitrarily occupied.
2) **Prioritizing the economical use of land**
The Chinese government requires central departments and local governments at all levels to optimize the allocation structure of construction land from two sources (existing construction land and new construction land) when formulating land use plans. The basic requirement for land use in urban and rural development is to strictly control the scale of new construction land and reuse the existing construction land as much as possible. The Chinese government believes that by improving the level of economical and intensive land use, less land input can also support sustainable economic and social development, and at the same time, the unreasonable occupation of cultivated land by urban and rural construction can be reduced.
3) **Coordinating related affairs**
The Chinese government requires that the general principle of resource allocation, that is, giving full play to the decisive role of the market and giving better play to the role of the government, should also be applied to cultivated land protection. In order to coordinate cultivated land protection with economic and social development and ecological civilization construction, as well as to unify the responsibilities, rights and interests of cultivated land protection, he Chinese government points out that the following should be done: strengthening the main responsibility of cultivated land protection, improving the interest adjustment mechanism, promoting both incentives and constraints, and improving the supervision and assessment system.
4) **Reforming and innovating**
The efforts of Chinese government on cultivated land protection is problem-orientated, emphasizing the need to constantly reform and innovate policy

measures to adapt to the macroeconomic and social development situation of the times it is in. In the contexts of entering a "new normal" economic development period and promoting supply-side structural reform, the focus of the Chinese government's reform and innovation of cultivated land protection policies mainly lies in grasping the relationship between economic development and cultivated land protection by improving the policy of balancing the occupation and replenishment of cultivated land, including: improving the permanent basic farmland control system, optimizing the management mode of dynamic balance of total cultivated land, implementing the differential policy of balancing the occupation and replenishment, and broadening the ways to replenish cultivated land as well as capital sources.

(4) **Main carrier: permanent basic farmland**

As the essence of cultivated land, permanent basic farmland is the main carrier for implementing the cultivated land protection policies to be mentioned next. To understand what permanent basic farmland is, we need to start with the introduction on its predecessor, basic farmland, as there is no essential difference between the two concepts. Nevertheless, the change in the name does reflect the Chinese government's increasing attention to cultivated land protection.

According to the *Regulations on Protection of Basic Farmland* adopted by the State Council in 1998, basic farmland refers to the cultivated land that cannot be occupied to meet the needs of population and socio-economic development for agricultural products in a certain period of time, and the parcels of basic farmland are determined according to the overall land use planning. The protection of basic farmland in China can be traced back to the 1980s, when some regions piloted the protection of basic farmland against the tense relationship between people and land as well as the threatened food security. By the early 1990s, hundreds of counties in more than 20 provinces had adopted the approach of designating basic farmland protection zones to protect basic farmland. In view of the effectiveness in protecting cultivated land, in 1992, the State Council declared to implement the basic farmland protection system nationwide.

In October 2008, the Third Plenary Session of the 17th Central Committee of the Communist Party of China introduced the concept of permanent basic farmland, which means basic farmland whose use cannot be changed under any circumstances and cannot be diverted to other uses in any way. The latest version of the *Land Administration Law*, which came into effect in 2020, formally establishes the protection of permanent basic farmland in the form of a law, proposing that "the country implements a permanent basic farmland protection system".

According to the *Land Administration Law*, the following kinds of cultivated land should be designated as permanent basic farmland in accordance with the overall land use planning, and a strict protection should be implemented for these permanent basic farmland parcels:

i. Cultivated land in the production bases of grain, cotton, oilseed, sugar and other important agricultural products, which are approved by the State Council's competent department of agriculture and rural affairs or the local governments at or above the county level;

ii. Cultivated land with good water conservancy and soil and water conservation facilities, including the built high-standard farmland and the medium and low yield farmland being transformed as well as that can be transformed;
iii. Vegetable production bases;
iv. Experimental plots for agricultural research and teaching;
v. Other kinds of cultivated land that shall be designated as permanent basic farmland according to the provisions of the State Council.

According to legal requirements, the permanent basic farmland designated by each province shall generally account for more than 80% of the cultivated land within its administrative area, and the specific proportion is determined by the State Council according to the actual situation of cultivated land resources in each province. The permanent basic farmland areas shall be designated with township as the unit, and the competent departments of natural resources and agriculture and rural affairs of the county-level government is jointly responsible for the organization and implementation of this work. In order to facilitate the strict administration, the central government has established a national database of permanent basic farmland, in which all the information of permanent basic farmland parcels is included. In addition, township governments are also required to publicize the location and scope of each permanent basic farmland parcel through setting up protection signs.

Towards the goal of designating more than 103 million hectares of permanent basic farmland set in the national land use planning, the central government carried out the designation of permanent basic farmland nationwide from 2015 to 2017. After completing this major task, the actual cultivated land parcels managed as permanent basic farmland is even a bit more than the planned scale, which are geographically located in 2887 counties across the country. The total number of map spots in the national permanent basic farmland database reached 45.4 million, and the database size reached 3 TB. As for the cultivated land type of permanent basic farmland parcels, the area of paddy field and irrigated land accounts for 48%, the land whose slope below 15 degrees accounts for 88%, meaning that the cultivated land quality of permanent basic farmland is at a very high level. In terms of its spatial layout, 6.49 million hectares of permanent basic farmland is located around the city, an increase of 2.09 million hectares compared with the previous. The proportion of cultivated land protected as permanent basic farmland around the city has increased from 45 to 60%, these permanent basic farmland parcels, together with forests, rivers, lakes and mountains, form an urban ecological barrier, become the physical boundary of urban development, and optimize the spatial pattern of urban and rural areas.

In conclusion, due to the large scale and high quality of permanent basic farmland and one of the important components of ecological barrier, a complete and special protection system for permanent basic farmland is the top priority of cultivated land protection and is regarded as the national will, rigid constraints, and the requirements of the times.

5.1.2 Policy Implementation

With the continuous optimization and upgrading of the goal of the cultivated land protection policy, the contents of the cultivated land protection policy are gradually enriched, and the policy tools used to achieve the policy goal are gradually diversified. The following part will correspond to the trinity goal of cultivated land protection policy, and introduce the policy measures oriented by each dimension respectively.

(1) **Quantity-orientated protection**

As previously mentioned, dynamic balance of total cultivated land is one of the core systems of cultivated land protection determined by the *Land Administration Law* promulgated in 1998. China has drawn a red line for its 120 million hectares of cultivated land. To ensure that it will never be crossed, on one hand, Chinese government strictly controls the occupation of cultivated land for non-agricultural purpose, especially prevents the occupation of high-quality permanent basic farmland, and on the other, implements a policy of balancing the occupation and replenishment of cultivated land.

1) **Policy of strictly controlling the occupation of cultivated land for non-agricultural purpose**
From the history of China's urbanization, the occupation of cultivated land by non-agricultural construction is the biggest threat to cultivated land resources, whether it is the expropriation of rural land for urban development, or the construction of industrial or residential buildings in rural areas. In order to prevent this phenomenon to the greatest extent, the Chinese government implements strict restrictive policies on the occupation of cultivated land by non-agricultural construction, mainly through planning and zoning control.

In China, urban construction land is divided into existing construction land and new construction land. The former refers to the land that is being used for urban development, while the latter usually refers to the land that can be used for urban development only through the expropriation of rural land. Obviously, the cultivated land occupied by non-agricultural construction is one of the important components of new construction land. Chinese governments at all levels emphasize giving full play to the overall control role of planning, when arranging the scale of new construction land for each region, the level of land intensive utilization and the ability to replenish cultivated land will be referred. For those regions with large stock of existing construction land, extensive utilization, and insufficient ability to replenish cultivated land, the quota they can obtain will be reduced. Besides, the Chinese government also focuses on optimizing the layout of construction land and minimizing the occupation of cultivated land, especially high-quality cultivated land, when selecting sites for major projects. Moreover, in 2017, the central government proposed to strengthen the conversion control of occupation of cultivated land by non-agricultural construction by establishing a land use conversion license system. At present, this system is being explored at the practical level.

The protection of permanent basic farmland is vital to strictly control the occupation of cultivated land for non-agricultural construction. Since permanent basic farmland is the main component of cultivated land, if the occupation of permanent basic farmland can be avoided in non-agricultural construction, it means that the "bull's nose" of quantity-orientated protection is grasped. For this reason, the Chinese government is committed to giving full play to the binding role of permanent basic farmland on all kinds of construction layout. It requires all regions and departments to fully connect with the layout of permanent basic farmland when preparing relevant plans for urban and rural construction, infrastructure and ecological construction. In principle, they shall not cross through the boundary of permanent basic farmland. According to the requirements of relevant policies, the cultivated land within the grain production functional areas and important agricultural product production protection areas shall be preferentially designated as permanent basic farmland, and a special protection shall be implemented. No unit or individual may occupy or change the use of these designated permanent basic farmland without authorization. Specifically, general construction projects shall not occupy permanent basic farmland. If it is really difficult to avoid permanent basic farmland in the site selection of major construction projects, the necessity and rationality of occupation and the feasibility of replenishment planning must be strictly demonstrated in the feasibility study stage. The scheme shall be pre-reviewed by the Ministry of Natural Resources, only after the approval can the procedures for agricultural land conversion and land expropriation be started.

In addition, in order to fundamentally alleviate the pressure on cultivated land occupied by non-agricultural construction, Chinese government has also vigorously improved the level of intensive land use towards the goal of reducing the total amount of construction land and the area of construction land occupied by unit GDP. The common measures in practice include: first, revitalizing the use of existing construction land, promoting the redevelopment of inefficient urban land, and guiding the overcapacity industries and "zombie enterprises" to release land through withdrawal from the market, transformation, merger and reorganization; second, improving the land use standard system, standardizing the land-saving evaluation of construction projects, and promoting the application of land-saving technologies and models; and last, strengthening the assessment and constraints on the goal of economical and intensive land use, realizing the reduction or zero growth of construction land in conditional areas, and promoting the new construction to occupy no or as little cultivated land as possible.

2) **Policy of balancing the occupation and replenishment of cultivated land**
Indeed, for a large developing country like China, it is impossible to realize urbanization and industrialization without occupying agricultural land. Therefore, the occupation of cultivated land for non-agricultural construction will occur at some times. The Chinese government has designed a policy of balancing the occupation and replenishment of cultivated land to deal with this situation, which

has become a key measure to achieve the strategic goal of quantity-orientated cultivated land protection.

According to the law, if non-agricultural construction occupies cultivated land, the land user must fulfill the obligation of replenishing cultivated land. For the land users who are unable to replenish the cultivated land of equivalent quantity and quality by themselves, they shall pay the cultivated land reclamation fee in full in accordance with the provisions of the local government. The local government will use this fee to replenish cultivated land, that is, to build high-standard farmland through land consolidation, reclamation and development, so as to ensure that the quantity and quality of cultivated land within their jurisdiction will not decline. More specifically, the standard of reclamation fee to be paid by land users shall be determined by the provincial governments according to the average cost of new cultivated land and the quality of occupied cultivated land, and the land user occupying permanent basic farmland shall pay twice the standard. As for the ways to replenish cultivated land, it is diversified, mainly including land remediation, high-standard farmland construction, linking the increase and decrease of urban and rural construction land, reclamation of industrial and mining wasteland left over by history, etc. At the same time, there are some restrictive requirements for replenishing cultivated land, for example, it is prohibited to reclaim seriously sandy land, to reclaim cultivated land on steep slopes above 25 degrees, and to reclaim cultivated land by deforestation.

According to the division of responsibilities, each provincial government is responsible for coordinating and implementing the annual task of replenishing cultivated land within its jurisdiction to ensure that the cultivated land occupied by construction is replenished in time with quality and quantity. The county government is responsible for the whole process management of land remediation and high standard farmland construction projects, and evaluating the quality of replenished cultivated land according to relevant technical regulations. The provincial government shall recheck to ensure that the quantity and quality of replenished cultivated land are in place.

The implementation of the task of replenishing cultivated land is mainly based on the self-balance of the county, supplemented by the adjustment within the province, and the final choice of the national appropriate overall planning. Specifically, if the county-level government is unable to balance the occupation and replenishment of cultivated land within its jurisdiction, it can seek supplement from other counties in the same city. If it is still unable to achieve the balance, it can turn to the areas with similar resource conditions within the province. The national overall planning is under exploration. According to the policy design, municipalities with serious shortage of cultivated land reserve resources can apply to the State Council for national overall planning if the scale of newly reclaimed cultivated land is insufficient to replenish the scale of cultivated land occupied by new construction, provinces with serious constraints on resources and environmental conditions and serious lack of capacity to replenish cultivated land may apply to the State Council for national overall planning for the shortage of replenished cultivated land caused by the implementation of major national construction projects. With the approval of the State Council, these provinces shall pay cross provincial replenishment cultivated land funds to the central finance according to the specified standards formulated based on the factors such as replenished cultivated land cost, resource protection compensation, management and protection expenses, and regional differences. The central finance shall make overall arrangements for the funds required for the implementation of the national task of overall replenished cultivated land, and implement the task of replenishing cultivated land in provinces rich in cultivated land reserve resources.

(2) **Quality-orientated protection**

1) **Policy of developing high-standard farmland on a large scale**

High standard farmland is usually designated as permanent basic farmland for special protection, the typical characteristics of which can be summarized as the following aspects: flat, centralized and continuous, perfect facilities, fertile soil, good ecology, strong disaster resistance, convenient for modern agricultural production and management, and can achieve stable yields despite drought or excessive rain.

Since the establishment of the land development and construction fund by the State Council in 1998, China has been exploring the path and mode of upgrading medium and low yield farmland and developing high standard farmland. In 2011, the release of the *National Plan for Developing High Standard Farmland in the Comprehensive Agricultural Development (2011–2020)* marked the rapid action of China's high standard farmland development. The plan not only sets the goal of developing 53 million hectares of high standard farmland by 2020, but also puts forward systematic measures. While the practice of developing high-standard farmland in recent years is mainly reflected in the following aspects:

Land consolidation. Determining the appropriate farming length and width of the plot with the consideration of the landform, crop types, mechanical operation, irrigation and drainage efficiency and other factors; building terraces in mountainous and hilly areas to enhance the ability of farmland to retain soil, water and fertilizer; leveling the land through filling with guest soil, stripping and backfilling topsoil; adjusting the surface slope to improve the farmland farming layer as well as the suitability of irrigation and drainage.

Soil improvement. Increase soil organic matter through deep tillage and subsoiling, straw returning to the field, increasing the application of organic fertilizer, planting green fertilizer and other ways, so as to improve the soil structure of degraded land and enhance its soil fertility; promoting reasonable rotation and reducing the obstacles of continuous cropping according to the production conditions, so as to improve the soil ecological environment; implementing soil testing and formula fertilization to promote soil nutrient balance.

Irrigation and drainage. Planning and constructing field irrigation and drainage projects according to the requirements of comprehensive treatment of drought, flood, waterlogging and saline alkali as well as equal emphasis on irrigation and drainage; Improving the field irrigation and drainage facilities system and building an ecological high-efficiency water-saving irrigation system, which could increase the effective irrigation area and improve the irrigation assurance rate, water efficiency and farmland flood control and drainage standards at the same time, so as to ensure the stable yields despite drought or excessive rain.

Field roads. Optimizing the layout of tractor roads and production roads in combination with regional production operations and the needs of agricultural machinery users; renovating field roads, reasonably increasing the pavement width, improving the load standard and accessibility of roads, so as to meet the requirements of agricultural machinery operation, production and logistics; constructing ecological field roads to reduce the adverse impact of hardened pavement and ancillary facilities on ecology.

Farmland power transmission and distribution. Improving farmland power grid and power transmission and distribution facilities according to the requirements of farmland modernization and management as well as combined with field roads, irrigation and drainage projects, so as to meet the power demand of farmland facilities, reduce agricultural production costs and improve the efficiency and benefits of agricultural production.

Technology services. Establishing long-term positioning monitoring points for high standard farmland quality to track and monitor the changes of farmland quality; promoting technical measures such as no tillage and less tillage and black land protection to protect and continuously improve the quality of cultivated land; promoting digital agriculture, improved varieties, green prevention of diseases and pests to improve the sustainable utilization level and comprehensive production capacity of farmland.

In a word, these measures have achieved remarkable positive results, such as solving the problems of fragmentation, decline in quality and lack of supporting facilities, promoting the large-scale, standardized and professional operation of agriculture, upgrading the agricultural mechanization, increasing the utilization efficiency of water and soil resources and the land output, promoting the transformation of agricultural operation and production, and improving the comprehensive efficiency and competitiveness of agriculture. By the end of 2020, China had completed the goal of developing 53 million hectares of high standard farmland, and the grain production capacity of high standard farmland increased by about 10–20%.

2) **Policy of protecting black land**

As the most precious soil resource on earth, black land refers to the land with black or dark humus topsoil, which is a high-quality land with good properties, high fertility and suitable for farming. Northeast China is one of the main black land zones in the world. According to relevant statistics, the typical black land area in this region has a cultivated land area of about 18.5 million hectares. However, for a long time in the past, due to over exploitation and unreasonable farming, there has been an increasingly serious problem of land degradation in the black land area of Northeast China, which poses a great threat to the sustainable development of agriculture and national food security. Facing this situation, in order to improve the comprehensive production capacity and sustainable development capacity of black land and promote the green and sustainable development of agriculture, the Chinese government has launched action to protect black land since the 1980s.

By the twenty-first century, the protection of black land in Northeast China has been significantly strengthened in terms of scale and intensity. The Chinese government has implemented five projects in this region: the pilot project for comprehensive control of soil and water loss, the project for comprehensive control of soil and water loss in sloping farmland, the national key construction project for soil and water conservation, the project for soil and water conservation in the northeast black land area within the national comprehensive agricultural development, and the project for comprehensive control of soil and water loss in erosion ditches in the northeast black land area. By 2018, the total investment had been 3.38 billion yuan, and the situation of 920, 660 hectares of soil erosion area and 1,935 erosion ditches has been improved. Since 2017, with the introduction of the *Northeast Black Land Protection Planning Outline (2017–2030)*, the protection of black land has progressed from focusing on water and soil control to focusing on improving the quality of cultivated land. In 2020, the Ministry of Agriculture and Rural Affairs and the Ministry of Finance jointly issued the *Northeast Black Land Conservation Tillage Plan (2020–2025)*, which aims to accelerate the promotion and application of conservation tillage from the technical aspect and continuously strengthen the strategic protection and utilization of black land. In 2021, seven relevant departments of the State Council jointly issued the *Implementation Plan of the National Black Land Protection Project (2021–2025)*, which focuses on the problem of poor quality of cultivated land in the black land area, and puts forward the means of systematic implementing soil erosion control, farmland infrastructure construction, and fertile tillage layer cultivation, so as to fundamentally reverse the degradation trend of black land.

Nowadays, China has formed a complete set of technical policy system in black land protection, and the main approaches are as follows: first, increasing the application of organic fertilizer and returning straw to the field, to increase the content of soil organic matter, improve soil physical and chemical properties, and continuously improve the basic fertility of cultivated land; Second, strengthening the comprehensive protection and management of sloping farmland and wind erosion and desertification land, to control soil erosion and nutrient loss and curb the degradation of black land and the decline of fertility; Third, carrying out demonstration of conservation tillage technology in some typical areas, and promoting technologies such as less or no tillage, straw mulching and subsoiling, to build a high standard tillage layer, improve the physical and chemical properties of black land, and enhance the ability of water and fertilizer conservation; Fourth, carrying out the action of zero growth in the use of chemical fertilizer and formulating scientific fertilizer formula and scientific irrigation system for crops; Fifth, developing mixed farms that combines planting and breeding, promoting the centralized collection and harmless treatment of livestock and poultry manure, to promote the combination of planting and breeding.

The black land protection in China has achieved remarkable results. It is estimated that during 2008–2018, the comprehensive quality of cultivated land in the typical black soil area of Northeast China has been steadily improved by 1.22 grades, realizing the transformation from medium and low land to medium and high land. However, the area of black cultivated land that has implemented comprehensive control measures accounts for a relatively low proportion, the soil and water loss of slope cultivated land is still heavy, the problems of thinning of cultivated layer and erosion ditch are still prominent, the downward trend of soil organic matter content has not been reversed, and the problems of local acidification and salinization still exist. There is still a long way to go to achieve the goal of 16.6 million hectares of black land protection by 2030.

(3) **Ecology-orientated protection**

1) **Policy of implementing rotation fallow**

Rotation fallow refers to the measures of changing crops or not farming for the purpose of protecting, nurturing and restoring soil fertility in a certain period of time in order to improve farming efficiency and realize the sustainable utilization of cultivated land. The implementation of rotation fallow can not only reduce the intensity of cultivated land use, realize the combination of land use and land cultivation, protect and improve soil fertility, enhance the aftereffect of grain and agricultural development, and enhance grain production capacity; but is conducive to the restoration of agricultural non-point source pollution, alleviate the pressure of ecological environment and promote the sustainable development of agriculture.

The national practice of rotation and fallow in China began with the pilot project carried out by the central government in some provinces in 2016. Specifically, the rotation pilot is to promote the "one main and four auxiliary" planting mode in the cold and cool area of Northeast China and the ecotone of agriculture and animal husbandry in North China. Among them, "one main" refers to the implementation of corn and soybean rotation, which aims to increase the supply of high-quality edible soybean and improve soil fertility at the same time. "Four auxiliary" refers to the implementation of rotation of potato, forage crops, drought and barren tolerant coarse grains, miscellaneous beans and oil crops, so as to optimize the agricultural production structure and meet the diversified consumption demand on the one hand; and improve soil physical and nutrient structure and maintain cultivated land productivity on the other hand.

The fallow pilot is based on the strategy of "adjusting measures to local conditions and implementing policies in different areas". For example, the seasonal fallow of "one season fallow and one season rain cultivation" is implemented in the groundwater funnel area with serious drought and water shortage, so as to promote drought and barren tolerant crops and reduce the amount of groundwater; in heavily polluted areas where heavy metals exceed the standard, protective isolation zones are established, pollution sources are blocked and controlled, and polluted farmland is repaired and treated, and at the same time, fallow is implemented for continuous years, and plants with high biomass and strong absorption and accumulation is preferentially planted; in areas with serious ecological degradation, the planting structure is adjusted to plant plants that prevent wind and sand, conserve water and protect the farming layer, agricultural activities are also reduced, so as to promote the improvement of the ecological environment.

In 2019, the first batch of pilot areas have successively completed tasks, the soil structure of these areas has been greatly improved, and the wind and sand fixation and water conservation capacity of cultivated land have been improved, which has played a positive role in repairing and improving the ecological environment. However, this batch of pilot projects also show various problems, which restrict the orderly promotion of policies. It mainly includes: the imbalance of compensation level affects the enthusiasm and initiative of farmers' participation; the compensation is mainly financial subsidies, which is difficult to meet the capital needs of long-term rotation and fallow; and the participation of farmers is mostly passive, lacking the motivation to take the initiative to improve and maintain land productivity.

2) **Policy of promoting conservation tillage**

Conservation tillage is an advanced agricultural farming technology that implements no tillage or less tillage on farmland, reduces soil tillage as much as possible, covers the surface with crop straw and stubble, reduces soil wind erosion and water erosion, and improves soil fertility and drought resistance. Supported by mechanical no tillage sowing, straw crushing and returning to the field, subsoiling and other technologies, it is regarded as an important sustainable agricultural development technology and a major reform of the traditional farming system.

Aware of the strategic significance of conservation tillage in promoting the sustainable use of cultivated land and the sustainable development of agriculture, the Chinese government has organized and implemented conservation tillage demonstration projects throughout the country since 2002. Through the three steps of building experimental demonstration areas, building extension areas and improving technical support capacity, the Chinese government has formed six types of conservation tillage areas (namely, Northeast Ridge Farming Area, Farming Pastoral Ecotone along the Great Wall, Northwest Loess Plateau Area, Northwest Oasis Agricultural Area, Huang Huai Hai Two Crop Flat Farming Area and South Flood and Drought Continuous Cropping Area) and a guiding technical model matching the regional planting system and natural ecological conditions. By the end of 2018, the scale of conservation tillage in China had reached 824, 200 hectares, of which the area of core technology application also showed a rapid growth, for example, the mechanized no tillage sowing area and mechanized straw returning area increased by 263% and 252% respectively compared with 2002.

Conservation tillage has produced obvious positive effects on the ecology-orientated protection of cultivated land in China, mainly reflected in: first, it can effectively reduce soil wind erosion, control farmland water and soil loss, inhibit farmland dust, enhance rainwater permeability and improve soil water content, so as to greatly reduce the loss of topsoil of cultivated land and reduce the frequency of dust storms, and consequently the agricultural ecological environment can be protected. Second, it can enhance the water suitability of soil, reduce the evaporation of water in soil, increase the water storage capacity of soil, and provide sufficient water resources for high and stable yield of crops. Third, it not only reduces the environmental pollution caused by straw incineration, but also reduces agricultural non-point source pollution by improving soil fertility and reducing the use of chemical fertilizer. Nevertheless, there is still room for the policy improvement in the technical model, machine and tool development, and farmers' participation.

5.2 Industrial and Mining Land Reclamation and Ecological Restoration

5.2.1 Background and Policy Evolution

(1) Threats to land use from mineral resource development

China is rich in mineral resources and is the world's largest producer, consumer and trading country of mineral resources. The basic position and role of mineral resources development and utilization in national economic development has been increasing, meeting the strong demand for mineral resources in national economic development and providing an important material guarantee for national energy security and economic development. However, the large-scale and high-intensity mineral resources development activities, which have long pursued the concept of "development over protection", have also caused China to pay a huge ecological and environmental cost, resulting in a large amount of land destroyed by mines, leaving behind a large number of mining ecological and environmental problems, causing serious damage to the surrounding ecological environment. On the one hand, the surface land resources and ecology are disturbed and damaged along with mining, such as digging and damage to occupied land, surface subsidence, etc., leading to collapse, landslide, mudslide, aquifer damage, subsidence, surface damage, etc.; on the other hand, the large amount of tailings and waste rock stockpiles lead to land occupation, dust, groundwater leakage pollution, and the production of a large amount of waste gas, waste water, waste residue and other harmful substances seriously pollute the air, water system and soil in mining areas, which in turn leads to the decline of the quality of the regional ecological environment and seriously restricts the sustainable development of resources, environment, population and society.

According to the national mining environment remote sensing survey and monitoring data released in 2019, the national mining-damaged land area is 3,610,500 hm^2, accounting for about 0.37% of the national land area, including 1,459,300 hm^2 of excavation-damaged land, 1,306,700 hm^2 of pressure-occupied land and 844,500 hm^2 of collapsed land. The area of land destroyed by mining in production mines under construction is 1,340,400 hm^2, and the area of land destroyed by mining in abandoned mines is 2,270,100 hm^2. According to the national mining geological environment survey data of the China Geological Survey with cities and counties as units, as of 2018, there are about 99,000 abandoned mines of various types in China, and the spatial distribution of abandoned mines nationwide is extremely uneven, with some areas being dense and others sparse, showing an overall trend of fewer large and medium-sized mines, more small mines, more non-metallic mines such as building materials and fewer energy and metal mines, and more in the east and less in the west.

The ecological and environmental problems of abandoned mines in China are characterized by various types, complex causes, large numbers, wide distribution, and serious hazards due to factors such as mine type, scale, mining method, and geological and environmental conditions of the mining area. The main ecological and environmental problems include mine geological disasters, destruction of land resources in mining areas, damage to regional groundwater systems and pollution of water and soil environments in mining areas. Among them, mining geological disasters mainly include ground collapse, ground fracture, collapse, landslide and mudslide. Mine ground collapse is the main ecological and environmental problem, especially the ground collapse of abandoned coal mines is the most serious. The destruction of land resources by abandoned mines not only aggravates the contradiction of land resource shortage in mining areas, but also leads to a serious decline in economic and ecological benefits of land. The mandatory dewatering and drainage during mining and the collapse and cracking of the upper part of the mining area have caused the leakage of overlying groundwater, which has seriously affected and damaged the regional groundwater system, resulting in a series of ecological and environmental problems such as the destruction of groundwater resources and the withering of vegetation in the mine area and surrounding areas. Especially in the abandoned coal mines in the plain basin area, the destruction of aquifers and changes in the conditions of groundwater replenishment, runoff and discharge caused by historical mining activities have caused a very serious drop in the groundwater level, which has seriously damaged the circulation of the groundwater system, exacerbated the contradiction of regional water shortage and affected the production and living water of local residents. Various solid slags and wastewater produced in the process of mineral resources development contain a large number of heavy metals and toxic and harmful elements, some of which are not treated to standard, unreasonably piled up and discharged, and spread to the soil and water bodies around the mine area through rainwater drenching and wind, causing serious pollution to the mine area and its downstream water and soil. Some toxic substances are not suitable for degradation and accumulate in the biological chain of the ecosystem, which eventually causes very serious ecological and environmental problems, especially the most serious soil and water pollution caused by acidic wastewater from abandoned metal mines.

According to the National Soil Pollution Status Survey Bulletin jointly released by the Ministry of Environmental Protection and the Ministry of Land and Resources in 2014, man-made activities in the development of industrial and mining industries are the main cause of soil pollution or exceedance. Of the 775 soil sites in 81 industrial waste sites surveyed, 34.9% exceeded the standard; of the 1,351 soil sites in 188 solid waste treatment and disposal sites surveyed, 21.3% exceeded the standard; and of the 1,672 soil sites in 70 mining areas surveyed, 33.4% exceeded the standard. At present, there are about 100,000 mines in China, and less than 1,000 of them are included in the national green mine list for announcement. The land damaged by mines can reach tens of millions of mu through the expansion of "point—line—surface—network". If these damaged lands are not reclaimed in time, they will pose a great threat to the surrounding environment. Since most of the high-quality farmland is located in low-lying flat areas, and there are often several mines around them, pollutants can migrate and transform with ground runoff or groundwater during heavy rainstorms, seriously polluting the farmland. Once the farmland is polluted, the cost of restoration is extremely high, and some of them can only passively change the land use and reduce the function of the land.

Therefore, under the reality of insufficient supply of land resources and degradation of ecological environment, the ecological protection and restoration of mining areas in China is facing serious challenges, and accelerating and effectively promoting the reclamation and ecological restoration of land damaged by mines is an important task that the country needs to implement without delay.

(2) **Requirements for industrial and mining land use to achieve carbon peak and neutrality targets**

President Xi Jinping made a solemn commitment to the world at the 75th session of the United Nations General Assembly that China will strive to peak its carbon dioxide emissions by 2030 and work towards carbon neutrality by 2060. To achieve this goal, the use of industrial and mining land also faces challenges.

Mineral mining not only causes the destruction of surface vegetation and changes in soil texture, but also damages the ecological environment, and these effects are also reflected in the "carbon effect". On the one hand, the destruction of vegetation affects the carbon absorption and transformation capacity of the mining area, on the other hand, the soil, which is one of the three major carbon pools on earth, is affected by mineral mining and its texture changes, which may affect the carbon cycle in the soil. Therefore, it is extremely important and urgent to scientifically implement mine ecological restoration and continuously improve the quality and stability of regional forests, grasses and other vegetation to the ecosystem.

Ecological restoration of mines can effectively enhance the carbon storage capacity of restored soils and carbon sequestration capacity of plants, and play an important role in achieving carbon peak and neutrality targets, which is reflected in the following four aspects: first, through ecological restoration, the damaged ecosystem can be alleviated, and the structure and function of the restored cropland, woodland, grassland and other ecosystems are relatively more complete than before, which can play a positive role in carbon sequestration, oxygen release, and buffering the impact of climate change. Second, in the process of ecological restoration, land remediation is required, and soil reconstruction, as an important part of land remediation, plays an important role in the accumulation of organic carbon in the soil, land remediation and other projects can effectively improve the quality of soil and increase the carbon storage potential in the restored area; third, because the construction land has the function of carbon source, the reclamation use of the waste construction land that has been destroyed or reached the production age into forest grass and wetlands can increase the vegetation cover, and realize the conversion of carbon source to carbon sink; fourth, conducting ecological management in the gangue mountain area not only can directly reduce carbon emissions, reduce the pollution of the environment, but also avoid the waste of land resources.

(3) **Policy evolution from land reclamation to ecological restoration**

In the era of planned economy, governments at all levels focused their efforts on mineral exploration and mining, and did not pay enough attention to the reclamation of damaged land and ecological restoration after mining. This trend was reversed in the mid-1980s as China transitioned from a planned to a market economy.

In 1988, the State Council issued the *Regulations on Land Reclamation*, which for the first time used the term land reclamation, defining land reclamation as the activity of taking remedial measures to bring land damaged by production and construction activities and natural disasters to a usable state. This document was revised in 2011 to provide a more comprehensive management approach to land destruction caused by production and construction and natural disasters, further clarifying the principle of "whoever destroys, whoever reclaims" and "whoever invests, whoever benefits", and defining the responsibility subject, funding solutions, and regulatory measures. In 2012, the Ministry of Land and Resources promulgated the *Measures on Implementing Land Reclamation Regulations*, proposing that land reclamation should take into account the social benefits, economic benefits and ecological benefits of land use after reclamation. If arable land is destroyed by production and construction activities and can be reclaimed as arable land, it should be reclaimed as arable land as a priority.

During the same period, land reclamation and environmental restoration and management of mines were juxtaposed, and the requirements for the latter were first reflected in the *Regulations on Mine Geological Environmental Protection* issued by the Ministry of Land and Resources in 2009, which applied to the prevention and restoration of ground collapse, ground fracture, collapse, landslide, aquifer damage, and topographic landscape damage caused by mineral resources exploration and mining activities. This document also puts forward the basic principles of "prevention is the main focus, prevention and treatment combined, whoever develops who protects, whoever destroys who treats, whoever invests who benefits", and clarifies that if the mining of mineral resources cause damage to the geological environment of the mine, the miner should be responsible for treatment and restoration, and the cost of treatment and restoration is included in the cost of production. Taking this as the starting point, the central government has gradually established the system of mine geological environment survey and evaluation, the systems of mine geological environment protection planning and the system of related mine geological environment protection and land reclamation program compilation and reporting, the system of mine geological environment treatment and restoration fund and related supervision system.

Over the years, land reclamation in mining areas has only been carried out in a narrow sense, i.e., focusing on a small area with the mining operation area as the core. This narrow sense of land reclamation in mining areas obviously does not meet the requirements of "overall protection, systematic restoration and comprehensive management". In 2016, the Ministry of Land and Resources took the lead in issuing the *Guidance on Strengthening the Restoration and Comprehensive Management of Mine Geological Environment*, which clarified the general requirements, main tasks and safeguard measures for strengthening the restoration and comprehensive management of geological environment of mine. The institutional reform of the State Council in 2018 adjusted the Ministry of Land and Resources to the Ministry of Natural Resources and established the Department of Ecological Restoration of Territorial Space, and the term "mine ecological restoration" has been widely used.

The ecological restoration of mines refers that, taking the ecosystem damaged by mineral resources mining as a whole, based on the importance of the ecosystem function in the area around the mine, the habitat environment and the economic and social development, and taking into account the natural conditions, topographic and geomorphological conditions, the ecological problems of the mine and their degree of harm, the ecological problems of mines caused by mineral resources mining activities, such as geological safety hazards, land destruction and vegetation damage, are repaired by natural forces or through artificial measures, so that the geological environment of mines can be stabilized, the damaged land can be reclaimed and used, the ecosystem function can be restored and improved, and it can be self-sustained and positively evolved to achieve a new ecological balance and sustainable development.

The ecological restoration of mines embodies an ecological logic with the following characteristics: following the laws of nature and ecological logic; taking reclamation of damaged land and restoration of geological environment as the basic content; focusing on natural restoration, aided by artificial restoration and ecological reconstruction; carrying out overall protection, systematic restoration and comprehensive management from the perspective of the ecosystem.

5.2.2 Policy Implementation

(1) Principles

The ecological restoration of mines is not just restoring damaged terrain or carrying out simple greening, but is a complex and systematic project integrating damage investigation, design planning and construction. The following principles generally need to be followed.

1) **Respect science, follow nature, and protect nature**. Respecting the law of natural ecosystem succession, changing the thinking of pure engineering restoration, adhering to the natural restoration as the main while artificial restoration as a supplement, maximizing the natural restoration capacity.

2) **Overall protection, systematic restoration and comprehensive management**. Considering the ecological function of the area where the mine is located and the characteristics that various ecological elements are interdependent, mutually influential and mutually restrictive, gradually repairing the damaged ecological function by systematic design and comprehensive management.
3) **According to local conditions, classified policies, and zoning governance**. Considering the diversity, complexity, multi-causal and regional characteristics of ecological problems in coal mines, giving full play to the leading role of territorial space planning, and following the purposes of land use determined by the planning.
4) **Restore cultivated land, integrate industries, and ensure safety**. For the ecological environment problems caused by mineral mining usually has the characteristics of large scale, involving many types of land, heavy degree and long time, fully considering the requirements of land reclamation, resource development and utilization, urban function construction, industrial import transformation, etc., and ensuring the geological stability and safety of the ecological restoration area through coordinated governance.
5) **Economically reasonable, technically feasible, and focusing on effectiveness**. In accordance with the principles of economic reasonableness and technical feasibility, reasonably determining the direction, mode and measures of ecological restoration, improving the efficiency of inputs and outputs, and maximizing the long-term benefits of restoration of abandoned mines.

(2) **Subjects of responsibility**

In accordance with the principle of who destroys and who manages, the entities who have obtained the mining rights should assume responsibility for the ecological restoration of the mines, and its responsibility for the ecological restoration of the mine is not exempt from the termination of this right. For those subjects of illegal mining, that is, in the case of unauthorized mining without a mining license or beyond the approved mining area mining subjects, they should bear the responsibility for ecological restoration in addition to the corresponding legal responsibility according to law.

For those mines that can not determine the entities responsible for restoration for historical reasons or the subjects of responsibility has been lost, as well as those were closed in response to the requirements of government policies and were determined to be repaired by the government at the time of closure, the government at the county level or above shall bear the responsibility for restoration and organize their implementation.

(3) **Modes**

1) **Factors affecting the selection of modes**. Ecological restoration of abandoned mines should take into account a variety of factors such as regional natural geographic and climatic conditions, ecosystem stability and types of abandoned mines.

First, the natural geographic and climatic conditions of the region determine the speed of ecological restoration. The regional water, heat, temperature and humidity conditions such as rainfall and temperature accumulation, chemical conditions such as geochemical element cycle, physical conditions such as material and energy cycle, and natural geographic conditions such as elevation, topography and slope determine the duration of ecological restoration of the mine. If the area affected by the abandoned mine has abundant rainfall, suitable temperature for plant and animal growth, sufficient chemical nutrients, smooth material and energy circulation, and low to medium altitude, gentle slope topography, etc., the ecosystem restoration can be accelerated and the restoration period can be shortened; on the contrary, the regional ecosystem restoration will be slower and the restoration period will be extended.

Second, the structure of the regional ecosystem and its stability determine the ecological restoration approach. Mining areas with good structural and functional stability of the original ecosystem generally have a high ecological threshold. On the one hand, under the effect of mining activities, it can still maintain the integrity of its own structure and function, and the system will not produce sudden changes, showing strong resistance to stress; on the other hand, after the external influence is eliminated, the ecosystem can adjust itself and repair itself naturally, showing strong self-restoration again. For example, some flat plains and hilly areas in eastern China have good natural background endowments, fertile soils, high water content, good surface vegetation, healthy biological population structure, and good stability of native ecosystems, and under moderate mineral development activities, the system can still maintain the stability and integrity of its own structure and function, and can reach the pre-disturbance state through natural restoration and artificial intervention within a period of time after the removal of disturbance; while for ecologically fragile and sensitive areas, such as the Southwest karst stone desertification area and Loess Plateau soil erosion area, the ecosystem stability is poor, and it is difficult for abandoned mines in these areas to recover to their previous state without artificial intervention conditions, therefore, ecological restoration of abandoned mines in such areas should be based on engineering measures, combining artificial restoration with natural restoration.

Last, the characteristics of abandoned mines, including their type, size, mining method and the physicochemical nature of the resulting problems, determine the ease of ecological restoration. The damage caused by energy and non-metal mine development to the regional ecological environment is mostly physical damage, such as ground collapse, mountain fragmentation and land destruction, and ecological restoration is relatively easy; the impact of metal mine development on the region is mostly chemical damage, such as water and soil environmental pollution, and ecological restoration is difficult. Large mines produce greater disturbance and damage effects than small mines, and the residual impact of large mines on regional ecology is greater, making ecological restoration more difficult; open-pit mines have a greater impact on the surface, and the collapse of mining areas and destruction of aquifers in shaft mines are more serious, making ecological restoration easier in open-pit mines and more difficult in shaft mines.

2) **Modes based on the land use purpose**. Following the principle of fully considering ecological, economic and social benefits, on the basis of comprehensive analysis of various natural factors such as regional soil, climate, geomorphology and biology and social factors such as socio-economic development level and planting habits, assessing the natural and economic attributes of abandoned mine land, combining the surrounding land use types, assessing the positive and negative environmental effects of abandoned mines and their reclamation potential, so as to determine its suitability as land for different purposes such as arable land, garden land, forest land, pasture land, etc., and to reasonably formulate the ecological restoration mode.

First is used as agricultural land. This mode is mainly applicable to the plain areas. For non-metallic abandoned mines in remote locations, if the conditions such as being agricultural land before mining, light soil and water pollution, small loss of soil quality, and no significant loss of soil fertility after mining, as well as rich water resources are met, land leveling measures can be taken to organize them into agricultural land and then, cultivating local advantageous crops to restore the production capacity of the land. For example, in the high diving level and steady sinking coal mining collapse areas in China's Huang-Huai-Hai, Northeast and North China Plains, it is suitable to carry out composite ecological restoration, that is, using coal gangue filling collapse pit to create land to develop agricultural planting in the less waterlogged or non-waterlogged collapse area, digging ponds to create land to develop aquaculture in the shallow waterlogged collapse area, and carrying out plantation forest planting in the poor soil quality or waste rock slag, tailings storage area.

Second is used as construction land. For abandoned mines located near towns or urban–rural areas, if conditions such as open-pit mining, flatter ground, gentler surface slope or shaft mining, backfilling of mining hollow areas and minor collapse areas have reached a stable state are met, corresponding engineering measures can be taken to carry out foundation stabilization treatment and use them as construction land after eliminating the potential danger of geological disasters such as avalanche slide flow. It is also possible to combine mining environment treatment with land development and utilization, and build them into commercial housing, industrial development zones, etc. to alleviate the problem of urban land tension and promote urban transformation and development.

Third is used as ecological land. For mining parks near towns, with good natural ecological landscape or with a long history of mining development and rich mining cultural heritage, it is possible to develop ecological landscape parks, mining theme parks, with special leisure tourism as the main focus, combining natural landscape resources with mining cultural resources to improve the ecological quality of the city and create a city tourism brand. This on the one hand meets the residents' demand for a better ecological environment, on the other hand promotes the mining culture, facilitates the transformation of the mining economy, and promotes the sustainable development of the mining economy.

Last is no longer use the land. For abandoned mines located in remote areas off the beaten track or ecologically fragile and sensitive areas, it is not advisable to carry out artificial remediation and restoration projects on a large scale or to reclaim the mine site for agricultural land or construction land. Natural restoration should be the main focus, mainly by means of sealing, limiting the impact of human activities on the ecological environment of the mine, and naturally restore the original structure and function of the ecosystem of the mine.

3) **Modes based on the zoning concept**. The number, type, development method, scale and induced ecological and environmental problems of abandoned mines vary in different ecological zones. Combining elements such as regional climatic characteristics, native ecosystem types, dominant ecological service functions, regional ecosystem sensitivity and distribution characteristics of abandoned mines in China, focusing on the impact of abandoned mines on ecological environment and ecosystem in different ecological zones, model types can be classified under the concept of zoning.

First is hilly and mountainous areas. For such areas, if there are geological hazards, measures should be taken to eliminate the hazards first; for sites with natural restoration conditions, priority should be given to natural mine ecological restoration; for sites that do not have natural restoration conditions, engineering measures should be taken to organize the site first, and then the site should be vegetated to restore the ecology. When greening the site, the selection of forest and grass species should be coordinated with the surrounding vegetation of the mine; for high and steep slopes with bare bedrock that do not have greening conditions, they can be temporarily sealed and set aside to avoid excessive treatment.

Second is plain and basin areas. For such areas, preventive measures should be taken to prevent ground subsidence and other geological disasters; sites with the potential for reclamation for agricultural land, priority should be given for reclamation as agricultural land after land consolidation through engineering measures; for sites that are difficult to restore to agricultural land, natural restoration or a combination of natural restoration and engineering measures can be used for vegetation greening and ecological improvement; for the mining-induced collapse waterlogged areas and abandoned mine waterlogged areas, the water surface planting and fishery farming can be developed after organizing with engineering measures.

Third is cities and surrounding areas. For such areas, priority should be given to eliminating mining geological hazards that threaten industrial and agricultural production and the safety of human settlements; sites with agricultural land reclamation potential should be given priority to reclamation as agricultural land after land consolidation through engineering measures; other sites that are difficult to restore as agricultural land should be built as urban ecological parks or ecological green areas after land consolidation, and sites with development conditions can be considered for consolidation as construction land. When creating urban ecological parks, the morphology of various sites should be fully considered, and on the basis of respecting the harmony of the surrounding ecosystem of the city, the planting and cultivation of characteristic trees and plants can be appropriately carried out to form characteristic ecological parks, but avoid creating too many artificial landscapes.

Last is desert and Gobi areas. For such areas, sealing and shelving should be carried out; for sites prone to wind and sand sources, appropriate engineering measures should be taken for wind and sand control, but avoid taking too many engineering measures to generate new ecological problems; sites with greening conditions should adopt natural restoration as the main method, supplemented by artificial restoration, to improve the ecology of mining areas.

(4) **Measures**

In order to achieve stability in the geological environment of mines, reclamation and utilization of damaged land, and restoration and improvement of ecosystem functions, the specific measures to be taken include:

1) taking measures to remove dangerous rocks, slope reduction, slope protection, construction of retaining facilities and other measures in and around the mine to eliminate the collapse, landslides, mudslides, ground subsidence and other potential geological hazards caused by the mining activities;
2) conducting topsoil stripping and centralized storage for potentially damaged arable land, forest land, and grassland, using them as much as possible to improve the soil of reclaimed land and taking treatment measures to dispose of solid waste to prevent or reduce soil contamination;
3) taking the measures such as the construction of dams, interception and drainage ditches, pools, sand ponds and other wastewater treatment in the mine and its surrounding area to reduce soil erosion and environmental pollution, the mine production wastewater and domestic wastewater can be treated separately to meet the standards and then discharged or recycled;
4) conducting ecological rehabilitation for the bare mountains after destruction of vegetation, conducting backfilling, reclamation or comprehensive use for mining areas that has collapsed and rock pits caused by mining activities, taking safety precautions for mining areas that can not be timely backfilled;
5) taking anti-leakage, anti-dispersion, dam failure and other measures for tailings ponds to prevent environmental pollution, eliminating safety hazards, and timely conducting land reclamation or ecological regeneration.

(5) **Technologies**

In the face of the intricate mining environmental damage problem, it is necessary to develop and use advanced technologies from the perspective of science, difference, advancement, and economy, so that the restoration benefits are balanced with financial and policy inputs. Although there are a variety of ecological restoration technologies, there are some basic common technologies, which are the key to ecological restoration.

1) **Geomorphic reshaping**. It refers to reshaping a new landform that is in harmony with the surrounding landscape by taking measures such as orderly disposal and land reshaping to eliminate and mitigate factors that have an impact on vegetation restoration and land productivity enhancement, taking into account the topographic and geomorphic characteristics of the mine site, the mining design, mining process and land destruction. In general, landform reshaping is the basis of land quality restoration in mining areas.
2) **Soil reconstruction**. It refers to reconstruct a suitable soil profile to restore and improve the productivity of reconstructed soil in a relatively short period of time as well as to improve the environmental quality of reconstructed soil, in the purpose of soil restoration or reconstruction of damaged land in mining areas, by adopting appropriate reconstructive technology techniques, and applying engineering measures and physical, chemical, biological and ecological measures.
3) **Vegetation restoration**. It refers to the selection of pioneer plants and suitable plants and other vegetation configurations, planting and care for different types and degrees of land damage in the mine, taking into account climate, altitude, slope, slope direction, surface material composition and effective soil thickness, etc., so as to make the restored plant communities sustainable and stable.
4) **Landscape reproduction**. It refers to rebuild a harmonious ecosystem with the surrounding landscape, following the concept of community of life, through the "point—line—surface—network" and "network—surface—line—point", which are two mutually reversible feedback pathways, fully considering the structure adjustment and optimal allocation of land resources, water resources, biological resources, human living environment in the process of landscape fragmentation and landscape integration.
5) **Biodiversity reorganization and conservation**. It refers to regulate the composition and structure of the biological population of the ecosystem and to gradually repair the ecosystem function in the process of geomorphic reshaping, soil reconstruction, vegetation restoration, landscape reproduction and ecosystem construction for extremely degraded ecosystems with broken structure and dysfunction, with the help of artificial support and induction, so as to induce the ecosystem to eventually evolve into a sustainable ecosystem that meets the intergenerational needs and values.

(6) Market-based approaches

China has a large historical debt in terms of mine ecological restoration, and the size of the areas where the mine ecological has been damaged that are in urgent need of restoration is huge. Since the law stipulates that for historical mine ecological problems, if it is difficult to identify the responsible subject, the local government at or above the county level shall organize the restoration, which has brought enormous financial pressure on the local government. The government's financial resources alone are far from being able to meet the demand, and the issue of funding has become a bottleneck limiting the ecological restoration of mines. In order to solve the outstanding problems of insufficient government investment, in accordance with the requirements of "building an environmental governance system in which the government is the leader, enterprises are the main body, and social organizations and the public participate", the Ministry of Natural Resources issued the *Opinions on Exploring the Use of Market-based Approaches to Promote Mine Ecological Restoration* in 2019, proposing a series of policies to stimulate social capital investment. It is hoped that through policy incentives, a market-oriented operation and scientific management model will be implemented to accelerate the ecological restoration of mines and achieve the unification of ecological, social and economic benefits.

1) **Factually verifying and determining the current status of categories of land use in mining areas**. For those agricultural land that really can not restore the original use due to mining collapse, it can be changed to other types of agricultural land or unused land, the required process is that the provincial department of natural resources in conjunction with relevant departments organize the verification, and obtain the consent of the land rights holders, then report to the Ministry of Natural Resources for approval. If this change involves arable land, it needs to be factually reduced, if it involves permanent basic farmland, it needs to be adjusted and replotted in accordance with the provisions and incorporated into the territorial spatial planning. It should be noted that the reduction of arable land does not exempt the entities who are responsible for causing the collapse from the legal due diligence obligations.
2) **Encouraging comprehensive rehabilitation and use of mining land**. If planning to convert the state-owned restored mine land into operating construction land, then, subject to the premise of territorial spatial planning, the local government can carry out pre-development of the land after the overall restoration and determine the land use right holder in separate lots by public competition; or it can simultaneously announce the mine ecological restoration plan and the land conveyance plan, and determine the same subject together to undertake both the restoration and development work by public competition, and sign the ecological restoration agreement and land conveyance contract respectively. If planning to convert the state-owned restored mine land into state-owned agricultural land, the local government can determine the entities who undertake the restoration work by agreement, and after the parties sign a contract for the operation of state-owned agricultural land, the latter engages in planting, forestry, animal husbandry or fisheries production.

   If the abandoned mine land is collectively owned, collective economic organizations can either carry out restoration by themselves or attract social capital to participate in the restoration. After completing restoration, for the collective-owned profit-oriented land registered by law that determined by the territorial spatial planning for industrial, commercial and other business purposes, the land owner can convey or lease it for the development of related industries.

   In addition, if developing tourism industry and constructing sightseeing platforms, stacks and other non-permanent ancillary facilities on the land after mine restoration, under the premise of not occupying permanent basic farmland and not damaging the ecological environment, natural landscape and not affect geological safety, the land can be managed according to the current purpose without being expropriated or transferred.

3) **Revitalizing the stock construction land in the mining areas**. After restoring the stock construction land of the mine as arable land, subject to acceptance, it means that the construction land quota is created, and this quota can be circled within the provincial area. Mining enterprises that are engaged in mining activities, if the stock construction land acquired by law has been restored to arable land and garden land, forest land, grassland and other agricultural land, after passing the acceptance, it can use the created construction land quotas in exchange for occupying the agricultural land due to new mining activities within the provincial area.
4) **Rationally using soil and rock materials in the abandoned mines**. In some restoration projects implemented by local governments for open-pit mines, there may be some new soil and rock materials generated from the restoration projects due to slope reduction and elimination of geological hazards, or itself there are some soil and rock materials left in situ, these soil and rock materials can be used for restoration projects without compensation; if there is still surplus, it can also be incorporated by the government into the public resources trading platform for external sales, with all sales proceeds used for ecological restoration in the region. If the implementation of the restoration project involves social investment entities, their reasonable benefits should be protected. In addition, on the basis of scientific assessment and demonstration, it is also necessary to simultaneously prepare a soil and stone utilization plan and a mine ecological restoration plan in accordance with the principle of "one mine, one policy", and implement it after the county-level natural resources department reports to the municipal natural resources department for review and approval.

5.3 Integrated Ecological Protection and Restoration of Territorial Space

5.3.1 Concept of Integrated Ecological Protection and Restoration

(1) **Challenges in ecological conservation and restoration faced by China**

Territorial space is a coupled human-earth system composed of two subsystems: natural geographic environment and human social activities. The essence of ecological restoration of territorial space is to restore and enhance the structure, processes, functions and services of damaged ecosystems through a series of engineering and biological measures, to harmonize human-earth relations and achieve healthy and stable ecosystems and substantial improvement of human ecological well-being. In order to cope with the adverse effects of unreasonable development and construction activities on natural ecosystems during rapid urbanization and industrialization, China has implemented a series of national land remediation and ecological protection and restoration projects since the 1980s, and has achieved certain results. However, most of the previous remediation and restoration work was aimed at a single element, taking ecosystem reconstruction as a way to create or promote ecosystem development with the assistance of human activities, with relatively single restoration objectives or objects, and insufficient systemic, holistic and comprehensive nature, which restricted the effectiveness of remediation and restoration. Consequently, China's natural ecosystems are still fragile in general, with insufficient ecological carrying capacity and environmental capacity, and the pressure of ecological protection brought by economic development is still greater, and the contradictions accumulated by the emphasis on development and light protection in some areas are increasingly becoming prominent.

1) **The problem of ecosystem quality function is prominent**. By 2020, the national pure tree forest area reaches 104.47 million hectares, accounting for 58.1% of the tree forest, a high percentage that leads to the instability of forest ecosystem. The national tree forest quality index is 0.62, which is still at a medium level overall. The grassland ecosystem as a whole is still fragile, and the area of moderate and severe degradation still accounts for more than 1/3. The ecological functions of some rivers, wetlands and lakes have been reduced or lost. The sandy land area of 172 million hectares and the soil erosion area of 274 million hectares are still serious. The area of mangrove forests has decreased by 40% compared with the 1950s, and the problems of decreasing coral reef coverage and decreasing seagrass bed cover are more prominent. The phenomenon of shrinking natural shoreline is still common, the function of disaster prevention and mitigation is degraded, and the overall situation of the near-shore marine ecosystem is not optimistic.
2) **The pressure on ecological protection is still greater**. In terms of ecology, China has a lot of historical debts, accumulated problems and real conflicts, and the ecological carrying capacity of some areas has reached or is close to the upper limit, so the task of ecological protection and restoration is very arduous, and it is not only a tough battle, but also a protracted one. In some places, there is still the phenomenon of "emphasis on economic development, light ecological protection", sacrificing the ecological environment in exchange for economic growth, and unreasonable development and utilization activities greatly squeeze out and destroy ecological space.
3) **Lack of systematic cognition on the ecological protection and restoration**. There is not enough understanding of the inner mechanism and laws of the community of life, and there is still a big gap between the implementation of the concept of holistic protection, systematic restoration and comprehensive management and requirements. The management system and coordination and linkage mechanism of equal rights and responsibilities have not yet been established, and the coordination of ecological protection and restoration faces

great pressure and resistance. The goals, construction content and governance measures of some ecological engineering are relatively single, and some projects still have the problem of patchwork, as well as the phenomenon of ignoring natural endowments such as water resources, soil, light and heat, native species, etc. The regional ecosystem did not show significant results in terms of overall improvement of service functions.

4) **Water resources guarantee faces challenges**. The structural contradiction in the water resources supply is outstanding, water resources are over-exploited in some areas, and economic and social water use has occupied a large amount of ecological water in rivers and lakes. Water ecological space has been encroached upon, and the ecological protection in basin area as well as the restoration of water security, water quality improvement, biodiversity protection faces serious challenges. Long-term large-scale over-exploitation of groundwater in some areas has formed groundwater leakage areas, causing ground subsidence, seawater intrusion and other ecological and environmental problems. Some cities have excessively dug lakes to attract water to create scenery, exacerbating water scarcity and destroying the cycle of water systems. The total amount of waste water discharged in the country remains high, and many rivers have pollutants entering them in excess of their capacity, and groundwater pollution is serious in some areas.
5) **Diversified investment mechanism has not yet been established**. Due to the obvious public welfare and external nature of ecological protection and restoration work, affected by low profitability and big project risks, coupled with the imperfect market-oriented investment mechanism and ecological protection compensation mechanism, as well as the lack of effective policies and measures to stimulate social capital to invest in ecological protection and restoration, resulting in the lack of effective ways to achieve the value of ecological products and the low willingness of social capital willing to enter. At present, the construction of the project is still mainly based on government input, with a single investment channel and insufficient overall capital investment. At the same time, ecological engineering construction projects are mostly laid out in remote and poor regions, and the lack of own financial resources in these areas restricts the implementation of the projects.
6) **Science and technology support capacity is not strong**. There is a lack in the aspects of standard system of ecological protection and restoration, new technology promotion, and transformation of scientific research results. There is a certain degree of disconnect between theoretical research and engineering practice, and the systemic and long-term effectiveness of key technologies and measures is insufficient. Science and technology service platform and service system is not sound, ecological protection and restoration industry is still in the cultivation stage. The capabilities of investigation, monitoring, evaluation and early warning to support ecological protection and restoration are insufficient, and the inter-departmental information sharing mechanism has not yet been established.

(2) **The concept of integrated ecological protection and restoration**

In November 2013, President Xi Jinping pointed out in the *Note on the Decision of the Central Committee of the Communist Party of China on Certain Major Issues Concerning Comprehensive and Deepened Reforms* that "we must realize that mountains, rivers, forests, fields and lakes are a community of life, and the lifeblood of people is in the fields, the lifeblood of fields is in rivers, the lifeblood of rivers is in mountains, the lifeblood of mountains is in soil, and the lifeblood of soil is in trees. If those who plant trees only plant trees, those who treat rivers only treat rivers, and those who protect fields only protect fields, they will easily lose sight of each other and eventually cause systemic damage to the ecology. It is necessary for a single department to be responsible for the usage regulation of all national land, and to unify the protection and restoration of mountains, rivers, forests, fields and lakes. This assertion reflects the new philosophy of China's top leaders regarding ecological protection and restoration.

This reflects an accurate grasp of the concept of natural values, that is, the elements of mountains, rivers, forests, fields, lakes and grasses are not isolated and independent from each other, but each element forms an organic whole through integration. Therefore, it is necessary to change the past restoration mode of categorical protection and single treatment to a holistic protection and enhancement of the ecosystem composed of multiple elements, while adhering to the concept of natural values and the concept of sustainable development, which drives the emergence of the system regarding an integrated protection and restoration of mountains, rivers, forests, fields, lakes and grasses.

5.3.2 Actions on the Integrated Ecological Protection and Restoration

(1) **Timeline**

In September 2015, the Central Committee of the Communist Party of China and the State Council issued the *Overall Plan for the Reform of the Ecological Civilization System*, proposing to establish the concept that mountains, rivers, forests, fields and lakes are a community of life. In November 2015, the Fifth Plenary Session of the 18th Central Committee of the Communist Party of China stated to build a solid ecological security barrier, insist on giving priority to conservation, focusing on natural restoration, implement ecological protection and restoration projects for mountains, rivers, forests, fields and lakes, and carry out large-scale land greening actions.

In October 2016, the Ministry of Finance, the Ministry of Land and Resources, and the Ministry of Environmental Protection jointly issued the *Notice on Promoting Ecological Protection and Restoration of Mountains, Rivers, Forests, Fields and Lakes*, which put forward clear requirements for carrying out ecological protection and restoration of mountains, rivers, forests, fields and lakes in all regions of the country.

In September 2017, the central government issued the *General Plan for the Establishment of National Park System*, which includes "grass" in the expression of the community of life, making ecological governance more compatible with the actual needs of the ecosystem. As of the end of 2020, the central government has carried out 25 pilot projects for ecological protection and restoration of mountains, rivers, forests, fields, lakes and grasses across the country. These projects involve 24 provinces and benefit 65 national-level poverty-stricken counties. The central government has issued a total of 50 billion yuan in awards and subsidies. The completed investment is nearly 170 billion yuan, and remarkable results have been received.

In June 2020, the National Development and Reform Commission and the Ministry of Natural Resources jointly issued the *National Master Plan for Major Projects for the Protection and Restoration of Important Ecosystems (2021–2035)*, which systematically planned for the protection and restoration of important ecosystems at the national level and put forward the general idea and main objectives in promoting the protection and restoration of natural ecosystems such as forests, grasslands, deserts, rivers, lakes, wetlands and oceans, as well as the overall layout, key tasks, major projects and supporting policies for the integrated protection and restoration of mountains, rivers, forests, fields, lakes and grasses. The Ministry of Natural Resources, in accordance with its responsibilities, has made ecological restoration planning for territorial space an important special plan for national territorial planning, requiring governments at all levels to prepare it.

In August 2020, in order to guide and regulate the implementation of the ecological protection and restoration project of mountains, rivers, forests, fields, lakes and grasses, as well as to improve the overall, systematic, scientific and operable ecological protection and restoration, in absorbing and drawing on advanced concepts and relevant standards of ecological protection and restoration at home and abroad, and summarizing the lessons learned from the pilot projects, the Ministry of Natural Resources, the Ministry of Finance and the Ministry of Ecology and the Environment jointly issued the *Guidelines for Projects of Ecological Protection and Restoration of Mountains, Rivers, Forests, Fields, Lakes and Grasses (for trial implementation)*. In addition, the relevant departments also actively promote the development of various technical standard documents, including implementation program preparation protocols, acceptance protocols, effect evaluation specifications, technical guidelines, adaptive management specifications, feasibility study preparation protocols and funding measurement specifications.

In the process of promoting the above actions, the conceptual connotation, objectives, tasks, concepts and organizational forms of ecological protection and restoration have been updated continuously, and developed towards multi-scale, multi-elements, multi-objectives, and multi-means, upgrading from simple soil and water management to integrated protection and restoration of mountains, rivers, forests, fields, lakes, and grasses, from microscopic farmland ecosystem and water ecosystem to village, local, regional, national and other spatial scales, from single element restoration and governance to comprehensive and systematic governance of all elements, from single ecological restoration to multi-objective collaborative governance of economy, society, ecology and culture, from the engineering means of end-of-pipe treatment and restoration to multiple means of source treatment, process coupling and comprehensive design, and from regional and sectoral autonomous governance to multi-level governance with national top-level design and multi-sectoral coordination.

(2) **Carriers**

There are two main carriers for the central government to implement the integrated ecological protection and restoration of territorial space.

1) **Major Projects for the Protection and Restoration of Important Ecosystems**. It refers to a series of major projects laid out in key areas such as Qinghai-Tibet Plateau Ecological Barrier Zone, Yellow River Key Ecological Zone, Yangtze River Key Ecological Zone, Northeast Forest Belt, Northern Anti-Sand Belt, Southern Hilly Mountain Belt, Coastal Belt, etc. They are embedded in the national ecological security strategic pattern, focusing on national key ecological function areas, ecological protection red line and national nature reserves as determined by the territorial spatial planning, highlighting the ecological support for major national strategies, taking into account the integrity of the ecosystem, the continuity of geographical units and the sustainability of economic and social development, and articulating with relevant ecological protection and restoration plans. The goal is to achieve fundamental improvement in the condition of natural ecosystems such as forests, grasslands, deserts, rivers and lakes, wetlands and oceans, significantly improve the quality of ecosystems and the ecological service functions, significantly enhance ecological stability, basically achieve a virtuous cycle of natural ecosystems, basically build the national ecological security barrier system, make the supply capacity of high-quality ecological products basically meet the needs of the people, and basically paint a beautiful picture of the harmonious coexistence of man and nature, by 2035.
2) **Projects of Ecological Protection and Restoration of Mountains, Rivers, Forests, Fields, Lakes, and Grasses**. It refers to the process and activities of overall protection, systematic restoration, and comprehensive management of the damaged and degraded ecosystem with declining service functions within a certain area, in accordance with the concept of mountains, rivers, forests, fields, lakes and grass as a community of life. It is based on the overall planning of the national land space and the ecological protection and restoration of the national land space and other related special planning, following the laws of natural ecosystem succession and the inherent mechanism, with the goals of improving the self-restoration capacity of the ecosystem, enhancing the stability of the ecosystem, and promoting the overall improvement of the quality of the natural ecosystem and the overall enhancement of the supply capacity of ecological products.

(3) **Principles**

The Chinese government has set several basic principles for regulating the implementation of the integrated ecological protection and restoration projects.

1) **Adhering to the priority of ecology and green development**. The Chinese government emphasizes that it should firmly establish the concept of lucid waters and lush mountains being invaluable assets, and consider the relationship between man and nature in an integrated manner in accordance with the requirements of good ecology. It should protect the legitimate rights and interests of relevant rights holders in accordance with the law, and promote the realization of the value of ecological products and the high-quality development of the ecological restoration industry, so as to meet the people's growing need for a beautiful ecological environment and the demand for quality ecological products.
2) **Adhering to natural restoration, with artificial restoration as a supplement**. The Chinese government emphasizes that it should follow the laws of natural ecosystem succession, give full play to the ability of nature to repair itself, protect biodiversity and ecological spatial diversity, and avoid excessive human intervention in ecosystems, and reasonably choose measures of conservation, protection, natural restoration, supplementary regeneration and ecological reconstruction according to the degree of degradation and damage, as well as the resilience of ecosystems, in order to restore ecosystem structure and function, enhance ecosystem stability and ecological products supply capacity, and strengthen the overall protection within a region.
3) **Adhering to the integrated planning and comprehensive management**. The Chinese government emphasizes the need to establish a long-term perspective, and in accordance with the idea of overall planning, overall design, phased deployment, and phased implementation, to scientifically determine the ecological protection and restoration objectives, reasonably layout the project works, coordinately implement various types of projects, and synergistically promote the integrated protection and restoration, so as to enhance the protection and restoration effect.
4) **Adhering to the problem-oriented and scientific restoration**. The Chinese government emphasizes the need to systematically sort out hidden dangers and risks by tracing their roots, to diagnose all-round ecological problems in natural ecosystems, and to improve the accuracy of problem identification and diagnosis. It is necessary to carry out protection and restoration according to local conditions, following the development and protection pattern as well as the control requirements of the territorial space, following the inherent mechanism of the ecosystem, targeting ecological problems and risks, and fully considering the regional ecological background and natural endowment. It should also strengthen the role of scientific and technological support, scientifically configurating the measures in the aspects of protection and restoration, natural and artificial, and biological and engineering, and improving the relevance of restoration measures.
5) **Adhering to obtain comprehensive benefits in an economic and reasonable manner**. The Chinese government emphasizes the need to optimize the

layout and timing of the project in accordance with the principles of financial possibility and technical feasibility, to improve the efficiency of the project by evaluating the suitability of the protection and restoration measures, to implement low-cost restoration and management as far as possible, to promote the healthy, stable, sustainable use and value realization of the ecosystem, and to achieve comprehensive ecological, social and economic benefits. It should also deepen the reform in the field of ecological protection and restoration, release policy dividends, broaden investment and financing channels, innovate diversified investment, construction and management modes, raise the awareness of ecological protection of all people, and promote the formation of a long-term mechanism of ecological protection and restoration led by the government with the participation of multiple subjects.

(4) **Contents**

The implementation of the integrated ecological protection and restoration projects mainly includes the following contents.

1) **Treatment and restoration of the mining environment**. In some areas of China, there are historical mining environmental problems that have not been effectively treated, resulting in geological environmental damage and pollution of the atmosphere, water bodies and soil, especially in some important ecological function areas, there are still some mining activities that pose a greater threat to the ecosystem. Therefore, it is necessary to actively promote the treatment and restoration of the mining environment, especially to focus on the treatment of abandoned mines in important ecological areas as well as residential living areas, to repair sensitive mining hills along the traffic routes, and to increase the efforts to restore greenery to those mines with serious vegetation damage and exposed rock pits.
2) **Land consolidation and pollution remediation**. Carrying out comprehensive improvement of ravines, slopes and hills is in important ecological areas from the two aspects of optimizing the pattern and improving the function, with specific projects including damaged land levelling, sandy and saline land management, conversion of sloping arable land to terraces, and reclamation and utilization of abandoned industrial and mining land. Especially for the already polluted land, it is necessary to prevent and control the risk of soil pollution with the integrated use of measures such as the source control, isolation buffer, and soil improvement.
3) **Biodiversity conservation**. Strengthening the ecological protection and restoration of rare and endangered plant and animal habitat areas, restoring the inter-regional ecological corridors that have been damaged to ensure connectivity and integrity, building biodiversity protection networks to drive overall ecological space restoration, and promoting the enhancement of ecosystem function.
4) **Watershed water environmental protection governance**. Carrying out ecological protection and restoration in the important river sources and water connotation areas, taking key watersheds as units to carry out systematic improvement,

taking a combination of engineering and biological measures, artificial treatment and natural restoration approaches to conduct the integrated management of the watershed water environment, and promoting its rest and recuperation for those rivers and lakes with important ecological functions.

5) **Comprehensive, systematic and integrated treatment and restoration**. In areas with rich ecosystem types, including the wetlands, grasslands and woodlands as a whole into major projects, rehabilitating and comprehensively improving the ecosystems that are concentrated, severely fragmented and functionally degraded, and gradually restoring the functions of ecosystem by means of land remediation, vegetation restoration, connection of river and lake system, shoreline environmental improvement, and wildlife habitat restoration.

(5) **Techniques**

1) **Technical process**. The technical process of conducting integrated ecological protection and restoration projects is generally divided into four stages: engineering planning, engineering design, engineering implementation, and management and maintenance. Among them, the engineering planning stage serves to identify and diagnose macroscopic problems at the landscape scale, set overall protection and restoration objectives, and determine the units of protection and restoration as well as the layout of engineering sub-projects; the engineering design stage mainly serves to diagnose ecological problems of each protection and restoration unit at the ecosystem scale, formulate the corresponding specific index system and standards, and determine the conservation and restoration mode and measures; the engineering implementation phase serves to design and implement the sub-projects at the site scale; the management and maintenance, monitoring and evaluation, adaptive management, and supervision and inspection are carried out throughout the whole process of ecological protection and restoration.
2) **Investigation of the status quo**. Conducting a detailed survey on the regional ecological function positioning, natural ecological and geographical conditions, and socio-economic conditions within the implementation area. Among them, the regional ecological functions include headwater conservation, soil and water conservation, biodiversity maintenance, wind prevention and sand fixation, etc. The natural ecological conditions include local climatic conditions, topography, hydrological characteristics, geological environment, physical, chemical properties and environmental quality of soil and water bodies; and the characteristics of the communities that constitute the ecosystem, including the species composition and characteristics of plant and animal communities, in particular, the species, numbers and habitats of important species such as dominant species, key species, indicator species, flagship species, pioneer species, and invasive species; and historical data with reference to ecosystem attributes and time series. Socio-economic conditions include local natural resource ownership and utilization, socio-economic development level, scope and intensity of human activities, and relevant ecological protection and restoration projects.

The sources of information for conducting the survey include the results of the national land survey, the evaluation of the carrying capacity of resources and environment and the suitability of territorial space development, and relevant planning, information from relevant departments on existing wildlife surveys, forestry surveys, ecological function zoning, ecological protection red lines, priority areas for biodiversity conservation, and nature reserves, as well as the results from relevant scientific research institutions and scientific field stations, and the collected local practical experience in ecological protection and restoration, opinions and suggestions from experts in related fields and the local public.

3) **Identification and diagnosis of ecological problems**. Considering the scale of the project construction, natural geographical conditions, natural succession law of the ecosystem, and referring to the historical state of the damaged ecosystem or the state of similar ecosystems in the vicinity, one or several local native ecosystems or similar ecosystems similar in environmental and natural conditions are identified as reference ecosystems. On the basis of the status quo survey, conducting gradient analysis, analogical analysis and comprehensive evaluation from large scale to small scale or from small scale to large scale, to accurately identify major ecological problems and the correlation, urgency and priority between problems, to determine relevant important ecosystems, species and key elements that need to be protected and restored, and to scientifically diagnose the area, distribution, extent, impact factors, causes and correlation with related ecosystems of damaged natural ecosystems.

   Specifically, the identification of ecological problems refers to the identification of the main ecological problems in the areas of ecological stress, ecosystem quality, ecosystem services, and ecological spatial patterns at the landscape scale for the implementation area, including identifying the problems of ecological stress and analyzing the causes in terms of climate change, biodiversity, land use structure and practices, water and soil environmental pollution caused by production and life, natural resource exploitation intensity, and pest invasion; identifying the problems of ecosystem quality and analyzing the causes in terms of food chain integrity, biodiversity, and structural and functional stability; identifying the problems of ecosystem services and analyzing the causes in terms of headwater conservation, soil and water conservation, biodiversity maintenance, and wind prevention and sand fixation; identifying the problems of ecological spatial pattern and analyzing the causes in terms of the habitat distribution of important species, connectivity of ecological corridors, ecological network structure, and important and sensitive ecological protection target points.

   The diagnosis of ecological problems refers to the diagnosis and analysis of the objects in need of protection, conservation, restoration and management, and their current status, as well as the severity and urgency of key ecological problems at the ecosystem scale, with reference to the properties of selected reference ecosystem (including physical geography, species composition, ecosystem structure, ecosystem function, etc.) and their ecological stresses. The focus is on two aspects: first, the evaluation of rare and endangered species and habitats, special ecosystem types and other objects that need to be protected and conserved, in terms of ecosystem integrity and connectivity, the type and degree of stress on important conservation targets; second, the evaluation of the type, degree of degradation and resilience of damaged ecosystems that need to be restored, in terms of vegetation, soil, water bodies, biodiversity and biological invasion. Furthermore, qualitative empirical analysis evaluation method, semi-quantitative or quantitative analysis evaluation method can be adopted according to the actual situation.

4) **Establishment of conservation and restoration objectives and standards**. Setting overall and specific targets for ecological protection and restoration by taking into account the socio-economic development, relevant plans and standards, regional ecological function positioning, ecological status quo, results of ecological problem identification and diagnosis, attributes of reference ecosystem, and according to different protection and restoration scales, levels and thresholds of restrictive factors; determining protection and restoration standards, proposing graded and phased binding and guiding indicators to achieve quantified targets. Setting up performance indicators for a specified period according to the performance management requirements. The binding indicators are mainly determined around the performance indicators in the construction of the project, and the data are sourced and measurable; the guiding indicators are proposed at the ecosystem and landscape scales, and are medium- and long-term goals that should serve the stability of ecosystems and the diversity of ecological spatial structures.

   Specifically, regarding the goal setting at the landscape scale, it should correspond to the scope of project implementation, focus on improving the regional dominant ecosystem services, put forward the overall goal of protection and restoration in terms of eliminating the impact of ecological stress, optimizing the ecological spatial pattern, unblocking the ecological network and improving the quality of the ecosystem, and set specific targets for ecological protection and restoration within the implementation period. Regarding the goal and standard setting at the ecosystem scale, it should correspond to the units of protection and restoration, focus on solving ecological process problems, put forward protection and restoration objectives and standards in terms of physical environment, species composition, ecosystem structure, ecosystem function, and ecological stress, according to the key attributes of the reference ecosystem, and set specific indicators for specific ecological problems, according to the actual project and relevant regulations. Regarding the goal and standard setting at the site scale, it should correspond to the sub-projects, take different measures for each unit of protection and restoration, and develop specific indicators according to the goal and standard at the ecosystem scale, combined with the actual project.

5) **Division of units and layout of engineering**. Dividing the conservation and restoration units according to the results of the current situation survey, problem identification and analysis, and the formulated conservation and restoration objectives. Those representative natural ecosystems, rare and endangered wildlife species and the habitats they depend on, natural relics of special significance, world natural and cultural heritage sites, scenic spots, forest parks,

geological parks, wetland parks, glacier parks, grassland parks, desert parks, aquatic germplasm resource reserves and drinking water source reserves should be classified as protection units.

Dividing the project types and clarifying the focus and content of protection and restoration according to the current status survey of each ecological protection and restoration unit, the diagnosis and analysis results of ecological problems and the specific goals set for protection and restoration. Sub-projects can also be set according to needs. Carrying out the spatial layout of engineering construction as well as arranging the engineering sub-projects for key ecological issues, in line with the requirements of correlation and synergy and according to the overall objectives and specific objectives, indicators and standards of protection and restoration for each unit. Carrying out source control, process blocking and end treatment in accordance with the priority order of ensuring flood control safety and geological safety and enhancing ecological functions, carrying out system restoration on the mountain and below the mountain, in the upper, middle and lower reaches of the watershed, and arranging the implementation of sub-projects in an orderly manner, according to the urgency and severity of ecological problems.

6) **Selection of protection and restoration models and measures**. Adopting the appropriate protection and restoration technology model for each type of ecological protection and restoration unit, according to the current situation survey, ecological problem identification and diagnosis results, and ecological protection and restoration objectives and standards. The common models are as follows, the first is ecological conservation, for representative natural ecosystems and rare and endangered wildlife species and their habitats, the ways of establishing nature reserves, removing stress factors, building ecological corridors, in situ and relocated conservation and breeding of rare and endangered species can be adopted to protect the integrity of ecosystems, improve the quality of ecosystems, protect biodiversity, and maintain the culture and traditional habits of indigenous people; the second is natural regeneration, for lightly damaged and resilient ecosystems, the ways of eliminating stress factors such as cutting off pollution sources, prohibiting inappropriate grazing and over-hunting, closing mountains and forests, and ensuring ecological flow can be adopted to strengthen protection measures and promote natural recovery of ecosystems; the third is assisted regeneration, for moderately damaged ecosystems, combined with natural recovery and on the basis of eliminating stress factors, the ways of small and medium intensity artificial auxiliary measures such as improving the physical environment, introducing suitable species with reference to the local ecosystem, and removing species that cause ecosystem degradation can be adopted to guide and promote the gradual recovery of ecosystem; the fourth is reconstruction, for severely damaged ecosystems, ecological reconstruction should be carried out on the basis of eliminating stress factors, focusing on landscape remodeling, habitat reconstruction, restoration of vegetation and fauna, and biodiversity reorganization, and among them, the key to habitat reconstruction is to eliminate limiting factors for vegetation (animal) growth, the key to vegetation reconstruction is

to first build suitable pioneer plant communities, and on this basis, to continuously optimize the community structure and promote the process of positive plant community succession, and the key to biodiversity reorganization is to introduce key animals and microorganisms to realize the construction of a complete food web of the ecosystem.

Designing multiple alternatives, and analyzing the ecological suitability, priority and timing of implementing the measures, based on the local natural conditions, ecological suitability, site conditions, construction seasons and the difficulty of the construction process, with fully incorporating the knowledge and experience of experts in relevant fields and local residents, as well as fully considering the interests, rights and satisfaction of local residents. Carrying out simulation and prediction of restoration methods and screening the relatively optimal ecological protection and restoration measures and technologies from the comprehensive evaluation of ecological and environmental impact and risk, economic and technical feasibility, and social acceptability.

7) **Estimation of funds and budgeting of investment**. Estimating the funds based on the overall objectives determined by the implementation plan and with the combination of the objectives and standards determined by each protection and restoration unit, the type and content of engineering construction, protection and restoration modes and measures, and the implementation period. Organizing the preparation of engineering design or sub-project construction design, and clarifying the construction schedule, funds, quality and safety and other control and supervision measures in accordance with the requirements of ecological protection and restoration of different territorial spaces, with reference to national, industry and other relevant standards, and taking into account the actual situation. The engineering design or sub-project construction design should address the specific problems of the ecosystem, the measures should be scientific and reasonable, economically feasible and technically operable, and the budget of project investment should be prepared by combining with the actual situation.

Chapter 6
Land Administration Policies

Shukui Tan, Siliang Wang, and Yang Liu

In a country like China, where land is under public ownership and at a stage of rapid urbanization, industrialization and agricultural modernization, land is valuable resource and important asset on which economic and social development depends, and governments at all levels are deeply involved in land use and have designed and implemented comprehensive and systematic land administration policies for this purpose. These policies aim at regulating land relations, organizing and monitoring land development, and protecting and rationalizing land resources. This chapter introduces some representative land administrative policies as follows: first, land survey, titling and registration policies, which are the basis for mapping out the land resources and protecting land property rights; second, the planned land supply and land reserve system, which is the policy basis for allocating and guaranteeing the land needed for urban development; third, land supervision and land violation governance policies, which are the basis for ensuring that land is used in an orderly manner and that the various land use policies are effectively implemented; and fourth, land taxation and finance policies, which are the basis for ensuring that land can create wealth and that wealth is distributed appropriately. For each type of policy, this chapter introduces its concept, connotation, rationale, and practice.

6.1 Land Survey, Land Titling and Land Registration

The prerequisite for effective land administration is to map the actual status of land resources, and to this end, the land survey should be regularly conducted. On this

S. Tan (✉)
Huazhong University of Science and Technology, Wuhan, China
e-mail: tansk@126.com

S. Wang · Y. Liu
Hunan University, Changsha, China

S. Tan and X. Huang (eds.), *Land Policy in China*, The Frontier of Public Administration in China, https://doi.org/10.1007/978-981-19-9895-9_6

basis, land titling and registration work should be done, especially the related system construction.

6.1.1 Land Survey System

(1) **Framework of land survey system**

Accurate land data information is an important basis for the preparation of national economic plans and the formulation of relevant policies. Land survey is a survey conducted to clearly describe the quantity, quality, distribution, utilization and tenure status of land.

The State Council issued the *Regulations on Land Survey* in 2008, marking the formal establishment of the land survey system. According to the Regulations, the purpose of the land survey is to comprehensively investigate the status of land resources and utilization, to grasp true and accurate basic data on land, to provide the basis for scientifically planning, rationally using and effectively protecting land resources, for implementing the strictest arable land protection system, and for strengthening and improving macro-control, and to promote comprehensive, coordinated and sustainable economic and social development. Land survey work is organized and implemented in accordance with the principles of "national unified leadership, division of work, local hierarchical responsibility, and joint participation of all parties". It is required for the central and local governments at all levels to share the burden of implementing the land survey.

The land survey implemented by the Chinese government consists of two types: the national land survey conducted every ten years, and the annual land change survey. The implementation of the land survey is to investigate the following contents: (1) the status and changes in land use, including land type, location, area, distribution and other conditions; (2) land tenure and its changes, including the land ownership and use rights; (3) land conditions, including the natural, socioeconomic and other conditions. It should be particularly noted that the focus of the survey on the status and changes in land use is to investigate the status and changes in basic farmland, including the amount, distribution and protection status of basic farmland. The implementation of the land survey should take a comprehensive survey approach, using field survey statistics, remote sensing monitoring and other means. The outcomes formed through the land survey are mainly in four forms, including data, graphics, texts and databases. According to the provisions, the outcomes of the land survey should be published to the community and accept public inquiries, except for those that should be confidential according to law, and these outcomes are an important basis for the preparation of national economic and social development planning and for engaging in the planning, management, protection, and utilization of land resources.

Land survey is a policy-oriented project with strong huge workload and many professional technologies involving in, which requires the participation of many departments and tens of thousands of engineers and technicians. Take the third national land survey, which will be introduced in the following, as an example, central departments such as National Development and Reform Commission, Ministry of Civil Affairs, Ministry of Finance, Ministry of Land and Resources, Ministry of Environmental Protection, Ministry of Housing and Urban–Rural Development, Ministry of Water Resources, Ministry of Agriculture, National Bureau of Statistics, National Forestry Administration, National Oceanic Administration, and National Bureau of Surveying, Mapping and Geographic Information were involved in this project.

(2) **Implementation of national land surveys**

Since the 1980s, the Chinese government has conducted three rounds of national land surveys.

1) **The first national land survey (1984–1997)**
In order to comprehensively investigate the type, quantity, quality, distribution and utilization of land nationwide and make scientific evaluation, the first national land survey was organized by the then Ministry of Agriculture, Animal Husbandry and Fisheries and other central departments in 1984, which lasted for more than ten years until the end of 1997, not only because of the technical constraints at that time, but also because of the difficulty in obtaining funding for the survey.
2) **The second national land survey (2007–2013)**
In 2007, the State Council decided to carry out the second national land survey from July 1 of that year. As a major survey on national conditions and national power, its purpose was to comprehensively investigate the national land use situation, grasp the real basic land data, and implement informationization and network management of the survey outcomes, establish and improve the land survey, statistical system and registration system, realize the socialization of land resource information services, and meet the needs of economic and social development, land macro-control and land resources management.
The main tasks of the survey included: (1) rural land survey, which was to investigate the type, location, scope, area distribution and tenure of each piece of land; (2) urban land survey, which was to investigate the location, scope, boundaries, quantity and use of each piece of land; (3) basic farmland survey, which was to match the basic farmland protection plots (blocks) with the map of current status of land use; (4) establishing the land use database and cadastral information system to realize the interconnection and sharing of survey information; (5) on the basis of the survey, constructing the statistical, monitoring and rapid updating mechanism of land resource change information.
Compared with the last survey, this survey adopted the unified national standard of land use classification for the first time, adopted the organization mode of unified government organization, local field survey and national quality control for the first time, and adopted the survey base map covering the national remote sensing image for the first time, which realized the consistency of map, data and field, thus comprehensively checking the national land use status and mastering the conditons of various land resources.
3) **The third national land survey (2018–2021)**

In September 2018, the State Council deployed to carry out the Third National Land Survey, a task to be successfully completed by August 2021. The objectives of this survey were to comprehensively refine and improve the basic national land use data, to ensure that the state can directly grasp the informative and accurate national land use status and land resource changes, to further improve the land survey, monitoring and statistical system, to realize the information management and sharing of outcomes, and to meet the needs of ecological civilization construction, spatial planning, supply-side structural reform, macro-control, natural resources management system reform and unified registration of rights, spatial use control of land and other works.

The main tasks of the third national land survey included: (a) to make field survey on the land type, area and tenure in accordance with the national unified standards, with the help of remote sensing, mapping, geographic information, internet and other technologies, using existing information in an integrated manner, and based on orthophoto maps, so as to fully grasp the distribution and utilization of various types of land, namely, arable land, garden land, forest land, grassland, commercial land, industrial and mining storage land, residential land, land for public administration and public services, transport land, water and land for water conservancy facilities, etc.; (b) to refine the survey of arable land, so as to have a comprehensive grasp of the quantity, quality, distribution and composition of arable land; (c) to conduct the survey of inefficient and idle land, so as to comprehensively map the land use status within the scope of cities, towns and development zones; (d) to establish the land survey database covering national, provincial, prefectural and county levels, which integrates images, land types, scope, area and tenure, and to improve the networked management system for interconnection and sharing at all levels; (e) to improve the investigation and statistics on the land resource change information as well as the mechanism for the all-weather and full-coverage remote sensing monitoring and rapid update.

6.1.2 *Land Titling and Registration System*

(1) **Rural land titling and registration**

Land titling refers to the confirmation and determination of land ownership, use rights and other rights, and is the clarification of the affiliation and content of rights related to land in accordance with laws and policies. Specific to rural land titling, it refers to the confirmation, registration and certification of collectively-owned land in rural areas through cadastral survey, ownership audit and other means to confirm the location, four boundaries, area, use and other information of rural land in accordance with the provisions of laws and policies.

The objects of rural land titling and registration are land rights such as rural collective land ownership and collective land use rights, among which, rural collective land use rights include residential land use rights, collective construction land use rights, etc. The implementation of the rural land titling and registration is a fundamental work to promote the reform and development of agriculture and rural areas.

Against the background of land fragmentation caused by the household responsibility system, this work reflects the central government's aim to protect farmers' land property rights and stimulate the flow of rural land, and is of great significance to safeguard farmers' legitimate rights and interests in land, realize the specialization and scale of agricultural production, smoothly promote industrialization, urbanization and agricultural modernization, strengthen rural social management and promote the integrated development of urban and rural areas.

Beginning in the late 1980s, the practice of rural land titling in China has gone through four stages.

First, the pilot and start-up from the late 1980s to 1993. During this period, the former State Land Administration Bureau launched the initial registration of rural collective land nationwide on a pilot basis in conjunction with the first national land survey, the main content was to register and issue certificates for the right to use residential land and the right to use collective construction land, and individual provinces initiated the registration and issuance of certificates for collective land ownership.

Second, the stagnation and wandering from 1993 to 1999. In 1993, the State Council abolished a series of fees, including that for rural land registration, in order to reduce the burden on farmers, and without a source of funding, the work of rural land registration almost came to a standstill.

Third, the deployment and restart again since 1999. In 1999, the Ministry of Land and Resources organized a study on the construction of the rural collective land tenure systems, proposing the idea of comprehensively confirming land ownership, regulating land use rights, guaranteeing landowners' rights to income, and strengthening land use control rights, on the premise of insisting on collective ownership of land, and striving to explore multiple forms of realization of collective land ownership system. In 2000 and 2001, research was further carried out to expand the coverage of registration and certification of collective land ownership. On this basis, in November 2001, the Ministry of Land and Resources comprehensively deployed to speed up the registration of collective land ownership throughout the country. In 2008, the Ministry of Land and Resources requested all regions to speed up the registration and issuance of certificates for rural residential land. Especially during the second national land survey, local governments in many regions promoted the work by combining the results of the second survey and annual remote sensing monitoring change survey.

Forth, the comprehensive and rapid promotion since 2010. In 2010, the central government clearly proposed for the first time to speed up the titling and registration of rural collective land ownership, residential land use rights and collective construction land use rights, and the work expenses were included in the financial budget. In 2011, the Ministry of Agriculture started to carry out pilot work in hundreds of counties with townships as units, and proposed to standardize the management of land rights titling and improve the policy on its organization, finance, and publicity. In 2013, the central government explicitly proposed to complete the task of land titling in rural areas in five years based on sound land contract management rights and ensuring farmers' basic rights and interests in land, to properly solve the problems of unclear land ownership and unclear land boundaries in rural areas. In 2014, three provinces, Shandong, Sichuan, and Anhui, were selected to take the lead in implementing pilot projects of rural land titling in the whole province. In 2017, the nationwide land titling began to be implemented. According to the data disclosed by the Ministry of Agriculture and Rural Affairs in 2020, 2,838 counties, 34,000 townships and more than 550,000 administrative villages in the country basically completed the work of titling and issuing certificates for contracted land, which resulted in the confirmation of rights of 1.5 billion mu of contracted land to 200 million farmers and the issuance of certificates for contracted land management, with the national rate of issuing certificates for contracted land in rural areas exceeding 96%. The titling work for other types of rural land is still in progress.

The Chinese government emphasizes the need to carry out the work of rural land titling and registration in an orderly manner in accordance with the law, based on relevant legal and policy documents as well as the provisions of local regulations and rules, in line with the principle of respecting history, focusing on reality, favoring production and life, and promoting social harmony and stability, on the basis of the results of the national land survey as well as the results of the annual land use change survey. The documents and information that are used as the basis for conducting rural land titling and registration include: approval documents and administrative decisions issued by the government or relevant administrative departments; mediation issued by the administrative department of land and resources of the government at or above the county level; judgments, rulings or mediation letters made by the courts and have entered into force; agreements reached between the parties in accordance with the law; cadastral survey results such as cadastral survey forms and land ownership boundary agreements; and other documents stipulated by laws and regulations.

(2) **Unified real estate registration system**

1) **The evolution of the system**

Real estate registration refers to the act that the owner of real estate rights, in accordance with the law and relevant provisions, records in the real estate register the changes in the ownership of real estate belonging to him/her with the registration department set up by the state according to law. Real estate registration is closely related to the resolution of conflicts of property rights, maintenance of market order, related tax collection, economic macro-control, and national rule of law construction, and thus has received widespread attention from the society.

Since the reform and opening up, the registration of real estate in China has been restoring and developing, and legalization and standardization have been enhancing, but it also present a fragmented state of multiple heads of responsibility. For example, regarding land registration, the department of natural resources was responsible for the registration of state-owned land use rights, collective land ownership, collective land use rights, and mortgage of land use rights without ground fixation, while the registration of land contract management rights was under the department of agriculture; the department of housing and urban–rural development was responsible for the registration of housing ownership and mortgage of housing ownership; the ownership and use rights of other natural resources such as forests, grasslands, sea areas, minerals were registered by different relevant administrative departments separately. This registration system, which was not uniform in terms of legal basis, registration authority, registration effectiveness, registration procedure and title certificate, was not conducive to registration and access to registration by the parties to the transaction, and the registration procedures and effectiveness adopted by each department were not the same, making registration a socially costly process, which brought many obstacles to real estate transactions.

Although the drawbacks of fragmented registration were brought to the attention of the central government at the beginning of the twentieth century, and the *Law on Property Rights* issued in 2007 clearly stated the principle that "the state shall implement a unified registration system for real estate", no substantial progress has been made over the years. With the in-depth reform of the administrative system, especially the promotion of the reform of delegating power and improving government services since the 18th National Congress of the Communist Party of China, the construction of a unified real estate registration system has been gradually accelerated. In 2013, the State Council clearly proposed to integrate the responsibilities of real estate registration, which are scattered in many departments, under one department, namely, the Ministry of Land and Resources is responsible for guiding and supervising the unified registration of real estate such as land, housing, grassland, forest land, and sea area nationwide, requiring the unification of four aspects: registration agencies, registration books, registration bases, and information platforms. Subsequently, the central government deployed 18 provinces across the country to carry out pilot projects of unified real estate registration. In 2015, the *Interim Regulations on Real Estate Registration* came into effect and the integration of real estate registration agencies was launched. In 2016, the State Council launched a special inspector for the unified registration of real estate, which accelerated the pace of work on the unified registration of real estate. In 2018, a nationwide unified registration system for real estate was initially completed. However, the system still faces problems such as lack of legal support, difficulties in information management, lack of uniformity in ownership information, and inadequate support facilities.

2) **Overview of the practice of implementing the system**

Real estate registration includes initial registration, change registration, transfer registration, cancellation registration, correction registration, objection registration, advance registration, seizure registration and other types of registration.

According to the regulations, real estate registration shall follow the principles of strict management, stability and continuity, and convenience to the public. The real estate rights already enjoyed by real estate rights holders according to the law are not affected by changes in the registry and registration procedures. Real estate rights that can be registered include: collective land ownership; ownership of buildings and structures such as houses; ownership of forests and trees; contractual land management rights such as arable land, forest land and grassland; construction land use rights; rural residential land use rights; sea use rights;

easement rights; mortgage rights; and other real estate rights that require registration under the law. Real estate registration is carried out a with real estate unit as the basic unit, and each real estate unit has a unique code.

Real estate registration agency shall establish a unified real estate register in accordance with the provisions of the department in charge of land and resources of State Council. Real estate register shall record the following matters: the location, boundary address, spatial boundaries, area, use and other natural conditions of real estate; the subject, type, content, source, duration, rights change and other ownership status of real estate rights; matters involving real estate rights restrictions and tips; other related matters.

The parties or their agents shall apply for real estate registration at the office of the real estate registration agency. Before the real estate registry records the application for registration in the real estate register, the applicant may withdraw the application for registration. The applicant shall submit the following materials and be responsible for the authenticity of the application materials: application for registration; proof materials and power of attorney to identify the applicants and their agents; relevant proof materials for real estate ownership source, documents to prove the reasons for registration, real estate ownership certificate; real estate boundary address, spatial boundaries, area and other materials; and other materials to explain the interests of others; other materials provided according to laws and administrative regulations.

After receiving the application materials for real estate registration, the real estate registration agency shall handle the application materials in accordance with the following cases respectively: if the application falls within the scope of registration duties, the application materials are complete and in legal form, or the applicant has submitted all the corrected application materials as required, the applicant shall be accepted and informed in writing; if there are errors in the application materials that can be corrected on the spot, the applicant shall be informed to correct them on the spot, after correction, the applicant shall be accepted and informed in writing; if the application materials are incomplete or do not meet the statutory form, the applicant shall be informed in writing on the spot that the application is not accepted, and a one-time notification of all the content to be corrected shall be made; if the application for registration of real estate does not belong to the scope of the agency responsible for registration, the applicant shall be informed in writing on the spot that the application is not accepted, and the applicant shall be informed to apply to the agency with registration rights.

After the real estate registration agency accepts the real estate registration application, it shall check in accordance with the following requirements: whether the real estate boundary, spatial boundaries, area and other materials are consistent with the conditions of the real estate applied for registration; whether the relevant supporting materials and documents are consistent with the content of the application for registration; whether the registration application violates the provisions of laws and administrative regulations. In one of the following cases, the real estate registration agency can conduct field view on the real estate applied for registration: the initial registration of ownership of buildings and structures such as houses; registration of mortgages on buildings under construction; registration of cancellation due to the loss of real estate; other circumstances under which real estate registration agency proposes the need for field view. For registration applications that may have disputes over ownership, or may involve the interests of others, the real estate registration agency may investigate with the applicant, interested parties or relevant agencies. When the real estate registration agency conducts field view or investigation, the applicant and the investigated person shall cooperate.

Real estate registry shall complete the real estate registration procedures within 30 working days from the date of acceptance of the registration application, unless otherwise provided by law. Registration matters are completed when the registration is recorded in the real estate register. Once the real estate registration agency has completed the registration, it shall issue a certificate of real estate title or a certificate of registration to the applicant in accordance with law.

6.2 Planned Land Supply and Land Reserve System

6.2.1 Planned Land Supply with Quota Control

(1) **Quota control in the construction land allocation**

Quota control in the construction land allocation refers to the process of maximizing the efficiency of land resource utilization by scientifically predicting the demand for various types of construction land within a certain region and period of time, formulating quotas for various types of construction land according to the local natural and social development conditions and the requirements of national economic development, and decomposing the construction land quotas according to the characteristics of regional land supply and demand. The quota control of construction land is not only related to the overall economic efficiency of resource allocation and affects economic growth, but also concerns the national policy of arable land protection and food security, thus it has an extremely important position in China's land supply management policy system.

The Quota control in the construction land allocation has a strong administrative overtone. The basic operation process can be summarized as follows: the central government determines the total amount of construction land quotas for the planning period at one time, while deciding the construction land quotas for each region, and decomposes them from the central to local levels until they reach the townships. In the process of quota allocation, the lower-level government can estimate a quota based on the local economic development demand for construction land, and then submit it to the higher-level government for approval, and only after the higher-level government's approval and determination can it finally take effect.

At present, Chinese central government has set three expected indicators, namely, the scale of new construction land, the total scale of construction land and the scale of urban industrial and mining land, and six binding indicators, namely, the amount of arable land retained, the area of protected basic farmland, the scale of arable land occupied by new construction, the amount of arable land replenished by reclamation and development, the scale of urban and rural construction land, and the scale of urban industrial and mining land per capita, the former of which refers to indicators that are expected to be achieved or should be achieved during the planning period, while the latter refers to indicators that must be achieved and cannot be broken during the planning period, the latter of which has a stronger directive than the former.

The quota control in the construction land allocation plays an important role in land management and even in social and economic fields. It is not only an important land management policy that can curb land market speculation and promote intensive land use; it is also an ecological protection policy that strengthens the protection of arable land and inhibits the non-agriculturalization of agricultural land; it is a macro-control policy that is conducive to the government's control of the land allocation and economic growth; it is also a regional coordination policy, which distributes regional quotas in a balanced manner and promotes coordinated regional development from the supply level. However, at the same time, this rigid quota control also has problems such as unpredictable long-term quota, lack of basis for quota allocation and strong subjectivity, rigidity of quota management does not match with actual demand, overly generalized policy and imbalanced regional distribution.

(2) **Reform of cross-regional transaction of quotas**

Construction land quota is the core concern of local development, however, the construction land quota control, which is mainly characterized by "unified allocation, hierarchical decomposition and directive management", is a strong planning management tool, although it is the highest level of regulation and control of the government based on the overall interests of society to promote the full realization of the operational goals of the land use system, which can ensure the fair allocation of construction land quota, but it excludes market competition and leads to the imbalance between the allocation of construction land quota and the real demand, especially it cannot meet the actual demand for construction land quota in developed areas.

In the context of ensuring food security and promoting ecological civilization, the pattern of "not enough to satisfy everyone" for the construction land quota will exist for a long time. During China's rapid urbanization, the allocation of construction land quotas relying on the general land use plan has played an important role in strictly protecting arable land and balancing arable land protection and construction land demand. However, this does not mean that the established quota allocation system does not need to be adjusted. As the economy in general shifts from high speed to high quality, optimizing the construction land quota allocation system is crucial to the regional resource factor allocation, and is also related to China's strategic goal of realizing the comprehensive construction of a socialist modern country.

In 2021, the General Office of the Central Committee of the Communist Party of China and the General Office of the State Council issued the *Action Plan for Building a High Standard Market System*, mentioning the need to carry out pilot for cross-regional transaction of land quotas, explore the establishment of a nationwide cross-regional transaction mechanism for construction land quotas, explore the establishment of a cross-regional transaction market for supplementary arable land quotas within provinces in places with conditions, and improve the trading rules and service system. In general, the practice in this area still needs to be advanced.

6.2.2 Land Reserve System

(1) **Definition of basic concepts**

Land reserve refers to the act of the competent department of land and resources acquire land in accordance with the law, organize pre-development and storage for supply, and the purpose of which is to regulate the land market and promote the rational use of land resources. Land reserve work is unified by the competent department of land and resources management, and the specific implementation of land reserve is undertaken by the land reserve agencies. The finance department is responsible for the supervision of land reserve funds and the assets formed.

Land reserve agencies are institutions that undertake land reserve work within the administrative jurisdiction, approved by the government at the county level or above, with independent legal personality, subordinate to the administrative division in charge of land and resources. The competent land and resources department implements the name recording management of land reserve agencies. The information of agencies that meet the requirements is reported to the Ministry of Land and Resources at each level and included in the national directory of land reserve agencies, which is updated regularly.

(2) **Implementation of land reserve system**

1) **Making a reserve plan**

First, according to national economic and social development planning, territorial planning, overall land use planning, urban and rural planning, the responsible department prepares a three-year rolling plan for land reserve, reasonably determines the scale of land reserve for the next three years, makes comprehensive arrangements for the land resources that can be collected and stored within three years in terms of total volume, structure, layout and timing, and gives priority to reserving vacant, inefficiently utilized and other stock of construction land.

Then, according to the needs of urban construction development and land market regulation, the relevant agencies are responsible for formulating the annual land reserve plan by combining the local social development plan, the three-year rolling plan for land reserve, the annual land supply plan, the local government debt limit and other factors. Its content shall include: carry-over of reserve land at the end of the previous year; annual plan for new reserve land; annual plan for pre-development of reserve land; annual plan for supply of reserve land; annual plan for temporary management and care of reserve land; and total annual demand for land reserve funds.

2) **Land that can be reserved**
Land in reserve must comply with the overall land use planning and urban and rural planning. Land that suffers from the situations such as pollution, heritage relics, mineral overburden, flooding potential, geological disaster risk shall not be reserved before it has been successfully treated. Land that can be included in the reserve includes: state-owned land recovered by law; acquired land; land acquired by exercising the right of first refusal; land that has undergone agricultural land conversion, expropriation approval procedures and completed the expropriation; other land acquired by law.

According to the regulations, the land that can be reserved must be land with clear property rights. Land reserve agencies should review the compliance of land acquisition methods and procedures, economic compensation, and land rights. Land shall not be compulsorily expropriated for the purpose of storage. If the acquisition method and procedures are not compliant, compensation is not in place, the land ownership is not clear, should apply for the relevant real estate registration procedures but has not yet done so, the land shall not be reserved.

6.3 Land Supervision System and Land Violation Governance

Although the land supervision system was not established only to rectify land violations, and the control of land violations does not only rely on the implementation of the land supervision system, the two are still inextricably linked.

6.3.1 Land Supervision System

The land supervision system is the application of the concept of administrative supervision in the field of land administration. The so-called administrative supervision refers to the establishment of a supervision team or the establishment of a supervision agency by a higher-level government to supervise and inspect the behavior of the relevant administrative agencies. The establishment of the land supervision system in China has undergone an evolutionary process over the past decade or so.

(1) **Background and evolution of land supervision system**

1) **The factual and institutional backgrounds of the land supervision system**
The fact that China was facing serious challenges due to government failure in arable land protection, a matter of national importance, is an essential reason

that prompted the central government to propose the land supervision system. On the one hand, land violations were increasing, and according to statistics, between 1999 and 2005, a total of 1,028,000 cases of land violations were found nationwide, involving an area of 321,000 hectares of land, with most of the illegal subjects being the government or at least involving the government; on the other hand, there were institutional flaws in the land administration system, it was difficult for the land supervision agencies, which was sub-departments within the local land administration departments, to effectively prevent and investigate problems such as illegal land use and management, resulting in the poor implementation of central policies and the persistent land violations. In order to strengthen the supervision of land violations, since 2004, the central government has carried out a centralized reform of land administration and implemented a vertical management model below the provincial level, bringing the land administration authority of local governments at all levels back to the provincial governments, yet the central government's supervision mechanism over provincial governments remained vacant, meaning that collusion in land use and management by provincial and sub-provincial governments was still possible.

2) **The emergency of the land supervision system and the original purpose of implementing this system**

As an institutional innovation, the idea of land supervision was first introduced in 2004. In October of that year, the State Council issued the *Decision on Deepening Reform and Strict Land Management*, which proposed "improving the land enforcement and supervision system and establishing a national land supervision system". After more than a year of planning, in July 2006, the General Office of the State Council issued the *Notice on Issues Related to the Establishment of the National Land Supervision System*, marking the formal establishment of the land supervision system. According to the design of the system, the central government establishes the Office of the State Chief Land Inspector in the Ministry of Land and Resources, and assigns the State Land Inspector Bureau to the localities to represent the central government stationed in each place to exercise land supervision and supervision duties. This positioning of responsibilities ensures the authority and independence of the supervision. Each stationed agency can send national land inspectors and staff to the relevant provinces and cities within its supervision area for supervision and supervision in due course.

The establishment of the land supervision system marks a major change in the Chinese land administration system, which is essentially a way to achieve effective land management and utilization by strengthening the government's internal control, and is characterized by government self-restraint. The core mechanism of its function is that the central government exercises special administrative supervision over local governments and adjusts the game relationship between the central and local governments. Its significance is reflected in three aspects. First, it is conducive to timely discovering and summarizing the experience of various regions, and supervising, helping, and supporting local governments to better fulfill their responsibilities for arable land protection targets. Second, it is conducive to strengthening the central government's supervision and supervision of the local government's implementation of regulatory policies, urging local governments to implement the central government's decisions and keep the smooth flow of government orders fully and accurately. Third, it is conducive to the orderly management and use of land in accordance with the law under a unified land policy, to ensure the effective implementation of land management laws and regulations nationwide.

3) **The new dynamics of the land supervision system**
At the beginning of the establishment of the land supervision system, the supervision agencies mainly focused on the implementation of local targets of responsibility for arable land protection, land law enforcement and other work. With the deepening of institutional reform and the continuous practice of the land supervision system, the work responsibilities have been newly enriched and developed in recent years, gradually moving towards more integrated multi-functional supervision and whole life cycle supervision in the construction of ecological civilization. The *Land Administration Law* amended in 2019 states that the agencies authorized by the State Council shall inspect the land use and land administration of provincial governments as well as municipal governments determined by the State Council, thereby enshrining the land supervision system into law as a formal system in the field of land administration. Based on this, the revised *Regulations for the Implementation of the Land Administration Law* further concretize the scope of supervision and institutional duties and powers, drawing out the basic framework of rules for the operation of land supervision, implying that the land supervision system has fully stepped into the rule of law.

(2) **Elements and implementation of land supervision system**

1) **Subject to implement land supervision system**
The subject of land supervision refers to the state authority that enjoys the power of state land supervision according to the authorization of laws and regulations, is able to independently engage in land supervision activities in its own name, and bears legal responsibility for the consequences of its actions. As has mentioned above, the subject of land supervision is the agency authorized by the State Council to specifically exercise land supervision and supervision power over the governments of provinces, autonomous regions, and municipalities directly under the Central Government, as well as the governments of cities determined by the State Council. Specifically, the State Council authorizes the Ministry of Natural Resources, which exercises supervisory and supervision authority on behalf of the State Council through the Chief Inspector of Natural Resources, who deploys supervision bureaus to localities to supervise and inspect the land use and management within the scope of the inspectors on behalf of the Chief Inspector. Currently, there are nine natural resources supervision bureaus nationwide.

2) **Objects to be supervised.**
According to the law, the objects to be supervised are the governments of provinces, autonomous regions, and municipalities directly under the Central

Government, as well as the governments of cities determined by the State Council, which means that the State Council can decide to include some prefecture-level municipal governments in the scope of supervision according to the needs of economic and social development and land management situation.

3) **Contents of land supervision**

The contents included in the land supervision are mainly the following aspects:

First, the situation of arable land protection. Given that arable land is a basic essential element of food production, the supervision agencies are responsible for monitoring and inspecting the provincial governments in fulfilling their target-oriented responsibilities for the protection of arable land and sound arable land protection system, in order to resolutely curb the non-agriculturalization of arable land and strictly control the phenomenon of not growing food on farmland.

Second, the situation of land economic and intensive use. Supervision agencies should adapt to the requirements of accelerating the transformation of the mode of economic development, strengthen the supervision of the field of land use, find and investigate the disorderly development of land, inefficient use, sloppy waste, loss of revenue and other issues by local government and relevant departments and entities, and promote high-quality economic and social development through rational development and use of land.

Third, the situation of preparation and implementation of territorial spatial planning. Supervision agencies should urge the establishment and supervise the implementation of the national territorial spatial planning system, relying on the basic national territorial spatial information platform, based on the evaluation of the carrying capacity of resources and environment and the suitability of territorial spatial development, strengthen the bottom-line constraints, focusing on the implementation of the ecological protection red line, permanent basic farmland, urban development boundary and other spatial control boundaries as well as the binding indicators, resolutely investigate and deal with the illegal and irregular behavior in the process of the preparation and implementation of the planning, and promote the construction of a territorial spatial layout and support system to serve and support high-quality development.

Fourth, the situation of implementation of major national decisions related to land management. Supervision agencies should toward the implementation of major decisions involving land management in the construction of ecological civilization, focusing on major special actions and major issues of widespread concern to the community to carry out supervision, focusing on promoting the resolution of outstanding issues and common problems, and urge the improvement of the institutional mechanism for natural resource management.

Fifth, the situation of implementation of land administration laws and administrative regulation. Supervision agencies should not only conduct strict investigation into the implementation of land administration laws and regulations and violations of land administration laws and regulations by local governments, but also make timely rationalization suggestions for unreasonable, imperfect and unsuitable land administration policies found in the supervision.

Last, the situation of land use and management in other aspects. Supervision agencies in practice should also target a particular aspect of the outstanding problems in the field of land management and major illegal and irregular problem clues, which are often obtained from the leadership instructions, departmental referrals, letters and visits, media disclosures, to carry out supervision and promote the resolution of the problems with larger impact.

4) **Types of land supervision**

In order to give full play to the three working mechanisms of land supervision, such as discovery mechanism, audit mechanism and correction mechanism, the supervision agencies mainly make use of the power of investigation, audit power, correction power and recommendation power granted by law to conduct land supervision, which includes three types in the practice, i.e., routine supervision, special supervision, and audit-based supervision.

Routine supervision refers to the comprehensive supervision and inspection of the land use and management behavior of the supervised area within a certain period of time by the supervision agency according to the relevant national laws, regulations and policies.

Special supervision refers to the special supervision and inspection of land violations with significant tendency and impact and information on land violations is mainly obtained through leading instructions, inspection findings, media disclosure and public reports.

Audit-based supervision refers to the daily approval and filing and centralized field verification of agricultural land conversion and land expropriation matters submitted by provincial governments to the State Council for approval and self-approval in accordance with the authority and procedures stipulated in relevant laws and regulations.

5) **Approaches to conduct land supervision**

There are several approaches for supervision agencies to conduct land supervision.

First is to investigate to know about situations that local governments have done in the implementation of major decisions and deployment of land management, the implementation of the main responsibility for the protection of arable land and the whole process of land use management, to find out whether there are illegal and irregular problems. Investigation methods include analysis through technical means of research and analysis, material review, or through media disclosure and mass reporting to find clues to the problem. In the process of conducting the investigation, the supervision agency has the right to the relevant entities and individuals to understand the relevant information on the matter of inspection. Assisting in and cooperating with the supervision agency is a legal obligation for the relevant entities and individuals, who should truthfully reflect the situation and provide relevant materials.

Second is rectification and correction. Supervision agencies in the conduct of supervision work, if the local government is found to result in problems in the management and use of land or to be ineffective in the implementation of major national decisions on land management, after the approval of the chief inspector, can propose the supervision opinion to the local government. Rectification work is organized and implemented by the local government. Local governments shall not falsely rectify, cope with rectification, delay rectification or rectification is not in place, but shall seriously organize rectification and report on rectification as a legal obligation.

Third is admonition. Admonition is an administrative measure for supervision agencies to meet with the local leaders or their relevant departments in charge, where exists the ineffective implementation of major decisions and deployments or prominent problems of violation of laws and regulations, through pointing out the relevant issues, listening to the situation, and making recommendations for rectification. According to the needs of the work, admonitions can take the form of centralized admonitions and individual admonitions. In practice, in addition to involving state secrets, commercial secrets and personal privacy, the admonition should be released to the public with relevant information, if necessary, media reporters can be invited to attend the admonition meeting, to accept social supervision and supervision of public opinion.

Last is accountability recommendations. In order to improve the effectiveness of the results of the supervision, institutionalize and legalize the work of accountability for land violations, the supervision agencies can make recommendations to the supervisory authorities, appointment and dismissal authorities and other relevant authorities to pursue responsibility in accordance with the law, forming a high-pressure situation of serious rectification. In addition, the supervision agencies has explored ways to strengthen collaboration with the central inspection, audit, environmental protection inspectors and other central supervision agencies, to achieve normalization of collaboration and coordination among departments, and to create a social atmosphere conducive to the work of the supervision.

6.3.2 Land Violation Governance

(1) **Land violation**

Land violation refers to the violation of land management laws and regulations by entities and individuals, i.e., failure to fulfill obligations under the land management law or abuse of rights and authority, and should be held legally responsible. According to the relevant laws, there are seven main forms of land violations: illegal land transfer in the forms of buying, selling or others; destruction of arable land; illegal occupation of land; refusal to fulfill the obligations of land reclamation; illegal approval of land; illegal appropriation or misappropriation of compensation for land expropriation; refusal to return the land.

Land violations present three distinctive features: first, arable land becomes the main carrier of violations, mainly because the weak ability and awareness of farmers to defend their rights provide space for illegal occupation of arable land; second, grassroots governments constitute the main subject of violations, because land is an important resource for local governments to develop the economy of their jurisdictions and obtain political achievements; third, the frequency of land violations is influenced by the level of economic development.

There are many factors behind the frequent land violations in China during the transition period, for example, the short-term concept of local officials to stimulate economic growth within a limited term of office makes them rely on land resources to a greater extent; the imperfect system of land laws and regulations makes it difficult to protect the legitimate rights and interests of farmers; the hollow external supervision system leads to ineffective constraints on local government actions; the unsound land management system leads to excessive power of local governments; the low degree of land marketization creates room for rent seeking.

The frequent and difficult-to-manage land violations seriously harm social and economic development, mainly in the following aspects: first, land violations are inevitably accompanied by corrupt behaviors such as abuse of power, and infringe on farmers' rights and interests, intensifying social conflicts; second, land violations disrupt the government's macro-control of land resources, hinder the implementation of land planning, and reduce the efficiency of land resources utilization; third, land violations increase damage to arable land and endanger food security.

(2) **Land inspection system**

The great harm makes the central government pay more and more attention to land violation control, which refers to the adoption of prevention, supervision and punishment to regulate the behavior of relevant subjects in land use or management activities, and the system formed by it is the land inspection system.

The so-called land inspection refers to the administrative law enforcement actions of the competent natural resources departments to inspect the implementation and compliance of land management laws and regulations by entities and individuals within the administrative region in accordance with the legal authority, procedures and methods, and to investigate and deal with violations of land management laws and regulations. It should be noted that land inspection and land supervision are two different systems, and their differences are mainly in the following aspects:

First, in terms of subject. The subject of land inspection is the competent department of natural resources of the government at or above the county level, which enjoys the authority of land administration according to law; while the subject of land supervision is the land supervision agency authorized by the central government.

Second, in terms of object. The object of land inspection is the management counterpart, i.e., all entities and individuals who have legal relations with land, and under certain conditions, also includes the local governments at all levels and the natural resources authorities exercising land administration power on behalf of the government; while the object of land supervision is the land use and management of provincial and city governments determined by the State Council. Although there is a crossover between the two, but the focus and tendency is different.

Third, in terms of authority. The function of land inspection is to inspect the implementation of land management laws and regulations and to impose legal sanctions, including administrative penalties and administrative sanctions, on violators of the law. The functions of land supervision mainly include the exercise of investigation, audit, correction and recommendation powers, and do not replace the inspection and administrative punishment and other management powers of natural resources authorities at all levels.

According to the *Land Administration Law* and the *Regulations for the Implementation of the Land Administration Law*, the competent department of natural resources of the government at or above the county level inspects violations of the laws and regulations on land management, and the competent department of agriculture and rural affairs at or above the county level inspects violations of the laws and regulations on rural residential land management. The staffs who undertake the land inspection tasks should be familiar with land management laws and regulations, loyalty, impartiality in law enforcement; and should be trained, qualified by the examination, and obtain administrative law enforcement documents before engaging in land inspection work.

The competent authorities, in performing their duties of inspection, have the right to take the following measures: questioning the entities and individuals involved in illegal cases; requesting the entities or individuals being inspected to provide documents and information on land rights for viewing or copying; entering the site where the suspected land violations occurs to take photographs and video; requesting the inspected entities or individuals to make explanations on issues related to land rights; entering the site where the land is illegally occupied by the inspected entities or individuals to conduct a survey; ordering the relevant parties to stop the ongoing land violations; suspending the land approval, registration and other procedures related to the illegal case during the investigation period; sealing documents and materials that may be transferred, destroyed, concealed or altered; and ordering the inspected entities or individual shall not sell and transfer the property related to the case during the investigation.

If the land inspection staff needs to enter the site to conduct surveys, require the relevant entities or individuals to provide documents, information and instructions, the relevant certification should be shown first. The relevant entities and individuals should support and cooperate with the competent authorities on the inspection of land violations, and provide work convenience, and shall not refuse and obstruct the relevant staffs to perform their duties in accordance with the law.

If the competent department in the inspection work finds the illegal acts of the state staff, it should deal with these acts according to law; if the department itself does not have the right to deal with, it shall transfer to the supervisory authority or relevant authorities according to law.

If the competent department in the inspection work finds the land violations that constitute a crime, the case shall be transferred to the relevant authorities to investigate the criminal responsibility of the relevant parties; if the act does not constitute a crime, it shall be given administrative punishment in accordance with the law.

6.4 Land Taxation and Land Finance

6.4.1 Land Taxation System in China

(1) Framework of land taxation system

Taxation is not only the main source of national revenue, but also an important means of macro-control of the national economy and resource allocation by the state. Land taxation is a way for the state to take land as the object of taxation and obtain part of the land revenue from land owners or users compulsorily, free of charge and fixed by virtue of political power according to law. Therefore, land taxation is an important part of state revenue on the one hand, and an important tool for the state to allocate land resources on the other. China has initially built up a relatively complete land taxation system covering all aspects and regulating the whole process of land use activities. The composition of this system can be understood from different perspectives.

1) According to the object of taxation, land taxes can be divided into land property tax, land revenue tax and land transfer tax. Among them, land property tax refers to the land tax based on the quantity or value of land as a kind of property possessed, controlled and earned by taxpayers, such as urban land use tax and land value-added tax; land income tax is the land tax based on the ordinary income from the land use, such as personal income tax and corporate income tax based on the amount of income when transferring or leasing real estate; land transfer tax is the land tax based on the amount of transfer occurring in the process of land transfer, such as value-added tax in the real estate industry.
2) According to whether land is directly taxed, land taxes can be divided into direct land tax and indirect land tax. Direct land tax is levied on the possession, use and transfer of land, and its tax revenue is directly related to land, including urban land use tax, land value-added tax, deed tax and arable land occupation tax, which are also the four taxes recognized by the central government as constituting land taxation. Indirect land tax refers to taxes whose tax objects are not the land itself but are closely related to the land use activities, including value-added tax, stamp duty, corporate income tax, personal income tax and urban maintenance and construction tax brought about by the development of the construction and real estate industries. It should be noted that some academic studies also consider property tax as a direct land tax due to the inextricable link between land and housing. According to the current inter-governmental revenue division standard, the revenue from these five direct land taxes is exclusively shared by local governments.
3) The categories of land tax can also be classified according to the land use segment to which the tax applies. The first category is the land tax applicable to the land acquisition, which only includes the arable land occupation tax; the second category is the land tax applicable to the land holding, which includes the urban land use tax and the property tax, and the third category is the land tax applicable to the land transfer, which includes the land value-added tax, urban maintenance

and construction tax, value-added tax, deed tax, stamp duty and various income taxes.

(2) **Introduction of major types of land taxes**

1) **Arable land occupation tax**
Arable land occupation tax is a tax levied by the state on entities and individuals who occupy arable land to construct buildings or structures or engage in non-agricultural construction, based on the actual area of arable land occupied and calculated according to the prescribed tax amount, which has the characteristics of one-time, specificity, restriction and development that are different from other taxes. The purpose of levying arable land occupation tax is to reasonably utilize land resources, strengthen land management and protect arable land. Its functions are mainly manifested in: using economic means to limit the indiscriminate occupation and abuse of arable land, while carrying out development of arable land and improvement of existing arable land, promoting the stable development of agricultural production, compensating for the loss of agricultural productivity caused by the occupation of arable land, and providing necessary financial support for the comprehensive and coordinated development of agriculture.
In April 1987, the State Council promulgated the *Provisional Regulations on the Arable Land Occupation Tax*, which aimed to restrict non-agricultural construction practices and protect arable land resources. In December 2018, the Standing Committee of the National People's Congress adopted the *Law on the Arable Land Occupation Tax*, so that there is a clear legal basis for the collection of the arable land occupation tax. The taxable amount of arable land occupation tax is the actual area of arable land occupied by the taxpayer multiplied by the applicable tax amount, which is related to the level of per capita arable land in the region, and a relatively lower standard can be applied in regions with a higher level of per capita arable land.
In the case of occupied basic farmland, the arable land occupied tax will be levied by a certain margin on top of the applicable local tax amount. In the case of occupied farmland for the construction of military facilities, schools, kindergartens, social welfare institutions, medical institutions, the arable land occupation tax is exempted. If the surviving families of rural martyrs, the surviving families of military personnel who died in the line of duty, disabled military personnel and rural residents who meet the conditions of rural minimum living security build new residential houses for their own use within the prescribed land use standards, they are also exempted from the arable land occupation tax. For the following cases, there are moderate reductions in the levy of arable land occupation tax, including: occupying arable land due to the construction of railroad lines, highway lines, runways of airports, aprons, ports, waterways, water conservancy projects, and rural residents occupy arable land within the prescribed land use standards for new residential houses for self-use.

2) **Urban land use tax**.
Urban land use tax refers to a tax levied by the state on entities and individuals using land within the scope of cities, counties, established towns and industrial

and mining areas, based on the actual area of land occupied by them and calculated according to the prescribed tax amount. The urban land use tax is the only tax applicable to the land holding, which is stable, long-term, non-one-time and relatively extensive. The purpose of levying urban land use tax is to rationalize the use of urban land, regulate the income of land grade difference, improve the efficiency of land use and strengthen land management.

In response to the requirements for land management imposed by the implementation of the urban land paid use system, the State Council issued the *Provisional Regulations of the People's Republic of China on Urban Land Use Tax* in September 1988, which has since been amended several times. According to the current version, the urban land use tax is calculated on an annual basis and paid in installments, and its collection is based on a differential fixed tax rate with a range of 1.5–30 RMB/m^2 per year for large cities, 1.2–24 RMB/m^2 per year for medium-sized cities, 0.9–18 RMB/m^2 per year for small cities, and 0.6–12 RMB/m^2 per year for counties, established towns and industrial and mining areas. The provincial government can determine the applicable tax range for the areas under its jurisdiction within the prescribed tax range, according to the conditions of municipal construction and economic prosperity. Municipal and county governments shall, according to the actual situation, divide the land in the region into several classes and set the corresponding applicable tax standards within the tax range determined by the provincial government, and report to the former for approval and implementation. Similarly, land used for several purposes is exempted from land use tax, such as, land used by state organs, people's organizations and military for their own use; land used by units allocated by the state treasury for their own use; land used by religious temples, parks and famous monuments for their own use; public land such as municipal streets, squares and green zones; productive land used directly for agriculture, forestry, animal husbandry and fishery.

3) **Land value-added tax**

Land value-added tax refers to a tax levied by the State on the entities and individuals who transfer real estate, including state-owned land use rights, buildings on the ground and their attachments, and receive income, based on the value added from the transfer of their real estate and calculated at the prescribed tax rate. The purpose of levying land value-added tax is to regulate the order of land and real estate market transactions, to reasonably regulate the gain from land appreciation and to safeguard the rights and interests of the country.

In view of the prevalence of speculation in the rapidly developing real estate market after the implementation of the urban land paid use system, which undermined the market order, the State Council issued the *Provisional Regulations of the People's Republic of China on Land Value-added Tax* in 1993, which was later amended in 2011. According to the current version, land value-added tax is levied on a per-by-case basis. The so-called value-added amount refers to the balance of the income obtained by the taxpayer from the transfer of real estate less the amount of legal deductions, where the income includes monetary income, income in kind and other income, and the legal deductions include the amount paid for acquiring the land use right, the costs and expenses of developing the land; the costs and expenses of construction of housing and supporting facilities, or the appraised price of old houses and buildings; and the amount of taxes related to the transfer of real estate. The land value-added tax is subject to a four-tier over-rate progressive tax rate, and the applicable tax rates are 30, 40, 50 and 60% respectively according to the ratio of the value-added amount relative to the amount of deductible items. The taxpayer is exempt from land value-added tax if any of the following situations apply: the taxpayer sells ordinary standard residential units and the value-added does not exceed 20% of the amount of deductible items, the real estate is requisitioned or repossessed due to national construction needs in accordance with the law.

4) **Deed tax**

Deed tax is a kind of tax levied on the recipient of the title when the title of real estate is transferred and changed due to the contract made between the parties, which has the characteristics of wide tax source, one-time levy and timely revenue collection. Through the taxation, the recipient of real estate gets a deed issued by the collecting authority in the name of the government as a proof to protect legal rights and interests. The role of deed tax is mainly reflected in the state's use of economic means to regulate real estate transactions, help local governments regulate the real estate market and increase local fiscal revenue.

The form of the deed tax system implemented in China today originated from the *Provisional Regulations of the People's Republic of China on Deed Tax* promulgated in 1997, and in August 2020, the Standing Committee of the National People's Congress adopted the *Law of the People's Republic of China on Deed Tax*, which has elevated the legal status of the tax collection. According to this law, the entities and individuals who acquire property rights from the transfer of real estate tenures are the taxpayers of the deed tax. Specifically, the acts that constitute the transfer of real estate tenures include: land use right conveyance, land use right transfer (e.g., sale, gift, swap), and housing sale, gift, swap. It should be noted that the so-called land use right transfer does not include the transfer of land contracting rights and land management rights. The deed tax rate applicable to each region is proposed by the provincial governments within the range of 3% to 5% and decided by the Standing Committee of the National People's Congress at the same level. Deed tax is calculated on the basis of the price of real estate. Due to the various ways of transfer of real estate tenures, the pricing methods are different. Specifically, the deed tax levied for land use right conveyance, land use right sale or housing sale is based on the transaction price stated in the contract of transfer of tenures, including the money to be delivered as well as the price corresponding to in-kind and other economic benefits; the deed tax levied for land use right swap or housing swap is based on the difference of the price of the swapped land use right or housing; the deed tax levied for land use right gift, housing gift or other acts of tenure transfer without price is based on the price approved by the taxation authority according to the law with reference to the market price of similar transactions. It should be noted that in the actual collection of the deed tax, a wide range of reduction or exemption clauses may also apply.

6.4.2 *Institutional Arrangements Related to Land Finance*

(1) **Collection and use of land conveyance revenue**

Land conveyance revenue is the total land proceeds obtained by the local government through the allocation of state-owned land use rights by way of conveyance, which is equal to the sum of costs for land expropriation compensation, land pre-development costs and net proceeds from land conveyance. Among them, the so-called land proceeds have the following categories: the total transaction proceeds determined by the conveyance of state-owned land use rights by tender, auction, listing and agreement; the land proceeds to be paid for the transfer of allocated state-owned land use rights or the use of the original allocated land for business construction in accordance with the law; the land proceeds to be paid for the realization and disposal of mortgaged allocated state-owned land use rights; the land proceeds to be paid for the transfer of welfare housing and affordable housing in accordance with the regulations; the land proceeds to be paid for the change in land use, plot ratio and other land use conditions of the conveyed state-owned land use rights. The land price to be paid; the land price to be paid for changing the land use, plot ratio and other land use conditions of the granted state-owned land use rights, as well as other income related to the conveyance or change of state-owned land use rights.

The central government has stipulated that the income and expenditure of land conveyance revenue are fully included in the management of local fund budgets since January 1, 2007. Under this arrangement, all the income is paid into the local treasury, and all the expenditure is arranged from the income of land conveyance through local fund budgets, and special accounts are set up in the local treasury to specifically account for the income and expenditure of land conveyance revenue. In May 2021, the Ministry of Finance required that the department responsible for the collection of land conveyance revenue be changed from the natural resources department to the taxation department, further bringing land conveyance revenue and expenditure into the regulatory track.

In terms of the use of land grant income, the following types of affairs are mainly involved: the first is expenses for land expropriation and demolition compensation, including land compensation, resettlement subsidy, compensation for ground attachment and crops, and compensation for demolition and relocation; the second is land development expenses, including preliminary land development expenditures and the costs related to preliminary land development in accordance with the provisions of the financial sector; the third is the expenditure for supporting agriculture and rural development, including the accrual of agricultural land development funds, expenditure on subsidies for the social security of expropriated peasants, expenditure on subsidies for maintaining the original living standards of expropriated peasants and expenditure on rural infrastructure construction; the fourth is expenditure for urban construction, including expenditure on construction of supporting facilities to improve the function of state-owned land use and urban infrastructure construction; the last is expenditure for other purposes, including land conveyance operational expenses, payment of land reimbursement fees for new construction land, accrual of state-owned land revenue fund, expenditure on urban affordable housing, payment of expenses for the resettlement of employee of state-owned enterprises that has gone bankrupt or been restructured.

In September 2020, the General Office of the CPC Central Committee and the General Office of the State Council issued the *Opinions on Adjusting and Improving the Use of Land Conveyance Revenue to Support Rural Revitalization*, pointing out that for a long time, land value-added revenue has been taken from rural areas and mainly used in urban areas, which has effectively promoted the rapid industrialization and urbanization, but the proportion of direct use in agriculture and rural affairs is low, and the support role for agricultural and rural development is insufficient. This document has emphasized the need to adjust the urban–rural distribution pattern of land conveyance revenue, steadily increase the proportion of land conveyance revenue for agriculture and rural affairs, focus on supporting the key tasks of rural revitalization, and provide strong support for the implementation of the rural revitalization strategy in accordance with the requirement of "taking from rural areas and mainly using it for rural affairs".

To this end, on the one hand, the central government is committed to establishing a fund transfer mechanism that is mainly retained by municipalities and counties and appropriately coordinated by the central and provincial governments. In other words, funds from land conveyance revenues for agriculture and rural affairs are mainly arranged and used by municipal and county governments, with emphasis on county governments, and county governments are given the autonomy to use the funds reasonably. At the same time, the provincial government coordinates a certain proportion of the funds from the land conveyance revenue for agriculture and rural affairs, and transfer the funds among the regions under its jurisdiction, focusing on supporting the rural revitalization of the main grain-producing and financially weak counties. The central government continues to coordinate the use of funds for the construction of water conservancy construction and land reimbursement fees for new construction land, in favor of the main grain-producing areas and central and western regions.

On the other hand, the central government emphasizes strengthening the integrated use of funds from land conveyance revenue for agricultural and rural affairs, proposing that it is allowed to break the management mode of itemized and scattered use according to the actual needs of rural revitalization, and integrate the use of funds from land conveyance revenues for agriculture and rural affairs, focusing on the construction of high-standard farmland, farmland water conservancy construction, modern seed industry upgrading, rural water supply guarantee, rural habitat environment improvement, comprehensive rural land improvement, arable land and permanent basic farmland protection, village public facilities construction and management, rural education, rural culture and spiritual civilization construction, as well as ecological protection and restoration directly related to agriculture and rural areas, and construction of food-for-work projects. At the same time, the central government requires strengthening the coordination between the funds from land conveyance revenue for agriculture and rural affairs and the general public budget input for agriculture, and continue to increase the financial expenditures for agriculture and rural affairs through the original channels to avoid the crowding-out effect on the general public budget input for agriculture, so as to ensure a real increase in input for agriculture and rural affairs.

(2) **Land finance and the local government debt**

Land finance, which refers to land-based finance that public land development rights are used as a basis to receive off-budgetary revenue, has long attracted worldwide attention. Since the reform of the tax-sharing system in 1994, land finance in China has become the major source in the local fiscal budget. With the development of urbanization and industrialization, the size of China's land finance has experienced growth at a rapid and unprecedented rate.

The so-called land financing refers to the local government relying on the local debt financing platform and financing from banks with land use rights as collateral, and using land conveyance revenue as a guarantee for repayment and a source of funds for repayment. The land mortgage revenue is actually the indebtedness obtained by local governments from bank loans with land as collateral, and is the borrowing that local governments must repay in the future.

In recent years, the large amount of bank credit leveraged by land mortgages has provided an important source of funds for promoting urbanization, and urban development has been able to raise urban land prices and create conditions for larger-scale land mortgages after urban development. The emergence and development of land mortgage is mainly due to the following three factors: First, the tax sharing reform in 1994 caused a shortage of local financial resources, and the original reliance on land revenue is increasingly constrained, so the city government that does not have the power to directly issue debt can only find another way, that is, through the financing platform to mortgage land to raise debt. Second, urban debt has a soft budget constraint in China, when local governments cannot repay their debts, it is expected that the central government will repay them for local governments, and local government debts have a special "rigidity of payment". Third, in the rapidly urbanizing China, land is a natural high-quality collateral, which can obtain more bank loans with the implicit endorsement of city governments. It follows that less constrained land collateral can lead to massive urban indebtedness.

Toward the end of 2017, the outstanding balance of Chinese local governments' debt was RMB 16.47 trillion. By the end of 2018, the total debt of local governments in China reached RMB 18.4 trillion, which is approached the ceiling of RMB 18.82 trillion of local governments' debt approved by the National People's Congress in 2017. However, the debt ratio (the ratio of the debt to GDP) is lower than the internationally accepted 100–120% warning line. Considering the hidden debts of local regions, local debts have potential risks.

Chapter 7
Outlook of China's Land Policies

Xianjin Huang, Xiao Lyu, Jun Yang, and Shandong Niu

Human society is currently facing many serious challenges such as global geostrategic tensions and the existential climate crisis, and the governments of all nations are making efforts to address them in the context of their own national conditions. China has developed a unique path, which is characteristically Chinese, in dealing with the many challenges. Among them, the land policy based on China's actual human-land relationship and the economic and social system has played an important role. Therefore, what is the future direction of China's land policy in light of global sustainable development, the harmonious coexistence of human beings and nature, and the deepening of China's ecological civilization construction strategy? This chapter first introduces the international value of China's land policy for global sustainable development and then proposes ideas for the improvement and refinement of China's land policy in the future based on the concept of ecological civilization and modernization for harmony between human beings and nature (Hongyu et al. 2020a, b).

7.1 International Value of China's Land Policies

The United Nations has made eradication of hunger, climate action, and poverty eradication as important targets in the Sustainable Development Goals (SDGs). China's land policy has made important contributions to global food security, climate

X. Huang (✉)
Nanjing University, Nanjing, China
e-mail: hxj369@nju.edu.cn

X. Lyu · S. Niu
Northeastern University, Shenyang, China

J. Yang
China University of Mining and Technology, Xuzhou, China

S. Tan and X. Huang (eds.), *Land Policy in China*, The Frontier of Public Administration in China, https://doi.org/10.1007/978-981-19-9895-9_7

change, and poverty alleviation by focusing on arable land protection, construction land control, and rural land system reform. This land policy adoption is a valuable contribution of China for global sustainable development.

7.1.1 Strict Arable Land Protection to Ensure Global Food Security

As a developing country with only 9% of the world's arable land but nearly 20% of the world's population, China's food security has been under global scrutiny. However, China does not have the concerns of Western societies, especially in the current situation where global climate change and the novel coronavirus pandemic pose major challenges to world food security, while the Chinese still have their rice bowls firmly in their own hands, and they are filled with China's own food. In 2020, the total national grain production was 669.50 billion Kg, achieving a "seventeenth consecutive bumper crop." It is undeniable that the increase in China's grain production is due to a combination of factors, but arable land is always the foundation of grain production and securing a certain area of arable land is the key to ensuring food security. Over the years, the Chinese government has formulated and introduced a series of strict arable land protection policies around one billion and eight hundred million acres of arable land red line, which has effectively curbed the rapid reduction of arable land. The Third National Land Survey in 2021 shows that China's arable land area is 1.9179 billion mu. China's strict arable land protection policies have provided solid support for the continuous improvement of food production, ensuring national food security and addressing various risk challenges, as well as making positive contributions to maintaining global food security.

At the same time, China's arable land protection policy is worth emulating by other countries around the world to achieve arable land protection and food security under sustainable development. Take the latest revision of the "Regulations on the Implementation of the Law of Land Administration of the People's Republic of China" in 2021 as an example, the relevant content of arable land protection is as follows.

(1) **Strictly prevent the "non-agriculturalization" and "non-grain" of arable land and build a firm line of defense for food production security**

On the basis of the relevant policies and laws, the "Regulations on the Implementation of the Low of Land Administration of the People's Republic of China" further clarify the institutional boundary of arable land use and strengthen special protection of arable land. It is clearly stipulated that the state implements special protection for arable land, strictly adheres to the red line of arable land protection, and strictly controls the conversion of arable land into other agricultural land such as forest, grassland, and garden land. Arable land should be given priority for production of grain and cotton, oil, sugar, vegetables, and other agricultural products. In accordance with the relevant state regulations needed to convert arable land into forest land, grassland, gardens, and other agricultural land, priority should be given to the use of arable land that cannot sustain long-term stable use.

(2) Improve the system of balance between the occupation and supplement of cultivated land and build a firm defense line for protecting arable land quantity

Relevant policy interpretation:

'the balance between occupation and supplement of cultivated land".

1. Sun Rui, Sun Ping, Wu Jinxi's research considered that balance of farmland occupation and compensation has to a certain extent suppressed the reduction of arable land and provided certain guarantee for scientific land use in China, which is a profound change in China's land management.

   Source: Sun Rui, Sun Ping, Wu Jinxi, et al. Effectiveness and limitations of cultivated land requisition-compensation balance policy in China. China Population, Resources and Environment, 2014, 24(03): 41–46.
2. Jiang Yu, Pu Lijie, Zhu Ming's research considered that the implementation of the balance of farmland occupation and compensation has curbed the momentum of rapid decline in the amount of arable land and, to a certain extent, has achieved harmonization of protecting arable land resources and ensuring economic development.

   Source: Jiang Yu, Pu Lijie, Zhu Ming, et al. Progress and review of the research of farmland requisition-compensation balance in China. Resources Science, 2019, 41(12): 2342–2355.
3. Shen Xiaoqiang, Wang Liping, Wu Cifang's research considered that China's balance of farmland occupation and compensation is a strict policy aimed at controlling the non-agriculturalization of arable land and replenishing the loss of arable land due to urban expansion through a top-down quota system.

   Source: Shen Xiaoqiang, Wang Liping, Wu Cifang, et al. Local interests or centralized targets? How China's local government implements the farmland policy of requisition–compensation balance. Land Use Policy, 2017, (67): 716–724.

The balance between the occupation and supplement of cultivated land is an important element of arable land protection in China. The "Regulations on the Implementation of the Law of Land Administration of the People's Republic of China" further improve the system of balance between the occupation and supplement of cultivated land, add specific requirements for acceptance of cultivated land, and standardize and refine the content of land preparation. For example, regarding the acceptance of cultivated land reclamation, the "Land Administration Law of the People's Republic of China" provides that the people's governments of provinces, autonomous regions, and municipalities directly under the Central Government shall supervise the units occupying cultivated land to reclaim cultivated land in accordance with the plan or organize the reclamation of cultivated land in accordance with the plan and ensure acceptance. On this basis, the "Regulations on the Implementation of the Law of Land Administration of the People's Republic of China" further clarified that the people's governments of provinces, autonomous regions, and municipalities directly under the Central Government shall organize the competent departments of natural resources and agriculture and rural areas to carry out acceptance of reclaimed arable land to ensure that the reclaimed arable land is implemented as per the plan. Permanent basic farmland designated should also be included in the national database of permanent basic farmland strictly managed. Occupation of arable land to supplement the situation should be announced to society in accordance with relevant state regulations. On land consolidation, the "Regulations on the Implementation of the Law of Land Administration of the People's Republic of China" provides that: the county-level people's government shall, in accordance with the requirements of the national land spatial planning on the integrated layout of agriculture, ecology, towns, and other functional space, develop a land consolidation program to promote the protection of arable land and the economical and intensive use of land. County, township (town) people's government should organize rural collective economic organizations, implement the land consolidation program, and idle land and abandoned land should be improved and transformed in a planned manner. Land consolidation of new arable land can be used as a supplement to the arable land occupied by construction.

Relevant policy interpretation:

"territorial spatial planning".

1. Liu Yansui, Zhou Yang's research considered that territorial spatial planning is generally regarded as an effective language to promote spatial governance and sustainable regional development. Optimizing the spatial development pattern of homeland and promoting sustainable socio-economic development have become important elements to enhance China's national governance capacity and ecological civilization construction.

   Source: Liu Yansui , Zhou Yang. Territory spatial planning and national governance system in China, Land Use Policy, 2021, (102): 105288.
2. Yue Wenze, Wu Tong, Wang Tianyu's research considered territorial spatial planning a spatial guideline for all kinds of development, utilization, and protection activities, a blueprint for sustainable development, an action guide for spatial development, a basic guarantee for high-quality development, and a basis for development and protection and construction activities.

Source: Yue Wenze, Wu Tong, Wang Tanyu, et al. "Double evaluations" for territorial spatial planning: Challenges and responses. Journal of Natural Resources, 2020, 35(10): 2299–2310.

(3) **Refine the system of arable land quality enhancement and protection to build a firm defense line of arable land quality and safety**

To ensure the quality of arable land, the "Land Administration Law of the People's Republic of China" requires that the people's governments at the provincial level shall take measures to ensure that the quality of arable land is not reduced, and that people's governments at all levels shall guide the rotation of fallow and prevention of soil pollution in accordance with local conditions. "The Regulations on the Implementation of the Law of Land Administration of the People's Republic of China" from the level of working principles and operational implementation level further clarified that local people's governments at or above the county level should take measures to prevent and control soil loss and pollution of arable land, planned transformation of low-yielding land, construction of high-standard farmland, improve the quality of arable land, protect black land and other high-quality arable land, and make reasonable arrangements for the use of soil in the cultivation layer of arable land occupied by construction, according to the law. If non-agricultural construction in accordance with the law occupies permanent basic farmland, the construction unit shall, in accordance with the provisions of the province, autonomous region, municipality directly under the Central Government, make the occupied arable land cultivation layer of soil available for new reclamation, as it shall do with poor quality land or other arable land soil that can be improved. At the same time, it is further clarified that local people's governments above the county level should strengthen the guidance and management of agricultural restructuring to prevent damage to the arable land cultivation layer; also, it should ensure that facility agricultural land is no longer used but should be organized to restore planting conditions.

(4) **Clarify the main body of responsibility for arable land protection and strengthen the legal responsibility for arable land protection**

"The Regulations on the Implementation of the Law of Land Administration of the People's Republic of China" clarify the main body responsible for the protection of arable land from the level of administrative regulations, that is, the people's governments of provinces, autonomous regions, and municipalities directly under the Central Government in their administrative regions, and the main person in charge is the first person responsible for the protection of arable land in their administrative regions. At the same time, the people's governments of provinces, autonomous regions, and municipalities directly under the Central Government shall determine the State Council's arable land holdings and permanent basic farmland protection tasks of decomposition, and implementation to specific plots and assess the implementation of the target of responsibility for arable land protection. In addition, to strengthen the crackdown on illegal acts and take "long teeth" measures to effectively protect arable land, the "Regulations on the Implementation of the Law of Land Administration of the People's Republic of China" increased the penalties for the "non-grain" of arable land and increased the penalty for illegal occupation of arable land and other acts for which fines can be levied. The amount of fines for illegal occupation of arable land has been increased. On the "non-grain" of arable land, it is clearly stipulated that the people's government at or above the county level responsible for natural resources departments shall rectify the deadline for illegal occupation of permanent basic agricultural land to develop forestry and fruit industry or digging ponds for fish farming. If no correction is made within the time limit, a fine of not less than 2 times but not more than 5 times of the cultivated land reclamation fee shall be imposed on the occupied area. Illegal occupation of arable land to destroy the planting conditions or the development of land caused by land desertification, salinization, and other acts can be combined with a fine; the amount of fine stipulated for arable land reclamation is more than 5 to 10 times. For the destruction of black land and other high-quality arable land, the penalty is heavier.

Relevant policy interpretation:

"permanent basic farmland protection".

1. Zhong Taiyang, Huang Xianjin, Chen Yi's research considered that during 2004–2007, the implementation of the basic farmland protection policy had a significant impact on the reduction of cropland loss, with each 1% increase in the basic farmland protection rate reducing the average annual cropland loss by 364.4 hm2 per province.

   Source: Zhong Taiyang, Huang Xianjin, Chen Yi. Arable land conversion effects of basic farmland protection policy. China Population, Resources and Environment, 2012, 22(01): 90–95.
2. Cheng Qianwen, Jinag Penghui, Cai Ling yan's research considered that the demarcation of permanent basic farmland guarantees a production baseline for China's agricultural development, ensures the easy occupation of high-quality farmland around cities, and strictly controls the use of arable land (especially high-quality farmland around cities) in the face of accelerated urban expansion.

   Source: Cheng Qianwen, Jinag Penghui, Cai Ling yan, et al. Delineation of a permanent basic farmland protection area around a city centre: Case study of Changzhou City, China. Land Use Policy, 2017, 60: 73–89.

7.1.2 *Strengthen the Control of Construction Land and Actively Respond to Global Climate Change*

Similar to the issue of food security, the expansion of construction land brought about by China's rapid urbanization and industrialization also received widespread attention from international organizations such as the World Bank and foreign scholars. American economist Stiglitz, winner of the Nobel Prize in economics, has listed China's urbanization and U.S. technology as two key factors affecting the course of human development in the twenty-first century. Urbanization includes the transformation of urban characteristics in multiple dimensions such as population, industry, space, and society; while land is the most important carrier of all social and economic activities, construction land is the most important support for urbanization. Therefore, expansion of construction land has become a common feature of urbanization in all countries around the world, and China is no exception. China's urbanization rate has grown rapidly from about 17.9% in 1978 during reform and opening up to nearly 63.9% in 2020, while the urban built-up area has expanded more than seven times. In April 2021, Chinese President Xi Jinping pledged at the Leaders' Climate Summit that China will strive to achieve carbon peaking by 2030 and carbon neutrality by 2060. This is a major strategic decision made by China based on its responsibility to promote the building of a global community of shared future and the inherent requirement to mitigate global warming to achieve sustainable development. For China, effectively controlling the area of construction land and optimizing the use of construction land based on a green concept has become an important issue. In fact, the Chinese government has been trying to explore effective ways to manage construction land, and policies related to construction land management are constantly being innovated and improved. The policy of "reduction," "greening," and "intensification" of construction land advocated by the Chinese government has an important positive effect on controlling global climate change. The relevant policies are also of reference value to other countries in the control of construction land.

(1) **Control the total amount and promote integrated development**

In accordance with the principles of gradual and orderly progress, land conservation, intensive development, and reasonable layout, the need is to gradually promote the scale of urban land from expansion to limited urban development boundary, optimize the spatial structure, scientifically determine the nature and functions of cities, determine development strategies and goals, development direction and scale, delineate urban development boundary, strengthen the control of per capita construction land index, improve the population density of built-up areas, and improve the efficiency of urban land use. The above measures will become the main tasks of total urban land use control. To truly implement these measures, the Chinese government has ensured the standardized and orderly implementation of land use planning by strengthening land use approval for construction projects, land supervision, and management and satellite remote sensing monitoring. In the approval of land use for various types of industries, the construction land control zoning determined by the general land use planning and the planned dominant use of the area where the parcel is located will be the basis for land use plan review, effectively enhancing the standardization and operability of the plan's implementation. Construction projects that violate the plan must be firmly investigated and punished according to the law. The three prongs of approval, monitoring, and strict investigation will ensure achievement of the total control target.

(2) **Reducing incremental amount and promoting balanced development**

The reduction of incremental land use is a guarantee for achieving a sustainable increase in land use conservation and intensification. The Chinese government proposes that the arrangement of new construction land indicators be linked to regional environmental capacity, land development intensity, industrial structure optimization, fulfillment of the responsibility goal of arable land protection, and the level of land conservation and intensive land use, as well as the use of land in accordance with the law. These indicators must also be coordinated with the arrangement of urban and rural construction land increase/decrease indicators and the scale of reclamation and utilization of abandoned industrial and mining land, and increase in the rate of land supply, the proportion of stock land in land supply, and the occupancy rate of construction land per unit of GDP. The weight of land conservation and land use reduction rate must be considered in the initial allocation of planning indicators. A mechanism must be established to match the indicators of the incremental land use plan and the task of revitalizing the stock of land. Besides, it must implement a policy of industrial land use with control, effectively guide industrial structure adjustment and upgrading, support the construction of national and provincial development parks, promote the construction of innovative parks and new industrialization demonstration bases, and focus on supporting land for key transportation, water conservancy, energy infrastructure above the provincial level and land for strategic emerging industries, high-end manufacturing, modern service industries, and land for livelihood such as guaranteed housing projects, so as to promote the innovative development capacity of various industries. At the same time, the need is for implementation of the annual land use plan index pre-delivery mechanism, the implementation of urban and county-wide land use index market-based allocation pilot, exploration of the market-based allocation mode, transaction mode, and revenue allocation management. It includes a sound industrial land-saving access system whereby there is strict control of the threshold of new industrial land supply. It also involves formulating and releasing the negative list of land access for construction projects, and strictly implement and dynamically adjust the directory of restricted land use projects and prohibited land use projects in Jiangsu Province. It aims to comprehensively implement the pre-application system for new industrial land and encourage localities to combine local industrial development orientation and transformation and upgrading needs to develop higher-than-standard mu average investment intensity of new industrial land for fixed assets, construction intensity, and output efficiency standards after industrial projects reach production.

(3) **Revitalize the stock and promote internal development**

Revitalizing the stock of construction land is the only way to release the potential of land and seek development when the total amount of land development is limited, and it is also a key step to improve the overall efficiency of land use. The issue of urban construction land stock requires a combination of institutional, legal, and economic tools. The Chinese government firstl carried out a census of construction land, researched and formulated technical specifications for construction land census, investigated the basic information of construction land, clarified the scope of low-utility land in cities and towns, and clarified the scale, distribution, direction of utilization, and timing of utilization of the stock of land that can be revitalized so as to lay a solid foundation for revitalizing and utilizing the stock of construction land. Second, it further deepened the reform of the land use system with compensation, giving full play to the decisive role of the market in the allocation of land resources, including expanding the scope of state-owned land use with compensation, revising the catalog of allocated land projects, reducing the allocation of non-public welfare land, and promoting the use of land for operating infrastructure and social public utilities with compensation. At the same time, localities are encouraged to moderately increase the price of industrial land in line with the needs of industrial restructuring and industrial transformation and upgrading. In addition, it strengthened the construction of land reserve institutions and the implementation of land reserve institutions' access name recording management. It promoted the enterprise land buyback system and established a new mechanism of land reserve management that combines the acquisition of reserves according to the application of market entities and the acquisition of reserves according to government functions. It prepared land reserve planning and annual plans, and increase the review and supervision of the scale of land reserves, the scale of financing and the timing of implementation. At the same time, in accordance with the principles of "clear property rights, integrated planning, benefit sharing and standardized operation," it hopes to actively promote the transformation of old towns, old mines, and "urban villages" to improve the population and industrial carrying capacity of urban land. To enhance urban service functions as the guide, it encouraged the transformation of the use of old factories and old plant facilities and improved the construction land "back two into three" mechanism. It classified guidance for areas with conditions, the use of independent development, and joint development mode to carry out "urban village" transformation.

(4) **Improve quality and promote high-quality development**

In the pre-development phase of land development, the need is for strict implementation of land supply policies. Based on the land use conditions agreed on in the land assignment contract, the whole process of dynamic assessment and supervision of construction project sites is implemented. Through sound industrial land access, comprehensive benefit assessment, land use rights withdrawal, and other mechanisms, project construction inputs, outputs, energy saving, environmental protection, employment, and other economic, social, and environmental factors have been included into the contract management. They reasonably determine the years of compensated use of industrial land according to the industrial life cycle and explore the scientific use of industrial land supply methods such as long-term lease, lease first and then let, and combination of lease and let. In the middle of development, on the one hand, it strictly implements land use standards, regularly issues revised industrial guideline catalogs and construction land index systems and establishes a land-saving evaluation system for construction project sites. On the other hand, it guides land development and utilization in three dimensions. It encourages land users to improve the utilization rate of land by adding floors to plants, renovating old plants and internal finishing, etc. under the premise of meeting the prescribed conditions. It promotes the composite use of land, three-dimensional use, comprehensive use of existing industrial land in line with the plan, does not allow for change of use, improves land utilization, and increases the volume ratio, at no additional land price. It encourages research and development of policies and measures to promote the development and use of underground space. It prescribes construction land use rights to be set up in the ground and underground stratification, acquisition, and use of the year with reference to the use of construction land use rights regarding surface regulations. These can be based on the local benchmark land price and the actual transaction of real estate and assessment to determine the minimum price standard for the stratification offer. In the later stages of development, the need is to actively carry out the evaluation of the economical and intensive use of land, the results of which in the development zone will be used as an important basis for upgrading and expanding the zone. In combination with the construction land census, the need is to promote the evaluation of the economical and intensive use of construction land in provinces, cities, counties, and central urban areas, and promote the economical and intensive use of land by all kinds of subjects.

7.1.3 Deepening Rural Land System Reform to Help Global Poverty Reduction and Development

Poverty not only seriously hinders the socio-economic development of poor countries but also is one of the root causes of current regional conflicts, the spread of terrorism, and environmental degradation. In a developing country, especially a large developing country like China with a huge geographical area and population size, poverty eradication is a difficult and systematic project. However, through continuous exploration and practice, China has established a relatively sound system of systems, organizations, and policies for poverty eradication and has accomplished the target of poverty eradication in the new era as scheduled, with nearly 100 million poor people rescued from poverty and achieving a major victory that has impressed the world. The effectiveness of China's poverty reduction not only benefits the Chinese people, but also contributes to the global cause of poverty eradication. Since China's poverty is mainly concentrated in rural areas because of the vast number of dormant land resources in the countryside, an important mission is to be able to activate these lands. Through the reform of the rural land system, the Chinese government has favorably promoted poverty reduction in rural areas and provided important lessons for various countries and regions around the world.

(1) **Trading of cross-regional indicators for replenishing arable land to help poor counties reduce poverty**

A system of achieving balance between occupation and supplement of cultivated land is key to achieve arable land protection in China, and this plays an important role in securing one billion and eight hundred million acres of arable land red line in China. However, differences in the level of economic development, arable land resource endowment, and reserve land resources have made it difficult to achieve a balance of arable land occupation and replenishment in economically developed regions, while relatively economically backward regions have more arable land reserve resources available for development, resulting in a spatial mismatch of resource demand. Based on this, the Chinese government proposes to explore national coordination of arable land replenishment. This can be implemented in accordance with the carrying capacity of resources and environment, the condition of arable land reserve resources, and the potential of new arable land for land improvement. Provinces with serious resource and environmental constraints and a serious shortage of capacity to replenish arable land can apply to the State Council for national coordination if the amount of newly reclaimed arable land is insufficient to replenish the amount of arable land occupied after new construction. The implementation of cross-regional supplemental arable land involves adjustment. Under the premise that ecological conditions allow, the need is to support the national key poverty-stricken areas rich in arable land reserve resources in an orderly manner to promote land improvement to increase arable land; supplemental arable land indicators can be transferred to economically developed areas within the province, supplemental arable land indicators transfer proceeds from the county government through budgetary arrangements for arable land protection, agricultural production, and rural economic and social development. Provincial (autonomous regions and municipalities directly under the Central Government) governments coordinate the protection of arable land and coordinated regional development; they support areas occupying arable land to pay for the transfer of supplementary arable land indicators based on the implementation of industrial transfer; they also provide support for infrastructure construction for counterpart areas of supplementary arable land; they mobilize the enthusiasm of farmers in supplementary arable land areas to protect arable land. This practice has largely supported the development of poor areas, enabling them to exchange resources for funds and achieve poverty reduction and elimination.

(2) **Reform the rural land acquisition system and protect the legitimate rights and interests of farmers**

Land in China's cities is owned by the state, and land in rural areas is collectively owned. Land expropriation is the only legal path to convert collective land into state land. Therefore, land expropriation is related to the vital interests of hundreds of millions of peasants. The Chinese government is only adding to, but also not subtracting from, the key issue of land expropriation, which is directly related to farmers' interests, further refining land expropriation procedures, improving the "Land Expropriation Compensation and Relocation Institution," reasonably dividing land expropriation powers among all levels of government in accordance with the principle of "equal rights and responsibilities," and optimizing and improving the efficiency of land expropriation. Requirements should be issued pre-announcement of land acquisition, and investigations should be based on the current situation of the proposed land expropriation and social stability risk assessment and on the results of social stability risk assessment. These must be combined with the status of land survey, the organization of natural resources, finance, agriculture, and rural areas, human resources and social security, and other relevant departments to develop land acquisition compensation and resettlement program. It must "protect the original standard of living of the expropriated farmers and ensure their long-term livelihood security"; It must ensure the land acquisition compensation and resettlement costs and follow the specific rules for allocation of specific provisions, where clear social security costs must be a separate expense, emphasizing that land acquisition compensation and resettlement costs must be in place in full. Provinces, autonomous regions, and municipalities directly under the Central Government are required to develop and publish comprehensive land prices, determine the land compensation fee for the expropriation of agricultural land, resettlement subsidy standards, development of land compensation fees, and resettlement subsidy distribution methods. At the same time, it is clear that social security costs are mainly used for eligible farmers who have been expropriated for social insurance contributions subsidies such as pension insurance, in accordance with the provisions of the provinces, autonomous regions, and municipalities directly under the Central Government separately. Application for land acquisition of local people's governments at or above the county level should involve timely implementation of land compensation, resettlement subsidies, rural villages, as well as other ground attachments and seedlings, such as compensation costs, and social security costs, and it must be ensured that the full amount is paid in place as earmarked. If the relevant costs are not fully in place, expropriation of land shall not be approved. The reform of the land acquisition system has safeguarded the fundamental interests of farmers, and farmers have received the value of their land.

(3) **Activating rural residential bases and increasing farmers' property income**

For a long time, Chinese farmers' property income has relied only on rent and savings income, and farmers' property investment methods were in a single state for a long time. With the improvement in China's rural financial system and the standardization of rural land transfer, especially under the reform of the residential base system, as per the "separation of the three rights." Once the confirmation of the qualification right of residential bases is completed, farmers can use the residential bases for mortgage and guarantee, which can increase their investment channels and realize the increase of their own property income. At the same time, farmers can voluntarily withdraw their idle house bases for compensation, and village collectives can transform their house bases and abandoned collective public welfare construction land into commercial collective-owned construction land in accordance with the law, which can be directly marketed under the premise of spatial planning and use control of the land. Farmers can also withdraw from their residential bases, and the local government will centrally build housing and replace it with that of farmers according to certain standards. Farmers will receive monetary compensation for their eligibility rights or a mixed compensation method of "housing replacement + monetary compensation" may be followed. The activation of rural residential bases has given farmers greater freedom of disposal and effectively increased their property income.

(4) **Exploring the market of commercial collective-owned construction land and visualizing rural collective income**

Rural commercial collective-owned construction land refers to rural construction land of production and business nature, including rural collective construction land used by rural collective economic organizations to set up enterprises using construction land determined by the overall land use planning of townships (towns) or to jointly hold enterprises and businesses with other units or individuals in the form of land use rights in shares or joint ventures. The market entry of rural commercial collective-owned construction land refers to the transfer of this land in the market, specifically including transfer, lease and shareholding, which is essentially the process of optimizing the allocation of the right to use rural commercial collective-owned construction land in the market. The newly revised "Land Administration Law of the People's Republic of China" of 2020 stipulates that commercial collective-owned construction land shall conform to the overall land use planning, urban and rural planning, and the planned use shall be for industrial or commercial purposes, etc. The land can be put on the market after it has been registered in accordance with the law before being put on the market, and the land can been put on the market with the consent of at least two-thirds of the members of the villagers' meeting or at least two-thirds of the villagers' representatives who are members of collective economic organizations, and arrangements have been made in the annual land use plan. The listing or market entry of rural commercial collective-owned construction land can, on the one hand, provide land resources for urban expansion and solve the problem of shortage of urban land resources and the contradiction between urban expansion and rural collective land occupation. On the other hand, it can solve the problem of farmers' income. The listing of commercial collective-owned construction land can improve farmers' property income, both in terms of one-time income and sustainable income. Therefore, the market entry of commercial collective-owned construction land largely visualizes the income of rural collectives, while also increasing farmers' income, and becomes an important channel to promote rural poverty reduction.

7.2 Reflections on China's Land Policy Facing Ecological Civilization

7.2.1 Promoting Land System Reform and Policy Innovation in Key Areas Based on the Concept of Ecological Civilization

In the face tighter resource constraints, serious environmental pollution and ecosystem degradation, the concept of ecological civilization must be established to respect, comply with, and protect nature. The construction of ecological civilization must be given prominence and integrated into all aspects and processes of economic, political, cultural, and social construction to build a Beautiful China. In the era of industrial civilization, the overemphasis on the dominant position of human value, the cognition of land value based on the economic value of land, and ignoring the limit of land carrying capacity made it difficult to match the new civilization development model. Ecological civilization reconsiders the relationship between man and nature, which is not only the civilization of human society but also the civilization of natural ecology (Zheng et al. 2020a, b).

Land resources are the material basis, spatial carrier, and constituent elements of ecological civilization construction; they are the key fields of ecological civilization construction. To promote ecological civilization, it is necessary to continue to deepen reform, change the way, adhere to equal emphasis on ensuring development and protecting resources, and develop resources and ecological construction at the same time. We should use the concept of ecological civilization to coordinate the management, development, and utilization of land resources, promote the formation of an industrial structure and growth mode for the economical and intensive use of land resources and the protection of the ecological environment, realize the consistency between the intensity and speed of land resources development and utilization and the renewal cycle and remediation and recovery cycle of land resources, and ensure the sustainable use of land resources. Presently, China has made certain achievements in the reform of land system and policy innovation in key areas, including the reform of rural "three pieces of land," comprehensive land consolidation, innovation of land policy for serving the development of new industries and new business forms, and innovation of land policy for major infrastructure. The land system has been continuously improved and developed making great contributions to the stability and economic development of the country. However, facing the requirements of the concept of ecological civilization at this stage, China's land system reform and policy innovation has tended to focus more on economic construction and development and less on the concept of ecological civilization. Therefore, in the future, land system reform and policy innovation in key areas of China must be promoted based on the concept of ecological civilization.

(1) **Under the guidance of ecological civilization, coordinating land development and utilization in key areas**

It is necessary to consciously take the concept of ecological civilization as the guidance, unify the understanding, change the way, and consider development, resource conservation, and ecological construction as the ultimate goals of land resource management. We should strengthen the top-level design and do a good job in work layout, so that all aspects of land resource management reflect ecological civilization. The ecological function of land resources should be emphasized, and land resources should be managed as an ecosystem and an ecological space. While carrying out land system reform and policy innovation in key areas, we should shoulder the important task of protecting the environment and realize the unity of economic, social, and ecological benefits of the development and utilization of land resources. Placing the construction of ecological civilization in a more prominent and consistent position, and making the management, development, and utilization of land resources more reasonable and orderly is the need of the hour.

(2) **Optimizing the pattern of land development based on the carrying capacity of resources and the environment**

Considering the geographical and geological conditions as the background, the resource and environmental carrying capacity as the basis, and regional functional advantages as the reference, territorial spatial planning must be conducted effectively. Taking this as a starting point, the need is to make overall arrangements and comprehensive arrangements for the reform of the "three pieces of land" in rural areas for the development and utilization of land resources, protection of the ecological environment, comprehensive land consolidation, and for the construction of major infrastructure. Optimization of land development must be promoted with a strict protection system. It is necessary to improve and implement the strictest cultivated protection system and the system of economical and intensive land use, establish and improve the system of compensated use of resources and the system of development compensation, strictly enforce the system of accountability for the protection and utilization of resources, and comprehensively strengthen the control of land development and utilization.

(3) **Improving the land resource management system and promoting the construction of ecological civilization**

To improve and perfect the land resource management system, we must ensure and promote the construction process of ecological civilization, First, it is necessary to adhere to (a) the organic combination of government management and market allocation, (b) classified management as the basis and comprehensive management as the orientation, (c) the integration of resource protection and resource development, and (d) the problem orientation and goal orientation, give play to the enthusiasm of the central and local governments, correctly handle the relationship between owners, managers, and users, and comprehensively and systematically promote the construction of an ecological civilization. Second, through "scientific planning, use control, market allocation, compensated use, unified registration, protection of rights and interests, source protection, unified rectification, comprehensive management, and strengthened supervision," these efforts should achieve "unified investigation and evaluation, unified confirmation and registration of rights, unified use control, unified supervision information platform, and unified rectification and repair" so as to comprehensively improve the protection, utilization, and management level of land resources, and promote coordination between the development and utilization of land resources and environmental protection. Third, following the ideas of strict prevention at the source, economic utilization, and comprehensive treatment, it is necessary to improve the ecological compensation mechanism of land resources, explore the establishment of a monitoring and early warning mechanism for the carrying capacity of resources and environment, and earnestly implement the strictest system for the protection and conservation of natural resources. Fourth, in accordance with the requirements of national coverage, whole-process supervision, scientific and technological support, and achieve a perfect, powerful, and effective system, it is necessary to establish a unified land resource supervision information platform, build a diversified supervision system with complete system and complementary functions, and strengthen the supervision of land resource protection and utilization. Fifth, it is necessary to adhere to the thinking and mode of governance to protect land resources, speed up the revision and formulation of relevant laws and regulations in the field of land resources, and establish an ecological civilization legal system that effectively restricts development behavior and promotes green, circular, and low-carbon development.

7.2.2 *Implementing the Strictest Cultivated Land Protection System and Economical and Intensive Land Use System in a Green Way*

Cultivated land resources are the fundamental source of ensuring the potential of agricultural production and an indispensable material condition for human survival and development. In recent years, all parts of China have implemented the strictest cultivated land protection system and the strictest economical and intensive land use system, strengthened the protection and quality construction of cultivated land and basic farmland, promoted the economical and intensive use of construction land, and achieved positive results. However, in some areas, problems still exist, such as occupying cultivated land, adjusting the occupation of basic farmland for construction, excessive expansion of the scale of construction land, extensive land development and utilization, low utilization efficiency and efficiency, and idle land, Especially, insufficient attention given to green transformation seriously restricts the sustainable use of cultivated land resources in China. The report of the 19th National Congress of the CPC mentioned "building an ecological system that respects nature and green development" (Xi 2017). Facing the concept of ecological civilization and the basic national conditions of large population and small land and insufficient land reserve resources, we must further deepen the implementation of the strictest cultivated land protection system and economical and intensive land use system in a green way.

(1) **Strengthening green and comprehensive protection of cultivated land resources according to the strategy of "storing grain in the land"**

In the new era, to strengthen the protection of cultivated land resources, the need is to strictly abide by the "red line of cultivated land" and ensure that the quality of cultivated land does not decline and productivity is improved. The key to this lies in improving the cultivated land protection system and security system and innovating diversified cultivated land protection mechanisms (Liu and Qiao 2014). On the one hand, before the breakthrough in the basic research of grain science and technology, the local way of storing grain in time for space has become the most realistic choice to ensure food security. In order to ensure the implementation of the strategy of "storing grain in the land," it is necessary to effectively protect cultivated land, ensure that the red line of cultivated land is not broken, and that basic farmland is not occupied, so as to truly preserve the grain production capacity and potential. On the other hand, considering the need for implementing "low-carbon economy" and "green development," there is a need to improve the utilization efficiency of cultivated land in the major grain producing areas. It is necessary to combine the actual situation of regional development and adopt differentiated regulation strategies to realize low-carbon and efficient development and utilization of cultivated land resources (Kuang et al. 2018). There is a need to develop a system protection concept of constructing a multi-community of cultivated land resources; clarifying the responsibility and interest connection between departments from the objective, process, and performance, alleviating the hidden contradictions between the central and the local governments, strengthening the provincial responsibility, compacting the territorial management of cities and counties, and promoting the efficient implementation of townships (towns). This can lead to the formation of a multi-governance cultivated land protection community dominated by farmers with social participation and government protection. This can optimize the institutional platform of the trinity of cultivated land resource protection. The need is to give full play to the policy effectiveness of the cultivated land protection system, so as to form a cultivated land protection system platform with consistent objectives, ecological priority, and dual incentives. We must also consider improving the intelligent supervision and management system of cultivated land resource protection by setting up intelligent supervision systems that connect the links in all directions with the intelligent cultivated land management platform as the core. By promoting the application and integration of the intelligent management system of natural resources a supervision system can be formed covering the protection business of resource stock change, occupation and reclamation balance supervision, real-time monitoring of permanent basic farmland, facility agricultural land, and the linkage between urban-land taking and rural-land giving (LUTRG) policy and land expropriation supervision (Niu and Fang 2019).

(2) **Internalizing land conservation and environmental protection as the core obligation of land use subjects**

Development is the absolute principle, and economy is the big strategy. The 18th National Congress of the CPC reiterated the basic national policy of resource conservation from the strategic height of the sustainable development of the Chinese nation, emphasizing that "every inch of land must be cherished," and "resource conservation should be promoted in an all-round way." We should widely mobilize all sectors of society, give full play to the enthusiasm, initiative, and creativity of Party committees, governments, departments, industries, and society at all levels, and constantly improve the target responsibility system for economical and intensive land use and accelerate the establishment of a joint responsibility mechanism for economical and intensive land use. We should speed up the establishment and improvement of a new pattern of land and resources management through "Party committee leadership, government responsibility, departmental coordination, public participation, and upper and lower linkage" to provide a strong institutional guarantee for the economical and intensive use of land. Through various media and other means, we should widely, transmit the sensible voice of economical and intensive land use to the entire society, so that it becomes a common concept embedded in the conscious action of every level of government, every unit, and every citizen, and the powerful force of the society to economize and intensify land use to the greatest extent. We must improve the land obligation system and realize the transformation of interests between land property rights subjects from game to a win–win (Hu 2014). While ensuring the complete property rights of rural collective land, the state should formulate and improve the corresponding land obligation system, resolutely implement the "strictest cultivated land protection system" and the "strictest land conservation system" and internalize land conservation and environmental protection as the core obligations of land users.

(3) **Establishing and improving the green utilization system of urban construction land and its supervision and management system**

As the material carrier of urban spatial composite function, green utilization of urban construction land produces high-quality and sustainable development of the urban system. In recent years, the carbon emission effect of urban construction land use has gradually attracted attention in all aspects of life. The excessive consumption of fossil fuels and the rapid expansion of cities have intensified greenhouse gas emissions, creating a negative impact on the comprehensive benefits of urban land use (Yuan et al. 2019). In the future, we need to strengthen control of the total amount and intensity of urban construction land, improve the efficiency and benefit of construction land use, change the land use mode, and enforce quality and efficiency of economic and social development. It is also necessary to strictly control the supply of construction land in large cities, limit the speed and scale of expansion of medium and small towns, and encourage the redevelopment of underused urban land. Second, we should comprehensively consider the problems and shortcomings in the development and utilization of urban construction land in different regions and implement policies such as industrial transformation, energy structure optimization, energy conservation, and environmental protection according to local conditions. For cities with low technological efficiency and no obvious technological catch-up effect, it is necessary to increase investment in high-tech research and development of enterprises and enhance the driving force of scientific and technological innovation. For regions with insignificant economies of scale and scope, it is necessary to speed up industrial structure adjustment and resource integration, reduce inter regional horizontal competition, improve the agglomeration capacity of green and low-carbon industries, and gradually form a development pattern with complementary advantages and clear division of labor between upstream and downstream industrial chains. We should reasonably guide foreign direct investment to low-carbon and environmental protection industries, improve clean technology in the use of urban construction land through technology introduction, cooperative research and development, and other channels, further improve foreign trade conditions, give priority to the export of low-carbon and low-pollution products, increase the import proportion of high carbon emission and high energy consumption goods, and reduce the embodied carbon emissions of industrial production through trade (Li et al. 2020).

7.2.3 *Strengthening the Overall Coordination of Land Protection and Utilization in Territorial Spatial Planning with a Good Governance Model*

Although the total amount of land resources in China is large, high-intensity development and utilization are limited, and regional distribution is extremely unbalanced. It is necessary to optimize the three major land and spatial layouts of urbanized areas, main agricultural production areas, and ecological function areas to realize the sustainable development of national economic security, food security, ecology, and security. These are facing multiple pressures to protect development, farmland, and ecology. It is necessary to take the new path of scientific protection and efficient utilization of land resources, cherish and make good use of every inch of land resources to support high-quality development and modernization.

(1) **Deepening the planning and use control of territorial space and building a new pattern of development and protection of territorial space**

Territorial spatial planning is a key measure to promote the construction of an ecological civilization, which reflects not only the fundamental requirements of ecological civilization construction, but also the practical needs of changing the way of governance of the territorial spatial structure (Dong 2019). In May 2019, *the Opinions of the CPC Central Committee and the State Council on Establishing a National Territory Spatial Planning System with Its Supervision and Implementation* was issued, which established the framework of the territorial spatial planning system in the new era, and comprehensively deployed the preparation and implementation of territorial spatial planning. In the context of territorial spatial planning, differentiated designs should be carried out according to the positioning of different functional areas, and attention should be paid to the policy objectives of each functional area and the coordination among them. Territorial space is the carrier of various natural resource elements and the ecological environment. Regulating the use of all territorial space is to coordinate the interactions among natural resources, economic and social development, and the ecological environment at different times and space scales. Faced with the development requirements of the new era such as "ecological civilization construction," "global space use control," and "space governance modernization," China's previous single-factor and sub-sectoral land use control has begun to transform into regulating the use of all territorial space. In the new era, China's implementation of regulating the use of all territorial space should be based on the concept of high-quality and sustainable development, with the goal of building a beautiful China, building a management and control mechanism with the spatial coordination of the three control lines of permanent basic farmland red line, ecological red line, and urban development boundary as the core, with access to space as the main line, and optimization of the license system for the development and utilization of territorial space as the premise. This control mechanism integrates territorial space access permits, full-factor transfer permits, and territorial space exit guidelines.

(2) **Implementing the integrated protection and restoration of "mountains, rivers, forests, farmlands, lakes, and grasslands" and innovating the value realization mechanism of ecological products**

Coordinated management of mountains, rivers, forests, farmland, lakes, and grassland systems is an important part of ecological civilization construction. In the report of the 19th National Congress of the CPC, it is mentioned, "we will adopt a holistic approach to conserving our mountains, rivers, forests, farmlands, lakes, and grasslands, implement the strictest possible systems for environmental protection," emphasizing that all kinds of natural resources are a unified whole. In the protection and restoration of a single type of ecosystem, the phenomenon of focusing on one part and neglecting the other, like the story of the "blind man and the elephant," can often cause systematic damage to the ecosystem. In the new era, faced with the problem of broken governance, it is more necessary to carry out the overall governance of natural resources and follow the concept of "mountains, rivers, forests, farmlands, lakes, and grasslands are a community of life" to realize harmonious coexistence between human and nature. Exploring and improving the value realization mechanism of eco-label products is an important direction for the reform of the ecological civilization management system; it is also a key measure for China to continuously deepen the reform of ecological civilization construction and organically combine the innovation of management systems and mechanisms. Since the 18th National Congress of the CPC, relevant policies have been introduced one after another, involving various aspects of ecological products; some regions have carried out a series of innovations, explorations, and practices, providing experience for the realization of the value of eco-label products. However, overall, the realization of eco-label product value still faces problems such as inconsistent understanding, unresolved economic externality dilemma, and lack of systematic policy guidance. It is necessary to further strengthen natural resource management and ecological environmental protection and improve the supply capacity of high-quality eco-label products. We should establish the value accounting and exchange mechanism of eco-label products, establish the value accounting system, price system and trading system of eco-label products, and realize the value-added of eco-label products. It is also necessary to actively explore and build a path to realize the value of diversified eco-label products that is led by the government, participated by enterprises and all sectors of society, is market-oriented and sustainable, so as to realize the multiplication, efficient transformation, and full release of the value of eco-label products.

(3) **Promoting the construction of a comprehensive platform of intelligent management and smart application and improving the modernization level of territory space governance**

The application of technological innovation is an important systematic support for the analysis and evaluation, planning, decision-making, optimal configuration, monitoring, and management of territory space. In the new era, on the one hand, the territory space governance is responsible for solving various problems left over from the "multiple planning" of the past; on the other hand, it is faced with a new situation, new tasks, and new requirements of the whole domain. All elements and all processes use control and space governance, which urgently need the effective support of information technology. Facing the new trend of social development and the new requirements of modernization of the unified territory space governance capacity, space governance should be based on the construction of ecological civilization, from the perspective of intelligent integration and innovation, comprehensive use of mobile internet, cloud computing, big data, internet of things, artificial intelligence, and other new generation information technology. Space governance should establish an interconnected "one network" of natural resources, a "one map" of three-dimensional natural resources, and a unified basic information platform for territory space and build a natural resource information database for regulatory decision-making, government services, and investigation and evaluation. To improve the integration, refinement, and intelligence of natural resource management, we should establish a national data infrastructure that serves all sectors of society, including natural resource background data and territorial space management and control rules, comprehensively improve the digital, networked, and intelligent technology level and support level of the whole business and whole process, and promote the intelligence of the whole process of the management and control of territorial space. At the same time, we must continue to improve technical standards and institutional systems, enhance the scientific nature of planning, and promote the innovative practice of new technologies through the participation of multiple subjects and collaborative innovation (Zhen et al. 2019).

7.3 Future of China's Land Policies Harmonization Between Humanity and Nature

7.3.1 Active Participation in the Reform and Construction of the Global Governance System

In 2012, to cope with the problem of agricultural resource ownership transaction caused by the rising trend of international agricultural product prices and the warming of agricultural investment, the Committee on World Food Security compiled *"the Responsible Governance of Land, Fishery and Forest Tenure within the Scope of National Food Security Voluntary Guidelines."* From this, we can observe the basic framework of the global land governance system, which comprises (a) the legal identification and distribution of land tenure rights and obligations; (b) the transfer and other changes of land ownership rights and obligations; and (c) the administrative management of land tenure. This reform framework expounds some basic principles in land management. For example, public welfare needs to be given priority in land management; ownership management must be taken as the basis of land governance; attention should be paid to comprehensive resource management; spatial planning must be supervised; and ownership dispute handling mechanism is essential (Liu and Chen 2014). These core ideas and principles are highly consistent with the policy reforms undertaken by the Chinese government and are the strategic direction and focus of China's participation in the reform and construction of the global governance system.

Public welfare takes precedence. The report of the 19th National Congress of the CPC pointed out that to ensure that all people have more sense of gain in joint construction and shared development, and to improve the distribution mechanism of land value-added income shared by the whole people, is an important issue for the party to lead the people to start a new journey of building a modern socialist country in all respects. The rational distribution principle of land incremental revenues should consider the efficiency of resource allocation and the fair distribution of wealth. First, market mechanisms and negotiation mechanisms must be introduced to build a primary distribution pattern that considers both efficiency and fairness, conflicts must be reduced in the process of value-added income distribution, and the goal of social equity must be realized. Second, the central and local governments should work together to regulate regional and urban and rural incomes and build an intra-generational distribution pattern. Finally, it is necessary to consider the construction of an intergenerational distribution pattern of sustainable development based on the intergenerational compensation fund and land development fund, realize the distribution pattern of land incremental revenues shared by the whole population, Zou et al. (2021) and establish a set of land incremental revenues distribution policy system that maintains social fairness and justice.

Tenure management needs to be strengthened. China's rural land tenure management is consistent with this principle. The policy of "separation of the three rights" of rural land in the new era stimulates land transfer by separating land contract right and operation right, improves the efficiency of land market allocation, and effectively promotes agricultural modernization. In the context of the reform of the property rights system of "separation of the three rights" of rural land, it is necessary to do a good job in the basic work of confirming, registering, and issuing certificates of rural land rights, so as to promote the realization of the strategic goal of rural revitalization. In addition, with the unconfirmed residential base and collective construction land as the focus of work, in accordance with the requirements for unified registration of real estate, it is necessary to speed up cadastral survey according to local conditions, actively resolve difficult problems, and for those who meet the registration conditions, go through the registration of real estate integrated with real estate in accordance with the laws and regulations.

We must focus on the comprehensive management of natural resources and improve the spatial planning system. The task at hand for the Chinese government is to identify ways to improve the management efficiency and synergistic effect of natural resource rules and regulations, so that natural resource management can better serve economic and social development, and better serve the construction of ecological civilization. Natural resource management can discuss neither resources in terms of resources nor ecology in terms of ecology, but can strengthen integrated management on the basis of comprehensive management, so as to achieve mutual connection, mutual feedback, and coordinated development between natural resource management and economic and social development, and improve human well-being (Ma et al. 2020). In the new era, the development, utilization, protection, and improvement of natural resources should be integrated as the starting point to realize optimization of the spatial development pattern and to realize rejuvenation and sustainable development of the Chinese nation. In the context of the modernization of the space governance system, the reconstruction direction of China's territorial spatial planning system is as follows: the development concept changes to "human-oriented" and "ecological civilization"; the strategic position changes to "macro guidance" and "strategic guidance"; and the structural system changes to "overall layout" and "hierarchical management." Under the background of the modernization of the space governance system, territorial spatial planning should be strategic and controllable, authoritative and legal, and systematic and scientific. In addition, the reconstruction of the current territorial spatial planning system urgently needs to resolve the core issues such as the improvement of the legal and regulatory system, the formulation of the regulation and standard system, the discipline construction, and the support of the theoretical method system (Meng et al. 2019).

The property dispute settlement mechanism should be strengthened. Due to the lack of detailed laws and regulations, the characteristics of concealment in form, suddenness in rights protection, large time span, difficulty in collecting evidence, and the complex relationship between the subjects involved in land property disputes make it challenging to resolve land property disputes in concrete practice. Therefore, in strengthening the mechanism for handling disputes over land property, it is necessary to consider the characteristics of disputes over land property in accordance with the principles of respecting history, facing reality, facilitating production and life, and complying with laws and regulations based on the existing land ownership dispute investigation and mediation mechanism, establish a three-level tenure dispute mediation platform at the city, county, and township levels, and a work mechanism for the mediation of tenure disputes that combine strips and blocks and inter-departmental linkages. It is necessary to further improve the relevant rules and regulations and standardize work procedures and work results; further there is a need to clarify problems at the operational level and improve the dispute resolution system and mechanism based on negotiation, administrative mediation, administrative adjudication, administrative reconsideration, and administrative litigation, to ensure that land property dispute mediation work has laid a solid policy foundation. We must also promote the establishment of a long-term dispute resolution mechanism based on the rule of virtue, supported by autonomy, and the rule of law as a barrier, Wang and Zhang (2020) by improving modernization of governance capabilities and maintaining social harmony and stability.

7.3.2 Accurately Serve the "3060" Goal of Carbon Peak and Carbon Neutrality

Presently, global climate change has become one of the biggest challenges to human development (Hu 2021). As a developing country with the largest carbon emission in the world, China has been committed to energy conservation and emission reduction and the development of a low-carbon and circular economy. On September 20, 2020, Chinese President Xi Jinping proposed at the general debate of the 75th United Nations General Assembly that "China will increase its nationally determined contribution, adopt more powerful policies and measures, and strive to peak carbon dioxide emissions before 2030, and strive to achieve carbon neutrality by 2060," as put forward the "3060" "double carbon" goal for China to deal with future climate change. In the context of the complex international situation after the spread of COVID-19, China's double carbon target demonstrates the responsibility of a major country to build a global community of a shared future for mankind and reflects China's firm determination to deal with global climate issues, injects new vitality into the global green recovery and development after COVID-19, and the important role it will play in promoting global climate action (Wang and Zhang 2020). The "3060" goal has shown the direction for China's future low-carbon transformation to promote high-quality economic development and ecological civilization construction and also put forward higher requirements for China's land use and management.

As China enters the new era, the mode of social production, economic development, and the development and utilization of territorial space should also enter a new historical stage. Low-carbon territorial space development will inevitably become one of the important tasks in the future development process. There are two main ways to realize low-carbon territorial space development: one is carbon emission reduction, and the other is carbon increase sink. The former takes the "source" as the starting point to reduce anthropogenic carbon emissions; the latter considers the "sink" and adopts reasonable and effective measures to fix more carbon in the terrestrial ecosystem. To this end, the following are recommended:

The first is to strengthen the supervision of the implementation of territorial spatial planning, guided by the increasing the capacity of carbon sinks, focusing on protection of high carbon sink areas, especially in southeastern China, and forest areas in Yunnan, Guangxi, Guangdong, Hunan, Jiangxi, and Fujian. In the preparation of territorial spatial planning and detailed territorial spatial planning, there is a need to establish a carbon sink impact assessment system and a carbon sink loss compensation mechanism, or a carbon sinks space compensation mechanism.

The second is to focus on the protection of the main carbon sink space and strengthen the control of the territorial space in the southeast region. The southeastern region is not only an important carbon source, but also an important carbon sink space. Therefore, it is necessary to strictly supervise the protection and restoration of natural ecosystems in this important carbon source and sinks space in the southeastern region, including the protection and restoration of forest land, cultivated land, grassland, and wetland systems. The concept of comprehensive land remediation should establish a sustainable social-ecological coupling system and strengthen the protection of biodiversity and ecosystems (Wang et al. 2020). From the perspective of land use structure optimization, the main ways to increase carbon sinks in the future are to increase the proportion of forest land, adjust the proportion of cultivated land, grassland, and construction land, pay attention to the carbon sink function of grassland and natural wetlands, and strictly control excessive conversion of grassland and forest land for construction (Lai and Huang 2011).

The third is to take the carbon peak as an opportunity to strengthen the management and control of the total amount of construction land. The reduction of non-construction land caused by the expansion of construction land is an important cause of carbon emissions from land use. Construction land is the accumulation area of industry, transportation, commercial services, and residential areas. This land shows high energy consumption and carbon emission intensity and carries low carbon sinks. It is the focus of carbon emission control and carbon emission reduction. Therefore, it is recommended to evaluate the carbon sources and sinks effect of the expansion of construction land, form a construction land scale control or urban growth boundary guidance idea based on carbon carrying capacity, Xu and Huang (2016) and explore the construction of a low-efficiency emission construction land pattern system. Further, we must formulate a carbon neutralization policy for major infrastructure and urban and rural construction land expansion and devise an innovative carbon compensation mechanism for construction land expansion.

The fourth is to explore and formulate carbon emission standards for land use based on carbon management and control. Combined with China's strategic deployment of the carbon peak and carbon neutralization, aiming at the impact of land use on carbon emissions, the need is formulate land use carbon emission standards for advantageous development areas and important carbon sink spaces, so as to combine carbon emission control with territorial space control and to provide institutional guarantee for the construction of a low-carbon territorial space pattern system.

7.3.3 Continue to Strengthen Land Policy to Promote Comprehensive Green Transformation of Economic and Social Development

With China's economy and society growing at a rapid pace, promoting comprehensive transformation of economic and social development has become important for China to achieve high-quality growth and a harmonious coexistence of humanity and nature. The *"14th Five-Year Plan for National Economic and Social Development of the People's Republic of China and the Outline of the Vision for 2035"* proposes to adhere to ecological priority and green development, promote high-level protection of the ecological environment, and accelerate green transformation of development methods. Among them, building a green development policy system and strengthening the construction of laws and policies for green development are important guarantees for achieving a comprehensive green transformation of economic and social development. Land resources are an important foundation for social and economic development. Promoting green transformation of land use patterns through land policy innovation and guiding the overall transformation of economic and social development are keys to transforming China's social and economic development patterns in the future. In the new era, the goal of China's social and economic development should be comprehensive green transformation. The need is to adhere to the development concepts of "harmonious coexistence between humanity and nature," consider "lucid waters and lush mountains as invaluable assets," and continue to strengthen land policies for achieving the comprehensive green transformation of economic and social development. This will inject a strong impetus into China's ecological civilization construction and sustainable development.

(1) **Improving the legal system support for green land use**

The green use of land is an inherent requirement to promote comprehensive green transformation of economic and social development. It is necessary to strengthen the supporting role of relevant laws in the green use of land and the comprehensive green transformation and development of the economy and society, and to promote the innovation of the concept and method of green land use. First, the value-laden role of the concept of green land use should be further strengthened in the existing laws such as the *Land Administration Law* and the *Chinese Civil Code*, and the rights and obligations of the central government, local governments, enterprises, individuals, and other relevant subjects in green land use should be clarified; the relevant content of cultivated land protection, rational use, and conservation of land should be refined; and the legal responsibility for land damage compensation and serious damage to the land ecological environment should be improved, so as to force land users to earnestly fulfill their obligations of green land use (Wei and Gan 2021). Second, the need is to formulate *the Spatial Planning Law* or further improve the relevant content of territorial spatial planning in the *Land Administration Law, Urban and Rural Planning Law,* and other laws, and take green land use as an important part of the "five-level and three-category" territorial spatial planning, thereby strengthening the support and supervision of the law on the green development and protection of territorial space. In addition, adjustments should also be made to the overlapping and conflicting contents of the current *Land Administration Law*, Urban and Rural Planning Law, *Environmental Protection Law,* and other relevant laws, so as to avoid conflicts between laws that lead to ambiguity of subject rights and obligations in actual implementation and other real issues.

(2) **Promoting comprehensive green transformation with a new round of territorial spatial planning**

As a guide for national spatial development and a spatial blueprint for sustainable development, territorial spatial planning is an important starting point for the construction of an ecological civilization and the promotion of comprehensive green transformation and development of the economy and society. The preparation and implementation of territorial spatial planning and the utilization and management of land resources and other national land resources from a macro perspective are conducive to the coordinated development of factors such as population, economy, land use, and ecological protection; they promote a rational layout for production space, living space, and ecological space and speed up the formation of green production methods and lifestyles, for comprehensive green transformation. In the new era, China's ecological civilization construction and comprehensive green transformation must adhere to territorial spatial planning, further improve the territorial spatial planning system, and run the concept of comprehensive green transformation and development throughout the planning. At the same time, to coordinate other space resources, systematic thinking is required to coordinate various elements of land space to ensure sustainable use of land. To this end, the formulation and implementation of territorial spatial planning should focus on combining goals and governance. In terms of resource management and control, the requirements for the implementation of the three control lines of the permanent basic farmland, the ecological red line, and the urban development boundary should be further clarified, and the spatial control boundary should be established to improve economical and intensive use of land. At the same time, attention should be paid to the quantitative management and control of comprehensive green transformation goals, and specific indicators such as land consumption, water consumption, energy consumption, carbon emission intensity, and regional land development intensity per unit of GDP should be formulated according to the national strategic goals and the actual conditions of different regions. They must also strengthen the management level of land resources. In terms of green space protection, based on territorial spatial planning, we should strengthen the protection and restoration of green ecological space, expand the scope of important ecological protection areas, and implement special plans to expand green infrastructure construction within the scope of production and living space, so as to achieve green integration of production, living, and ecological space (Zhao 2020). Following the guidelines of territorial spatial planning, we must optimize the layout of production, living, and ecological space, and evaluate green indicators to effectively improve the efficiency of government resource management and social governance. These also promote the rational allocation of land use space, the development mode to green development, high quality development and transformation, and thereby promote comprehensive green transformation of the whole society.

(3) **The transformation of land use pattern promotes comprehensive green transformation of economic and social development**

As the basic resource of economic and social development, rational and efficient allocation of land resources profoundly affects all aspects of the transformation of social development. Since the reform and opening up, China's city-centered development model and land use model had its share of disadvantages. With increased urbanization, a large number of rural people moved to cities to work or settle down. On the one hand, the relationship between urban people and land continued to deteriorate. On the other hand, due to the increasing population, the production intensity and living space density in urban areas became much higher than that in rural areas. Chinese cities then faced serious problems such as deteriorating air quality and deteriorating living environment. In addition, the long-term disorderly development and expansion of construction land occupied the development space of other land such as ecological land, resulting in serious damage to the ecological environment and low space utilization efficiency, which are not conducive to China's green and high-quality development. Therefore, transforming land use patterns, improving land use efficiency, and realizing the harmony and unity of man and nature on the premise of maintaining a reasonable economic growth rate have become important concepts for land use and management in China.

The transformation of land use patterns is an important engine for the comprehensive green transformation of China's current urban and rural development model, production and lifestyle, and industrial structure. On the one hand, by strictly controlling the increment, revitalizing the stock, optimizing the structure, improving efficiency, comprehensive utilization, and standard, land use mode can be transformed from incremental expansion to stock revitalization and efficient increment to resolve the problems of blind and unwieldy urban expansion in China. It can also resolve the problem of extensive and idle rural construction land, reduce conflicts between people and land, and reduce damage to the ecological environment. Thereby, it can lead to efficient allocation of land resources between urban and rural areas and between production, ecology, and living spaces, and break through the development problems caused by land resource constraints. On the other hand, the green transformation of land use patterns indicates the wide application of environmentally friendly new technologies and new products in land use and management, which is not only conducive to promoting comprehensive transformation of China's production and lifestyle and building a new pattern of harmonious development between man and nature but also conducive to the comprehensive transformation and upgrading of the industrial structure and the continuous advancement of supply-side structural reforms. Therefore, we must pay attention to the important role of land use transformation in economic and social development and promote comprehensive green transformation of China's economic and social development with intensive, efficient, and green land use. The change of land use pattern is not only a change of concept and behavior, but also a change of system and policy. Promoting the change of land use pattern means re-examining the current national conditions of land resources in China, changing the traditional concept of extensive development, and establishing a new concept of green land use. Specific measures should focus on delineating the boundary of permanent basic farmland, actively adjusting the layout and utilization of construction land, strengthening land consolidation, establishing a green and recyclable land use system, strengthening land composite utilization and three-dimensional development, and improving the comprehensive benefits of land use (Yu et al. 2017). In addition, as an important subject of land management, the Chinese government should intensify efforts to promote the green transformation of land use methods, adopt "economic + ecological" multi-objective assessment on the performance of local governments and gradually promote the transformation of local governments' development model of "making money from the land." They must also ensure that local governments under the "principal-agent" system act in accordance with the central government's intentions.

References

Dong Z (2019) Ten relations of territorial planning in the new era. Resour Sci 41(9):1589–1599

Hu A ( ) China's goal of achieving carbon peak by 2030 and its main approaches. J Beijing Univ Technol (social Sciences Edition) 21(03):1–15

Hu C (2014) The dilemma and innovation of China's rural land conservation and intensive use system. Rural Econ 03:41–45

Kunag B, Lu X, Han J et al (2018) Regional differences and dynamic evolution of cultivated land use efficiency in major grain producing areas in low carbon perspective. Trans Chinese Soc Agri Eng 34(11):1–8

Lai L, Huang X (2011) Research on carbon emission effects of land use in China. Nanjing University Press, Nanjing, pp 169–174

Li G, Wang J, Cao Y et al (2020) Dynamic changes and influencing factors of urban construction: land use efficiency under carbon emission constraint in Fujian Province. China Land Sci 34(04):69–77

Liu L, Chen L (2014) Clarifying ownership and planning space: Looking at global land governance trends from the perspective of "land reform" in Africa. Resour Guide 12:48–49

Liu Y, Qiao L (2014) Innovating system and policy of arable land conservation under the new-type urbanization in China. Econ Geogr 34(4):1–6

Lu W, Zhang T, Jiang Q (2017) To promote the urban green development by way of land use change: Taking the exploration and practice of Shanghai as an example. Environ Prot 45(04):59–64

Ma Y, Li X, Wu C et al (2020) Build system for integrated management of natural resources. Macroeconomic Manag (11): 57–62, 71

Meng P, Wang Q, Lang H et al (2019) Analysis of the challenges and reform orientation of territorial spatial planning system in China under the background of spatial governance system modernization: reviews from the serial research of territorial spatial governance. China Land Sci 33(11):8–14

Niu S, Fang B (2019) Cultivated land protection system in China from 1949 to 2019: historical evolution, realistic origin exploration and path optimization. China Land Sci 33(10):1–12

Wang R, Han B, Sun R et al (2020) International ecological restoration concepts and enlightenment to China's integrated land consolidation in the new period. Land Econ Res 6(1):117–140

Wang C, Zhang Y (2020) Implementation pathway and policy system of carbon neutrality vision. Chinese J Environ Manag 12(06):58–64
Wang C, Zhang Y (2020) Implementation pathway and policy system of carbon neutrality vision. Chinese J Environ Manag 12(06):58–64
Wei Y, Gan Z, Chen J et al (2021) Study on eco-friendly land use. China Land Sci 35(10):27–34
Xi J (2017) Decisive victory in building a moderately prosperous society in all respects and winning the great victory of socialism with Chinese characteristics for a new era: report at the 19th National Congress of the Chinese Communist Party. People's Publishing House, Beijing, pp 19, 50, 25, 51.
Xu X, Huang X (2016) The study on population carrying capacity of Yangtze River Economic Belt based on carbon's peak values. Modern Urban Stud 30(5):33–38
Yuan K, Gan C, Yang H et al (2019) Validation of the EKC and characteristics decomposition between construction land expansion and carbon emission: a case study of Wuhan City. China Land Sci 33(01):56–64
Zhao Y (2020) The path of land spatial planning under the guidance of green development concept. China Land 10:31–32
Zhen F, Zhang S, Qin X et al (2019) From informational empowerment to comprehensive empowerment: exploring the ideas of smart territorial spatial planning. J Nat Resour 34(10):2060–2072
Zheng H, Wu C, Xu Z et al (2020a) The reflection and rebuilding of land-value cognition for ecological civilization construction. China Land Sci 34(04): 10–17
Zheng H, Wu C, Xu Z et al (2020b) The reflection and rebuilding of land-value cognition for ecological civilization construction. China Land Sci 34(04): 10–17
Zou X, Shi X, Ma X (2021) Distribution of incremental land revenue since the founding of the Communist Party of China: policy evolution, theoretical argument and reform logic. China Land Sci 35(08):15–22